DISCOVERING *The* WESTERN PAST

A Look at the Evidence   Volume II: Since 1650

MERRY E. WIESNER
University of Wisconsin—Milwaukee

JULIUS R. RUFF
Marquette University

WILLIAM BRUCE WHEELER
University of Tennessee, Knoxville

Houghton Mifflin Company   Boston

Dallas   Geneva, Illinois   Palo Alto   Princeton, New Jersey

Text Acknowledgments

Pages 9–10: Extract from Francis William Coker, ed., *Readings in Political Philosophy*. Used with the approval of Yale University. Pages 12–16: Extract from THE MEMOIRS OF THE DUKE OF SAINT SIMON ON THE REIGN OF LOUIS XIV, translated by Bayle St. John. Used by permission of the publisher, Unwin Hyman. Page 35: Extract from T. D. Kendrick, ed. and trans., *The Lisbon Earthquake*. Used by permission of Harper & Row, Publishers, Inc. Pages 42–43: Extract from Denis Diderot, *The Encyclopedia: Selections*, ed. and trans. Stephen J. Gendzier. Published by Harper & Row. Used by permission of Stephen J. Gendzier. Page 64: Figures from E. E. Rich and C. H. Wilson, eds., *The Cambridge Economic History of Europe*, vol. 5, *The Economic Organization of Early Modern Europe*. Used by permission of Cambridge University Press. Page 65: Table from Catherine Lis and Hugo Soly, *Poverty and Capitalism in Pre-Industrial Europe* (Brighton, England: The Harvester Press, 1979). Copyright © 1979, The Harvester Press, Ltd. Used by permission. Page 67: Table from Jean-Noël Biraben, "Certain Demographic Characteristics of the Plague Epidemic in France, 1720–1722." Reprinted by permission of *Daedalus*, Journal of the American Academy of Arts and Sciences. *Historical Population Studies*, vol. 97, no. 2, Spring 1968, Boston, MA.

Text acknowledgments continue following page 395.

Cover: *Bacon's Picture Map of London, 1908* (detail). Photograph courtesy of The British Library.

Printed in the U.S.A.

Library of Congress Catalog Card Number: 88-81367

ISBN: 0-395-47586-4

CDEFGHIJ-VH-9543210/89

CONTENTS

PREFACE

The title of this book begins with a verb, a choice that reflects our basic philosophy about history. History is not simply something one learns about; it is something one does. One discovers the past, and what makes this pursuit exciting is not only the past that is discovered but the process of discovery itself. This process can be simultaneously exhilarating and frustrating, enlightening and confusing, but it is always challenging enough to convince those of us who are professional historians to spend our lives at it.

The recognition that history involves discovery as much as physics or astronomy does is often unshared by students, whose classroom experience of history frequently does not extend beyond listening to lectures and reading textbooks. The primary goal of *Discovering the Western Past: A Look at the Evidence* is to allow students enrolled in the Western Civilization course to *do* history in the same way we as historians do—to examine a group of original sources in order to answer a question about the past. We feel that contact with original sources is an excellent means of communicating the excitement of doing history, but incorporating complete works or a collection of documents into a Western Civilization course can be problematic for many instructors.

The evidence in this book thus differs from that in most source collections in its variety. We have included such visual evidence as coins, paintings, aerial photographs, cartoons, buildings, architectural plans, maps, and political posters. In choosing written evidence we again have tried to offer a broad sample—songs, plays, poems, court records, notarial contracts, statistical data, and work regulations all supplement letters, newspapers, speeches, autobiographies, and other more traditional sources.

In order for students to learn history the way we as historians do, they must not only be confronted with the evidence; they must also learn how to use that evidence to arrive at a conclusion. In other words, they must learn historical methodology. Too often methodology (or even the notion that historians *have* a methodology) is reserved for upper-level majors or graduate students; beginning students are simply presented with historical facts and interpretations without being shown how these were unearthed or formulated. They may learn that historians hold different interpretations of the significance of an event or individual or different ideas about causation, but they are not informed of how historians come to such conclusions.

Thus, along with evidence, we have provided explicit suggestions about how one might analyze that evidence, guiding students as they reach their own conclusions. As they work through the various chapters, students will discover not only that the sources of historical information are wide-ranging, but that the methodologies appropriate to understanding and using them are equally diverse. By doing it themselves, students will learn how intellectual historians handle philosophical treatises, economic historians quantitative data, social historians court records, and political and diplomatic historians theoretical treatises and memoirs. They will also be asked to consider the limitations of their evidence, to explore what historical questions it cannot answer as well as those it can. Instead of passive observers, students become active participants.

Following an approach that we have found successful in many different classroom situations, we have divided each chapter into five parts: The Problem, Sources and Method, The Evidence, Questions to Consider, and Epilogue. The section called "The Problem" presents the general historical background and context for the evidence offered and concludes with the central question or questions explored in the chapter. The section titled "Sources and Method" provides specific information about the sources and suggests ways in which students might best study and analyze this primary evidence. It also discusses how previous historians have evaluated such sources and mentions any major disputes about methodology or interpretation. "The Evidence" forms the core of each chapter, presenting a variety of original sources for students to use in completing the central task. In "Questions to Consider," suggestions are offered about connections among the sources, and students are guided to draw deductions from the evidence. The final section, "Epilogue," traces both the immediate effects of the issue under discussion and its impact on later developments.

Within this framework, we have tried to present a series of historical issues and events of significance to the instructor as well as of interest to the student. We have also aimed to provide a balance among political, social, diplomatic, intellectual, and cultural history. In other words, we have attempted to create a kind of historical sampler that we believe will help students learn the methods and skills used by historians. Not only will these skills—analyzing arguments, developing hypotheses, comparing evidence, testing conclusions, and reevaluting material—enable students to master historical content; they will also provide the necessary foundation for a productive, meaningful life beyond college.

Discovering the Western Past is designed to accommodate any format of the Western Civilization course, from the small lecture/discussion class of a liberal arts or community college to the large lecture with discussions led by teaching assistants of a sizable university. The chapters may be used for individual assignments, team projects, class discussions, papers, and exams. Each is self-contained, so that any combination may be assigned. The book is not intended to replace a standard textbook, and it was written to accompany any Western Civilization text the instructor chooses. The Instructor's Manual provided with the book offers further suggestions for class discussion as well as a variety of ways in which students' learning may be evaluated and annotated lists of suggestions for further reading.

In the completion of this book, the authors received assistance from a number of persons. All three authors would like to acknowledge the initial work on this project by Professors Carol L. Lansing and Michael J. McDonald of the University of Tennessee, Knoxville. The organization and concepts that they proposed for these volumes provided a foundation for the work of the present authors. Our colleagues and students at the University of Wisconsin—Milwaukee, Marquette University, and the University of Tennessee, Knoxville have been generous with their ideas and time. Merry E. Wiesner (-Hanks) wishes especially to thank Ann Healy and Carolyn Ashbaugh for their critiques and suggestions and Neil Wiesner-Hanks and Kai Wiesner-Hanks for their help in maintaining the author's perspective. Julius R. Ruff wishes to acknowledge the assistance of the Reverend John Patrick Donnelly, S.J., Joseph Mikolajczak, Michael Sibalis, Laura B. Ruff, and Julia B. Ruff. Edwin Trainer of the University of Tennessee, Knoxville has been especially supportive, as has Palmira Brummett, who offered invaluable assistance on the non-Western perspective.

We wish particularly to acknowledge the following historians, who read and commented on the manuscript through its stages of development:

Susan Amussen, *Connecticut College*

James G. Baughman, *Jefferson Community College*

Rebecca Boehling, *University of Dayton*

John Bohnstedt, *California State University, Fresno*

Ronald Brown, *Charles County Community College*

Craig Buettinger, *Jacksonville University*

Helen Callahan, *Augusta College*

Gerald Herman, *Northeastern University*

Jean Knoll, *De Paul University*

Sharon Strocchia, *Emory University*

Finally, we wish to thank the staff of Houghton Mifflin Company for their enthusiastic support.

M.E.W.   J.R.R.   W.B.W.

CHAPTER ONE
STAGING ABSOLUTISM

THE PROBLEM

The "Age of Absolutism" is the label historians often apply to the history of Europe in the seventeenth and eighteenth centuries. In many ways it is an appropriate description; although the seventeenth-century conflict between king and Parliament in England resulted in the Civil War (1642–1648) and Glorious Revolution (1688), which severely limited royal power and created parliamentary government, most European monarchs of this era aspired to absolute authority in their realms.

The royal absolutism that evolved in seventeenth-century Europe represents an important step in governmental development. In constructing absolutist states, monarchs and their ministers both created new organs of administration and built on existing institutions of government to supplant the regional authorities of the medieval state with more centralized state power. In principle, this centralized authority was subject to the absolute authority of the monarch; in practice, royal authority was nowhere as encompassing as that of a modern dictator. Poor communi-cation systems, the persistence of traditional privileges that exempted whole regions or social groups from full royal authority, and other factors all set limits on royal power. Nevertheless, monarchs of the era strove for the ideal of absolute royal power, and France was the model in their work of state building.

French monarchs of the seventeenth and early eighteenth centuries more fully developed the system of absolute monarchy. In these rulers' efforts to overcome impediments to royal authority we can learn much about the creation of absolutism in Europe. Rulers in Prussia, Austria, Russia, and many smaller states sought not only the real power of the French kings but also the elaborate court ceremony and dazzling palaces that symbolized that power.

Absolutism in France was the work of Henry IV (r. 1589–1610), Louis XIII (r. 1610–1643) and his minister Cardinal Richelieu, and Louis XIV (r. 1643–1715). These rulers established a system of centralized royal political authority that destroyed many remnants of the feudal monarchy. The reward for their endeavors was great: with Europe's largest population and immense wealth, France was potentially the mightiest country on the continent in 1600 and its natural leader, if only these national strengths could be unified and directed by a strong government. Creation of such a government around an absolute monarch was the aim of French rulers, but they confronted formidable problems, common to many early modern states, in achieving their goal. Nobles everywhere still held considerable power, in part a legacy of the system of feudal monarchy. In France they possessed military power, which they used in the religious civil wars of the sixteenth century and in their Fronde revolt against growing royal power in the mid-seventeenth century. Nobles also exercised considerable political power through such representative bodies as the Estates General and provincial assemblies, which gave form to their claims for a voice in government. Moreover, nobles served as the judges of the great law courts, the *parlements*, that had to register all royal edicts before they could take effect.

A second obstacle to national unity and royal authority in many states, in an age that equated national unity with religious uniformity, was the presence of a large and influential religious minority. In France the Protestant minority was known as the Huguenots. Not only did they forswear the Catholic religion of the king and the majority of his subjects, but they possessed military power in their rights, under the Edict of Nantes,[1] to fortify their cities.

A third and major impediment to unifying a country under absolute royal authority lay in regional differences. The medieval monarchy of France had been built province by province over several centuries, and the kingdom was not well integrated. Some provinces, like Brittany in the north, retained local estates or assemblies with which the monarch actually had to bargain for taxes. Many provinces had their own cultural heritage that separated them from the king's government centered in Paris. These differences might be as simple as matters of local custom, but also as complex as unique systems of civil law. A particular problem was the persistence of local dialects, which made the French of royal officials a foreign and incomprehensible tongue in large portions of the kingdom.

The only unifying principle that could overcome all these centrifugal forces was royal authority. The task in the seventeenth century was to build a theoretical basis for a truly powerful monarch, to endow the king with tangible power that gave substance to theory, and to place the sovereign in a setting that would never permit the country to forget his new power.

To establish an abstract basis for absolutism, royal authority had to be strengthened and reinforced by a veritable cult of kingship. Seventeenth-century French statesmen

1. **Edict of Nantes:** In this 1598 decree, King Henry IV sought to end the civil warfare between French Catholics and Huguenots. He granted the Protestants basic protection, in the event of renewed fighting, by allowing them to fortify some 200 of their cities. The edict also accorded the Protestants freedom of belief with some restrictions and civil rights equal to those of Catholic Frenchmen.

built on medieval foundations in this task. Medieval kings had possessed limited tangible authority but substantial religious prestige; their vassals had rendered them religious oaths of loyalty. French monarchs since Pepin the Short had been anointed in a biblically inspired coronation ceremony in which they received not only the communion bread the Catholic Church administered to all believers, but also the wine normally reserved for clerics; once crowned, they claimed to possess mystical religious powers to heal with the royal touch. All these trappings served to endow the monarch with almost divine powers, separating him from and raising him above his subjects. Many seventeenth-century thinkers emphasized this traditional divine dimension of royal power. Others, as you will see, found more practical grounds for great royal power.

To achieve greater royal power, Henry IV reestablished peace after the religious civil warfare of the late sixteenth century and Cardinal Richelieu curbed the military power of the nobility. With the creation of loyal provincial administrators, the *intendants*, and a system of political patronage that he directed, the Cardinal also established firmer central control in the name of Louis XIII. Richelieu, moreover, ended Huguenot political power by crushing their revolt in 1628, and he intervened in the Thirty Years' War to establish France as a chief European power.

The reign of Louis XIV completed the process of consolidating royal authority in France. Louis XIV created much of the administrative apparatus necessary to centralize the state. The king brought the nobility under even greater control, building in Europe's largest army a force that could defeat any aristocratic revolt and creating in Versailles a court life that drew nobles near to the king, away from provincial plotting, where their actions could be observed. The king also sought to extend royal authority by expanding France's borders through a series of wars and to eliminate completely the Huguenot minority by revoking their religious freedoms embodied in the Edict of Nantes.

The king supplemented his military and political work of state building with other projects to integrate France more completely as one nation. With royal patronage, authors and scholars flourished and, by the example of their often excellent works, extended the French dialect in the country at the expense of provincial tongues. In the king's name, his finance minister, Jean-Baptiste Colbert (1619–1683) sought to realize a vision of a unified French economy. He designed mercantilist policies to favor French trade and to build French industry, and he improved transportation to bind the country together as one unit. The result of Louis's policies, therefore, was not only a stronger king and a more powerful France but a more unified country as well.

Far more than previous French monarchs, Louis XIV addressed the third task in establishing absolutism. In modern terms it consisted of effective public relations, which required visible evidence of the new royal authority. The stage setting for the royal

[3]

display of the symbols of absolute authority was Versailles, the site of a new royal palace. Built between 1661 and 1682, the palace itself was massive, with a façade one-quarter mile long pierced by 2,143 windows. It was set in a park of 37,000 acres, of which 6,000 acres were embellished with formal gardens. These gardens contained 1,400 fountains that required massive hydraulic works to supply them with water, an artificial lake one mile long for royal boating parties, and 200 statues. The palace grounds contained various smaller palaces as well, including Marly, where the king could entertain small, select groups, away from the main palace that was the center of a court life embracing almost 20,000 persons (9,000 soldiers billeted in the town; and 5,000 royal servants, 1,000 nobles and their 4,000 servants, plus the royal family, all housed in the main palace). Because the royal ministers and their secretaries also were in residence, Versailles was much more than a palace: it was the capital of France.

Royal architects deliberately designed the palace to impart a message to all who entered. As a guidebook of 1681 by Laurent Morellet noted regarding the palace's art:

The subjects of painting which complete the decorations of the ceilings are of heroes and illustrious men, taken from history and fable, who have deserved the titles of Magnanimous, of Great, of Fathers of the People, of Liberal, of Just, of August and Victorious, and who have possessed all the Virtues which we have seen appear in the Person of our Great Monarch during the fortunate course of his reign; so that everything remarkable which one sees in the Château and in the garden always has some relationship with the great actions of His Majesty.[2]

The court ritual and etiquette enacted in this setting departed markedly from the simpler court life of Louis XIII and were designed to complement the physical presence of the palace itself in teaching the lesson of a new royal power.

In this chapter we will analyze royal absolutism in France. What was the theoretical basis for absolute royal authority? What was traditional and what was new in the justification of royal power as expressed in late sixteenth- and seventeenth-century France? How did such early modern kings as Louis XIV communicate their absolute power in the various ceremonies and symbols of royal authority presented in the evidence that follows?

SOURCES AND METHOD

This chapter assembles several kinds of sources, each demanding a different kind of historical analysis. Two works of political theory that were

2. Laurent Morellet, *Explication historique de ce qu'il y a de plus remarquable dans la maison royale de Versailles et en celle de Monsieur à Saint-Cloud* (Paris, 1681), quoted in Robert W. Hartle, "Louis XIV and the Mirror of Antiquity" in Steven G. Reinhardt and Vaughn L. Glasgow, eds., *The Sun King: Louis XIV and the New World* (New Orleans: Louisiana State Museum Foundation, 1984), p. 111.

influential in the formation of absolutism open the evidence. To analyze these works effectively, you will need some brief background information on their authors and on the problems these thinkers discussed.

Jean Bodin (1530–1596) was a law professor, an attorney, and a legal official. His interests transcended his legal education, however. He brought a wide reading in Hebrew, Greek, Italian, and German to the central problem addressed in his major work, *The Six Books of the Republic* (1576), that of establishing the well-ordered state. Writing during the religious wars of the sixteenth century when government in France all but broke down, Bodin offered answers to this crisis. Especially novel for the sixteenth century was his call for religious toleration. Although at least formally a Catholic[3] and recognizing unity in religion as a strong unifying factor for a country, Bodin was unwilling to advocate force in eliminating Protestantism from France. He believed that acceptance was by far the better policy.

Bodin's political thought was also significant, and his *Republic* immediately was recognized as an important work. Published in several editions and translated into Latin, Italian, Spanish, and German, the *Republic*

influenced a circle of men, the *Politiques*, who advised Henry IV. In seeking to explain how to establish the well-ordered state, Bodin contributed much in the process to Western political theory. Perhaps his most important idea was that there was nothing divine about governing power. Men created governments solely to ensure their physical and material security; to meet those needs, the ruling power had to exercise a sovereignty on which Bodin placed few limits.[4] Indeed, Bodin's concept of the ruler's power is his most important contribution to political thought. In the brief selection from Jean Bodin's complex work, examine his conception of the sovereign power required to establish a well-ordered state in France and contrast this conception with the feudal state still partially existing in his time.

The second work of political theory was written by Jacques Bénigne Bossuet (1627–1704), Bishop of Meaux. A great orator who preached at the court of Louis XIV, Bossuet was entrusted with the education of the king's son and heir, the Dauphin. He wrote three works for that prince's instruction, including the one excerpted in this chapter, *Politics Drawn from the Very Words of the Holy Scripture* (1678).

As tutor to the Dauphin and royal preacher, Bossuet expressed what has been called the *divine right* theory of kingship: that is, the king was

---

3. Bodin's religious thought evolved in the course of his life. Although he was brought up a Catholic and was briefly a Carmelite friar, his knowledge of Hebrew and early regard for the Old Testament led some to suspect he was a Jew. Writings of his middle years indicate some Calvinist leanings. Later in life, his thought seems to have moved beyond traditional Catholic and Protestant Christianity. He was nevertheless deeply religious.

4. Bodin saw the sovereign power limited by natural law and the need to respect property (which meant that the ruler could not tax without his subjects' consent) and the family.

God's deputy on earth, and to oppose him was to oppose divine law. Here, of course, the bishop was drawing on those medieval beliefs and practices imputing certain divine powers to the king. Because Bossuet was an influential member of the court of Louis XIV, his ideas on royal authority carried considerable weight. Trained as a theologian, he buttressed his political theories with scriptural authority. In this selection, determine the extent of the royal link to God. Why might such a theory be particularly useful to Louis XIV?

Source 3 is a selection from the *Memoirs* of Louis de Rouvroy, Duke of Saint-Simon (1675–1755). Saint-Simon's memoirs of court life are extensive, comprising forty-one volumes in the main French edition. They constitute both a remarkable record of life at Versailles and, because of their style, an important example of French literature. As useful and important as the *Memoirs* are, however, they must be read with care. All of us, consciously or unconsciously, have biases and opinions, and memoirists are no exception. In fact, memoir literature illustrates problems that students of history should be aware of in all they read. The way in which authors present events, even what they choose to include or omit from their accounts, reflects their opinions. Because memoir writers often recount events in which they participated, they may have especially strong views about what they relate. Thus, to use Saint-Simon's work profitably, it is essential to understand his point of view. We must also ask if the memoir writer was in a position to know firsthand

what he or she is relating or is simply recounting less reliable rumors.

Saint-Simon came from an old noble family recently risen to prominence when his father became a royal favorite. Ironically, no one was more deeply opposed to the policies of Louis XIV, which aimed at destroying the traditional feudal power of the nobility in the name of royal authority, than this man whose position rested on that very authority. Saint-Simon was, quite simply, a defender of the older style of kingship in which sovereignty was limited by the monarch's need to consult with his vassals. His memoirs reflect this view and are often critical of the king. But even with his critical view of the king and his court, Saint-Simon was an important figure there, an individual privy to state business and court gossip, who gives us a remarkable picture of life at Versailles. Analyze the court etiquette and ritual Saint-Simon describes as a nonverbal message from the king to his most powerful subjects. For example, what message did the royal waking and dressing ceremony convey to the most powerful and privileged persons in France, who crowded the royal bedroom and vied for the privilege of helping the king dress? What message did their very presence convey in turn to Louis XIV? Recall Bossuet's ideas of kingship. Why might public religious ritual such as that attending the royal rising be part of the agenda of a king not particularly noted for his piety during the first half of his life?

Studied closely, the three different kinds of written evidence presented—the work of a sixteenth-century political theorist, the writings of a contemporary supporter, and the memoirs of one of the king's opponents—reveal much about the growing power of the French monarchy. What common themes do you find in these works? What were the sources of the king's political authority? From these written sources we move on to pictorial evidence of the symbols of royal authority. Symbols, as you know, are concrete objects possessing a meaning beyond what is immediately apparent. We are all aware of the power of symbols, particularly in our age of electronic media, and we all, perhaps unconsciously, analyze them to some extent. Take a simple example drawn from modern advertising: the lion appears frequently as an image in advertisements for banks and other financial institutions. The lion's presence is intended to convey to us the strength of the financial institution, to inspire our faith in the latter's ability to protect our funds. Using this kind of analysis, you can determine the total meaning of the symbols associated with Louis XIV.

Consider the painting presented as the fourth piece of evidence, *Louis XIV Taking Up Personal Government in 1661*. Louis XIV had been king in name since the age of five after his father's death in 1643, but only in 1661, as an adult, did he assume full power. Remember that such art was generally commissioned by the king and often had an instructional purpose. What do the following elements symbolize: the portrayal of Louis XIV as a Roman emperor; the positioning of a figure representing France on his left; the crowning of

the king with a wreath of flowers; the figure of Time (note the hourglass and scythe) holding a tapestry over the royal head; and the presence of herald angels hovering above?

Now go on to the other pictures and perform the same kind of analysis, always trying to identify the symbolic message the painter or architect wished to convey. For Source 5 study the royal pose and such seemingly superficial elements in the picture as the king's dress and the background details. Ask yourself what ideas these were intended to convey. Source 6 presents the insignia Louis XIV chose as his personal symbol, which decorated much of Versailles. Reflect on Louis's reasons for this choice in reading his explanation:

The symbol that I have adopted and that you see all around you represents the duties of a Prince and inspires me always to fulfill them. I chose for an emblem the Sun which, according to the rules of this art [heraldry], is the noblest of all, and which, by the brightness that surrounds it, by the light it lends to the other stars that constitute, after a fashion, its court, by the universal good it does, endlessly promoting life, joy, and growth, by its perpetual and regular movement, by its constant and invariable course, is assuredly the most dazzling and most beautiful image of the monarch.[5]

With Sources 8 through 13, we turn to analysis of architecture, which of course also served to symbolize royal power. You must ask

5. Quoted in Reinhardt and Glasgow, *The Sun King*, p. 181.

yourself how great that concept was as you look at the pictures of Versailles. The palace, after all, was not only the royal residence but also the setting for the conduct of government, including the king's reception of foreign ambassadors. At the most basic level, notice the scale of the palace. What impression might its size have been intended to convey? At a second level, examine decorative details of the palace. Why might the balustrade at the palace entry have been decorated with statuary symbolizing Magnificence, Justice, Wisdom, Prudence, Diligence, Peace, Europe, Asia, Renown, Abundance, Force, Generosity, Wealth, Authority, Fame, America, Africa, and Victory?

Observe the views of the palace's interior, considering the functions of the rooms and their details. Source 10 offers a view of the royal chapel at Versailles. Richly decorated in marble and complemented with ceiling paintings such as that depicting the Trinity, the chapel was the site of daily masses as well as of royal marriages and celebrations of victories. Note that the king attended mass in the royal gallery, joining the rest of the court on the main floor only when the mass celebrant was a bishop. Why might such a magnificent setting be part of the palace? More important, what significance do you place on the position the king chose for himself in this grand setting?

Sources 11 and 12 present the sites of the royal rising ceremony described by Saint-Simon. The royal bedroom, Source 11, was richly decorated in gilt, red, and white, and was complemented by paintings of biblical scenes. Notice the rich decoration of the Bull's Eye Window Antechamber, just outside the bedroom, where the courtiers daily awaited the king's arising. Why were the rooms decorated in such a fashion?

Source 13 offers an artist's view of Marly. Again, notice the scale of this palace, reflecting that it was, according to Saint-Simon, a weekend getaway spot for Louis XIV and selected favorites. How might the king have used invitations to this château with the closeness to the royal person they entailed? Examine details of the palace. The central château had twelve apartments, four of which were reserved for the royal family, the others for its guests. The twelve pavilions around the lake in the center of the château's grounds each housed two guest apartments and represented the twelve signs of the zodiac. What symbolic importance might you attach to this?

Finally, return to Source 7, which recreates the pageant known as the Carousel of 1662, one of many such entertainments at court. The scale of such festivals could be huge. In 1662, 12,197 costumed people took part in a celebration that included a parade through the streets of Paris and games. Costumed as ancient Romans, Persians, and others, the participants must have made quite an impression on their audience. What kind of impression do you think it was?

What common message runs through the art and architecture you have analyzed? As you unravel the message woven into this visual evidence, combine it with the evidence you derived from Saint-Simon's portrayal of court life and the political theory of absolutism. Remember, too, the unstated message: that the monarchy of Louis XIV possessed in Europe's largest army the ultimate means for persuading its subjects to accept the divine powers of the king. You should be able to determine from all this material what was new in this conception of royal authority and the ways in which the new authority was expressed.

THE EVIDENCE

Source 1 from Francis William Coker, editor, Readings in Political Philosophy *(New York: Macmillan, 1926), pp. 235–236.*

1. From Jean Bodin, *The Six Books of the Republic*, Book I, 1576

The first and principal function of sovereignty is to give laws to the citizens generally and individually, and, it must be added, not necessarily with the consent of superiors, equals, or inferiors. If the consent of superiors is required, then the prince is clearly a subject; if he must have the consent of equals, then others share his authority; if the consent of inferiors—the people or the senate—is necessary, then he lacks supreme authority. . . .

It may be objected that custom does not get its power from the judgment or command of the prince, and yet has almost the force of law, so that it would seem that the prince is master of law, the people of custom. Custom, insensibly, yet with the full compliance of all, passes gradually into the character of men, and acquires force with the lapse of time. Law, on the other hand, comes forth in one moment at the order of him who has the power to command, and often in opposition to the desire and approval of those whom it governs. Wherefore, Chrysostom[6] likens law to a tyrant and custom to a king. Moreover, the power of law is far greater than that of custom, for customs may be superseded by laws, but laws are not supplanted by customs; it is within the power and function of magistrates to restore the operation of laws which by custom are obsolescent. Custom proposes neither rewards nor penalties; laws carry one or the other, unless it be a permissive law which nullifies the penalty of some other law. In short, a custom has compelling force only as long as the prince, by adding his endorsement and sanction to the custom, makes it a law.

---

6. **Chrysostom:** Saint John Chrysostom (ca 347–407), an early Father of the Greek Church whose religion led him into conflict with the Eastern Roman emperor.

It is thus clear that laws and customs depend for their force upon the will of those who hold supreme power in the state. This first and chief mark of sovereignty is, therefore, of such sort that it cannot be transferred to subjects, though the prince or people sometimes confer upon one of the citizens the power to frame laws (*legum condendarum*), which then have the same force as if they had been framed by the prince himself. The Lacedæmonians bestowed such power upon Lycurgus, the Athenians upon Solon;[7] each stood as deputy for his state, and the fulfilment of his function depended upon the pleasure not of himself but of the people; his legislation had no force save as the people confirmed it by their assent. The former composed and wrote the laws, the people enacted and commanded them.

Under this supreme power of ordaining and abrogating laws, it is clear that all other functions of sovereignty are included; that it may be truly said that supreme authority in the state is comprised in this one thing—namely, to give laws to all and each of the citizens, and to receive none from them. For to declare war or make peace, though seeming to involve what is alien to the term law, is yet accomplished by law, that is by decree of the supreme power. It is also the prerogative of sovereignty to receive appeals from the highest magistrates, to confer authority upon the greater magistrates and to withdraw it from them, to allow exemption from taxes, to bestow other immunities, to grant dispensations from the laws, to exercise power of life and death, to fix the value, name and form of money, to compel all citizens to observe their oaths: all of these attributes are derived from the supreme power of commanding and forbidding—that is, from the authority to give law to the citizens collectively and individually, and to receive law from no one save immortal God. A duke, therefore, who gives laws to all his subjects, but receives law from the emperor, Pope, or king, or has a co-partner in authority, lacks sovereignty.

Source 2 from Richard H. Powers, editor and translator, Readings in European Civilization Since 1500 *(Boston: Houghton Mifflin, 1961) pp. 129–130.*

2. From Jacques Bénigne Bossuet, *Politics Drawn from the Very Words of the Holy Scriptures*, 1678

TO MONSEIGNEUR LE DAUPHIN

God is the King of kings. It is for Him to instruct and direct kings as His ministers. Heed then, Monseigneur, the lessons which He gives them in His Scriptures, and learn . . . the rules and examples on which they ought to base their conduct. . . .

7. **Lacedæmonians:** the Spartans of ancient Greece. **Lycurgus:** traditional author of the Spartan constitution. **Solon:** sixth century B.C. Athenean lawgiver.

BOOK II: OR AUTHORITY. . .

CONCLUSION: Accordingly we have established by means of Scriptures that monarchical government comes from God. . . . That when government was established among men He chose hereditary monarchy as the most natural and most durable form. That excluding the sex born to obey[8] from the sovereign power was only natural. . . .

BOOK III: THE NATURE OF ROYAL AUTHORITY. . .

FIRST ARTICLE: Its essential characteristics. . . . First, royal authority is sacred; Second, it is paternal; Third, it is absolute; Fourth, it is subject to reason. . . .

SECOND ARTICLE: Royal authority is sacred.

FIRST PROPOSITION: God establishes kings as his ministers and reigns over people through them.—We have already seen that all power comes from God. . . .

Therefore princes act as ministers of God and as His lieutenants on earth. It is through them that he exercises His empire. . . .

Thus we have seen that the royal throne is not the throne of a man, but the throne of God himself. So in Scriptures we find "God has chosen my son Solomon to sit upon the throne of the kingdom of Jehovah over Israel." And further, "Solomon sat on the throne of Jehovah as king."

And in order that we should not think that to have kings established by God is peculiar to the Israelites, here is what Ecclesiastes says: "God gives each people its governor; and Israel is manifestly reserved to Him.". . .

SECOND PROPOSITION: The person of the king is sacred.—It follows from all the above that the person of kings is sacred. . . . God has had them anointed by His prophets with a sacred ointment, as He has had His pontiffs and His altars anointed.

But even before actually being anointed, they are sacred by virtue of their charge, as representatives of His divine majesty, delegated by His providence to execute His design. . . .

The title of *christ* is given to kings, one sees them called *christs* or the Lord's *anointed* everywhere.

Bearing this venerable name, even the prophets revered them, and looked upon them as associated with the sovereign empire of God, whose authority they exercise on earth. . . .

THIRD PROPOSITION: Religion and conscience demand that we obey the prince.—After having said that the prince is the minister of God Saint Paul concluded: "Accordingly it is necessary that you subject yourself to him out of fear of his anger, but also because of the obligation of your conscience. . . ."

---

8. **Sex born to obey:** women. The Salic Law, mistakenly attributed to the medieval Salian Franks, precluded women from inheriting the crown of France.

And furthermore: "Servants, obey your temporal masters in all things. . . ." Saint Peter said: "Therefore submit yourselves to the order established among men for the love of God; be subjected to the king as to God . . . be subjected to those to whom He gives His authority and who are sent by Him to reward good deeds and to punish evil ones."

Even if kings fail in this duty, their charge and their ministry must be respected. For Scriptures tell us: "Obey your masters, not only those who are mild and good, but also those who are peevish and unjust."

Thus there is something religious in the respect which one renders the prince. Service to God and respect for kings are one thing. . . .

Thus it is in the spirit of Christianity for kings to be paid a kind of religious respect. . . .

BOOK IV: CONTINUATION OF THE CHARACTERISTICS OF ROYALTY

FIRST ARTICLE: Royal authority is absolute.

FIRST PROPOSITION: The prince need render account to no one for what he orders. . . .

SECOND PROPOSITION: When the prince has judged there is no other judgment. . . . Princes are gods.

Source 3 from Bayle St. John, translator, The Memoirs of the Duke of Saint-Simon on the Reign of Louis XIV and the Regency, *8th ed. (London: George Allen, 1913), vol. 2, pp. 363–365, vol. 3, pp. 221–27.*

3. The Duke of Saint-Simon on the Reign of Louis XIV

[On the creation of Versailles and the nature of its court life]

He [Louis XIV] early showed a disinclination for Paris. The troubles that had taken place there during the minority made him regard the place as dangerous;[9] he wished, too, to render himself venerable by hiding himself from the eyes of the multitude; all these considerations fixed him at St. Germains[10] soon after the death of the Queen, his mother. It was to that place he began to attract the world by fêtes and gallantries, and by making it felt that he wished to be often seen.

9. During the Fronde revolt of 1648–1653, the royal government lost control of Paris to the crowds and the royal family was forced to flee the city. Because Louis XIV was a minor (only ten years of age) when the revolt erupted, the government was administered by his mother, Anne of Austria, and her chief minister, Cardinal Mazarin.

10. **St. Germain-en-Laye:** site of a royal château, overlooking the Seine and dating from the twelfth century, where Louis XIV was born. The court fled there in 1649 during the Fronde.

His love for Madame de la Vallière,[11] which was at first kept secret, occasioned frequent excursions to Versailles, then a little card castle, which had been built by Louis XIII—annoyed, and his suite still more so, at being frequently obliged to sleep in a wretched inn there, after he had been out hunting in the forest of Saint Leger. That monarch rarely slept at Versailles more than one night, and then from necessity; the King, his son, slept there, so that he might be more in private with his mistress; pleasures unknown to the hero and just man, worthy son of Saint Louis, who built the little château.[12]

These excursions of Louis XIV by degrees gave birth to those immense buildings he erected at Versailles; and their convenience for a numerous court, so different from the apartments at St. Germains, led him to take up his abode there entirely shortly after the death of the Queen.[13] He built an infinite number of apartments, which were asked for by those who wished to pay their court to him; whereas at St. Germains nearly everybody was obliged to lodge in the town, and the few who found accommodation at the château were strangely inconvenienced.

The frequent fêtes, the private promenades at Versailles, the journeys, were means on which the King seized in order to distinguish or mortify the courtiers, and thus render them more assiduous in pleasing him. He felt that of real favours he had not enough to bestow; in order to keep up the spirit of devotion, he therefore unceasingly invented all sorts of ideal ones, little preferences and petty distinctions, which answered his purpose as well.

He was exceedingly jealous of the attention paid him. Not only did he notice the presence of the most distinguished courtiers, but those of inferior degree also. He looked to the right and to the left, not only upon rising but upon going to bed, at his meals, in passing through his apartments, or his gardens of Versailles, where alone the courtiers were allowed to follow him; he saw and noticed everybody; not one escaped him, not even those who hoped to remain unnoticed. He marked well all absentees from the court, found out the reason of their absence, and never lost an opportunity of acting towards them as the occasion might seem to justify. With some of the courtiers (the most distinguished), it was a demerit not to make the court their ordinary abode; with others 'twas a fault to come but rarely; for those who never or scarcely ever came it was certain disgrace.

Louis XIV took great pains to be well informed of all that passed everywhere; in the public places, in the private houses, in society and familiar intercourse. His spies and tell-tales were infinite. He had them of all species;

---

11. **Madame de la Vallière:** Louise de la Baume le Blanc, Duchesse de la Vallière (1644–1710), the king's first mistress.

12. Saint-Simon greatly admired Louis XIII, whom he had never met, and for over half a century attended annual memorial services for the king at the royal tombs in the basilica of St. Denis.

13. Anne of Austria (1601–1666), the mother of Louis XIV.

many who were ignorant that their information reached him; others who knew it; others who wrote to him direct, sending their letters through channels he indicated; and all these letters were seen by him alone, and always before everything else; others who sometimes spoke to him secretly in his cabinet, entering by the back stairs. These unknown means ruined an infinite number of people of all classes, who never could discover the cause; often ruined them very unjustly; for the King, once prejudiced, never altered his opinion or so rarely, that nothing was more rare.

[*On the royal day and court etiquette*]
[*The royal day begins*]

At eight o'clock the chief valet de chambre on duty, who alone had slept in the royal chamber, and who had dressed himself, awoke the King. The chief physician, the chief surgeon, and the nurse (as long as she lived), entered at the same time. The latter kissed the King; the others rubbed and often changed his shirt, because he was in the habit of sweating a great deal. At the quarter, the grand chamberlain was called (or, in his absence, the first gentleman of the chamber), and those who had, what was called the *grandes entrées*. The chamberlain (or chief gentleman) drew back the curtains which had been closed again, and presented the holy water from the vase, at the head of the bed. These gentlemen stayed but a moment, and that was the time to speak to the King, if any one had anything to ask of him; in which case the rest stood aside. When, contrary to custom, nobody had aught to say, they were there but for a few moments. He who had opened the curtains and presented the holy water, presented also a prayer-book. Then all passed into the cabinet of the council. A very short religious service being over, the King called, they re-entered. The same officer gave him his dressing-gown; immediately after, other privileged courtiers entered, and then everybody, in time to find the King putting on his shoes and stockings, for he did almost everything himself and with address and grace. Every other day we saw him shave himself; and he had a little short wig in which he always appeared, even in bed, and on medicine days. He often spoke of the chase, and sometimes said a word to somebody. No toilette table was near him; he had simply a mirror held before him.

As soon as he was dressed, he prayed to God, at the side of his bed, where all the clergy present knelt, the cardinals without cushions, all the laity remaining standing; and the captain of the guards came to the balustrade during the prayer, after which the King passed into his cabinet.

He found there, or was followed by all who had the entrée, a very numerous company, for it included everybody in any office. He gave orders to each for the day; thus within a half a quarter of an hour it was known what he meant to do; and then all this crowd left directly. The bastards, a few favourites, and the valets alone were left. It was then a good opportunity for talking with the King; for example, about plans of gardens and buildings; and conversation lasted more or less according to the person engaged in it.

All the Court meantime waited for the King in the gallery, the captain of the guard being alone in the chamber seated at the door of the cabinet.

[*The business of government*]

On Sunday, and often on Monday, there was a council of state; on Tuesday a finance council; on Wednesday council of state; on Saturday finance council. Rarely were two held in one day or any on Thursday or Friday. Once or twice a month there was a council of despatches[14] on Monday morning; but the order that the Secretaries of State took every morning between the King's rising and his mass, much abridged this kind of business. All the ministers were seated according to rank, except at the council of despatches, where all stood except the sons of France, the Chancellor, and the Duc de Beauvilliers.[15]

[*The royal luncheon*]

The dinner was always *au petit couvert*, that is, the King ate by himself in his chamber upon a square table in front of the middle window. It was more or less abundant, for he ordered in the morning whether it was to be "a little," or "very little" service. But even at this last, there were always many dishes, and three courses without counting the fruit. The dinner being ready, the principal courtiers entered; then all who were known; and the first gentlemen of the chamber on duty, informed the King.

I have seen, but very rarely, Monseigneur[16] and his sons standing at their dinners, the King not offering them a seat. I have continually seen there the Princes of the blood and the cardinals. I have often seen there also Monsieur,[17] either on arriving from St. Cloud to see the King, or arriving from the council of despatches (the only one he entered), give the King his napkin and remain standing. A little while afterwards, the King, seeing that he did not go away, asked him if he would not sit down; he bowed, and the King ordered a seat to be brought for him. A stool was put behind him. Some moments after the King said, "Nay then, sit down, my brother." Monsieur bowed and seated himself until the end of the dinner, when he presented the napkin.

[*The day ends*]

At ten o'clock his supper was served. The captain of the guard announced this to him. A quarter of an hour after the King came to supper, and from

---

14. **Council of Despatches:** the royal council in which ministers discussed the letters from the provincial administrators of France, the *intendants*.

15. **Duc de Beauvilliers:** Paul de Beauvilliers, Duc de St. Aignan (1648–1714), friend of Saint-Simon and tutor of Louis XIV's grandsons, the dukes of Burgundy, Anjou, and Berry.

16. **Monseigneur:** Louis, Dauphin de France (1661–1711), son of Louis XIV and heir to the throne.

17. **Monsieur:** Philippe, Duc d'Orléans (1640–1701), Louis XIV's only sibling. His permanent residence was at the Château of St. Cloud near Paris.

the ante-chamber of Madame de Maintenon[18] to the table again, any one spoke to him who wished. This supper was always on a grand scale, the royal household (that is, the sons and daughters of France), at table, and a large number of courtiers and ladies present, sitting or standing, and on the evening before the journey to Marly all those ladies who wished to take part in it. That was called presenting yourself for Marly. Men asked in the morning, simply saying to the King, "Sire, Marly." In later years the King grew tired of this, and a valet wrote up in the gallery the names of those who asked. The ladies continued to present themselves.

After supper the King stood some moments, his back to the balustrade of the foot of his bed, encircled by all his Court; then, with bows to the ladies, passed into his cabinet, where on arriving, he gave his orders. He passed a little less than an hour there, seated in an arm-chair, with his legitimate children and bastards, his grandchildren, legitimate and otherwise, and their husbands or wives. Monsieur in another arm-chair; the princesses upon stools, Monseigneur and all the other princes standing.

The King, wishing to retire, went and fed his dogs; then said good night, passed into his chamber to the *ruelle*[19] of his bed, where he said his prayers, as in the morning, then undressed. He said good night with an inclination of the head, and whilst everybody was leaving the room stood at the corner of the mantelpiece, where he gave the order to the colonel of the guards alone. Then commenced what was called the *petit coucher*, at which only the specially privileged remained. That was short. They did not leave until he got into bed. It was a moment to speak to him. Then all left if they saw any one buckle to the King. For ten or twelve years before he died the *petit coucher* ceased, in consequence of a long attack of gout he had had; so that the Court was finished at the rising from supper.

18. **Madame de Maintenon:** Françoise d'Aubigné, Marquise de Maintenon (1635–1719) married Louis XIV after the death of his first wife, Marie Thérèse of Spain.

19. **ruelle:** the area in the bedchamber in which the bed was located and in which the king received persons of high rank.

4. **Charles Le Brun,** *Louis XIV Taking Up Personal Government,* ca 1680, **from the Ceiling of the Hall of Mirrors at Versailles**

5. **Hyacinthe-François-Honoré-Pierre-André Rigaud,** *Louis XIV,*
King of France and Navarre, 1701

7. Rousselet, Louis XIV as "Roman Emperor" in an engraving from the Carousel of 1662

6. Mask of Apollo, God of Light, 17th century

[19]

8. Garden Façade of Versailles

9. Aerial View of Versailles

[21]

Sources 10 through 12 from Château de Versailles/Cliché des Musées Nationaux-Paris.

10. The Royal Chapel at Versailles

11. Reconstruction of the King's Chamber at Versailles, after 1701

12. Antechamber of the Bull's Eye Window at Versailles

13. Pierre Denis Martin, *Château of Marly,* **1724**

QUESTIONS TO CONSIDER

Louis XIV is reputed to have said, "I am the state." Whether the king actually uttered those words is immaterial for our purpose; they neatly summarize the unifying theme in all this chapter's evidence, which demonstrates how royal power was defined as absolute and how that authority was expressed in deeds, art, and architecture.

Consider first the theories of royal authority, comparing the political ideas of Bodin and Bossuet. What are the origins of sovereignty for Bodin and Bossuet? How do they differ? Why can Bodin be said to have justified absolutism on the basis of expediency, that is, that absolute royal power was the only way to ensure order? Do the two thinkers ultimately arrive at the same conclusions? What is the difference between Bodin's conclusion that the royal power permitted the king to hand down laws to his subjects and receive them from no one and Bossuet's definition of the king as virtually a god on earth?

Royal ceremony and etiquette enforced this view of the king. Consider Saint-Simon's *Memoirs* again. The selection describes only limited aspects of court etiquette, but it conveys to us a vivid image of court life. Who was the center of this court made up of the country's most prominent nobles? Analyze individual elements of court ceremony. How does each contribute to a consistent message? Consider the royal dining ritual. To reinforce the lesson of royal power, who was kept standing during the king's luncheon? Who had the task, for most commoners performed by an ordinary waiter, of handing the king his napkin? A message of royal power is being expressed here in a way that is almost theatrical.

Indeed, the image of theater can be useful in further structuring your analysis. The stage setting for this royal display, the palace of Versailles, shows the work of a skilled director in creating a remarkably uniform message in landscape and architecture alike. Who do you suppose that director was? Examine his statement at Versailles. Look first at the exterior views of both Versailles (Sources 8 and 9) and Marly (Source 13). How do the grounds add to the expression of royal power? What view of nature might they suggest to a visitor? How did the stage set enhance the play described by Saint-Simon? How did it encourage the French to accept the authority of Louis XIV?

Look next at the interior of the palace. It was, of course, a royal residence. But do you find much evidence of its function as a place to live in? Examine the royal bedroom and its outer room (Sources 11 and 12). Modern bedrooms are generally intimate in size and decoration; how does the king's differ? Why? Notice, too, the art and use of symbols in the palace. Why might the king's artists and architects have decorated the palace so richly with Biblical and classical heroes and themes (Sources 8, 9, 10, 11, 12)?

Finally, consider the principal actor, Louis XIV. Notice how his self-presentation is consistent with the trappings of the stage set. We find him consciously acting a role in Source 7, portraying an emperor in the Carousel of 1662. That engraving embodies a great deal of indirect information. What details reinforce the aura of royal power? Why should the king be mounted and in Roman costume? What strikes you about the king's attitude atop the prancing horse? Compare this picture with the Le Brun (Source 4) and Rigaud (Source 5) paintings. What elements do you find these pictures to have in common? How does the royal emblem of the sun (Source 6) contribute to the common message?

With these considerations in mind, return now to the central questions of this chapter. What was the theoretical explanation of royal power expressed in late sixteenth- and seventeenth-century France? How did such early modern kings as Louis XIV communicate their absolute power in the various ceremonies, displays, and symbols of royal authority presented in the evidence?

EPILOGUE

We all know that any successful act produces imitators. In the seventeenth century the monarchy of Louis XIV for a long time looked like the most successful regime in Europe. Royal absolutism had seemingly unified France. Out of that unity came a military power that threatened to overwhelm Europe; an economic strength, based on mercantilism, that increased French wealth; and an intellectual life that gave the culture of seventeenth- and eighteenth-century Europe a distinctly French accent. Imitators of Louis XIV's work were therefore numerous. At the very least, kings sought physically to express the unifying and centralizing monarchical principle of government in palaces recreating Versailles.[20]

But the work of such monarchs as Louis XIV involved far more than the construction of elaborate palaces in which to stage the theater of their court lives. The act of focusing the state on the figure of the monarch began the transition to the centralized modern style of government and marked the beginning of the end of the decentralized medieval state that bound subjects in an almost contractual relationship to their ruler. The king now emerged as theoretically all-powerful and also as a symbol of national unity.

The monarchs of the age did their work of state building so effectively that the unity and centralization they created often survived the monarchy itself. The French monarchy, for example, succumbed to a revolution in 1789 that in large part stemmed from

20. Palaces consciously modeled on Versailles multiplied in the late seventeenth and early eighteenth centuries. They included the Schönbrunn Palace in Vienna (1694), the Royal Palace in Berlin (begun in 1698), Ludwigsburg Palace in Württemberg, Germany (1704–1733), the Würzburg Residenz in Franconia, Germany (1719–1744), and the Stupinigi Palace (1729–1733) near Turin, Italy.

the bankruptcy of the royal government after too many years of over-spending on wars and court life in the name of royal glory. But the unified state endured, strong enough to retain its sense of unity despite challenges in war and changes of government that introduced a new politics of mass participation.

The methods employed by Louis XIV and other monarchs also transcended their age. Modern governments understand the importance of ritual, symbolism, and display in creating the sense of national unity that was part of the absolute monarch's goal. Ritual may now be centered on important national observances. The parades on such days as July 4 in the United States, July 14 in France (commemorating one of the earliest victories of the Revolution of 1789), and the anniversary of the October 1917 Revolution in the Soviet Union all differ in form from the rituals of Louis XIV. They are designed for a new political age, one of mass participation in politics, in which the loyalty of the whole people, not just an elite group, must be won. But their purpose remains the same: to win loyalty to the existing political order.

Modern states also use symbolism to build political loyalty. Artwork on public buildings in Washington, D.C. and the capital cities of other republics, for example, often employs classical themes. The purpose of such artwork is to suggest to citizens that their government perpetuates the republican rectitude of Athens and Rome. Display also is part of the political agenda of modern governments, even among governments of new arrivals in the community of nations. This is why newly independent, developing nations of the twentieth century expend large portions of their meager resources on such things as grand new capital cities, the most sophisticated military weaponry, and the latest aircraft for the national airline. These are symbols of their government's successes and thus the basis for these regimes' claims on their peoples' loyalty. These modern rituals, symbols, and displays perform the same function for modern rulers as Versailles did for the Sun King.

CHAPTER TWO

THE ENLIGHTENMENT

CONFRONTS THE DIVINE:

THE DEBATE OVER

THE LISBON EARTHQUAKE

THE PROBLEM

Because Roman Catholics observe November 1 as All Saints' Day, a holy day obliging their attendance at the mass in commemoration of all the church's saints, most of the population of Lisbon, Portugal was either at church or preparing to attend services on the sunny morning of Saturday, November 1, 1755. At 9:30 A.M., however, a loud rumbling noise disrupted the peaceful morning. Then three great seismic shocks rocked the city and ended its citizens' religious devotions. Churches and homes alike tumbled during this earthquake whose shocks were felt as far away as Switzerland and northern France, and many persons perished. Other disasters resulting from the earthquake soon increased the loss of life. Fires spread from the hearths of the damaged city and burned for almost a week before they could be extinguished. The trembling of the earth created ocean waves 15 to 20 feet high that swept up the Tagus River on which Lisbon is situated and broke over the city's waterfront. The combined destruction of earthquake, fires, and tidal waves left about 10,000 to 15,000 dead on that holy day of November 1.[1]

Natural disasters such as this always have perplexed the human mind. What is the reason for them? Why do they happen where they do? For religious persons of the Judeo-Christian West in the eighteenth century, what was the explanation for such evils as earthquakes in a world they believed was governed by a benevolent God? The Lisbon earthquake was a remarkable catalyst to thought and debate in its time, prompting contemporary thinkers to propose a variety of answers to these eternal questions.

Certainly the Lisbon earthquake was not the most destructive in human history; far more devastating

---

1. Estimates on the earthquake toll vary greatly, ranging as high as 60,000 persons. T. D. Kendrick, the author of a modern study, *The Lisbon Earthquake* (Philadelphia: J. B. Lippincott, 1957), accepts 10,000–15,000 as the probable number of dead, and, indeed, as the city's population was only about 275,000, the figure of 60,000 dead is difficult to accept.

quakes have occurred.[2] What made this disaster worthy of note was its location and its timing. Because the 1755 earthquake struck a major capital and international trading center, it captured the attention of all informed Europeans.[3] These educated Europeans recorded their reactions to the disaster in a period of intellectual change, and their writings relevant to the earthquake and the broader issue of humankind's understanding of the physical world provide us a unique look into the evolution of Western thought.

By the year 1755, Europe approached the culmination of an intellectual revolution underway since the sixteenth century. Scientific discoveries of the sixteenth and seventeenth centuries, which your textbook describes as the Scientific Revolution, produced a wholly new outlook on the physical world that gained increasing acceptance among educated Europeans. The result of the sixteenth- and seventeenth-century work of Nicholas Copernicus, Johannes Kepler, Galileo Galilei, René Descartes, Sir Isaac Newton,

2. A number of twentieth-century earthquakes, for which we have more accurate casualty counts, have clearly been more devastating. For example, the quake that struck Yokohama, Japan on September 1, 1923 took about 200,000 lives; another in Tangshan, China on July 28, 1976 killed about 242,000 persons.

3. Other earthquakes of the period either struck on the fringes of the West, as in Jamaica in 1692 and Peru in 1746, or in isolated parts of Europe, as in Sicily in 1693. The few that had occurred in major cities—like London's quakes of 1750—had been slight in comparison to Lisbon's.

and others was a growing certainty that the physical world could be understood through the ability of human reason to discern immutable mathematical laws that governed it. No longer did intellectuals explain the world in terms of supernatural action. The physical world increasingly appeared to be a great machine, and many eighteenth-century thinkers, called Deists in their religious outlook, posited a novel relationship between God and the physical world. The movements of the world-machine might have been created by God, but Deists believed that they could not be interrupted by Him. Some thinkers also had faith that a divine plan governed the world, affirming that all would be well. But all agreed that nothing happened in such a world without sufficient cause or reason. This was a true revolution in thought, espoused by intellectuals called *philosophes*, who sought to apply their faith in the existence of reasonable and comprehensible natural laws to all aspects of the human experience.

The Enlightenment's concept of a machinelike universe contradicted much in the traditional Judeo-Christian concept of God. Most important, perhaps, Enlightenment thought precluded any belief in divine intervention in the physical world. Miracles, for example, simply were impossible for the *philosophes* because they violated natural laws of cause and effect. Traditional religious beliefs, however, were not without their defenders. Often these defenders were clergymen who, using the

Chapter 2

The

Enlightenment

Confronts the

Divine: The

Debate Over

the Lisbon

Earthquake

same tools of reason employed by the Enlightenment's exponents, strongly disagreed with the *philosophes*. In Catholic Europe, members of the Society of Jesus, or Jesuits, were important defenders of traditional beliefs; in France they even published an influential monthly journal for their cause, the *Journal de Trevoux*. Clergymen in Protestant countries also espoused traditional beliefs concerning a divine presence in the world.

Debate between the proponents of these two differing visions of this world's relationship to God had been underway for years before the Lisbon earthquake. That disaster elicited from theologians very predictable explanations, as we will see. The *philosophes*, however, differed markedly among themselves on the earthquake's significance. By reading selections on the exchange of ideas oc-casioned by the Lisbon earthquake, the background on how some of these ideas developed, and the later implications of these thoughts, you will gain a deeper understanding of eighteenth-century thought about God and His relationship to the world. This was a key issue for the age, and one widely debated. Examining it allows us to learn a great deal about the Enlightenment by posing basic questions to the sources presented in this chapter: Why did the Lisbon earthquake present such an intellectual crisis for eighteenth-century thinkers? How did theologians explain the disaster within the framework of their beliefs? How did Enlightenment thinkers explain it? In what direction was their thought on the physical world and its relationship to divine forces leading them?

SOURCES AND METHOD

The problem at hand presents you with questions in the history of ideas, or what historians call "intellectual history." For generations, intellectual historians wrote about the ideas of the past without asking a question that seems central to historians today: "Who, in a certain period, held a particular set of ideas?" More precisely, "How representative were these ideas of the society as a whole?" In other words, "How broad was the impact of these ideas in their own time?"

As your text probably notes, literacy was not widespread in eighteenth-century Europe, so that the majority of the continent's population never had access to the ideas of the Scientific Revolution or the Enlightenment. Indeed, historians in recent years have come to recognize the persistence of a culture of the people, a popular culture, sometimes pre-Christian in its roots, that coexisted with the ideas of the *philosophes*. The intellectual world of the unlettered was one inhabited by witches and warlocks, in which people readily accepted supernatural explanations for physical phenomena. Such people might be frightened almost to death by an earthquake, but they took little part in the discussion of its philosophical ramifications presented here.

If the majority of the population of eighteenth-century Europe had little or no access to the ideas we will examine, are those ideas still relevant to our study of the past? The answer is certainly yes, though we must take care not to attribute the ideas to all persons. We are discussing ideas that were current among the small, educated elite of the eighteenth century. We must recognize, however, that this privileged group had tremendous influence in a societal and governmental system that accorded little role to anyone born outside that class. Moreover, such persons were the opinionmakers of their age. Their ideas would have had considerable influence among those with some education among the middle classes. Thus the thought of this minority of Europe's total population had an impact well outside the boundaries of the social group from which it arose and thus is quite worthy of study.

The evidence that follows has been chosen to present you with a broad sample of the thought of Europe's eighteenth-century intellectual elite and the background of its development. The Lisbon earthquake raised the immediate problem of explaining the disaster. This question involved large issues, chief among them the relationship of the physical world to God. Did God intervene in the world's daily operation, as theologians argued? Was He, as Deists said,

like a watchmaker who created a world-machine and then stood back, letting it operate on its own? Or was no divine hand at work in the world at all? In reading these selections, you should gain an understanding of why the Lisbon disaster preoccupied so many eighteenth-century thinkers.

Sources 1 and 2 represent a tendency perhaps as old as humankind, that is, the attempt to explain natural phenomena in terms of supernatural or divine forces. Source 1, "An Opinion on the True Cause of the Earthquake," was a pamphlet written by a Roman Catholic priest, the Jesuit Gabriel Malagrida (1689–1761). Born in Italy, Malagrida spent much of his life in missionary work in Portugal's Brazilian colony and lived in Lisbon after 1754. It is not insignificant that he was a Jesuit; the Society of Jesus was one of the most influential orders in the early modern Roman Catholic church. The absolute loyalty of the Jesuits to the papacy, combined with their energy and preaching ability, had done much to stem the spread of sixteenth-century European Protestantism. In subsequent centuries the order's excellent schools had strengthened Catholicism, as had the influence its members wielded as spiritual advisors to monarchs. Malagrida in every way typified his order. He was an excellent preacher, well connected at court, and consequently his attempt to justify the earthquake in theological terms had an impact in Catholic Portugal. How did he account for the earthquake?

Chapter 2

The

Enlightenment

Confronts the

Divine: The

Debate Over

the Lisbon

Earthquake

Source 2 is a sermon by John Wesley (1703–1791), one of the most influential English Protestant leaders of the eighteenth century. Ordained a priest of the Church of England, Wesley experienced a religious conversion in 1738 that led him to found a new Protestant faith, Methodism. Wesley preached widely in the cause of his faith; he is estimated to have journeyed 250,000 miles in the course of delivering 40,000 sermons, often to large audiences. Because many of his sermons were published in pamphlet form, he reached an even larger public than those able to attend his sermons. According to this influential Protestant clergyman, what was the cause of the Lisbon earthquake? How might future earthquakes be avoided?

With Source 3 we encounter the thought of the Enlightenment. Voltaire was the pen name of François-Marie Arouet (1694–1778), one of the greatest of the *philosophes*. Born the son of a Parisian notary, Voltaire received a traditional education from French Jesuits but early developed an independence of thought and an irreverence toward established creeds and institutions that plunged him into difficulties. In 1717 the royal government imprisoned him for eleven months for alleged insults to the regent of France. In 1726 his writings provoked the authorities once again, and he avoided a second, lengthy imprisonment by agreeing to leave France for an extended stay in England. Voltaire remained in England over two years.

The lack of official tolerance for Voltaire's early writings defined the theme that became a constant in his writings: the cause of toleration. In England, he believed he found a much freer and more tolerant society than that in France, and his *Letters Concerning the English Nation* (published 1733) contrasted France very unfavorably with England. The book also reflected the deep impact of the ideas of the English thinkers Newton and Locke on Voltaire. He would go on to write an extensive popular version of Newtonian physics, *Elements of the Philosophy of Newton* (1736), but in the earlier work we find a brief summary of Newton's thought. What sort of world did Newton describe? What was the relationship of God to this world? In what ways does Voltaire express a Deistic interpretation of God's relationship to the physical world?

Source 4 is a passage from the poem "An Essay on Man" by Alexander Pope (1688–1744), an English poet whose acquaintance Voltaire made during his English sojourn. As a member of England's Roman Catholic minority, Pope was excluded from educational opportunities open to Protestants, and he was largely self-taught. "An Essay on Man," published in 1734, is therefore remarkable as a summary of philosophical speculation of the day on God's relationship to the world described by Newton. What is that relationship, according to Pope? Why does Pope tell his readers to accept the world as they find it?

Source 5 is an excerpt from the *Encyclopedia: The Rational Dictionary of the Sciences, the Arts, and the Crafts*, edited by Denis Diderot. Conceived as an attempt to summarize the knowledge of the eighteenth century and especially the results of the Scientific Revolution, the *Encyclopedia* also served to recapitulate Enlightenment thought. Many of the chief *philosophes*, including Voltaire, wrote its articles and brought to the work their criticism of institutions of their age. Immediate controversy was the result. Church authorities sought to stop publication of the *Encyclopedia*, but slowly, over the years 1751 to 1772, the work appeared in seventeen volumes of text and eleven volumes of illustrations. The entry reproduced here as Source 5 is on the subject "Observation." What methods of research did its anonymous author urge scientific researchers to adopt? How does this article reflect the Scientific Revolution? Is there any role for the intervention of God in this method of amassing knowledge?

In Source 6 we have evidence of the effort to apply these methods of research. This selection is the work of Georges Louis Leclerc, Comte de Buffon (1707–1788), a nobleman and scientist who served as director of the French royal botanical gardens in Paris. In addition, he devoted himself for forty years to writing a forty-four–volume *Natural History*, his attempt to summarize and popularize the results of the Scientific Revolution. Although Buffon may not have been a particularly original thinker and his observation of earthquakes clearly was confined to their aboveground effects, his work was a great success, becoming something of a bestseller that greatly influenced his age. Certainly we cannot scientifi-

cally accept Buffon's explanation of earthquakes today. But what approach to the physical world does his work represent? Would he in any way be able to accept the ideas of Malagrida or Wesley? Does Buffon see any evidence of divine design? How does his concept of the world grow out of Newton's science?

In Source 7 we encounter a rather different Voltaire from the man who discussed Newton. In his "Poem on the Lisbon Disaster, or An Examination of that Axiom 'All Is Well,'" published twenty years after *Letters*, we have the work of an older Voltaire, whose words reflect a growing doubt about the ideas of the early Enlightenment on the relationship of the physical world to God. What is Voltaire's view of God's role in the physical world in this poem he wrote on receiving the news of the Lisbon disaster? Why can Voltaire accept neither a theological nor a Deistic explanation of the event? What possible implications for the later Enlightenment's views on God do you find in this work of the influential Voltaire?

Voltaire's Lisbon poem elicited a forceful response in the form of a letter from Jean-Jacques Rousseau (1712–1778). Born in Geneva, Switzerland, Rousseau was the child of a mother who died shortly after his birth, and his subsequent haphazard upbringing was followed by a wandering life that permitted few lasting relationships. His works, including *The Social Contract*, a work of political theory, and *Emile*, a work of educational philosophy, rank Rousseau among the eighteenth century's greatest thinkers. But he was not part

Chapter 2

The

Enlightenment

Confronts the

Divine: The

Debate Over

the Lisbon

Earthquake

of the company of the *philosophes* and ultimately disassociated himself from them. Rousseau's works glorify the simplicity to be found in nature, and in many ways he was a precursor of the Romantic movement in early nineteenth-century literature, which consciously sought to negate the Enlightenment.

It was only natural for Rousseau, therefore, to have intellectual differences with Voltaire. When he wrote his letter in 1755, however, Rousseau's great work was still in the future and he was as yet relatively unknown. His letter to Voltaire, already an internationally known thinker, was thus rather audacious. What does Rousseau find wrong in Voltaire's view of the Lisbon earthquake? What relationship between God and humans does Rousseau express?

The author of Source 9, "The Essay on Miracles," was David Hume (1711–1776), a Scottish philosopher who lived for a time in France and who briefly befriended Rousseau. (Hume offered Rousseau a home when the latter was expelled from Bern, Switzerland for his ideas. Rousseau soon quarreled with Hume, however, as he did with many persons.) Hume's thought reflects the Enlightenment search for hard, observable facts to justify conclusions, whether historical, philosophical, or theological. Could Hume find evidence of the God of Malagrida and Wesley on one hand or of the God of Newton and the early Voltaire on the other? According to Hume, is any divine scheme at work in the world?

If Hume represents the skepticism of the Enlightenment, Baron d'Holbach, a German-born nobleman who passed much of his life in France, perhaps reflects a logical culmination of Enlightenment thought about the physical world. What room is there for a divinity in Holbach's view, which sees the world as an "uninterrupted succession of causes and effects" in which "matter always existed." Why do you think Holbach's contemporaries, including Voltaire, criticized his position as atheistic?

As you read these selections, you should be able to answer the central questions of this chapter: Why did the Lisbon earthquake pose such an intellectual crisis for eighteenth-century thinkers? How did theologians explain the disaster? How did Enlightenment thinkers explain it? In what direction was their thought on the physical world and its relationship to divine forces leading them?

THE EVIDENCE

Source 1 from T. D. Kendrick, The Lisbon Earthquake *(Philadelphia: Lippincott, 1957), pp. 137–138. Translated by T. D. Kendrick.*

1. Gabriel Malagrida, "An Opinion on the True Cause of the Earthquake," 1756

Learn, O Lisbon, that the destroyers of our houses, palaces, churches, and convents, the cause of the death of so many people and of the flames that devoured such vast treasures, are your abominable sins, and not comets, stars, vapours and exhalations, and similar natural phenomena. Tragic Lisbon is now a mound of ruins. Would that it were less difficult to think of some method of restoring the place; but it has been abandoned, and the refugees from the city live in despair. As for the dead, what a great harvest of sinful souls such disasters send to Hell! It is scandalous to pretend the earthquake was just a natural event, for if that be true, there is no need to repent and to try to avert the wrath of God, and not even the Devil himself could invent a false idea more likely to lead us all to irreparable ruin. Holy people had prophesied the earthquake was coming, yet the city continued in its sinful ways without a care for the future. Now, indeed, the case of Lisbon is desperate. It is necessary to devote all our strength and purpose to the task of repentance. Would to God we could see as much determination and fervour for this necessary exercise as are devoted to the erection of huts and new buildings! Does being billeted in the country outside the city areas put us outside the jurisdiction of God?[4] God undoubtedly desires to exercise His love and mercy, but be sure that wherever we are, He is watching us, scourge in hand.

---

4. Many of Lisbon's citizens fled the danger of the city for the countryside and remained there in shacks and tents until the earthquake danger passed.

Chapter 2

The

Enlightenment

Confronts the

Divine: The

Debate Over

the Lisbon

Earthquake

Source 2 from The Works of John Wesley, vol. 11 (Grand Rapids, Mich.: Zondervan, 1958), pp. 1–2, 6–7, 8, 11.

2. John Wesley, "Some Serious Thoughts Occasioned by the Late Earthquake at Lisbon," 1755

Tua res agitur, paries quum proximus ardet.[5]

Thinking men generally allow that the greater part of modern Christians are not more virtuous than the ancient Heathens; perhaps less so; since public spirit, love of our country, generous honesty, and simple truth, are scarce anywhere to be found. On the contrary, covetousness, ambition, various injustice, luxury, and falsehood in every kind, have infected every rank and denomination of people, the Clergy themselves not excepted. Now, they who believe there is a God are apt to believe he is not well pleased with this. Nay, they think, he has intimated it very plainly, in many parts of the Christian world. How many hundred thousand men have been swept away by war, in Europe only, within half a century![6] How many thousands, within little more than this, hath the earth opened her mouth and swallowed up! Numbers sunk at Port-Royal, and rose no more! Many thousands went quick into the pit at Lima! The whole city of Catanea, in Sicily, and every inhabitant of it, perished together.[7] Nothing but heaps of ashes and cinders show where it stood. Not so much as one Lot escaped out of Sodom![8]

And what shall we say of the late accounts from Portugal? That some thousand houses, and many thousand persons, are no more! that a fair city is now in ruinous heaps! Is there indeed a God that judges the world? And is he now making inquisition for blood? If so, it is not surprising, he should

5. From the Roman poet Horace: "'Tis your own interest that calls, when flames invade your neighbor's walls."

6. Intense warfare did mark the half-century preceding the earthquake. The great Northern War (1700–1716) pitted Sweden against Russia. In the War of the Spanish Succession (1702–1714), France and Spain fought against England, Holland, the armies of the Holy Roman Emperor, and most of the German states. In the War of the Polish Succession (1733–1735), Spain and France confronted Russia and the forces of the Holy Roman Emperor. Almost all of Europe was involved in the War of the Austrian Succession (1740–1748) in which France, Spain, Prussia, and a number of the German states fought England and Austria. At the time Wesley wrote, fighting between English and French forces had already broken out in North America that would lead to the Seven Years War of 1756–1763. And these were only the major wars! Minor conflicts also raged. One historian reckoned that all of Europe was at peace for only two years in the century spanning 1700–1800.

7. Wesley refers here to the earthquakes of 1692, 1693, and 1746 mentioned in note 3.

8. In the Bible's book of Genesis, chapters 11–14 and 19, God destroyed Sodom and Gomorrah with fire because of their wickedness. Abraham's nephew, Lot, a resident of Sodom, was warned of the destruction and escaped.

begin there, where so much blood has been poured on the ground like water! where so many brave men have been murdered, in the most base and cowardly as well as barbarous manner, almost every day, as well as every night, while none regarded or laid it to heart.[9] "Let them hunt and destroy the precious life, so we may secure our stores of gold and precious stones."[10] How long has their blood been crying from the earth! Yea, how long has that bloody *House of Mercy*,[11] the scandal not only of all religion, but even of human nature, stood to insult both heaven and earth! "And shall I not visit for these things, saith the Lord? Shall not my soul be avenged on such a city as this?" . . .

But alas! why should we not be convinced sooner, while that conviction may avail, that it is not chance which governs the world? Why should we not now, before London is as Lisbon, Lima, or Catanea, acknowledge the hand of the Almighty, arising to maintain his own cause? Why, we have a general answer always ready, to screen us from any such conviction: "All these things are purely natural and accidental; the result of natural causes." But there are two objections to this answer: First, it is untrue: Secondly, it is uncomfortable.

First. If by affirming, "All this is purely natural," you mean, it is not providential, or that God has nothing to do with it, this is not true, that is, supposing the Bible to be true. For supposing this, you may descant ever so long on the natural causes of murrain, winds, thunder, lightning, and yet you are altogether wide of the mark, you prove nothing at all, unless you can prove that God never works in or by natural causes. But this you cannot prove; nay, none can doubt of his so working, who allows the Scripture to be of God. For this asserts, in the clearest and strongest terms, that "all things" (in nature) "serve him;" that (by or without a train of natural causes) He "sendeth his rain on the earth;" that He "bringeth the winds out of his treasures," and "maketh a way for the lightning and the thunder;" in general, that "fire and hail, snow and vapour, wind and storm, fulfil his word." Therefore, allowing there are natural causes of all these, they are still under the direction of the Lord of nature: Nay, what is nature itself, but the art of God, or God's method of acting in the material world? . . . .

9. In this sentence Wesley is referring to the executions resulting from trials by the Portuguese Inquisition. The Inquisition was a system of Roman Catholic courts created to identify and judge heretics. Like all continental European courts of the day, these courts could torture the defendant to gather evidence against him or her. Civil, not church, authorities, however, executed sentences.

10. **Precious stones:** "Merchants who have lived in Portugal inform us that the King has a large building filled with diamonds; and more gold stored up, coined and uncoined, than all the other monarchs of Europe." [Wesley's note] This may or may not have been true, but Lisbon certainly received gold from New World mines and diamonds from mines discovered in the Portuguese colony of Brazil in the 1730s.

11. **House of Mercy:** "The title which the Inquisition of Portugal (if not in other countries also) takes to itself." [Wesley's note]

Chapter 2

The

Enlightenment

Confronts the

Divine: The

Debate Over

the Lisbon

Earthquake

A Second objection to your answer is, It is extremely uncomfortable. For if things really be as you affirm; if all these afflictive incidents entirely depend on the fortuitous concourse and agency of blind, material causes; what hope, what help, what resource is left for the poor sufferers by them? . . .

What defence do you find from thousands of gold and silver? You cannot fly; for you cannot quit the earth, unless you will leave your dear body behind you. And while you are on the earth, you know not where to flee to, neither where to flee from. You may buy intelligence, where the shock was yesterday, but not where it will be to-morrow,—to-day. It comes! The roof trembles! The beams crack! The ground rocks to and fro! Hoarse thunder resounds from the bowels of the earth! And all these are but the beginning of sorrows. Now, what help? What wisdom can prevent, what strength resist, the blow? What money can purchase, I will not say deliverance, but an hour's reprieve? Poor honourable fool, where are now thy titles? Wealthy fool, where is now thy golden god? If any thing can help, it must be prayer. But what wilt thou pray to? Not to the God of heaven; you suppose him to have nothing to do with earthquakes. . . .

But how shall we secure the favour of this great God? How, but by worshipping him in spirit and in truth; by uniformly imitating Him we worship, in all his imitable perfections? without which the most accurate systems of opinions, all external modes of religion, are idle cobwebs of the brain, dull farce and empty show. Now, God is love: Love God then, and you are a true worshipper. Love mankind, and God is your God, your Father, and your Friend. But see that you deceive not your own soul; for this is not a point of small importance. And by this you may know: If you love God, then you are happy in God; if you love God, riches, honours, and the pleasures of sense are no more to you than bubbles on the water: You look on dress and equipage, as the tassels of a fool's cap; diversions, as the bells on a fool's coat. If you love God, God is in all your thoughts, and your whole life is a sacrifice to him. And if you love mankind, it is your own design, desire, and endeavour, to spread virtue and happiness all around you; to lessen the present sorrows, and increase the joys, of every child of man; and, if it be possible, to bring them with you to the rivers of pleasure that are at God's right hand for evermore.

Source 3 from Voltaire, Letters Concerning the English Nation *(New York: Burt Franklin Reprints, 1974), pp. 65–66, 96–97, 100, 103, 105–106.*

3. Voltaire on Newtonian Physics, 1733

Not long since, the trite and frivolous Question following was debated in a very polite and learned Company, *viz.* (namely) who was the greatest Man, *Cæsar, Alexander, Tamerlane, Cromwell,* & *c.*[12]

Some Body answer'd, that Sir *Isaac Newton* excell'd them all. The Gentleman's Assertion was very just; for if true Greatness consists in having receiv'd from Heaven a mighty Genius, and in having employ'd it to enlighten our own Minds and that of others; a Man like Sir *Isaac Newton*, whose equal is hardly found in a thousand Years, is the truly great Man. And those Politicians and Conquerors, (and all ages produce some) were generally so many illustrious wicked Men. That Man claims our Respect, who commands over the Minds of the rest of the World by the Force of Truth, not those who enslave their Fellow Creatures; He who is acquainted with the Universe, not They who deface it. . . .

The Discoveries which gain'd Sir *Isaac Newton* so universal a Reputation, relate to the System of the World, to Light, to Geometrical Infinites; and lastly to Chronology, with which he us'd to amuse himself after the Fatigue of his severer Studies.

I will now acquaint you (without Prolixity if possible) with the few Things I have been able to comprehend of all these sublime Ideas. With Regard to the System of our World, Disputes were a long Time maintain'd, on the Cause that turns the Planets, and keeps them in their Orbits; and on those Causes which make all Bodies here below descend towards the Surface of the Earth.

Having . . . destroy'd the *Cartesian* Vortices,[13] he despair'd of ever being able to discover, whether there is a secret Principle in Nature which, at the same Time, is the Cause of the Motion of all celestial Bodies, and that of Gravity on the Earth. But being retir'd in 1666, upon Account of the Plague,

12. **Julius Caesar** (102–44 B.C.) dominated Rome during the last years of the republic. **Alexander the Great** (356–323 B.C.) was the king of Macedonia who led the Greeks on wars of conquest to create an empire including modern Greece, Turkey, Egypt, and much of the Middle East to the borders of India. **Tamerlane** (ca 1336–1405) was a Mongol chieftain who created an empire embracing parts of southern Russia, Turkey, the Middle East, Afghanistan, Pakistan and northern India. **Oliver Cromwell** (1599–1658) led Parliament's armies against the king in the English Civil War. After the king's defeat and execution, he ruled England as virtual dictator.

13. **Cartesian vortices:** René Descartes (1546–1650), a French philosopher and mathematician, accounted for planetary motion in terms of vortices, that is, a rapid movement of cosmic bodies in a fluid or ether around an axis. Newtonian physics with its law of gravity dispensed with such theories.

Chapter 2

The

Enlightenment

Confronts the

Divine: The

Debate Over

the Lisbon

Earthquake

to a Solitude near *Cambridge*; as he was walking one Day in his Garden, and saw some Fruits fall from a Tree, he fell into a profound Meditation on that Gravity, the Cause of which had so long been sought, but in vain, by all the Philosophers, whilst the Vulgar think there is nothing mysterious in it. He said to himself, that from what height soever, in our Hemisphere, those Bodies might descend, their Fall wou'd certainly be in the Progression discover'd by *Galileo*;[14] and the Spaces they run thro' would be as the Square of the Times. Why may not this Power which causes heavy Bodies to descend, and is the same without any sensible Diminution at the remotest Distance from the Center of the Earth, or on the Summits of the highest Mountains; Why, said Sir *Isaac*, may not this Power extend as high as the Moon? And in Case, its Influence reaches so far, is it not very probable that this Power retains it in its Orbit, and determines its Motion? But in case the Moon obeys this Principle (whatever it be) may we not conclude very naturally, that the rest of the Planets are equally subject to it? In case this Power exists (which besides is prov'd) it must increase in an inverse *Ratio* of the Squares of the Distances. All therefore that remains is, to examine how far a heavy Body, which should fall upon the Earth from a moderate height, would go; and how far in the same time, a Body which should fall from the Orbit of the Moon, would descend. To find this, nothing is wanted but the Measure of the Earth, and the Distance of the Moon from it.

This is Attraction, the great Spring by which all Nature is mov'd. Sir *Isaac Newton* after having demonstrated the Existence of this Principle, plainly foresaw that its very Name wou'd offend; and therefore this Philosopher in more Places than one of his Books, gives the Reader some Caution about it. He bids him beware of confounding this Name with what the Ancients call'd occult Qualities; but to be satisfied with knowing that there is in all Bodies a central Force which acts to the utmost Limits of the Universe, according to the invariable Laws of Mechanicks.

Give me Leave once more to introduce Sir *Isaac* speaking: . . . "The Spring that I discover'd was more hidden and more universal, and for that very Reason Mankind ought to thank me the more. I have discover'd a new Property of Matter, one of the Secrets of the Creator; and have calculated and discover'd the Effects of it. After this shall People quarrel with me about the Name I give it."

Vortices may be call'd an occult Quality because their Existence was never prov'd: Attraction on the contrary is a real Thing, because its Effects are demonstrated, and the Proportions of it are calculated. The Cause of this Cause is among the *Arcana*[15] of the Almighty.

Procedes huc, & non amplius.
Hither thou shalt go, and no farther.

14. **Galileo Galilei:** Italian astronomer, mathematician, and physicist (1564–1642) whose work was an important contribution to the Scientific Revolution. He developed the mathematical explanation of the rates at which bodies fall to earth in his law of falling bodies.

15. **Arcana:** secrets or mysteries.

Source 4 from A. W. Ward, editor. The Poetical Works of Alexander Pope *(London: Macmillan, 1879), pp. 199–200.*

4. From Alexander Pope, "An Essay on Man," 1734

All are but parts of one stupendous whole,
Whose body Nature is, and God the soul;
That, chang'd thro' all, and yet in all the same;
Great in the earth, as in th' ethereal[16] frame;
Warms in the sun, refreshes in the breeze,
Glows in the stars, and blossoms in the trees,
Lives thro' all life, extends thro' all extent,
Spreads undivided, operates unspent;
Breathes in our soul, informs our mortal part,
As full, as perfect, in a hair as heart:
As full, as perfect, in vile Man that mourns,
As the rapt Seraph[17] that adores and burns:
To him no high, no low, no great, no small;
He fills, he bounds, connects, and equals all.

Cease then, nor Order Imperfection name:
Our proper bliss depends on what we blame.
Know thy own point: This kind, this due degree
Of blindness, weakness, Heav'n bestows on thee;
Submit.—In this, or any other sphere,
Secure to be as blest as thou canst bear:
Safe in the hand of one disposing Pow'r,
Or in the natal, or the mortal hour.
All Nature is but Art, unknown to thee;
All Chance, Direction, which thou canst not see;
All Discord, Harmony not understood;
All partial Evil, universal Good:
And, spite of Pride, in erring Reason's spite,
One truth is clear, WHATEVER IS, IS RIGHT.

16. **ethereal:** heavenly.
17. **Seraph:** one of the heavenly creatures hovering around the throne of God described in Isaiah 6.

Chapter 2

The

Enlightenment

Confronts the

Divine: The

Debate Over

the Lisbon

Earthquake

Source 5 from Denis Diderot, The Encyclopedia: Selections, *edited and translated by Stephen J. Gendzier (New York: Harper & Row, 1967),* pp. 175–177.

5. From the *Encyclopedia*, Anonymous Entry on "Observation," ca 1765

OBSERVATION (*Gram. Physic. Med.*) is the attention of the soul focused on objects offered by nature. An experiment is the result of this same attention directed toward phenomena produced by the labors of man. We must, therefore, include within the meaning of the generic noun *observation* the examination of all natural effects, not only of those that present themselves at once and without intermediary to our sight but also those we would not be able to discover without the hand of a worker, provided that this hand has not changed, altered, or disfigured them. The work necessary to reach a mine does not prevent the examination that is made of the metal's distribution, position, quantity, and color from being a simple *observation*. It is also by *observation* that we know the interior geography, that we estimate the number, position, and nature of the layers of earth, although we are obliged to resort to instruments for the excavation that allows us to see the mine. We must not consider as an *experiment* the opening of cadavers, the dissection of plants or animals, and certain analyses or mechanical sorting of mineral matter that scientists are obliged to do in order to be able to *observe* the parts that enter into their composition. The telescope of astronomers, the magnifying glass of the naturalist, and the microscope of the physicist do not prevent the knowledge acquired by these means from being the exact product of *observation*. All these preparations, these instruments only serve to render the different objects of *observation* more concrete, to remove the obstacles that prevent us from perceiving them, or to pierce the veil that hides them. But no change results from this, and there is not the slightest alteration in the nature of the *observed* object. It appears, nevertheless, such as it is; and this is the main difference between an *observation* and an *experiment* which decomposes, combines, and thereby gives use to rather different phenomena from those which nature presents. . . .

Observation is the primary foundation of all the sciences, the most reliable way to arrive at one's goal, the principal means of extending the periphery of scientific knowledge and of illuminating all its points. The facts, whatever they are, constitute the true wealth of the philosopher and the subject of *observation*: the historian collects them, the theoretical physicist combines them, and the experimenter verifies the results of their synthesis. Several facts taken separately appear dry, sterile, and unfruitful. The moment we compare them, they acquire a certain power, assume a vitality that everywhere results from the mutual harmony, from the reciprocal support, and from a chain that binds them together. The connection of these facts and the general cause that links them together are some of the objects of reasoning, theories, and systems, while the facts are the materials. The moment a certain number of them have been gathered, some people hasten to construct; and the building is the more solid as the materials are more numerous and each one of them finds a more appropriate place.

Source 6 from Georges Louis Leclerc, Comte de Buffon, Histoire naturelle, générale et particulière, avec description du cabinet du roi, *vol. 1 (Paris: De l'Imprimerie Royale, 1749), pp. 526–529. Translated by Julius R. Ruff.*

6. From Georges Louis Leclerc, Comte de Buffon, *Natural History, General and Specific,* ca 1750

There are two kinds of earthquakes. One type is caused by the action of subterranean fires and by the explosion of volcanoes and is only felt over small distances when volcanoes are active or when they erupt. When the materials which make subterranean fires begin to ferment, to heat up, and to ignite, the fire expands on all sides and, if it does not naturally find outlets, it heaves up the ground and makes a passage by throwing out the earth in its way. This produces a volcano, the effects of which repeat themselves and endure in proportion to the inflammable materials.

But there is another kind of earthquake, very different as regards its effects and perhaps as regards its causes. These are the earthquakes which are felt over long distances and which shake a large area of terrain without the appearance of a new volcano or an eruption. We have examples of earthquakes which are felt at the same time in England, France, Germany, and as far away as Hungary. These earthquakes always extend over an area much longer than it is wide. They shake a band or zone of the earth with varying force in different locations. They are almost always accompanied by a muffled sound, similar to that of a large, quickly rolling coach.

To understand more fully the causes of this kind of earthquake, it is necessary to remember that all inflammable and explosive materials produce . . . a great deal of air in igniting.[18] This air produced by the fire is in a very highly rarefied state and, because of its state of compression in the depths of the earth, it must produce very violent effects. Let us therefore suppose that at a very great depth, say 600 to 1200 feet, there are found pyrites and other sulphurous materials and that by the fermentation produced by the filtration of water or by other causes, these materials ignite. Let us see what

18. Buffon advanced this description of combustion a quarter of a century before the great French chemist Antoine Laurent Lavoisier (1743–1794) accurately described combustion and the role of oxygen in this process.

Chapter 2

The

Enlightenment

Confronts the

Divine: The

Debate Over

the Lisbon

Earthquake

must happen. These materials are not regularly arranged in horizontal strata . . . they are, on the contrary, in perpendicular clefts in the caverns . . . where water can penetrate and have an effect. These materials ignite, producing a large quantity of air, the force of which, compressed in a small space like a cavern, not only will shake the terrain above but will look for routes of escape. . . . The routes which are available are caverns and cuts by water and subterranean streams. The rarefied air will rush violently through all of these passages which are open to it. It will form a raging wind in its subterranean paths, the noise of which will be heard on the earth's surface, and it will be accompanied by shock and concussions. This subterranean wind produced by the fire will extend as far as the subterranean cavities and cuts, and will cause a tremor the violence of which will depend on the distance from the source and the narrowness of the passages through which the wind passes. . . . This air will produce no eruption or volcano because it will have found enough space in which to expand or indeed because it will have found escapes and will have left the earth in the form of wind or vapor.[19]

Source 7 from Oeuvres complètes de Voltaire, *nouvelle edition, vol. 9 (Paris: Garnier frères, 1877), p. 470. Translated by Julius R. Ruff.*

7. From Voltaire, "Poem on the Lisbon Disaster, or An Examination of that Axiom 'All Is Well,'" 1755

Oh, miserable mortals! Oh wretched earth!
Oh, dreadful assembly of all mankind!
Eternal sermon of useless sufferings!
Deluded philosophers who cry, "All is well,"
Hasten, contemplate these frightful ruins,
This wreck, these shreds, these wretched ashes of the dead;
These women and children heaped on one another,
These scattered members under broken marble;
One-hundred thousand unfortunates devoured by the earth,[20]
Who, bleeding, lacerated, and still alive,
Buried under their roofs without aid in their anguish,

19. The article on "Earthquakes" in the *Encyclopedia* edited by Diderot also explains this phenomenon with a theory of subterranean fire. Modern geologists have shown earthquakes to be the result of stresses in the earth's crust. Interestingly, however, modern research also has shown that the eighteenth-century theories of subterranean fire were not entirely incorrect: the earth does have a liquid core of practically molten rock.

20. Voltaire wrote this poem on hearing the first news of the disaster. Those first reports grossly exaggerated the number of deaths, as does the poem.

End their sad days!
In answer to the half-formed cries of their dying voices,
At the frightful sight of their smoking ashes,
Will you say: "This is result of eternal laws
Directing the acts of a free and good God!"
Will you say, in seeing this mass of victims:
"God is revenged, their death is the price for their crimes?"
What crime, what error did these children,
Crushed and bloody on their mothers' breasts, commit?
Did Lisbon, which is no more, have more vices
Than London and Paris immersed in their pleasures?
Lisbon is destroyed, and they dance in Paris!

Source 8 from Theodore Bestermann, editor, Voltaire's Correspondence, *vol. 30 (Geneva: Institût et Musée Voltaire, 1958), pp. 102–115. Translated by Julius R. Ruff.*

8. From Jean-Jacques Rousseau's Letter to Voltaire Regarding the Poem on the Lisbon Earthquake, August 18, 1756

All my complaints are . . . against your poem on the Lisbon disaster, because I expected from it evidence more worthy of the humanity which apparently inspired you to write it. You reproach Pope[21] and Leibnitz[22] with belittling our misfortunes by affirming that all is well, but you so burden the list of our miseries that you further disparage our condition. Instead of the consolations that I expected, you only vex me. It might be said that you fear that I don't feel my unhappiness enough, and that you are trying to soothe me by proving that all is bad.

Do not be mistaken, Monsieur, it happens that everything is contrary to what you propose. This optimism which you find so cruel consoles me still in the same woes that you force on me as unbearable. Pope's poem[23] alleviates my difficulties and inclines me to patience; yours makes my afflictions worse, prompts me to grumble, and, leading me beyond a shattered hope, reduces me to despair. . . .

21. Alexander Pope, whose "Essay on Man" is Source 4 in this chapter.
22. **Gottfried Wilhelm von Leibnitz:** a German mathematician and philosopher (1646–1716), the author of *Essays on Theodicy*, in which he examined the origins of evil in the world. Leibnitz saw the universe operating according to a divine plan and therefore this was the best of all possible worlds. He was not a total optimist, however, because he recognized the existence of evil. Incompletely understanding the thought of Leibnitz, Voltaire satirized him as a blind optimist in his novel *Candide* (1759).
23. **Pope's poem:** "An Essay on Man."

Chapter 2

The

Enlightenment

Confronts the

Divine: The

Debate Over

the Lisbon

Earthquake

"Have patience, man," Pope and Leibnitz tell me, "your woes are a necessary effect of your nature and of the constitution of the universe. The eternal and beneficent Being who governs the universe wished to protect you. Of all the possible plans, he chose that combining the minimum evil and the maximum good. If it is necessary to say the same thing more bluntly, God has done no better for mankind because (He) can do not better."

Now what does your poem tell me? "Suffer forever unfortunate one. If a God created you, He is doubtlessly all powerful and could have prevented all your woes. Don't ever hope that your woes will end, because you would never know why you exist, if it is not to suffer and die. . . ."

I do not see how one can search for the source of moral evil anywhere but in man. . . . Moreover . . . the majority of our physical misfortunes are also our work. Without leaving your Lisbon subject, concede, for example, that it was hardly nature that there brought together twenty-thousand houses of six or seven stories. If the residents of this large city had been more evenly dispersed and less densely housed, the losses would have been fewer or perhaps none at all. Everyone would have fled at the first shock. But many obstinately remained . . . to expose themselves to additional earth tremors because what they would have had to leave behind was worth more than what they could carry away. How many unfortunates perished in this disaster through the desire to fetch their clothing, papers, or money? . . .

There are often events that afflict us . . . that lose a lot of their horror when we examine them closely. I learned in *Zadig*,[24] and nature daily confirms my lesson, that a rapid death is not always a true misfortune, and that it can sometimes be considered a relative blessing. Of the many persons crushed under Lisbon's ruins, some without doubt escaped greater misfortunes, and . . . it is not certain that a single one of these unfortunates suffered more than if, in the normal course of events, he had awaited [a more normal] death to overtake him after long agonies. Was death [in the ruins] a sadder end than that of a dying person overburdened with useless treatments, whose notary[25] and heirs do not allow him a respite, whom the doctors kill in his own bed at their leisure, and whom the barbarous priests artfully try to make relish death? For me, I see everywhere that the misfortunes nature imposes upon us are less cruel than those which we add to them. . . .

I cannot prevent myself, Monsieur, from noting . . . a strange contrast between you and me as regards the subject of this letter. Satiated with glory . . . you live free in the midst of affluence.[26] Certain of your immortality, you peacefully philosophize on the nature of the soul, and, if your body or

24. **Zadig:** a story published by Voltaire in 1747 that still reflected some faith on his part that a divine order for the world assured that all would work out for the best. In the story, Zadig, the main character, endures a lengthy series of misfortunes.

25. **notary:** in France and other Continental countries, a professional person specializing in drafting wills and inventorying the property involved in them as well as drawing up other property arrangements.

26. Voltaire had prospered from his publishings and also had invested well. He owned property in Geneva, Switzerland and a large estate at Ferney, France, on the Swiss border.

heart suffer, you have Tronchin[27] as doctor and friend. You however find only evil on earth. And I, an obscure and poor man tormented with an incurable illness, meditate with pleasure in my seclusion and find that all is well. What is the source of this apparent contradiction? You explained it yourself: you revel but I hope, and hope beautifies everything.

. . . I have suffered too much in this life not to look forward to another. No metaphysical subtleties cause me to doubt a time of immortality for the soul and a beneficent providence. I sense it, I believe it, I wish it, I hope for it, I will uphold it until my last gasp. . . .

> I am, with respect, Monsieur,
>
> Jean-Jacques Rousseau

Source 9 from David Hume, Essays: Moral, Political and Literary *(Oxford: Oxford University Press, 1963), pp. 519–521, 524–526, 540–541.*

9. David Hume, "The Essay on Miracles," 1748

There is, in Dr. Tillotson's[28] writings, an argument against the *real presence*,[29] which is as concise, and elegant, and strong, as any argument can possibly be supposed against a doctrine so little worthy of a serious refutation. It is acknowledged on all hands, says that learned prelate, that the authority, either of the Scripture or of tradition, is founded merely on the testimony of the Apostles, who were eye-witnesses to those miracles of our Saviour, by which he proved his divine mission. Our evidence, then, for the truth of the *Christian* religion, is less than the evidence for the truth of our senses; because, even in the first authors of our religion, it was no greater; and it is evident it must diminish in passing from them to their disciples; nor can any one rest such confidence in their testimony as in the immediate object of his senses. But a weaker evidence can never destroy a stronger; and therefore, were the doctrine of the real presence ever so clearly revealed in Scripture, it were directly contrary to the rules of just reasoning to give our assent to it. It contradicts sense, though both the Scripture and tradition, on which it is supposed to be built, carry not such evidence with them as sense, when they are considered merely as external evidences, and are not brought home to every one's breast by the immediate operation of the Holy Spirit.

Nothing is so convenient as a decisive argument of this kind, which must at least *silence* the most arrogant bigotry and superstition, and free us from

27. **Theodore Tronchin:** a physician (1709–1781) of Geneva, Switzerland. A pioneer in smallpox inoculation in Switzerland, he was a member of Voltaire's circle.
28. **Dr. John Tillotson:** Archbishop of Canterbury (1630–1694), that is, spiritual leader of the Church of England.
29. **real presence:** the presence of Jesus Christ on earth after his death.

Chapter 2

The

Enlightenment

Confronts the

Divine: The

Debate Over

the Lisbon

Earthquake

their impertinent solicitations. I flatter myself that I have discovered an argument of a like nature, which, if just, will, with the wise and learned, be an everlasting check to all kinds of superstitious delusion, and consequently will be useful as long as the world endures; for so long, I presume, will the accounts of miracles and prodigies be found in all history, sacred and profane.

Though experience be our only guide in reasoning concerning matters of fact, it must be acknowledged, that this guide is not altogether infallible, but in some cases is apt to lead us into errors. One who in our climate should expect better weather in any week of June than in one of December, would reason justly and conformably to experience; but it is certain that he may happen, in the event, to find himself mistaken. However, we may observe that, in such a case, he would have no cause to complain of experience, because it commonly informs us beforehand of the uncertainty, by that contrariety of events which we may learn from a diligent observation. All effects follow not with like certainty from their supposed causes. Some events are found, in all countries and all ages, to have been constantly conjoined together: others are found to have been more variable, and sometimes to disappoint our expectations; so that in our reasonings concerning matter of fact, there are all imaginable degrees of assurance, from the highest certainty to the lowest species of moral evidence.

A wise man, therefore, proportions his belief to the evidence. In such conclusions as are founded on an infallible experience, he expects the event with the last degree of assurance, and regards his past experience as a full *proof* of the future existence of that event. In other cases he proceeds with more caution: he weighs the opposite experiments: he considers which side is supported by the greater number of experiments: to that side he inclines with doubt and hesitation; and when at last he fixes his judgment, the evidence exceeds not what we properly call *probability*. All probability, then, supposes an opposition of experiments and observations, where the one side is found to overbalance the other, and to produce a degree of evidence proportioned to the superiority. A hundred instances or experiments on one side, and fifty on another, afford a doubtful expectation of any event; though a hundred uniform experiments, with only one that is contradictory, reasonably beget a pretty strong degree of assurance. In all cases, we must balance the opposite experiments, where they are opposite, and deduct the smaller number from the greater, in order to know the exact force of the superior evidence. . . .

A miracle is a violation of the laws of nature; and as a firm and unalterable experience has established these laws, the proof against a miracle, from the very nature of the fact, is as entire as any argument from experience can possibly be imagined. Why is it more than probable that all men must die; that lead cannot, of itself, remain suspended in the air; that fire consumes wood, and is extinguished by water; unless it be that these events are found agreeable to the laws of nature, and there is required a violation of these laws, or, in other words, a miracle to prevent them? Nothing is esteemed a miracle, if it ever happen in the common course of nature. It is no miracle that a man, seemingly in good health, should die on a sudden; because such a kind of death, though more unusual than any other, has yet been frequently observed to happen. But it is a miracle that a dead man should come to life; because that has never been observed in any age or country. There must, therefore, be an uniform experience against every miraculous event, otherwise the event would not merit that appellation. And as an uniform experience amounts to a proof, there is here a direct and full *proof*, from the nature of the fact, against the existence of any miracle. . . .

The plain consequence is (and it is a general maxim worthy of our attention), "That no testimony is sufficient to establish a miracle, unless the testimony be of such a kind, that its falsehood would be more miraculous than the fact which it endeavours to establish: and even in that case there is a mutual destruction of arguments, and the superior only gives us an assurance suitable to that degree of force which remains after deducting the inferior." When any one tells me that he saw a dead man restored to life, I immediately consider with myself whether it be more probable that this person should either deceive or be deceived, or that the fact which he relates should really have happened. I weigh the one miracle against the other; and according to the superiority which I discover, I pronounce my decision, and always reject the greater miracle. If the falsehood of his testimony would be more miraculous than the event which he relates, then, and not till then, can he pretend to command my belief or opinion.

Upon the whole, then, it appears, that no testimony for any kind of miracle has ever amounted to a probability, much less to a proof; and that, even supposing it amounted to a proof, it would be opposed by another proof, derived from the very nature of the fact which it would endeavour to establish. It is experience only which gives authority to human testimony; and it is the same experience which assures us of the laws of nature. When, therefore, these two kinds of experience are contrary, we have nothing to do but to subtract the one from the other, and embrace an opinion either on one side or the other, with that assurance which arises from the remainder. But according to the principle here explained, this subtraction with regard to all popular religions amounts to an entire annihilation; and therefore we may establish it as a maxim, that no human testimony can have such force as to prove a miracle, and make it a just foundation for any such system of religion. . . .

What we have said of miracles, may be applied without any variation to prophecies; and, indeed, all prophecies are real miracles, and as such, only can be admitted as proofs of any revelation. If it did not exceed the capacity of human nature to foretell future events, it would be absurd to employ any prophecy as an argument for a divine mission or authority from heaven. So that, upon the whole, we may conclude, that the *Christian Religion* not only

Chapter 2

The

Enlightenment

Confronts the

Divine: The

Debate Over

the Lisbon

Earthquake

was at first attended with miracles, but even at this day cannot be believed by any reasonable person without one. Mere reason is insufficient to convince us of its veracity: and whoever is moved by *Faith* to assent to it, is conscious of a continued miracle in his own person, which subverts all the principles of his understanding, and gives him a determination to believe what is most contrary to custom and experience.

Source 10 from Paul-Henry Thiry, Baron d'Holbach, The System of Nature, *translated by H. D. Robinson (Boston: J. P. Mendum, 1853), pp. viii–ix, 12–13, 15, 19–23.*

10. From Paul-Henry Thiry, Baron d'Holbach, *The System of Nature*, 1770

Preface

The source of man's unhappiness is his ignorance of Nature. The pertinacity with which he clings to blind opinions imbibed in his infancy, which interweave themselves with his existence, the consequent prejudice that warps his mind, that prevents its expansion, that renders him the slave of fiction, appears to doom him to continual errour. He resembles a child destitute of experience, full of idle notions: a dangerous leaven mixes itself with all his knowledge: it is of necessity obscure, it is vacillating and false:—He takes the tone of his ideas on the authority of others, who are themselves in errour, or else have an interest in deceiving him. To remove this Cimmerian darkness,[30] these barriers to the improvement of his condition; to disentangle him from the clouds of errour that envelop him, that obscure the path he ought to tread; to guide him out of this Cretan labyrinth,[31] requires the clue of Ariadne,[32] with all the love she could bestow on Theseus. It exacts more than common exertion; it needs a most determined, a most undaunted courage—it is never effected but by a persevering resolution to act, to think for himself; to examine with rigour and impartiality the opinions he has adopted. . . .

Man seeks to range out of his sphere: notwithstanding the reiterated checks his ambitious folly experiences, he still attempts the impossible; strives to

30. **Cimmerian darkness:** in Greek mythology, the Cimmerians were a people inhabiting a land of perpetual darkness.
31. **Cretan labyrinth:** according to Greek mythology, there existed on the island of Crete a structure of winding passages leading to a monster with the body of a man and the head of a bull, the Minotaur. This monster was annually fed seven young men and seven young women from Athens as that city's tribute to the rulers of Crete.
32. **Ariadne:** daughter of the King of Crete, fell in love with Theseus, an Athenean hero and one of the youths sent by Athens to be offered to the Minotaur. Ariadne gave Theseus a ball of thread which he unwound as he penetrated the labyrinth and there killed the Minotaur. He then followed the thread back out of the labyrinth.

carry his researches beyond the visible world; and hunts out misery in imaginary regions. He would be a metaphysician before he has become a practical philosopher. He quits the contemplation of realities to meditate on chimeras. He neglects experience to feed on conjecture, to indulge in hypothesis. He dares not cultivate his reason, because from his earliest days he has been taught to consider it criminal. He pretends to know his fate in the indistinct abodes of another life, before he has considered of the means by which he is to render himself happy in the world he inhabits: in short, man disdains the study of Nature, except it be partially. . . .

The most important of our duties, then, is to seek means by which we may destroy delusions that can never do more than mislead us. The remedies for these evils must be sought for in Nature herself; it is only in the abundance of her resources, that we can rationally expect to find antidotes to the mischiefs brought upon us by an ill-directed, by an over-powering enthusiasm. It is time these remedies were sought; it is time to look the evil boldly in the face, to examine its foundations, to scrutinize its super-structure: reason, with its faithful guide experience, must attack in their entrenchments those prejudices to which the human race has but too long been the victim. For this purpose reason must be restored to its proper rank,—it must be rescued from the evil company with which it is associated. . . .

Truth speaks not to these perverse beings [the enemies of the human race]:—her voice can only be heard by generous minds accustomed to reflection, whose sensibilities make them lament the numberless calamities showered on the earth by political and religious tyranny—whose enlightened minds contemplate with horrour the immensity, the ponderosity of that series of misfortunes with which errour has in all ages overwhelmed mankind. . . .

Of Nature

. . . The *civilized man*, is he whom experience and social life have enabled to draw from nature the means of his own happiness; because he has learned to oppose resistance to those impulses he receives from exterior beings, when experience has taught him they would be injurious to his welfare.

The *enlightened man*, is man in his maturity, in his perfection; who is capable of pursuing his own happiness; because he has learned to examine, to think for himself, and not to take that for truth upon the authority of others, which experience has taught him examination will frequently prove erroneous. . . .

It necessarily results, that man in his researches ought always to fall back on experience, and natural philosophy: These are what he should consult in his religion—in his morals—in his legislation—in his political government—in the arts—in the sciences—in his pleasures—in his misfortunes. Experience teaches that Nature acts by simple, uniform, and invariable laws. It is by his senses man is bound to this universal Nature; it is by his senses he must penetrate her secrets; it is from his senses he must draw experience of her laws. Whenever, therefore, he either fails to acquire experience or quits its path, he stumbles into an abyss, his imagination leads him astray. . . .

Chapter 2

The

Enlightenment

Confronts the

Divine: The

Debate Over

the Lisbon

Earthquake

Man did not understand that Nature, equal in her distributions, entirely destitute of goodness or malice, follows only necessary and immutable laws, when she either produces beings or destroys them, when she causes those to suffer, whose organization creates sensibility; when she scatters among them good and evil; when she subjects them to incessant change—he did not perceive it was in the bosom of Nature herself, that it was in her abundance he ought to seek to satisfy his wants; for remedies against his pains; for the means of rendering himself happy: he expected to derive these benefits from imaginary beings, whom he erroneously imagined to be the authors of his pleasures, the cause of his misfortunes. From hence it is clear that to his ignorance of Nature, man owes the creation of those illusive powers under which he has so long trembled with fear; that superstitious worship, which has been the source of all his misery. . . .

The universe, that vast assemblage of every thing that exists, presents only matter and motion: the whole offers to our contemplation nothing but an immense, an uninterrupted succession of causes and effects; some of these causes are known to us, because they strike immediately on our senses; others are unknown to us, because they act upon us by effects, frequently very remote from their original cause. . . .

Of Motion and Its Origin

. . . Observation and reflection ought to convince us, that every thing in Nature is in continual motion. . . . Thus, the idea of Nature necessarily includes that of motion. But, it will be asked, from whence did she receive her motion? Our reply is, from herself, since she is the great whole, out of which, consequently, nothing can exist. . . .

If they [natural philosophers] had viewed Nature uninfluenced by prejudice, they must have been long since convinced, that matter acts by its own peculiar energy, and needs not any exterior impulse to set it in motion. They would have perceived, that whenever mixed bodies were placed in a capacity to act on each other, motion was instantly engendered, and that these mixtures acted with a force capable of producing the most surprising effects. If filings of iron, sulphur and water be mixed together, these bodies thus capacitated to act on each other, are heated by degrees, and ultimately produce a violent combustion. If flour be wetted with water, and the mixture closed up, it will be found, after some little lapse of time, by the aid of a microscope, to have produced organized beings that enjoy life, of which the water and the flour were believed incapable: it is thus that inanimate matter can pass into life, or animate matter, which is in itself only an assemblage of motion. Reasoning from analogy, the production of a man, independent of the ordinary means, would not be more marvellous than that of an insect with flour and water. . . .

Those who admit a cause exterior to matter, are obliged to suppose, that this cause produced all the motion by which matter is agitated in giving it existence. This supposition rests on another, namely, that matter could begin to exist; a hypothesis that, until this moment, has never been demonstrated by any thing like solid proof. To produce from nothing, or the *Creation*, is a term that cannot give us the most slender idea of the formation of the universe; it presents no sense, upon which the mind can fasten itself.

Motion becomes still more obscure, when creation, or the formation of matter, is attributed to a *spiritual* being, that is to say, to a being which has no analogy, no point of contact, with it; to a being which has neither extent, nor parts, and cannot, therefore, be susceptible of motion, as we understand the term; this being only the change of one body relatively to another body, in which the body moved, presents successively different parts to different points of space. Moreover, as all the world are nearly agreed that matter can never be totally annihilated, or cease to exist, how can we understand, that that which cannot cease to be, could ever have had a beginning?

If, therefore, it be asked, whence came matter? it is a very reasonable reply to say, it has always existed. . . .

Let us, therefore, content ourselves with saying *that* which is supported by our experience, and by all the evidence we are capable of understanding; against the truth of which, not a shadow of proof such as our reason can admit, has ever been adduced; which has been maintained by philosophers in every age; which theologians themselves have not denied, but which many of them have upheld; namely, that *matter always existed; that it moves by virtue of its essence; that all the phenomena of Nature is ascribable to the diversified motion of the variety of matter she contains; and which, like the phenix,*[33] *is continually regenerating out of her own ashes.*

QUESTIONS TO CONSIDER

The selections that you have read allow you to trace one of the major issues raised by the *philosophes* as they sought to use the discoveries of the Scientific Revolution to comprehend the physical world more completely. Your consideration of this issue—the relationship of God to the physical world—should give you some clear understanding of the thought of the *philosophes* and its implications.

Consider first the traditional views expressed by Catholic and Protestant theologians. What caused the Lisbon earthquake, according to Malagrida? Did he foresee further disaster overtaking the city? Can you find in his pamphlet possible remedies for the city's misery from which Lisbon residents might have derived comfort?

---

33. **phenix:** the common modern spelling is "phoenix." In Egyptian mythology, the phoenix was a large bird, living a life span of 500 to 600 years in the Arabian desert. At the end of its life the phoenix was consumed in fire and from its ashes a new phoenix arose.

Chapter 2

The

Enlightenment

Confronts the

Divine: The

Debate Over

the Lisbon

Earthquake

Contrast Malagrida's view of the plight of Lisbon with that of John Wesley, bearing in mind, of course, the latter's Protestantism. What cause did Wesley ascribe to the earthquake? Did he see any way to avoid such disasters? Despite their obvious differences, do you find any similarity in outlook in Malagrida and Wesley?

Now move on to Enlightenment sources, which are arranged to permit you to trace the development of the *philosophes'* responses to the disaster and the implications of their thought. Voltaire's distillation of Newton's physics in Source 3 is fundamental to understanding the Enlightenment because Newton's work provided the basis for the *philosophes'* understanding of the world in which they lived. Through what method did Newton propose to understand the physical world? What relationships did he find governing the physical world? In what way did Newton's ideas provide a governing theory to explain much of that physical world? Why might you expect those influenced by Newton to describe the physical world as a machine?

Source 4, Alexander Pope's "An Essay on Man," represents an early-eighteenth-century attempt to balance a belief in God with the new scientific discoveries of Newton and others. How does Pope reflect traditional religion? What elements of sixteenth- and seventeenth-century scientific thought do you find in Pope? Most important, what role does God play in the world, according to Pope? What effect does that divine role have on humankind?

Reconsider the entry on "Observation" from the *Encyclopedia*. What view of reason does the article offer to its readers? How does Buffon attempt to apply this vision in his selection on earthquakes? What sort of causal pattern does he find for earthquakes? Despite his explanation of earthquakes, which is recognized today as incorrect, is there any room for a divine role in Buffon's explanation of these disasters? With whose view do you more closely identify, that of Buffon or Malagrida?

Voltaire's "Poem on the Lisbon Disaster" is the reaction of the Enlightenment's most celebrated thinker to the earthquake. Contrast it with the account he had written earlier of Newton's science. How had Voltaire's point of view changed during this interval? How does Voltaire respond to the views of his friend Alexander Pope? What response does he have to the theological explanation of the quake? Do you detect a growing skepticism in the thought of the older Voltaire? If so, in what ways? What response to Voltaire does Jean-Jacques Rousseau make in his letter? What similarities in thinking with earlier selections do you find in Rousseau?

Next examine Source 9, the selection by David Hume. Compare Voltaire's skepticism about a divine role in the world with the position Hume takes in "The Essay on Miracles." Also contrast Hume with Rousseau; how might intellectual differences have helped to cause their break? Where had Enlightenment skepticism, evident in Voltaire's later thought, led Hume? What religious implications of the Enlightenment's search to apply human reason to all issues do you find in Hume's work? Is any room left here for a divine role in the natural order? Trace this tendency in the thought of Baron d'Holbach, whose ideas shocked even some *philosophes*. Where have the principles of the Enlightenment led in Holbach's *System of Nature*? As we noted earlier, some of Holbach's contemporaries called him an atheist. How else might you describe his thought?

Your answers in carefully considering these questions should provide you with the basis for responding to the main questions posed in this chapter: Why did the Lisbon earthquake pose such an intellectual crisis for eighteenth-century thinkers? How did theologians explain the disaster? How did Enlightenment thinkers explain it? In what direction was their thought on the physical world and its relationship to divine forces leading them?

EPILOGUE

The difference in outlook between Malagrida and Wesley on one hand and the older and skeptical Voltaire and the Baron d'Holbach on the other is immense, and it represents a long intellectual journey for eighteenth-century thinkers. The culmination of this journey represented the success of the Scientific Revolution in modeling for the Western mind a method of searching for reasonable, scientific explanations of natural phenomena as well as imparting its faith in human ability to find these answers.

The Enlightenment, however, meant much more than even this. The implications of a movement ultimately unprepared, as we have seen, to accept traditional religion were tremendous beyond the fields of theology and natural science. Enlightenment skepticism in matters religious is controversial even to the present day. Its search for reasonable and comprehensible natural laws to govern all aspects of the human ex-

perience helped to change the Western world. Though a new and grander Lisbon arose out of the old city's ruins, much else did not long survive the intellectual crisis of mid-century that earthquake embodied. Disappointment greeted the *philosophes'* search for rational laws governing humankind's own creations on earth, and they called for changes in those institutions. Their failure to discover a basis in reason for divine-right rule (see Chapter 1) led many *philosophes* to call for the reform of monarchy. In his *Social Contract*, for example, Rousseau argued for a new governing principle in which the general will of the people should govern. In the criminal justice practiced by governments of the day, the *philosophes* found a brutal system in which courts might employ torture to force defendants to testify against themselves and in which capital punishment was common. Many *philosophes* argued against the barbarism of such a system. In the work of the Italian thinker Cesare Bonesana, Marchese di Beccarria (1738–1794), the Enlightenment produced a strong statement

Chapter 2

The

Enlightenment

Confronts the

Divine: The

Debate Over

the Lisbon

Earthquake

against the death penalty and in favor of punishments based on prison terms graduated to fit the offense.

In religious matters, *philosophes* everywhere found an intolerance that to them seemed irrational, and Voltaire led their call for toleration and freedom of thought. Not even economic affairs escaped the attention of the *philosophes*. Eighteenth-century economic life was still dominated by guilds (see Chapter 5) that set prices and government mercantilist policies that regulated trade. Adam Smith (1723–1790), a Scottish economist, led many Enlightenment thinkers in calling for a free economy. Let the natural laws of the economy work unimpeded and unregulated and the needs of all would be met, they argued. Everywhere the *philosophes* looked, they saw the need for reform. The existence today in the modern West of much of what they called for testifies to the wide-ranging influence of their thought.

A further casualty of the earthquake in Portugal was the Society of Jesus, one of the great opponents of much of Enlightenment thought. The disaster enhanced the power of the Marquis of Pombal, chief minister of Portugal's weak-willed monarch, Joseph I, because he led the relief and rebuilding efforts in the devastated city. The Portuguese version of that eighteenth-century phenomenon described in your text as the "enlightened despot," Pombal wielded more and more royal power even though he never wore the crown.

Your text recounts the careers of a number of enlightened despots, including Frederick the Great of Prussia and Joseph II of Austria. Like these rulers, Pombal had a vision of a government that was first of all absolute in power and only secondarily reforming in its policies. He found the great power of the Catholic church in Portugal a formidable obstacle to his hopes of building the secular strength of the state. Armed with greater prestige after the earthquake, Pombal attacked the greatest bastion of clerical power, the Society of Jesus, and expelled almost all of Portugal's Jesuits on September 1, 1759. In 1761 he ordered the execution of Gabriel Malagrida, the Society's most visible Portuguese spokesman. Malagrida's ideas stood in the way of reconstruction because he preached a need for spiritual regeneration and focused people's attentions on the next life. Pombal, in contrast, required all of Portugal's energies for rebuilding in the here and now. Other Catholic countries duplicated the Portuguese expulsion of the Jesuits. Local political or theological issues were often at the root of such expulsions, but they resulted in the worldwide abolition of the Society of Jesus from 1773 to 1814.[34]

The postearthquake Western world, thanks to the natural forces of the Lisbon disaster and the intellectual forces of the Enlightenment, would be considerably transformed on a number of levels. The fruits of Enlightenment thought are still with us in many forms.

---

34. On the French experience, see Dale Van Kley, *The Jansenists and the Expulsion of the Jesuits from France* (New Haven: Yale University Press, 1974).

CHAPTER THREE
A STATISTICAL VIEW
OF EUROPEAN RURAL LIFE,
1600–1800

Chapter 2 gave us a glimpse into the intellectual currents circulating among the educated upper classes of eighteenth-century Europe. Such groups have left historians ample evidence of their intellectual milieu in the works of figures like Voltaire as well as copious records of their lives and activities in correspondence, autobiographies, and other written sources. As a consequence, historians have been able to describe in great detail both the thought and the daily routine of Europe's opinion molders and governing classes. No matter how much influence these groups wielded, however, ultimately they represented only a small minority of the total population of their countries.

Most Europeans in the seventeenth and eighteenth centuries were illiterate, or barely literate, a "silent majority" because they left none of the conventional written records that have long provided historians their raw material in reconstructing the world of the privileged classes. Moreover, the majority of the population was rural, earning its living from the land, far from London, Paris, Venice, Vienna, and the other great urban centers that traditionally have attracted the research efforts of historians. Consequently we know a great deal about Voltaire as a member of the European elite, for example, but very little about the many peasants who worked his estate at Ferney—or about any other peasants, for that matter.

Only relatively recently have historians developed the methodological skills to penetrate the world of the majority of early modern Europe, the nonelites who left no written records of their own. Twentieth-century French scholars led the way in research in this area, and consequently the largest body of materials now available is devoted to France. Here two groups of French scholars have advanced our knowledge. One

Chapter 3
A Statistical
View of
European
Rural Life,
1600–1800

school, associated with the historical journal *Annales: Economies, sociétés, civilisations*, attempts to write "total history." Their search to understand the entirety of human existence, not just the actions of generals and kings and the thought of the great philosophers, has led them into many interesting lines of research, including studies of climatic changes and of literacy.[1] Because the ability to read and write largely defines the relationships an individual or a group forms with the wider world, the presence or absence of literacy is a fundamental issue in studying historic populations. Based on the frequency with which persons were able to sign their names to such documents as marital registers and court records, these historians have reconstructed the literacy pattern of western Europe during the seventeenth and eighteenth centuries. A more literate north and a less literate south characterized western Europe at this time, a regional difference that can be attributed largely to religious factors: northern European countries like England and Sweden were Protestant and emphasized individual reading of the Bible as an integral part of religious practice. Throughout Europe an inverse relationship existed between the ability to read and write on the one hand and personal wealth and social class on the other.

A second school of French researchers has focused attention on historical demography, that is, the historical study of population.[2] Because regular census data on populations is largely a nineteenth-century development, these historians have reconstructed the past by means of other data, as you will see.

English and other historians followed the French lead, with the result that our knowledge of Europe's unlettered majority has grown immensely over the past four decades. Whatever their nationalities, however, historians examining Europe's ill-educated majority have adopted a common approach in reconstructing the past. Because little information exists for any given seventeenth- or eighteenth-century individual, historians have employed the technique of *collective biography*: they attempt to reconstruct the life of a community or social group and often express the results of their studies statistically.

The picture that emerges from these statistical studies is one of deep poverty for Europe's farming majority, a poverty that left them utterly at the mercy of nature. This is how the French demographic historian, Pierre Goubert, draws on his many years of study to describe the lifestyle of poorer French peasants in the late seventeenth century:

> The humble day-labourer, with a garden, a plot of land, a couple of sheep,

---

1. The journal *Annales* espoused this approach to history from its founding in 1929 by the French historians Marc Bloch and Lucien Febvre. The influence of this approach to historical study grew immensely after World War Two.

2. Historical demography is a relatively new field of study, too. The major early works of the French pioneers in the field date only from the 1950s.

working seasonally for other people, spinning or woodworking at home, would live in the classic cottage, the *chaumine enfumée* (smoky cottage) specified by La Fontaine,[3] and these would certainly have been the commonest dwellings in France at that time. Made of stone or daub, depending on the region, but always with a solid chimney, stone surrounds for door and windows, it would be built around a simple frame of local wood, and roofed with reeds, rye straw, heather, or fern, topped with some large stones to protect the thatch from the wind. Inside there would be a single room, square or elongated (sometimes with a stable at one end). Beneath its occupants' bare feet (they put clogs on to go out) would be a floor of trodden earth, sometimes strewn with reeds or branches, all pretty well soaked with rain, damp from the walls, and chicken urine and droppings. The "hearth," the heart of the house, usually had a hook and a pot; there they warmed themselves, when the door was not open to make the chimney draw. Wind, rain, small animals, and every sort of parasite—creeping, scratching, jumping—came in all the time. Apart from cold (which they could protect themselves from by means of old cloaks, flea-ridden blankets, and *poches* [sacks]), their chief enemy was *arsin*, fire.[4]

The methodology that allows historians to portray the details of a vanished way of life in this manner consists of two basic operations: first compiling their statistical data and then analyzing it, that is, asking the right questions of their figures. Their goal is to understand the life of rural farming poor, to learn if any change in that life occurred over time, and to attempt to explain changes through other sets of data. Your objective in this chapter is to ask and respond to the kinds of questions of statistical data that historians pose to understand better the lifestyle of Europe's majority from 1600 to 1800. What were the natural forces that affected these people? How can we measure the effects of these forces on Europe's farming population? Can we discern any changes that might have allowed Europe's "silent majority" to escape the grip of these natural forces?

SOURCES AND METHOD

The evidence in this chapter has been selected to present you with a wide variety of the forms in which historians advance the statistical results of their research: tables and graphs. Analyzing these materials jointly will allow you to understand more fully the lives led by seventeenth- and eighteenth-century Europeans.

Source 1 presents data on European agricultural productivity for the grains wheat, rye, and barley, the

3. **Jean de La Fontaine** (1621–1695): a French poet and author of fables often describing rural life.

4. Pierre Goubert, *The French Peasantry in the Seventeenth Century*, trans. Ian Patterson (New York: Cambridge University Press, 1986), p. 37.

Chapter 3

A Statistical

View of

European

Rural Life,

1600–1800

mainstays of European diet during the period 1600–1800. The data are arranged by regions and expressed in terms of yield ratios. *Yield ratios* are a basic statistical tool employed by historians of agriculture that express the number of bushels harvested from one bushel of seed. Thus, from 1600 to 1649 in Zone I, 1 bushel of grain seed produced 6.7 bushels at harvest. To put this data in perspective, you need to understand that modern farming methods on amply watered wheat fields in the U.S. Midwest produce yield ratios of at least 40:1 and often much higher. What do you conclude about the productivity of agriculture in the period that is the subject of this chapter? Which areas of Europe were most and least productive? Which areas showed the greatest advance toward a more productive farming? Given such an agriculture, why would you not be surprised to find the majority of the population occupied with farming?

Source 2 presents the dietary consequences of agriculture as a table representing the theoretical diet in 1800 of the population of the southern Netherlands (modern Belgium), one of the more prosperous regions of Europe in the early modern period. To interpret this data, you need to know that nutritionists tell us that about 2,400 calories daily are necessary for an adult male to sustain physically strenuous labor. For a balanced, nutritionally complete diet, about 15 percent of those calories should be in the form of protein and 33 to 50 percent of these should be of animal origin. Fats, essential to

sustain body temperature, should represent 25 to 30 percent of the diet; carbohydrates, 55 to 60 percent. The vitamins contained in fresh fruits, vegetables, and milk also are essential. What do you find in this diet of one of the most prosperous parts of Europe? What foodstuffs are most prominently featured? What dietary deficiencies do you note? What health consequences do you think such a diet would have in the southern Netherlands?

We must understand, too, that the diet presented in Source 2 represents the ideal, not the norm. Weather factors often affected European farming, resulting in diminished agricultural yields. Insufficient or excessive rainfall, abnormally low temperatures, and other climatological phenomena all influenced the harvest. The graphs in Source 3 represent some of the most interesting research of modern historians—the study of weather and its consequences. Their work is showing us the climatic differences that have affected the West over the last millennium. Diagram 1 in Source 3 presents temperature data from England in the eighteenth century as evidence of general European temperature trends. In what years were the spring and summer temperatures abnormally cool? Diagram 2 presents the effects of temperature trends by showing simultaneously the dates of grape harvests and the advance of glaciers in the Alps. An especially extended period of glacial advance indicates a period of cool weather, as does an unusually late grape harvest. Diagram 3 draws on the data kept by the French along with other early modern European governments on the price of food, the ultimate consequence of weather trends. How do seasonal temperatures correlate with wheat prices? In what years did weather adversely affect agriculture and drive up prices?

The data presented in Source 4 may seem abstract to twentieth-century readers, who, after all, live in a society in which social welfare agencies prevent actual starvation among the poor despite price increases for dietary essentials. We must remember that such agencies are relatively recent additions to Western life; two centuries ago they did not exist. The graph in Source 4 presents the consequences of periodic food price increases for a French wagoner. You should understand that the graph assigns a value of 100 to wages and prices in the period 1726–1735, establishing that period as the base "index" for the graph. An index of 155 for the price of wheat in Arles in the late 1740s thus represents a 55 percent increase over wheat prices of the base period. What do you observe in long-term salary trends? What do you note about the long-term trends in the price of the wheat essential in making bread, the dietary staple of the poor? What sorts of conditions did the wagoners of Bas-Provence experience in the 1730s, the late 1740s, and especially from the 1760s into the late 1780s?

Poverty and dietary insufficiencies breed a multitude of maladies. But many epidemic diseases struck even well-fed populations. None of these was more feared in medieval and early modern Europe than the bubonic plague. Physicians knew no cure for this fatal illness that had ravaged Europe since its first appearance there in the fourteenth century. By the eighteenth century, Europeans at least understood somewhat the importance of quarantining districts afflicted by the plague as a means of stemming its spread. The table in Source 5 represents plague mortalities in southern France in 1720–1721 as the disease spread. Plague broke out first in the large port of Marseilles and spread to much of the surrounding region, grievously afflicting some towns and not others. Quarantines restricted the disease to the southern part of France, and the Marseilles epidemic was the last great outbreak of the plague in the modern West to date. In what towns did the greatest portion of the population die? What impact would such losses have had on the towns?

Disease was common in early modern Europe, as were famine conditions. When disease coincided with agricultural failure, the result could be what historians call a *demographic* or *population crisis*, a period when deaths exceed births and the population declines. Information on such crises in the population history of Europe has been amassed laboriously by historians using records left by the literate members of early modern society about the largely illiterate majority. Priests, for example, kept parish registers of baptisms, marriages, and burials, which, in the hands of

Chapter 3

A Statistical

View of

European

Rural Life,

1600–1800

skilled historical demographers, permit the scholarly reconstitution of the history of past populations.

The data presented in Source 6 present evidence of the last great demographic crisis to afflict all of Europe, which occurred in the 1740s. As in the graph in Source 4, the researchers have established values around a base period to which a value of 100 is assigned. Thus, in Source 6, 100 represents the average number of births annually in 1735–1744. An index number of 106 for births in England during the year 1740 indicates simply that births that year were 6 percent higher than the average. Similarly, an index of 89 for 1735 indicates births were 89 percent of the base period total.

At what rate was Europe's population growing prior to the 1740s? What reasons might account for this trend? In what years, as revealed in an abnormally high death rate, did demographic crises strike the various European countries? Consult the data on births and marriages. Did the crisis have a greater, more lasting effect than simply the deaths resulting from it? What happened to marriage and birth rates in the wake of the crisis? How might these developments affect a society's ability to replace its losses?

Inadequate means of transportation also affected the conditions of the population in early modern Europe. An area experiencing poor harvests might confront outright starvation simply because of the impossibility of moving food supplies to it from prosperous neighboring areas. Source 7 presents demographic data from Bresles-en-Beauvaisis, a town in northern France, for the seventeenth and early eighteenth centuries. Compare the graphs of food prices and births and burials. In what years were food prices high? In what years did burials exceed births? What do you think caused the excessive burials? How often, over the period 1655–1745, did burials exceed births? Do you think this population grew much in this period?

Our data thus far suggest that a very high death rate affected early modern Europeans. But death did not claim all equally. Examine Source 8, which presents data on infant and child mortality in several parts of France. Approximately what percentage of eighteenth-century French children might hope to live to age ten?

Source 9 employs the statistical tool of average life expectancy to show living conditions in Colyton, England. Average life expectancy is a statistical construct in which the life spans of all persons born at a given point in time are averaged together. In deriving such averages, historians of population as well as public health specialists average the life spans of the infant dying within minutes or hours of birth and the old person who reaches the age of eighty or ninety. The resulting figure offers a perspective on how well a given society provides for the health and welfare of its members. For purposes of comparison, the average life expectancy in modern England in the 1980s is 70.2 years for males and 76.2 years for females, whereas in some impoverished Third World countries today life expectancy is roughly 43 years for both men and women.

The Colyton figures show average life expectancy for years of high, low, and average death rates. How do such life expectancies compare with those of modern England and the modern Third World? What role do you think infant mortality had in keeping average life expectancy low?

The lives of early modern Europeans clearly were affected by the fortunes of agriculture. But even in noncrisis years the regular rhythm of the agricultural year ruled early modern rural Europeans' lives. The rural French experience was probably typical of Europe as a whole: the year opened with January and February, cold months when agricultural labor was light because of weather conditions. Food reserves, however, were beginning to shrink at this time, and farmers often slaughtered pigs and other livestock because fodder for the animals was running low. By March, April, and May the fruits of the previous autumn's harvests were dwindling for humans, too, as agricultural labor resumed with plowing and planting. Late May and June, after the crops were planted, might bring a slight respite from work. But late summer and early autumn brought the more taxing labor of the harvest. In these months epidemics of disease as well as health problems resulting from the drinking of impure water and the eating of partially ripened fruits and vegetables made necessary

by summer shortages affected the health of the rural population. Once the harvest was in, of course, winter's rigors resumed.

Source 10 presents the seasonal incidence of death in four areas in France. How does the death rate reflect the impact of the agricultural year and climatic conditions on French people? Note that the graph for Morannes distinguishes the deaths of the young from the old. When did children die? Why? In Sources 11 and 12, you find data on marriages and conceptions in rural France. To analyze the marriage data, you must remember that France is largely a Catholic country and you should understand that the Church forbade marriages during Advent (the period in late November and December for four Sundays before Christmas on December 25) and Lent (the period of forty weekdays before Easter beginning on Ash Wednesday, usually in March and early April). Bearing in mind these religious strictures and the agricultural cycle, determine when rural Frenchmen married and why they chose the months they did. Why would these months in the agricultural cycle be propitious times for wedding feasts? When did French rural couples conceive their children? How might the agricultural cycle affect reproduction?

Your task in this chapter is to reconstruct the lifestyle of Europe's majority using the statistical sets provided. Use the mode of analysis suggested in this section, taking care to: (1) Study each data set, observing changes over time—for instance,

Chapter 3
A Statistical
View of
European
Rural Life,
1600–1800

increased agricultural productivity in some areas. (2) Once you have identified a change, seek an explanation in the other data sets. For example, what weather trends affected areas with improved agricultural output? How might they help to account for increased productivity? What role might diet have played? (3) Pose basic questions of your data. What trends were affecting the population?

Making use of this methodology, you should be able to answer the central questions of this chapter: What were the natural forces that affected these people? How can we measure the effects of these forces on Europe's farming population? Can we discern any changes that might have allowed Europe's "silent majority" to escape the grip of these natural forces?

THE EVIDENCE

Source 1 from E. E. Rich and C. H. Wilson, editors, The Cambridge Economic History of Europe, *vol. 5,* The Economic Organization of Early Modern Europe *(New York: Cambridge University Press, 1977), p. 81.*

1. Combined Yield Ratios of Wheat, Rue, and Barley, 1500–1820

Period	Zone I[a]	Zone II[b]	Zone III[c]	Zone IV[d]
1600–1649	6.7:1	—	4.5:1	4.0:1
1650–1699	9.3	6.2:1	4.1	3.8
1700–1749	—	6.3	4.1	3.5
1750–1799	10.1	7.0	5.1	4.7
1800–1820	11.1	6.2	5.4	—

a. Zone I: England, Low Countries.
b. Zone II: France, Spain, Italy.
c. Zone III: Germany, Switzerland, Scandinavia.
d. Zone IV: Russia, Poland, Czechoslovakia, Hungary.

Source 2 from Catherine Lis and Hugo Soly, Poverty and Capitalism in Pre-Industrial Europe (Atlantic Highlands, N.J.: Humanities Press, 1979), p. 182.

2. Average Diet in the Southern Netherlands, ca 1800

CONSUMPTION PER PERSON PER DAY

Foodstuffs	Quantity	Number of calories	Constituents (grams)		
			Proteins	*Fats*	*Carbohydrates*
Bread[a]	500 grams	1,250	35.3	14.6	257.9
Potatoes	700 grams	490	11.4	0.5	106
Meat	27 grams	60	5.0	4.5	—
Butter	27 grams	205	0.1	22.7	—
Cheese	1 gram	3	0.2	0.1	—
Fish	6 grams	13	2.5	1.1	—
Sugar	5 grams	17	—	—	4.4
Syrup	3 grams	7	—	—	—
Rice	1 gram	3	—	—	—
Eggs	0.137	10	0.8	0.7	—
Milk	0.082 litre	5	2.7	3	3.8
Buttermilk	0.411 litre	122	12.2	1.5	14.0
Vegetables	0.030 litre	45	3.0	0.2	7.5
Total		2,230	73.2	48.9	393.6
Beer	0.500 litre	225	or	or	or
Gin	0.016 litre	45			
Wine	0.012 litre	8	14%	10%	76%
Grand Total		2,508			

a. Mixed loaves consisting of two-thirds rye and one-third wheat.

Sources 3 and 4 adapted from Ernest Labrousse, et al., Histoire économique et sociale de la France, vol. II, Des derniers temps de l'âge seigneurial aux préludes de l'âge industriel (1660–1789) (Paris: Presses Universitaires de la France, 1970), pp. 392, 537.

3. Wheat Prices and Weather, France, 1699–1789

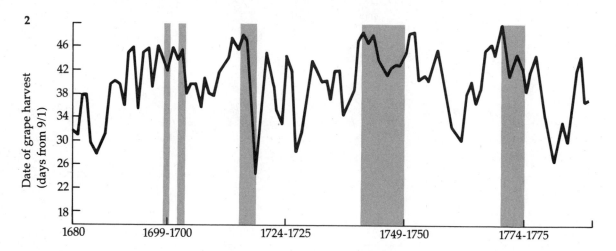

1. Spring and summer temperatures for England (two-year moving averages; temperature scale in Fahrenheit; graph of temperatures inverted for better comparison with the graph of grape harvests).

2. Dates of grape harvests (counted in days from September 1, in moving two-year averages); glacial maximums in the Alps shown in shading.

3. Price of wheat per *setier* of Paris in *livres tournois* (French currency of eighteenth century).

4. Contrast Between Fixed Salary of a Typical Agricultural Worker and Price of Wheat in Bas-Provence, France, 1726–1789

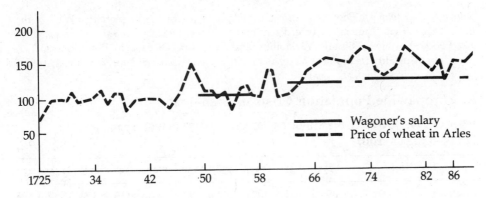

Source 5 from Jean-Noël Biraben, "Certain Demographic Characteristics of the Plague Epidemic in France, 1720–1722," Daedalus, *Spring 1968, pp. 541–542.*

5. Epidemics: The Plague in Southern France, 1720–1721

Place	Approximate Preplague Population	Date of First Appearance of Plague	Number of Plague Deaths	Percentage of Population Killed
Marseilles and envirorons	90,000	20 June 1720	39,334	43.7
Vitrolles	770	2 August	210	27.3
Gignac	470	15 August	42	8.9
Septèmes	940	26 August	200	21.3
Gaubert	500	4 September	29	5.8
Nans	500	27 September	125	25.0
Auriol	3,200	3 October	1,319	41.2
Villars Brancas	300	9 October	12	4.0
Martigues	6,000	1 November	2,200	36.7
Arles	22,000	26 November	9,400	42.7
Orgon	1,700	29 December	105	6.2
La Valette	1,600	20 February 1721	1,068	64.3
Trinquetaille les Arles	1,157	11 June	80	6.9
St. Nazaire (Sanary)	1,200	1 July	51	4.2
La Roquebrussane	997	14 August	201	20.1

Chapter 3

A Statistical

View of

European

Rural Life,

1600–1800

[Sources 6–12 are assembled to reflect the combined effects of the agricultural cycle and disease on population.]

Source 6 from John D. Post, "Climatic Variability and the European Mortality Wave of the Early 1740s," The Journal of Interdisciplinary History, *vol. 15 (1984), no. 10 (table 1) and* Food Shortage, Climatic Variability, and Epidemic Disease in Preindustrial Europe: The Mortality Peak in the Early 1740s *(Ithaca, N.Y.: Cornell University Press, 1985), pp. 46, 48 (tables 2 and 3).*

6. Europewide Population Crisis of 1740–1742

INDEXES OF ANNUAL NUMBER OF DEATHS IN EUROPE, 1735–1744 (1735–1744 = 100)

Location	1735	1736	1737	1738	1739	1740	1741	1742	1743	1744
England	89	94	102	92	93	106	118	124	98	85
Scotland	88	96	109	88	93	122	116	107	90	91
Ireland (Dublin)	93	89	94	106	93	140	119	99	93	72
France	80	93	93	96	109	123	116	111	94	83
Low Countries	83	95	102	93	97	99	149	98	98	84
Germany	84	116	114	99	98	112	110	96	92	78
Austria (Vienna)	88	112	108	118	98	111	105	105	87	69
Switzerland	86	100	115	84	85	108	100	123	112	87
Italy	94	115	96	87	86	100	107	112	108	95
Sweden[a]	70[b]	82	102	92	93	108	98	118	131	76
Finland	64	75	104	85	97	157	95	136	112	74
Norway	68	74	88	83	83	92	149	187	100	76
Denmark	81	102	114	100	96	114	112	103	95	83
Unweighted average	82	96	103	94	94	115	115	117	101	81

a. Base period 1736–1744.
b. Index number derived from Stockholm and nine Swedish counties.

INDEXES OF ANNUAL NUMBER OF BIRTHS IN EUROPE, 1735–1744 (1735–1744 = 100)

Location	1735	1736	1737	1738	1739	1740	1741	1742	1743	1744
England	105	103	101	103	105	100	93	91	99	100
France	100	101	106	100	105	99	99	95	96	99
Low Countries	106	105	106	105	102	97	88	94	101	95
Germany	103	100	93	97	104	96	91	99	108	109
Austria (Vienna)	114	110	111	109	120	106	81	78	84	88
Switzerland	106	99	106	103	102	97	100	94	96	97
Italy	99	93	100	101	102	101	99	103	98	103
Sweden[a]	99[b]	92	94	104	113	100	99	98	92	107
Finland	105	111	110	113	112	104	98	74	78	96
Norway	100	105	105	97	108	103	95	90	95	102
Denmark	101	99	96	102	102	99	94	97	103	106
Unweighted average	103	102	103	103	107	100	94	92	95	100

a. Base period 1736–1744.
b. Index number derived from Stockholm and nine Swedish counties.

INDEXES OF ANNUAL NUMBER OF MARRIAGES IN EUROPE, 1735–1744 (1735–1744 = 100)

Location	1735	1736	1737	1738	1739	1740	1741	1742	1743	1744
England	104	95	100	100	103	98	88	97	107	107
France	93	94	99	101	97	96	96	101	122	101
Low Countries	108	107	101	99	103	86	90	107	102	99
Germany	97	93	97	99	104	88	101	115	109	97
Switzerland	102	99	102	105	96	99	88	97	114	98
Italy	99	93	101	104	101	99	97	92	104	111
Finland	105	106	105	103	95	93	78	75	101	140
Unweighted average	101	98	101	102	100	94	91	98	108	108

Chapter 3
A Statistical
View of
European
Rural Life,
1600–1800

Source 7 adapted from Pierre Goubert and Daniel Roche, Les français et l'Ancien Régime, *vol. I (Paris: Armand Colin, 1984), p. 45.*

7. Local Crises at Bresles-en-Beauvaisis, France, late 17th and early 18th centuries

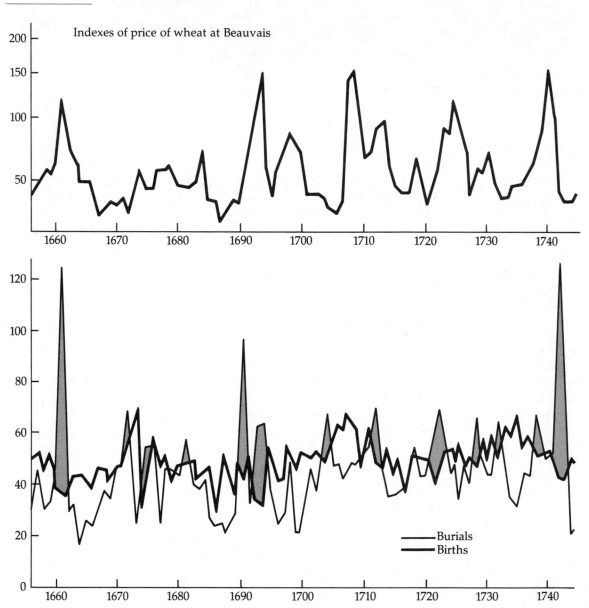

Source 8 from Pierre Goubert, "Legitimate Fecundity and Infant Mortality in France During the Eighteenth Century: A Comparison," Daedalus, Spring 1968, pp. 599–600.

8. Infant and Child Mortality in France: Children Living to the Age of 10 Years

Brittany:

Saint-Aubin (1748–1789)	580 of 1,000
La Guerche (1720–1790)	510 of 1,000
Saint-Méen (1720–1792)	463 of 1,000

Elsewhere (Southwest and Normandy):

Thézels (1747–1782)	645 of 1,000
Azereix (18th century)	639 of 1,000
Crulai (1674–1742)	672 of 1,000

Source 9 from E. A. Wrigley, "Mortality in Pre-Industrial England: The Example of Colyton, Devon, Over Three Centuries," Daedalus, Spring 1968, p. 574.

9. Life Expectancy in Colyton, England, in Years

Period	High Mortality	Low Mortality	Midpoint
1538–1624	40.6	45.8	43.2
1625–1699	34.9	38.9	36.9
1700–1774	38.4	45.1	41.8

Chapter 3
A Statistical
View of
European
Rural Life,
1600–1800

Source 10 from François Lebrun, Les hommes et la morte en Anjou aux 17ᵉ et 18ᵉ siècles. Essai de démographie et de psychologie historiques *(Paris and The Hague: Mouton, 1971), p. 190.*

10. Seasonal Incidence of Mortality in Several Rural Areas of France, 17th and 18th centuries

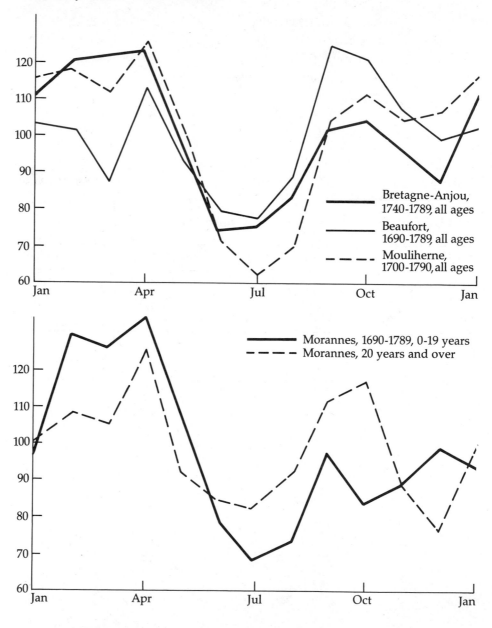

Sources 11 and 12 from Pierre Guillaume and Jean-Pierre Poussou, Demographie historique *(Paris: Armand Colin, 1970), p. 184; p. 172.*

11. Seasonal Incidence of Marriage in France, Showing the Three Most Common Months (1–3) and the Three Least Common Months (10–12), by Location

Parishes	Period of Observation	1	2	3	10	11	12
Thézels-Saint-Sernin (Lot)	1700–1792	Feb.	Nov.	June	Sept.	Aug.	Dec.
Castelnau-de-Montratier (Lot)	1716–1789	Feb.	Nov.	Jan.	Aug.	March	Dec.
La Rochelle, Saint-Barthélemy parish	1677–1685	Feb.	Jan.	July	April	March	Dec.
Chef-Boutonne (Deux-Sèvres)	1722–1792	Feb.	Jan.	Nov.	Aug.	March	Dec.
Avits (Tarn)	1692–1717	Feb.	June	Jan.	Aug.	March	Dec.
Lyon	1750–1774	Feb.	Jan.	Nov.	April	March	Dec.
Saint-Romain-d'Urfé (Loire)	1740–1749	Nov.	Feb.	Jan.	April	March	Dec.
Bonneuil-sur-Marne (Seine)	1680–1790	Nov.	Jan.	Feb.	Aug.	March	Dec.
Bagneux (Seine)	1691–1789	Feb.	Nov.	Jan.	April	Dec.	March
Paris {	1728–1737	Feb.	Nov.	Jan.	April	March	Dec.
	1778–1787	Feb.	Nov.	Jan.	Aug.	March	Dec.
Crulai (Orne)	1675–1798	Nov.	Feb.	Jan.	April	March	Dec.

12. Seasonal Incidence of Conceptions in France, Showing the Three Most Common Months (1–3) and the Three Least Common Months (10–12), by Location

Parishes	Period of Observation	1	2	3	10	11	12
Thézels-Saint-Sernin (Lot)	1700–1792	June	May	July	Oct.	March	Sept.
Castelnau-de-Montratier (Lot)	1716–1789	June	May	April	Aug.	Sept.	March
Divillac (Lot)	1671–1692	June	May	April	Aug.	March	Nov.
Ile de Ré, 8 parishes	1764–1773	June	Jan.	April	Aug.	Sept.	Oct.
La Rochelle, Saint-Barthélemy parish	1677–1685	Feb.	June	May	Oct.	Dec.	Sept.
Chef-Boutonne (Deux-Sèvres)	1722–1792	June	May	April	Aug.	Oct.	Sept.
Avits (Tarn)	1692–1717	June	Jan.	Nov.	Feb.	Sept.	Oct.
Saint-Romain-d'Urfé (Loire)	1740–1749	June	May	July	Oct.	Sept.	Nov.
Crulai (Orne)	1700–1799	June	May	April	Sept.	Nov.	Oct.

Chapter 3

A Statistical

View of

European

Rural Life,

1600–1800

Each of the sources of evidence you considered in this chapter represents a piece of a puzzle that, when assembled, presents a picture of the life of the rural majority of seventeenth- and eighteenth-century Europe. Let us now begin to fit those pieces together.

Consider first what the various sources tell you about the health of seventeenth- and eighteenth-century Europeans in "average" times. How did the productivity of farming compare to that of today? What sort of diet did it provide Europeans of those centuries? Why would you not be surprised to learn that modern scientists have found evidence that nutritionally based ailments like rickets abounded among these people and that historians have discovered that they were of much shorter stature than twentieth-century Europeans? What would you conclude about this population's resistance to disease?

Next you should determine the frequency with which a physically vulnerable population faced the physical stress of nonaverage times. Note in Source 5 how disastrous an epidemic could be in early modern times. Then recall the sanitary conditions described by Pierre Goubert earlier in this chapter. How common do you think diseases other than the plague must have been, given such sanitary conditions and the physical condition of the population? To arrive at a partial answer to this question, count the demographic crises at Bresles-en-Beauvaisis in the 1655–1745 period. How many times did burials exceed deaths in this period? How often, on the average, did crises combining disease and food shortage recur? To generalize from the French case, reflect how much more productive agriculture in the French zone of Europe was than in some other parts of the Continent and consult the tables in Source 6. What groups in society, based on the evidence in Sources 8 through 10, were most vulnerable to disease and poor nutrition?

If demographic crises recurred with some frequency, especially in the seventeenth century, the effects were felt for years afterward. What effect did demographic crises have on later rates of marriages and births, according to the data in Source 6? Why do you think that population experienced little growth in the seventeenth and eighteenth centuries?

You should also consider the effect that climate and agricultural life had on those who survived the threats to life in seventeenth- and eighteenth-century Europe. How did the cycle of agriculture affect such basic events of human life as marriage and reproduction?

Finally, reconsider the full range of evidence to determine the possibilities for change in this lifestyle. What chance did scientific farming methods have to influence the agricultural methods of a widely illiterate European majority? Compare the overall literacy rate in northern Europe (higher than that in southern Europe) with eighteenth-century improvements in agricultural productivity. What correlation between increased literacy rates and farm output would you expect? If farm productivity could have been improved, what sort of effects do you think Western Europe would have experienced?

As you formulate answers to these questions that transcend the lessons of the individual pieces of evidence and lead you to general conclusions, you should be on the way to putting together the puzzle. As you do so, you should be able to answer the main questions of this chapter. What were the natural forces that affected the majority of seventeenth- and eighteenth-century Europeans? How can we measure the effects of these forces on Europe's farming population? Can we discern any changes that might have allowed Europe's "silent majority" to escape the grip of these natural forces?

EPILOGUE

The world we have sketched here was, until the late eighteenth century, one of limited literacy, poverty, and precarious existence characterized by a stagnant or slowly growing population. Educational levels improved slowly in the late eighteenth century and more rapidly along with the spread of public education in the nineteenth century. But the biggest change was the transformation of the demographic system of Western Europe.

After a century and a half of little growth, Europe's population rapidly expanded after about 1750. The population of England and Wales increased more than fivefold between 1750 and 1900 and that of France almost doubled in the same period. Other countries experienced similar dramatic population increases.

This population explosion was primarily the result of a reduced mortality rate. In particular, losses of life to famine and disease decreased. Famines declined in frequency and severity for several reasons. Some Western European farmers applied more scientific techniques to improve their output, first in England and Holland but later elsewhere. New crops of American origin, like corn and the potato, were introduced to European agriculture. Yielding more food per acre than wheat and often cultivable on marginal lands unsuited for that grain, these crops also increased the food supply. All these developments were part of a phenomenon that many textbooks call the Agricultural Revolution, a process that greatly reduced the numbers of deaths from starvation or the effects of malnutrition.

Deaths from diseases also diminished in the eighteenth century, when physicians began inoculation for smallpox and more effective quarantining of infectious diseases. As a result of the more bountiful and reliable food supply and reduced mortality from disease, the population swelled.

A second transformation of society, the Industrial Revolution, also dramatically altered the lifestyle we examined in this chapter. Beginning in England in the late eighteenth century and later elsewhere in Europe, the Industrial Revolution drew

Chapter 3

A Statistical

View of

European

Rural Life,

1600–1800

increasing numbers of people away from agriculture to employment in factories and residence in the cities that grew up around the new plants (see Chapters 5 and 7). The Agricultural Revolution aided this process by creating harvests so productive that a farming minority of the population could feed an urbanized majority employed in manufacturing and service industries. The result was an increasingly urbanized Europe.

The Industrial Revolution also helped to destroy the demographic system we explored in this chapter. Improved transportation, like the railroads made possible by the modern steel industry, permitted food products to be moved rapidly to areas in need of them and to eliminate the local famines we examined in Source 9. Some historians also argue that at least in England the Industrial Revolution may also have helped to increase the birth rate. Because marriage has always depended on the existence of the financial means to establish a new household, industrialization may have created the wealth necessary to allow more women than ever before to marry and to have children.

A variety of factors combined in the nineteenth and early twentieth centuries to alter beyond recognition the rural world we have explored. Its isolation bred of illiteracy, its poverty rooted in an unproductive agriculture, and its high mortality now represent a lifestyle foreign to modern Europe, a Western society preserved only in museums and history books.

CHAPTER FOUR

A DAY IN
THE FRENCH REVOLUTION:
JULY 14, 1789

Tuesday dawned cool and cloudy in Paris. Leaden skies threatening heavy rainfall cast little light into the narrow, crowded streets of the capital. But that rain held off until evening, thereby providing the opportunity for events to occur in the city's streets and squares that set off a fundamental change in the political history of France and the West as a whole. When rain finally fell, sending Parisians scurrying home, the forces of King Louis XVI had lost control of the capital and the principle of royal absolutism was clearly in decline.

On that Tuesday, July 14, 1789, the people of Paris seized the great fortress and prison on the city's eastern edge known as the Bastille. Construction of the Bastille had begun in 1370 as part of the eastern defenses of Paris. The fortress had eight towers set in walls about 100 feet high and 10 feet thick. Its only entrance was by two drawbridges across a moat that was dry in 1789; by that date the Bastille had been obsolete as a fort for several centuries. Developments in modern artillery had rendered its walls vulnerable, and the growth of Paris meant that the Bastille was no longer on the city's periphery but instead was surrounded by the streets of the suburb known as the Faubourg Saint-Antoine.

As early as the fifteenth century, the monarchy had confined prisoners in the Bastille, but the systematic use of the old fort as a prison began during the ministry of Cardinal Richelieu in the early seventeenth century. The Bastille was used to confine persons whose offenses were not punishable under the regular criminal laws of France, and received political prisoners held without trial under royal orders known as *lettres de cachet*. Religious dissenters joined the prison's inmates during the reign of Louis XV (1715–1774). The nature of this prison gave it a particularly evil reputation in the eighteenth century, but one

[77]

that was little warranted by 1789. Although the Bastille had a capacity for forty-two prisoners in cells, with room for additional inmates in a dungeon that had been unused for twenty years, it held only seven prisoners on July 14, 1789. These seven—four forgers, two victims of mental illness, and one murder suspect locked away at the behest of his noble family—hardly seemed victims of injustice. Indeed, the monarchy was considering plans to demolish this structure, whose usefulness had ended when the Paris crowd captured it.

The origins of this mass action, the first—but not the last—of its kind in Paris during the Revolution, may be found in a political and economic crisis that had kept France in turmoil during the preceding thirty months. As a consequence of the costly wars of the eighteenth century and a system of taxation that largely exempted the clergy and nobility from fiscal obligations, the French monarchy faced bankruptcy by 1787.[1] Several finance ministers struggled with the crown's fiscal problems, but all eventually arrived at the same solution: fundamental financial reform that would tax the Church and nobility, not simply the commoners. In proposing such changes, however, the royal ministers encountered constitutional problems. The proposed reforms violated traditional rights of the clergy

1. France's successful intervention in the American War of Independence played no small part in this debt. The American war cost France 2 billion livres, a figure about four times the government's tax receipts in 1788. By that year interest payments on the government's debts consumed 51 percent of its receipts.

and nobility, and the king was forced to call for the meeting of a French representative body—the Estates General, which had not met since 1614—to consider reform.[2]

The election campaign for the Estates General stirred up the country, creating expectations of change, and French voters did not return a legislature prepared simply to approve tax reform and go home. Some representatives of the clergy and nobility resisted any change. More seriously, the monarchy confronted the defiant members of the Third Estate, representing the commoners, who demanded tax reform and greater political equality.[3] They declared themselves a National Assembly, the rightful representatives of the French people, and then, on June 20, 1789, in their Tennis Court oath called for a constitution to limit royal power. This defiance of royal authority was really the first act of revolution.

The king vacillated at first in the face of such defiance but then resolved on two steps. On June 22, 1789 he signed orders for the movement of troops into the region of Paris and Versailles to regain control. Those assigned were largely foreign soldiers (Swiss and German regiments especially) in French service, who presumably would be more will-

2. Royal failure to call the Estates General was deliberate: the body was an obstacle to royal absolutism.

3. Representatives of the clergy constituted the First Estate of the Estates General; representatives of the nobility made up the Second Estate of what had been traditionally a three-house legislature. In 1789 the king required this traditional style of meeting, which gave great voice to the small minority of the population who were clerics and nobles.

ing to use force on civilians than would French soldiers. Such troop movements, however, could not be kept secret. There was growing fear in Versailles and Paris of a royal coup in early July directed against the defiant National Assembly and its supporters in the capital.

The king's second step was the dismissal of Jacques Necker as royal finance minister on July 11, 1789. Popular opinion regarded Necker as a liberal financial genius whose skills kept the government solvent, stabilized financial markets, and kept Paris supplied with food. But he and the ministers associated with him were replaced with officials more fully committed to Louis's impending use of force to reestablish royal authority.

Political events of the preceding months and a rapid rise in bread prices caused by recent bad harvests had heightened tension in Paris even before the king reached this decision. The concurrence of political and economic unrest already had led to large-scale rioting on April 27–28, 1789, when rumors spread that a wallpaper manufacturer, Reveillon, had advocated reduction of workers' wages.[4] Troops had been needed to

restore order in the capital in April. News of Necker's firing reached Paris about 9:00 A.M. on July 12, a Sunday when the population's release from normal weekday duties favored the spread of rumor and political agitation. One of the agitators, the demagogic Camille Desmoulins, effectively directed the thoughts of many Parisians to action when he said to his listeners at the popular gathering place, the Palais Royal:

> Citizens, you know that the Nation had asked for Necker to be retained, and he has been driven out! Could you be more insolently flouted? After such an act they will dare anything, and they may perhaps be planning and preparing a Saint-Bartholomew massacre of patriots for this very night! . . . To arms! To arms![5]

Demonstrations broke out in Paris by the middle of the day on July 12, bolstered by the adherence of the French Guards, a unit charged with keeping order in the city, to the cause of the crowds. By evening fighting took place between demonstrators and units of the foreign troops ordered to Paris by the king, and their commanders withdrew royal forces from the city. Unrest continued through the night without opposition. At about 1:00 A.M. on July 13, crowds began to burn the tax stations along the wall surrounding Paris, since the majority of the commoners blamed the tax on goods entering the

4. Reveillon was one of Paris's largest manufacturers; his wallpaper works employed about 300 persons. He had not, however, precisely advocated a reduction of wages in a speech he gave at his local assembly to elect representatives to the Estates General. On April 23, Reveillon had said that if the price of bread could be reduced, worker's wages would follow, resulting in a lower cost for the goods they produced. Sources vary widely on the human cost of the rioting. Jacques Godechot, *The Taking of the Bastille: July 14, 1789* (trans. Jean Stewart; New York: Scribner's, 1970, p. 147), accepts a figure of 300 dead.

5. Quoted by Godechot, pp. 187–188. **Saint-Bartholomew Massacre:** on August 24, 1572, Catholic forces killed several thousand Protestants all over France during the French wars of religion.

capital for higher food prices. At 6:00 A.M. crowds attacked a monastery where they believed food was stored.

As disorder grew in the capital, on the morning of July 13 the men who had served as electors of the Parisian deputies to the Estates General assembled at the Paris city hall and implemented two important decisions.[6] First, they constituted a committee from their ranks to administer the city, in effect creating a revolutionary municipal government; second, they called for the founding of a "civic militia." The militia's stated purpose was to keep order in the capital, but the formation of such an armed force, obeying the orders of the electors rather than the king, was another revolutionary act.

The creation of the militia, soon to be called the *National Guard*, required arms, and the search for guns and ammunition became the next object of crowd action. On the morning of July 14, a large crowd forced its way into the *Invalides*, an old soldiers' home/barracks, and seized all of the 32,000 muskets stored there. Muskets were of little value without gun-

powder and musket balls, however, and the crowd found few of these commodities at the Invalides. They surged on that morning to the Bastille, where royal officers earlier had transferred 250 barrels of powder for safekeeping as Paris grew restive. Defending the fortress against a growing crowd were eighty-two *invalides* (older or partially disabled soldiers fit only for garrison duty) and thirty-two soldiers of the Swiss regiments in French service. After two deputations from the crowd failed to secure the commander's surrender, the attack began about 1:30 P.M. By 5:00 P.M. the Bastille and its supplies had fallen to the crowd.

You now have a summary of what the crowd did on July 14, 1789. Such mass actions were common in early modern Europe. Your problem in this chapter is to analyze the evidence presented here to answer basic questions about the crowd. Why were the people of Paris angry in mid-July 1789? How were Parisians mobilized for action? Who comprised the crowd that stormed the Bastille?

This chapter presents a variety of evidence to assist you in answering the basic questions about the atmosphere in Paris in July 1789 that produced

6. Rules for Estates General elections in Paris required that voters in each of the city's sixty electoral districts select electors, who in turn would vote for representatives to the Estates General.

the attack on the Bastille. The first pieces of evidence you encounter in the chapter are visual. You already have analyzed such sources in Chapter 1, and you should examine the pictures presented in this chapter to reconstruct the physical setting for the events of 1789. In analyzing the evidence, your objective should be to derive answers to this question: What features of the physical layout of Paris were conducive to the spread of rumors and agitation?

Sources 1 and 2 offer views of the Palais Royal, the property of the Duke of Orléans, a member of the royal family. On the grounds of this palace the duke developed a commercial and entertainment area lined with shops and cafés. The palace and its grounds were outside of police jurisdiction because they belonged to the duke and so attracted political agitators, prostitutes, and criminals like pickpockets. Much of the politically active population of Paris would have been familiar with the grounds of the Palais Royal. What role might such a site have played on July 14, 1789? Why might the significance of the Palais Royal for the political climate of 1789 have been so great that a few historians have seen it as evidence of a plot by its owner to foment a revolution that might benefit his own political ambitions?

Figure 3 shows the rue du Fer-à-Moulin, a street typical of many of those of eighteenth-century Paris at the time of the Revolution. In 1789 much of the Parisian population of about 600,000 still lived in such streets, crowded inside the boundaries set by the city's former medieval fortifications. To accommodate this dense population, residential buildings were six or seven stories high and crowded, with an average of almost thirty residents in each one. Try to imagine life in these buildings and streets. Do you think people would have spent a great deal of time in the streets? Why? What sorts of exchanges of information might have occurred in streets like these?

Source 4 introduces a new form of evidence, architectural drawings of residential buildings, to enhance your understanding of the physical aspect of Paris in 1789. The floor plan for 18, rue Contrescarpe is of a house very near the Bastille. Such multistoried structures typically had a ground floor rented out to a merchant or craftsman who maintained a shop that opened on the street. A craftsman might have rented a workshop behind the shop on the ground floor, too. Access to the residential upper floors was through the gate opening onto the street at the end of the passage leading to the interior courtyard. Each building's numerous residents would cross the courtyard daily going in and out or fetching water from the well. All would have needed to mount the staircase to rooms whose prices decreased as the number of steps separating them from the ground increased. As a consequence of this pricing procedure, a master craftsman might occupy a large apartment on the first floor up these stairs; his employees, the tiny rooms in the attic. Reflect on this living situation. How might news and rumor have spread in such a setting? How might a crowd be mobilized there? Why might the economic power of an employer and his residential proximity to his workers in such buildings permit an employer committed to a political cause to draw his workers along with him?

This chapter also presents quantitative data in the form of graphs, tables, and a map similar to that which you analyzed in Chapter 3. The information presented here is essential to understanding which social groups participated in the events of July 14, 1789 and why. As we found in Chapter 3, the largely illiterate

[81]

majority of pre-nineteenth-century Europe left few conventional written records, like letters and diaries, which might allow historians to interpret their thought. Historians' ingenuity, however, has allowed them to understand these people through other sources. In constructing the data sets on food prices in this chapter, historians drew on a rich source for understanding seventeenth- and eighteenth-century life. Because early modern governments recognized a correlation between high food prices during periods of dearth on one hand and riots and other acts of public disorder on the other, they kept close watch on such prices. Their effort generated excellent records of food prices, especially of the cost of wheat, the essential ingredient for the bread that was the staple of early modern diets. Look at the graphs numbered 5 and 6 among the evidence for this chapter. Although the two researchers used slightly different measures of wheat in assembling their data, you are presented with significant price trends: long-term trends in wheat prices for France as a whole are in Source 5 and short-term trends for Paris alone are in Source 6. Analyze the price trends presented here. Between the 1730s and mid-1780s, the highest prices were the result of failed harvests in the early 1770s. During that period the rural poor in some regions of the country resorted at times to eating boiled grass or acorns when bread became too scarce and costly. How did prices in 1789 in Paris and France compare with those of the 1770s? Imagine yourself a Frenchman aged

forty in 1789. What would your memory of food prices be? How would those of 1789 strike you? Consult Source 7, a table. How would price trends in 1788–1789 have affected your family's income?

Historians drew on a second kind of source—tax data—in formulating the map presenting the composition of the various Paris sections by income (Source 8). These data are your basis for understanding the economic structure of Paris's population and, most important for our purposes, the economic background of the crowd members who stormed the Bastille. For centuries, historians and government officials held that the lowest and most criminal elements composed these crowds. Indeed, eighteenth-century French police records use a phrase that may be translated as "the scum of the people" in describing the composition of crowds. What do we find about the Bastille crowd, however? We may assume that geographic proximity to the Bastille drew many people to that citadel on July 14. But what sort of neighborhoods sent their residents to the Bastille? To analyze Source 8, you need to know that "active citizens" were those citizens allowed to vote under the 1791 Constitution (by virtue of paying taxes worth three days' labor) and that those eligible for administrative function were the most affluent of active citizens, paying taxes worth at least ten days' labor.

Other data might also allow historians further to identify the members of the crowd, if not by name, at least by social group. Police records of those arrested in unsuccessful rebellions that provide personal data on participants have been systematically exploited only recently by historians. But the Bastille attack began a successful revolution, and the crowd members became heroes and heroines who received the title *Vainqueurs de la Bastille* ("Conquerors of the Bastille") and state pensions if they had been disabled in the attack. The list of these persons is one among many functions of the administrative and fiscal record keeping of a modern state, but it provides you, in the table that is Source 9, with an occupational listing of the Bastille's conquerors. From a distance of two hundred years, it is probably impossible to reconstruct the precise income of each conqueror. Moreover, each trade, like the cabinetmaking common in the Faubourg St. Antoine, would have shown a variety of incomes within the ranks of its practitioners—another frustration. We do know, however, that in skilled trades the self-employed tended to be masters of their trades and therefore probably more affluent than journeymen wage earners or apprentices employed by others. Examine the table. What were the most common trades of the Bastille's attackers? Who predominated, wage earners or the self-employed? What conclusion do you draw from the fact that most of the conquerors had definite trades and were not unskilled or poor?

Written sources can supplement quantitative evidence and supply historians with information on public opinion in Paris during the month of July 1789. This chapter presents several types of such evidence, which you have not previously analyzed. Source 10 is another part of the massive bureaucratic record generated by modern states, in this case a petition addressed to the French national legislature by a woman seeking compensation for her and her husband as conquerors of the Bastille. In reading her petition, ask yourself how her account further contributes to your knowledge of the crowd's composition. Combine this analysis with the understanding that the division of household labor in the eighteenth century gave housewives the major marketing responsibility. Why might women be involved in crowd actions in 1789 or at other points in the Revolution?

Next you will read a travel account, a literary form very common in the early modern period. Europe's curiosity about the outside world grew with the Age of Exploration during the sixteenth century, and a large reading audience developed for accounts by European travelers. The usefulness of such works in reconstructing a society varies, however, according to the intelligence and observational skills of their authors. In the case of Arthur Young, whose Paris report is excerpted as Source 11, we have the work of a master of the travel genre.

Arthur Young (1741–1820) was a wealthy and educated Englishman who sought out and publicized the latest agricultural techniques. Before visiting France to examine French farming, a journey that produced the selection here, Young published descriptions of his travels through England, Wales, and Ireland and was well known as an agricultural expert and as an economist. The record of his travels in France is valuable, therefore, for several reasons. Young's fame and his knowledge of the French language gained him access to many prominent Frenchmen. The observational skills he had honed on earlier trips allowed him quickly to appreciate the economic problems of France and to assess public reaction to them. Finally, as luck would have it, his journey took him through France in the years 1787, 1788, and 1789, so that he was present in the country during the early days of the Revolution. His account, consequently, is extremely useful in understanding the events of the year 1789. Young tells us a great deal about modern politics and the spread of revolution. Thanks to parish schools that offered inexpensive elementary education, the population of Paris was much more literate than the rural population of France. How did Young find this literacy affecting politics in the capital? How did political news spread to provincial cities like Metz? Do you find in any of this description a political life that in some ways presages that of our modern age?

The third kind of written evidence presented in this chapter is diplomatic correspondence. The letters of ambassadors to their home governments long have been useful sources for historians. Their utility derives from the very functions of ambassadors. Since the posting of the first permanent ambassadors by Italian Renaissance states, these officials performed several roles. First, they represented their countries' interests to foreign courts, and thus we can identify the policies of their states in ambassadors' correspondence with their superiors. Additionally, from their earliest days ambassadors kept their governments informed of conditions in their host countries that might affect international relations; they functioned almost like spies, gathering all available information for use by their governments. In this regard, the British ambassador's reports to his superiors in the Foreign Office are extremely important. In 1789 France was a major power that had long been in conflict with England and one most influential in achieving American victory over the English in the War of Independence. As a result, information on political events in France was crucial to English policymakers, and their ambassador supplied detailed reports on France. As with all sources, however, the historian must approach such correspondence with a critical eye. Was the ambassador writing from firsthand knowledge of events? Is his information verified by other sources? How would you assess the reliability of the Duke of Dorset, the English ambassador to France, whose letters are Source 12 among the evidence? What do they tell you about events in Paris?

The fourth written source in this chapter is an excerpt from the journal and diary literature written by many educated persons in the centuries before our own. The historical utility of such sources again depends on their authors' activities and abilities to record accurately events of their times.

In the journal of the Parisian book-seller Siméon-Prosper Hardy we have the work of a reasonably well-educated man who was something of a busybody, alert for all news. Hardy was also a cautious man who took no part in the dangerous events of July 14 and whose residence was far from the Bastille, however. He can therefore be relied on only for noting general trends in Paris, not for details on the Bastille attack. What picture of general events does the selection in Source 13 from his journal present?

All these sources should fit together in your mind like the pieces of a puzzle, allowing you to reconstruct the state of public opinion in Paris in July 1789, to determine how crowds were mobilized, and to understand who stormed the Bastille on July 14.

Source 1 from Musée Carnavalet, Paris.

1. Henri Monnier, *The Palais Royal*

Source 2 from Bibliothèque Nationale, Paris; Vinck Collection.

2. Camille Desmoulins Speaking to the Crowds at the Palais Royal, July 12, 1789

Source 4 adapted from David Garrioch, Neighborhood and Community in Paris, 1740–1790 (New York: Cambridge University Press, 1986), p. 222.

4. Plan of a Typical Parisian Residential Building, 18, rue Contrescarpe, Faubourg St. Antoine

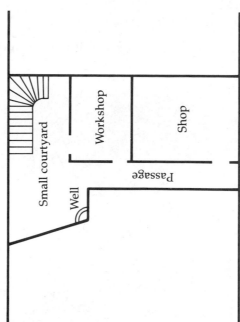

Source 3 from Musée Carnavalet, Paris.

3. Rue du Fer-à-Moulin, 1870

Source 5 adapted from Ernest Labrousse, Ruggiero Romano, and F.-G. Dreyfus, Le prix du froment en France au temps de la monnaie stable (1726–1913) *(Paris: Ecole des Haute Etudes en Sciences Sociales, 1970), p. xiv, and Jacques Godechot,* The Taking of the Bastille, July 14, 1789 *(New York: Scribner's, 1970), p. 13.*

5. Average Price of a Hectoliter (100 liters) of Wheat in France, 1726–1790

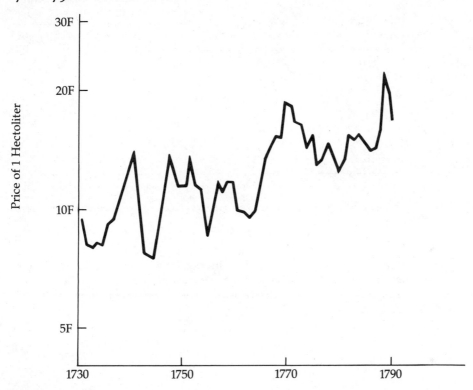

Source 6 from Jacques Godechot, The Taking of the Bastille, July 14, 1789 *(New York: Scribner's, 1970), p. 13.*

6. Price of 100 Kilograms of Wheat in Paris, 1770–1790

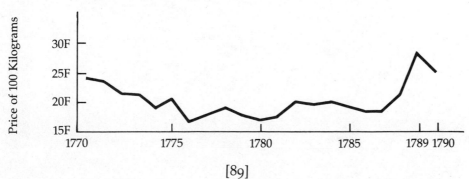

Source 7 from George Rudé, "Prices, Wages and Popular Movements in Paris During the French Revolution," Economic History Review, 2nd ser., vol. 6 (1953), p. 248.

7. Bread and the Wage Earner's Budget[a]

Occupation	Effective Daily Wage in Sous (s)[b]	Expenditure on Bread as Percentage of Income with Bread at	
		9s (Aug 1788)	14½s (Feb–July 1789)
Laborer in Reveillon wallpaper works	15	60	97
Builder's laborer	18	50	80
Journeyman mason	24	37	60
Journeyman, locksmith, carpenter, etc.	30	30	48
Sculptor, goldsmith	60	15	24

[a]The price of the 4-pound loaf consumed daily by a workingman and his family as the main element in their diet.
[b]"Effective" wage represents the daily wage adjusted for 111 days of nonwork per calendar year for religious observation, etc.

Source 8 from Marcel Reinhard, Nouvelle histoire de Paris: La Révolution *(Paris: Distributed by Hachette for the Association pour la publication d'une Histoire de Paris, 1971), pp. 66–67 (map), and George Rudé,* The Crowd in the French Revolution *(New York: Oxford University Press, 1959), pp. 244–245 (key).*

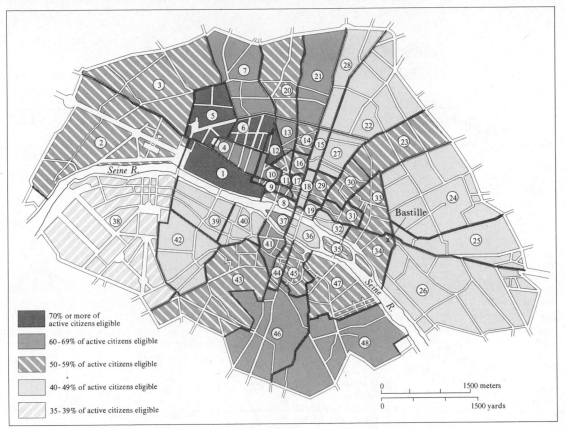

Legend:
- ▓ 70% or more of active citizens eligible
- ▓ 60 - 69% of active citizens eligible
- ▨ 50 - 59% of active citizens eligible
- ░ 40 - 49% of active citizens eligible
- ▨ 35 - 39% of active citizens eligible

Section[a]	Bastille July[b]	Section	Bastille July	Section	Bastille July
1. Tuileries	2	18. Lombards	5	35. Île Saint-Louis	—
2. Champs Élysées	—	19. Arcis	3	36. Notre Dame	1
3. Roule	2	20. Faubourg Montmartre	—	37. Henri IV	2
4. Palais Royal	1	21. Poissonière	1	38. Invalides	5
5. Vendôme	1	22. Bondy	4	39. Fontaine de Grenelle	2
6. Bibliothèque	2	23. Temple	9	40. Quatre Nations	6
7. Grange Batelière	2	24. Popincour	87	41. Théâtre Français	6
8. Louvre	1	25. Montreuil	139	42. Croix Rouge	2
9. Oratoire	2	26. Quinze Vingts	193	43. Luxembourg	7
10. Halle au Blé	6	27. Gravilliers	3	44. Thermes de Julien	3
11. Postes	4	28. Faubourg St. Denis	1	45. Sainte-Genevieve	10
12. Louis XIV	—	29. Beaubourg	5	46. Observatoire	3
13. Fontaine Montmorency	—	30. Enfants Rouges	2	47. Jardin des Plantes	3
14. Bonne Nouvelle	—	31. Roi de Sicile	3	48. Gobelins Outside Paris	3
15. Ponceau	3	32. Hôtel de Ville	18		
16. Mauconseil	4	33. Place Royale	17	*Total*	602
17. Marché des Innocents	6	34. Arsenal	23		

[a]Names of sections are as in 1790–1791.
[b]Numbers arrested, killed, wounded, or participated in the attack on the Bastille.

Source 9 from George Rudé, The Crowd in the French Revolution *(New York: Oxford University Press, 1959), pp. 246–248.*

9. Trades of the Bastille Insurgents, 1789

Trade	Participants (no.)	Trade	Participants (no.)	Trade	Participants (no.)
1. Food, Drink		Cabinet makers	48 (9)	*9. Leather*	
Bakers	5	Chandlers	—	Curriers	—
Brewers	2 (1)[a]	Fancy ware	9 (1)	Leather, skin dressers	2
Butchers	5 (3)	Joiners	49 (8)	*10. Print and Paper*	
Cafés, restaurants	4	Upholsterers	4 (1)	Bookbinders	—
Chocolate	—	*5. Transport*		Booksellers	—
Cooks	2 (2)	Bargemen	3 (3)	Papermakers	1
Fruit vendors	—	Blacksmiths	—	Printers	8 (4)
Grocers	—	Carters	5 (5)	*11. Glass, Pottery*	
Innkeepers	2	Coachmen	2 (1)	Earthenware	1
Pastry chefs	4	Farriers	4 (1)	Potters	7
Tobacco	—	Harness, saddlers	5	Royal Glass factory	1 (1)
Wine merchants	11	Porters	16 (16)	*12. Miscellaneous*	
2. Building, Roads		Riverside workers	5 (5)	Actors, artists, musicians, etc.	—
Carpenters	3	Shipyard workers	5 (5)	Beggars	—
Glaziers	—	Wheelwrights	—	Bourgeois	—
Locksmiths	41 (8)	*6. Metal*		Businessmen	4
Monumental masons	9 (1)	Braziers	7 (1)	Charcoal burners	3
Navvies	2 (2)	Buttonmakers	3	Civil servants	—
Painters	4	Cutlers	—	Clerks	5
Paviors	—	Edge-tool makers	2	Domestic servants, cleaners	—
Plasterers	—	Engravers, gilders	13	Deputies	—
Quarrymen	—	Founders	9 (2)	Fishermen	2 (1)
Sawyers	4 (1)	Goldsmiths	6 (1)	Housewives	—
Sculptors	20 (1)	Instrument makers	—	Journalists, publishers	—
Stonecutters	4 (4)	Jewelers	5	Laborers	2 (2)
Stonemasons	7 (5)	Mechanics	—	Launderers	3 (1)
Surveyors	—	Nailsmiths	9 (1)	Newsagents, vendors	—
Tilers	—	Pewterers	2	Peasants	—
3. Dress		Stovemakers	5 (3)	Priests	—
Beltmakers	—	Tinsmiths	5 (2)	Professional (lawyers, doctors)	—
Boot and shoe	28 (5)	Watchmakers	3	Shopkeepers, assistants	22 (1)
Dressmakers	—	*7. Wood*		"Smugglers"	—
Dyers, cleaners	3	Coopers	3 (1)	Teachers	1
Florists, gardeners	6 (3)	Turners	10	Trades	56 (1)
Furriers	2 (1)	*8. Textiles*		Army, police, National Guard:	
Hairdressers	10	Cotton	—	a. Officers	—
Hatters	9 (4)	Gauze	22 (22)	b. Others	77
Ribbon weavers	3 (3)	Silk	1 (1)		
Stocking weavers	4 (4)	Weavers	1	*Total*	662 (149)
Tailors	7 (1)				
4. Furnishing					
Basketmakers	2				
Boxmakers	1				

[a]Figures in parentheses represent insurgents who probably were wage-earners (i.e., not self-employed).

Source 10 from Darline Gay Levy, Harriet Branson Applewhite, and Mary Durham Johnson, editors and translators, Women in Revolutionary Paris, 1789–1795 *(Urbana: University of Illinois Press, 1979), pp. 29–30.*

10. Petition Addressed by Marguerite Pinaigre to the French National Assembly

Legislators:

The person named here, Margueritte Piningre [*sic*], wife of Sieur Bernard Vener, one of the Vainqueurs de la Bastille, has the honor of appearing today before your august assembly to reclaim the execution of the decree issued by the Constituent Assembly in his [her husband's] favor in 1789. This intrepid citizen, who has the misfortune of being crippled for the rest of his days without ever being able to work again in his life because of wounds received on all parts of his body, yes, Legislators, not only has this dear citizen fought in the conquest of the Bastille with the greatest courage, but furthermore, his *citoyenne*[7] wife, who is present here, worked equally hard with all her might, both of them having resolved to triumph or to die. It is she who ran to several wineshops to fill her apron with bottles, both broken and unbroken, which she gave to the authorities to be used as shot in the cannon used to break the chain on the drawbridge of the Bastille. Therefore, by virtue of these legitimate claims the petitioner believes herself justified in coming before the National Assembly today to advise it concerning the non-execution of laws relative to conquerors who were severely maimed, as was the petitioner's husband. This law awards a pension to those who are really crippled and without the means for earning their living. Such is the situation of the latter, who is offering to provide evidence in the form of authentic statements. Nevertheless, he still has not been awarded this pension which he so richly deserves, he as well as his wife, as a consequence of the dangers they faced. The only gratification which this citizen has received is a small sum of four hundred *livres*, which since 1789 has barely sufficed to care for him and to help him get over the severe wounds he suffered.

Under these circumstances, and in the light of such a compelling account, the petitioner dares hope, Messieurs, for your justice and your usual generosity. May you be willing to take under urgent consideration the object of a request which is becoming as pressing as it is urgent—assuming that surely you would not allow one of the most zealous and intrepid Vainqueurs de la Bastille to languish any longer bent under the weight of the indigence to which he is presently reduced, along with his wife and his children, who

---

7. **citoyenne:** citizeness. As an expression of revolutionary equality, during the Revolution, the terms of address "citizen" and "citizeness" replaced the traditional "Monsieur" and "Madame," based as they were on "My Lord" and "My Lady."

expect his every minute to be his last—because from this period [July 14, 1789] on he has always been ill and continues to suffer cruelly every day. The petitioner expects the favor of the representatives of the French nation, to whom she will never cease to offer her most heart-felt gratitude.

[signed] Marguerite Pinaigre

Source 11 from Arthur Young, Travels in France During the Years 1787, 1788 and 1789, *edited by Jeffry Kaplow (Gloucester, MA: Peter Smith, 1976), pp. 104–105, 130, 145–146.*

11. Arthur Young's Report from France

[*June 1789 (in Paris)*]

THE 9TH.—The business going forward at present in the pamphlet shops of Paris is incredible. I went to the Palais Royal to see what new things were published, and to procure a catalogue of all. Every hour produces something new. Thirteen came out to-day, sixteen yesterday, and ninety-two last week. We think sometimes that Debrett's or Stockdale's shops at London are crouded, but they are mere deserts, compared to Desenne's, and some others here, in which one can scarcely squeeze from the door to the counter. The price of printing two years ago was from 27 liv. to 30 liv.[8] per sheet, but now it is from 60 liv. to 80 liv. This spirit of reading political tracts, they say, spreads into the provinces, so that all the presses of France are equally employed. Nineteen-twentieths of these productions are in favour of liberty, and commonly violent against the clergy and nobility; I have to-day bespoken[9] many of this description, that have reputation; but enquiring for such as had appeared on the other side of the question, to my astonishment I find there are but two or three that have merit enough to be known. Is it not wonderful,[10] that while the press teems with the most levelling and even seditious principles, which put in execution would overturn the monarchy, nothing in reply appears, and not the least step is taken by the court to restrain this extreme licentiousness of publication? It is easy to conceive the spirit that must thus be raised among the people. But the coffee-houses in the Palais Royal present yet more singular and astonishing spectacles; they are not only crouded within, but other expectant crouds are at the doors and windows, listening *à gorge déployée*[11] to certain orators, who from chairs or

8. **livre:** the main unit of Old Regime currency, made up of 20 sous (s). Each sou contained 12 deniers (d); 6 livres equaled 1 écu.
9. **bespoken:** Young employs an archaic usage of this word whose meaning here may most clearly be rendered as "encountered."
10. **wonderful:** another older usage. Young does not state approval here but indicates that the contents of the press were surprising.
11. **à gorge déployée:** enthusiastically.

tables harangue each his little audience: the eagerness with which they are heard, and the thunder of applause they receive for every sentiment of more than common hardiness or violence against the present government, cannot easily be imagined. I am all amazement at the ministry permitting such nests and hot-beds of sedition and revolt, which disseminate amongst the people, every hour, principles that by and by must be opposed with vigour, and therefore it seems little short of madness to allow the propagation at present.

THE 10TH.—Every thing conspires to render the present period in France critical: the want of bread is terrible: accounts arrive every moment from the provinces of riots and disturbances, and calling in the military, to preserve the peace of the markets. The prices reported are the same as I found at Abbeville and Amiens 5s. (2½d.) a pound for white bread, and 3½s. to 4s. for the common sort, eaten by the poor: these rates are beyond their faculties, and occasion great misery.

THE 26TH.—Every hour that passes seems to give the people fresh spirit: the meetings at the Palais Royal are more numerous, more violent, and more assured; and in the assembly of electors, at Paris, for sending a deputation to the National Assembly, the language that was talked, by all ranks of people, was nothing less than a revolution in the government, and the establishment of a free constitution: what they mean by a free constitution, is easily understood—*a republic*; for the doctrine of the times runs every day more and more to that point; yet they profess, that the kingdom ought to be a monarchy too; or, at least, that there ought to be a king. In the streets one is stunned by the hawkers of seditious pamphlets, and descriptions of pretended events, that all tend to keep the people equally ignorant and alarmed. The supineness, and even stupidity of the court, is without example: the moment demands the greatest decision—and yesterday, while it was actually a question, whether he should be a Doge of Venice,[12] or a King of France, the King went a hunting! The spectacle of the Palais Royal presented this night, till eleven o'clock, and, as we afterwards heard, almost till morning, is curious. The croud was prodigious, and fireworks of all sorts were played off, and all the building was illuminated: these were said to be rejoicings on account of the Duc d'Orléans[13] and the nobility joining the commons; but

12. **Doge of Venice:** in principle the head of Venetian government, the Doge in reality was a figurehead.
13. **Duc of Orléans:** Louis Philippe Joseph, Duke of Orléans (1747–1793), was a member of the royal family who played an equivocal role in the Revolution's early years. As a member of the Assembly of Notables, he opposed new royal taxing authority. On June 25, 1789, the duke answered the call of the Third Estate of the Estates General for noblemen to join it, in defiance of royal order, as the National Assembly. This is the event celebrated in Young's account. The duke's ownership of the Palais Royal has led generations of historians to accuse him of inciting the revolutionary agitation that took place there. Before his death in the Reign of Terror, he served as a member of the legislature and in 1792 cast his vote for the death of Louis XVI.

united with the excessive freedom, and even licentiousness of the orators, who harangue the people; with the general movement which before was threatening, all this bustle and noise, which will not leave them a moment tranquil, has a prodigious effect in preparing them for whatever purposes the leaders of the commons shall have in view; consequently they are grossly and diametrically opposite to the interests of the court;—but all these are blind and infatuated.

> [*July 1789 (on the road at Metz, a city*
> *about 150 miles east of Paris)*]

THE 14TH.—They have a *cabinet littéraire*[14] at Metz, something like that I described at Nantes, but not on so great a plan; and they admit any person to read or go in and out for a day, on paying 4s. To this I eagerly resorted, and the news from Paris, both in the public prints, and by the information of a gentleman, I found to be interesting. Versailles and Paris are surrounded by troops: 35,000 men are assembled, and 20,000 more on the road, large trains of artillery collected, and all the preparations of war. The assembling of such a number of troops has added to the scarcity of bread; and the magazines[15] that have been made for their support are not easily by the people distinguished from those they suspect of being collected by monopolists. This has aggravated their evils almost to madness; so that the confusion and tumult of the capital are extreme.

Source 12 from Keith Michael Baker, editor, Readings in Western Civilizations, *vol. 7,* The Old Regime and the Revolution *(Chicago: University of Chicago Press, 1987), pp. 193–196.*

12. Report of the British Ambassador, the Duke of Dorset, to the Foreign Office in London

(*25th June, 1789.*) The reports concerning the scarcity of corn[16] in the neighbourhood of Paris have but too much foundation: the deficiency of this material article extends to the distance of 15 leagues[17] round the City and is so severely felt that Administration has been obliged to supply the different great Markets, by sending corn from the Magazines of the *Ecole Militaire*[18] originally intended for the consumption of the Capital: in regard to the other

14. **cabinet littéraire:** reading room.
15. **magazines:** storage depots.
16. **corn:** in British usage, this word refers to wheat, not American corn or maize.
17. **league:** a unit of distance equal to about 3 miles in English-speaking countries.
18. **Ecole Militaire:** the Military School in Paris.

Provinces of the Kingdom there is no further apprehension, as they are sufficiently supplied 'till the ensuing harvest which has every appearance of being very plentifull. . . .

The French Guards have, in some few instances within these few days, shewn a great reluctance to act and some of the men have declared that if they should be called upon to quell any disturbance they will, if compelled to fire, take care not to do any mischief. The Archbishop of Paris was very ill-treated last night by the mob at Versailles: his coach was broke to pieces and his horses much bruised: if the Guards had not protected him he must himself have been inevitably destroyed.

The people now are disposed to any desperate act of violence in support of the *Assemblée Nationale*.[19] I shall not fail to send Your Grace immediate intelligence of any momentous occurrence during this critical state of affairs. . . .

(*16th July, 1789.*) I wrote to Your Grace on the 12th Inst. by a messenger extraordinary to inform you of the removal of M. Necker from His Majesty's Councils: I have now to lay before Your Grace an account of the general revolt, with the extraordinary circumstances attending it, that has been the immediate consequence of that step. On Sunday evening a slight skirmish happened in the Place de Louis XV, in which two Dragoons[20] were killed, and two wounded of the Duc de Choiseuil's Regiment: after which all the troops left the Capital, and the populace remained unmolested masters of everything: much to their credit however, uncontrouled as they now were, no material mischief was done; their whole attention being confined to the burning of some of the Barriers. Very early on Monday morning the Convent of St. Lazare was forced, in which, besides a considerable quantity of corn, were found arms and ammunition supposed to have been conveyed thither as a place of security, at different periods from the Arsenal: and now a general consternation was seen throughout the Town: all shops were shut; all public and private works at a stand still and scarcely a person to be seen in the Streets excepting the armed *Bourgeoisie*, a temporary police for the protection of private property, to replace the established one which no longer had any influence.

In the morning of Tuesday the Hospital of Invalids was summonsed to surrender and was taken possession of after a very slight resistance: all the cannon, small arms and ammunition were immediately seized upon, and every one who chose to arm himself was supplied with what was necessary . . . in the evening a large detachment with two pieces of cannon went to the Bastille to demand the ammunition that was there, the *Gardes Bourgeoises*[21] not being then sufficiently provided: a flag of truce was sent on before and

19. **Assemblée Nationale:** the National Assembly.
20. **Dragoon:** cavalryman equipped with both a sabre and a short musket and therefore capable of fighting either mounted or on foot.
21. **Gardes Bourgeoises:** the civic militia formed by the Parisian electors on July 13.

was answered from within, notwithstanding which the governor (the Marquis de Launay) contrary to all precedent fired upon the people and killed several: this proceeding so enraged the populace that they rushed to the very gates with a determination to force their way through if possible: upon this the Governor agreed to let in a certain number of them on condition that they should not commit any violence: these terms being acceded to, a detachment of about 40 in number advanced and were admitted, but the drawbridge was immediately drawn up again and the whole party instantly massacred: this breach of honor aggravated by so glaring an act of inhumanity excited a spirit of revenge and tumult such as might naturally be expected: the two pieces of cannon were immediately placed against the Gate and very soon made a breach which, with the disaffection that as is supposed prevailed within, produced a sudden surrender of that Fortress: M. de Launay, the principal gunner, the tailer, and two old invalids who had been noticed as being more active than the rest were seized and carried to the *Hôtel de Ville*[22] where, after a very summary trial before the tribunal there, the inferior objects were put to death and M. de Launay had also his head cut off at the Place de Grève, but with circumstances of barbarity too shocking to relate. . . . In the course of the same evening the whole of the *Gardes Françoises*[23] joined the Bourgeoisie with all their cannon, arms and ammunition: the Regiments that were encamped in the *Champ de Mars*,[24] by an Order from Government left the ground at 2 o'Clock yesterday morning and fell back to Sêve, leaving all their camp equipage behind them; the magazines of powder and corn at the *Ecole Militaire* were immediately taken possession of and a *Garde Bourgeoise* appointed to protect them. Nothing could exceed the regularity and good order with which all this extraordinary business has been conducted: of this I have myself been a witness upon several occasions during the last three days as I have passed through the streets, nor had I at any moment reason to be alarmed for my personal safety.

Source 13 from Marcel Le Clère, editor, Paris de la préhistoire à nos jour *(Paris: Editions Bordessoules, 1985), p. 411. Translated by Julius R. Ruff.*

13. The Bookseller Hardy on the Background of the Bastille Attack

On Sunday, July 12, between five and six in the evening the news arrived from Versailles that Monsieur Necker, Minister of State and Director General of Finances, at the king's order had given up his office and had left incognito

22. **Hôtel de Ville:** the Paris city hall.
23. **Gardes Françaises:** the French Guards, the unit normally charged with Parisian security, whose loyalty to the king had begun to erode as early as June 28, 1789.
24. **Champ de Mars:** the large parade ground in Paris in front of the Military School.

for Switzerland the previous night at one hour past midnight. If one believed the rumors, his departure came after he had told His Majesty that he deplored the disasters with which France was going to be overwhelmed, and warned him that before long there would, perhaps, not be a single *écu* left in the treasury. The resulting public outcry that worthy ministers had been dismissed and had been replaced by others who had no merit at all in public opinion led to the cancellation of all theatrical performances and the refunding of ticket prices to their audiences. This unexpected event causes a great clamor and spreads dread to all minds. In the Palais Royal, the Tuileries,[25] and in the Champs Elysées occurs an astonishing meeting of citizens of all social stations which results in the movements of large numbers of troops and guards charged with the city's security. People reported that various tragic events, of which I am unable to get precise details, had occurred in the Place Louis XV and on the Tuileries terrace. All the residents of the capital and its suburbs spend most of the night in the greatest anxiety.

QUESTIONS TO CONSIDER

Crowd violence was not uncommon in early modern Europe, and historians have recently shown that such violence, rather than reflecting blind rage, often represented the expression of very definite ideas. Recall the political crisis of June and July 1789. The National Assembly was defying the king, and many Parisians supported this stand. Both the legislators at Versailles and the people of Paris knew that royal troops were moving in the latter's direction. They correctly connected these military steps with Necker's dismissal and believed that the king was beginning a coup to suppress demands for change in France. How might political problems coinciding with other difficulties have helped to produce the Bastille attack? Your problem in this chapter is to reconstruct the nature

and spread of certain ideas in Paris on July 14, 1789 by bringing together the various pieces of evidence presented here.

Consider first the physical setting of this historical drama. Examine the picture of the Palais Royal. How many people could congregate here in fair weather like that experienced on July 12–14? What effect did Camille Desmoulins appear to have on the crowd? If political agitation and rumors spread beyond the Palais Royal, what physical features of Paris, visible in the city's streets and residences, would have been conducive to their dispersion throughout the city? What conditions did Parisians encounter in the streets? How would these conditions affect the spread of news? What features of the floor plans of typical Parisian houses might have permitted the mobilization of all residents in a political cause? Combine all these facts and

25. **Tuileries:** the gardens of the Tuileries Palace, open to the public. To their west was the Place Louis XV (now the Place de la Concorde) and an area still undeveloped in the eighteenth century, the Champs Elysées.

you should have an idea of the nature of political activity in the city in 1789.

Next, consider the prices for wheat in Paris. You need to know what these prices represented to Parisians in terms of daily survival. How might food prices have inspired the agitation made possible by the city's physical layout? Examine both national and Parisian trends in wheat prices. What impact did rising bread prices have on the budgets of even skilled workers like journeymen masons and locksmiths? What do you suppose their response to such prices might have been? Remember that Jacques Necker, who was widely regarded as an important factor in keeping Paris supplied with food, was dismissed on July 11.

Examine next the social background of the Bastille's attackers. Refer to the map and the table showing the trades and residences of Bastille insurgents to determine which groups felt the problems of 1789 most acutely. What social groups were represented in the crowd? What was their economic standing? What parts of the city did they come from? Why do you suppose such groups, rather than other residents of the city, were moved to action? What factors conducive to the mobilization of the insurgents would you expect to find among them? Why would you expect them to be accustomed to organization in trades still governed by guilds? Why would you expect them

to have been involved in the business activities of Parisian streets and markets?

As you complete this analysis, you should have an understanding of the composition of the Bastille crowd, how it was mobilized, and why the population might be agitated by food problems in 1789. Remember that the food price crisis coincided with a political crisis. Consult the written sources to understand the conjunction of these problems. How does Arthur Young show the response of Parisian public opinion to all of this? Were the effects of the crisis felt beyond Paris? Look at the works of the British ambassador and the bookseller Hardy. What do they tell us about developments in Paris? Considering that the Bastille fell to a group of armed rebels, how do you account for the ambassador's assurances that he felt safe? Refer to your findings on the crowd's composition in answering this question and remember the creation of a civil guard made up of middle-class citizens. What social group controlled Paris by the time rain fell on July 14?

By combining these sources, both the traditional written accounts long used by historians and the sociological material that establishes the composition of the crowd, you should be able now to answer the central questions of this chapter. What stirred Parisians to mass action? Who was in that crowd on July 14, 1789?

EPILOGUE

The fall of the Bastille to a popular attack whose genesis you have analyzed in this chapter was an event charged with both practical and symbolic significance. On the practical level, capturing the Bastille provided the crowd with the gunpowder it sought and made regaining control of Paris virtually impossible for the royal army. In consequence, the king's resolve to oppose the National Assembly evaporated along with his hopes of controlling Paris. Louis XVI announced to the National Assembly on July 15 that troops would be removed from the region of the capital; on July 16 he recalled Necker as finance minister. On the following day, July 17, the king went to Paris, where his actions publicly confirmed royal recognition and acceptance of the events of the preceding days. First he received the keys to the city from its new mayor, Jean-Sylvan Bailly, representative of the electors of Paris who now controlled the capital. At the city hall he affixed to his hat the blue, white, and red cockade,[26] composed of the blue and red of the Paris coat of arms and the white of the monarchy. That cockade would become the symbol of the Revolution and its colors would come to form a new national flag.

With these actions Louis XVI effectively surrendered control of events to the citizen rebels of Paris. Although we now know that his private sentiments remained steadfastly opposed to the widening Revolution, his public acquiescence was plain to Frenchmen of all political persuasions. The king's brother, the Count of Artois, left the country on the evening of July 16, the first of thousands who would flee the growing Revolution out of fear or hatred for what it represented. At the same time, towns and cities all over France imitated Paris by forming revolutionary governments and National Guards to consolidate the overthrow of the old regime in municipal administration. Disorder spread among peasants in the countryside, prompting the National Assembly to end all societal privileges on August 4, 1789. The Revolution had won its first great victory, a fact even the king later recognized. Planning an escape in 1792, Louis said that, in hindsight, he should have fled Paris on July 14, 1789 to rally his forces and undo the Revolution. He stated, "I know I missed my opportunity: that was on July 14th. I ought to have gone away then. . . . I missed my opportunity, and I've never found it again."[27]

The symbolic importance of the Bastille's fall also is great. Despite its small prisoner census by 1789, the old fortress-prison symbolized royal power to eighteenth-century Frenchmen. The Paris government conferred the job of physically smashing this symbol on an enterprising contractor who demolished the prison and sought his fortune by marketing its remains for souvenirs. Many of its stones he shipped for a fee to local

26. **cockade:** a rosette of ribbons often worn on the hat as a kind of badge in the eighteenth century.

27. Quoted in Godechot, p. 257.

governments around France, and he peddled paperweights, inkpots, and other objects made of "Bastille irons" to gullible customers. Masonry taken from the prison was used in a Parisian bridge so that citizens could tread on the "stone of tyranny." Lafayette sent a key to the Bastille to George Washington as a symbol of the victory of liberty. This key hangs today at Mount Vernon. And on July 14, 1790, the city of Paris honored 954 citizens who had taken part in the prison's capture as conquerors of the Bastille.

Eighteenth-century Frenchmen recognized the great symbolic importance of July 14, 1789, and France commemorated the anniversary of the Bastille's fall throughout its Revolution. Future generations recognized the event's importance, too. In 1880 the Third Republic made July 14 the great national holiday, observed in France with as much patriotic fervor as Americans observe July 4.

CHAPTER FIVE

LABOR OLD AND NEW:

THE IMPACT OF

THE INDUSTRIAL REVOLUTION

THE PROBLEM

The main difficulty did not . . . lie so much in the invention of a proper self-acting mechanism for drawing and twisting cotton as in the distribution of the different members of the apparatus into one cooperative body, in impelling each organ with its appropriate delicacy and speed, and above all, in training human beings to renounce their desultory habits of work, to identify themselves with the unvarying regularity of work of the complex automation. It requires in fact a man of Napoleonic nerve and ambition to subdue refractory tempers of work people accustomed to irregular spasms of diligence, and to urge on his multifarious and intricate constructions in the face of prejudice, passion, and envy.

This is how Andrew Ure, an early and enthusiastic analyst of the Industrial Revolution, characterized the problems of industrial management in his book *The Philosophy of Manufacturers* (1835). In these few sentences Ure identified the essence of the Industrial Revolution. As most

Western Civilization courses correctly emphasize, the period of history this label describes did indeed represent an economic and technological revolution of the greatest magnitude. The manner in which the West produced its goods changed more in the century from 1750 to 1850 than in all the previous centuries of human history, making necessary, as Ure says, the solution of tremendous problems of technology and integration of industrial processes.

But the Industrial Revolution had another impact, one that Ure did not neglect, though he approached it from the managerial point of view in emphasizing the manager's need to train his employees. That Ure thought the disciplining of the workforce was perhaps the manager's chief problem suggests the broad social impact of industrialization. The first generations of factory laborers encountered a world of work dramatically transformed from that of their fathers and mothers, a laboring situation with which most were totally unfamiliar.

[103]

Chapter 5
Labor Old
and New:
The Impact of
the Industrial
Revolution

The work life of the preindustrial laborer certainly had not been easy. Workdays were long, typically dawn to dusk, six days per week, and it was common for wives and children to labor alongside their husbands and fathers as part of a household economy. Indeed, for agricultural workers and craftsmen alike, labor took up so much of their time that little remained for other daily activities. The material rewards of labor often were meager, too; we saw the mass poverty of preindustrial Europe in Chapter 3. But preindustrial work, however long, hard, and unrewarding, had characteristics that distinguished it from early industrial labor.

Preindustrial work usually was conducted in and around the worker's residence. Such labor afforded the worker occasional variety and, in some instances, a measure of control over the pace of work. We may see this effect if we examine the various types of preindustrial workers. Agricultural workers certainly experienced periods of intensive labor, especially at spring plowing and at harvest time, but periods of less intensive labor, especially in the winter months, punctuated their work year and brought them a bit of respite from their duties.

Many of the skilled craftsmen who produced the consumer goods of preindustrial Europe also enjoyed some measure of control over their tasks. True, most crafts were organized into guilds that required their members to undergo a training process, known as *apprenticeship*; these guilds also regulated the quality and pricing of the goods produced by members. But a man's successful completion of training, generally demonstrated by crafting a *masterpiece* as an example of his skill, gained him a mastership and the right to produce the articles of his trade as his own employer. His production unit often included his family and apprentices and more experienced day workers, called *journeymen*, under his supervision. The master set the pace for himself and his workers, who, particularly in Catholic countries, might look forward to a number of religious holidays, civic festivals, and fairs to interrupt their year's labor.

In the later centuries of the preindustrial era, another kind of labor began to emerge. Called the *putting-out system*, this form of employment became common in textile production. A merchant would purchase the raw material, often wool, and deliver it to various rural workers who would spin, weave, dye, and finish the cloth using traditional methods. Often workers were farm families who took in textile work to supplement their incomes. Merchants sought such rural workers because they worked cheaply and because they were beyond the jurisdiction of urban authorities, who limited textile production to guild members. The putting-out system allowed merchants to gather large numbers of workers under their control and thus organize production more efficiently. Even workers in this more disciplined mode of production enjoyed some freedom in organizing their work, however, despite the low wages that often kept them in poverty. For example, consider a weaver employed as part of the putting-out system. He might accord himself "holy Monday," that is, a prolongation of the Sabbath, by taking the first day of the week off. He might also take a few hours off on Tuesday and Wednesday as well, completing his week's required production only by working all night Thursday and Friday. No matter how he scheduled his work time, however, the choice was his. He had some control over his labor.

Indeed, all these factors that somewhat lessened the intensity of preindustrial labor have led some historians to idealize preindustrial work. It is important that we do not follow their example. By perhaps the most important measure of a laborer's work life—the standard of living it supports—it is by no means certain that early industrial employment represented an overall worsening of workers' living conditions. Historians continue to debate the issue of standard of living, examining diverse data on wages, diet, and housing; the problem clearly is a complex one. Whereas the preindustrial skilled craftsman was generally well rewarded for his work, the agricultural laborer and putting-out worker usually were not, and peasant families on the Continent sometimes lived a subsistence existence. For some rural workers, early industrial labor may actually have improved their standard of living.

Industrial labor, however, definitely brought all those employed in the new mills, factories, and mines a new style of work. Hours in the new establishments remained long, but the work year was interrupted by

fewer holidays because factory owners could maximize returns on their massive investments in plants and machines only by using them to their fullest. Labor by whole families often continued, too, but the factory system separated them from their homes, and the tasks and workplaces of family members were very different. Husbands endured the heaviest labor in textile mills or mines. Their wives, research has shown, most often remained at home, keeping house, caring for young children and often laboring many hours in low-paying tasks that could be done at home—"slop work," that is, needle trades, bookbinding, millinery, or other such occupations. Only a minority of married women worked in early mills and mines. Children and unmarried women, however, went out to work in mills, where their hands were better suited to intricate machinery than men's, or in mines, where their small stature allowed them to move more easily than men through low mine tunnels. Their wages always were very low.

Most significantly, perhaps, the worker lost control over the pace of his or her work. Modern factory production dictated that workers serve these new machines that had taken over the productive role. Barring breakdowns, the machine's pace never varied; the new work was monotonous. Workers found themselves endlessly repeating the same tasks in the production process with little autonomy. In addition, industrial work imposed a new punctuality on workers. For the factory system to function smoothly, all had to be at

Chapter 5

Labor Old

and New:

The Impact of

the Industrial

Revolution

their work stations on time and re-main there except during scheduled breaks. "Holy Monday" and un-scheduled leisure time threatened the smooth operation of an industrial establishment. Early mines and fac-tories posed significant safety prob-lems, too, as we will see.

How did the first generations of industrial workers respond to such fundamental changes? Some adapted. Others proved incapable of adjusting to the new working conditions, and absenteeism (especially on Mon-days), chronic tardiness, and work-ers' inability to keep pace with ma-chines plagued many early mills. Many other workers experienced a growing inner alienation, identified by such early observers of industri-alism as Karl Marx, that manifested itself in various forms of asocial be-havior. When economic conditions were good and jobs were plentiful, early mills had problems with fre-quent employee resignations. Some mills experienced as much as 100 per-cent annual employee turnover.

Other new social problems also ac-companied industrialization. Urban expansion accompanied the factory system (see Chapter 7), reflecting the movement of many rural families to growing cities in search of factory employment. Such moves separated the new arrivals from friends and from the social controls of village life. In the city they often found not only the poverty of early industrial work but also the anonymity of urban life and the wealth of modern society dis-played by the privileged classes. The result was a rapid rise of crimes against property accompanying ur-ban growth. Older social problems

persisted, too. Preindustrial workers frequently consumed alcohol in ex-cess as an escape from their tedious work lives. Indeed, "holy Monday" often reflected the effects of a work-er's weekend of alcohol abuse. The early industrial age was little differ-ent. One English clergyman de-scribed to a committee of Parliament the sight of twelve-year-old coal min-ers staggering with drink.

The human response to this fun-damental change in work thus as-sumed many forms, but these did not include organized resistance to the machine age by industrial workers. Those employed in early mills and mines often were illiterate and con-sequently difficult to mobilize for col-lective actions such as strikes. More-over, laws like the English Com-bination Acts (1799, 1800) and the French Le Chapelier Law (1791) ac-tually forbade worker organizations; the few early unions were illegal and secretive. The only overt resistance to industrialization, therefore, came not from industrial workers but from one group of preindustrial laborers, namely, the artisans. This class had a high rate of literacy and thus were aware that the new machines ulti-mately threatened both their liveli-hoods and their work autonomy. They lashed out with acts of machine smashing. English machine smashers were called *Luddites* after one Ned Ludd, who supposedly originated their movement.

Machine smashing, of course, could not stop industrialization, and workers in early mines and mills be-came the objects of an increasingly stringent discipline aimed at forcing their acceptance of the new labor.

Overseers beat child laborers. Managers fined or dismissed adults and sometimes blacklisted particularly difficult workers to deny them any employment.

In this chapter you will be asked to contrast the working conditions of the preindustrial and industrial ages. How did industrial labor differ from preindustrial work? How did such labor evolve? What effects did the new labor have on the first generations of men, women, and children in Europe's mills and mines?

SOURCES AND METHOD

The central questions of this chapter require your analysis of both preindustrial and industrial labor. As an aid to this analysis, the evidence for this chapter is accordingly divided into two groups, one relating to the preindustrial age (the "old labor") and the other to the industrial era (the "new labor").

The evidence on the old labor opens with a summary of holidays in a textile-producing city, Lille, France, in the seventeenth century. How would you characterize the pace of labor in Lille, a city whose work calendar was not unusual in Catholic Europe?

Source 2 presents excerpts from guild regulations in the Prussian woolen industry. The Industrial Revolution began in England in the mid-eighteenth century but affected the Continent much later, only in the first decades of the nineteenth century. Thus these guild regulations dating from 1797 describe the traditional labor of many Europeans. In reading them, ask yourself what sort of labor conditions these regulations sustained. A worker's demonstration of his mastery of all the processes of producing wool cloth won him the "freedom of the guild" and its privi-

leges. The latter involved the right to establish his own production unit and market his goods, as well as guild assistance when old age or illness prevented work. What sort of limits on the activities of guild members accompanied these freedoms? What do you think were the reasons for these restrictions? What efforts to protect both the consumer and the guild members' market can you discern in these restrictions? Why was the putting-out system explicitly forbidden to guild members? What specifically in all these restrictions seems intended to create a protected monopoly for producers?

Source 3 describes another facet of the old style of labor in textile production, namely, the putting-out system. It is the work of François-Alexandre Frédéric, Duke of La Rochefoucauld-Liancourt (1747–1827), an astute observer of the social and economic problems of his day who applied his energy and wealth in various reform schemes, including experimental farms and an early cotton mill. La Rochefoucauld wrote persuasively on the need for improved poor relief and better education for all Frenchmen. His social status as a duke may have limited his knowledge of the working conditions of those employed in textiles in

Chapter 5

Labor Old

and New:

The Impact of

the Industrial

Revolution

Rouen, but he does provide a good description of this method of production in this excerpt from his travel account of 1781 to 1783. Who was employed in textiles in Rouen? What does the duke tell you about the quantity of production in Rouen, despite the continued use of hand looms? How did the organization of this work, the quantity of production, and the destinations of its products foreshadow certain features of the industrial age?

Source 4, "The Clothier's Delight," is a popular song, a type of source you have not yet studied in Volume II. Historians examine songs as evidence of popular culture to understand the attitudes and lives of men and women who were often illiterate and therefore left little written record of their activities. We must understand that such songs may exaggerate their message a bit to achieve their desired effect among unsophisticated audiences. Nevertheless we do have in this song some evidence of broad trends in the putting-out system and the concerns of those employed in it by English clothiers. Who controlled the material in this production process? Were the weavers and other textile workers the independent producers described in the guild regulations? Why did the workers view the clothiers as adversaries? How did the clothiers control the workers?

In the testimony of Mrs. Britton offered in Source 5, you encounter for the first time a piece of evidence you will analyze several times in this chapter, the record of hearings on early industrial working conditions conducted by legislative committees.

From such records committee members drew up recommendations that often resulted in legislation to improve working conditions in early mills, factories, and mines. These records have a great advantage for the historian because they also offer a glimpse into the world of the illiterate laboring poor of an earlier age. Secretaries to the investigating committees often took down the testimony of witnesses verbatim, providing an enduring record of all the difficulties of labor in the early industrial era. Mrs. Britton labored in the old style as agricultural worker, but she brought a unique perspective to her testimony to a committee of the British Parliament because she once had worked in a factory also. What were the work conditions and the standard of living of agricultural workers like Mrs. Britton and her husband? How did agricultural labor compare with factory labor for Mrs. Britton?

Next, consider the evidence on the new labor, that is, the work of the industrial age. Sources 6 and 7 in this section are regulations governing the conditions of work in early industrial enterprises. In using such material, the historian must remember that it describes the behavior prescribed by persons in authority; such regulations may not describe the actual comportment of those whose behavior the statutes aimed to control. Indeed, we can assume frequent conflict between the prescribed rules and the actual behavior of working people as workers adapted to the new conditions of industrial work.

Examine the work code for the foundry and engineering works in

Moabit, an industrial suburb of Berlin, Germany in 1844 (Source 6). What sort of habits did these regulations seek to inculcate in the foundry workers? Notice also the pay practices described in paragraph 18. Why would management have adopted these? What disadvantages did they represent for the worker?

The apprenticeship agreement for girls as silk workers in rural Tarare, France (Source 7) retains the terminology of the old labor in designating new workers as apprentices, but it lays down industrial-age work rules for governing young women. Examine the agreement carefully, noting its disciplinary features. How long was the apprenticeship? When were wages paid? What happened if a girl left before the completion of her apprenticeship? What were the work hours? In what ways did management seek to increase production? Such mills as this were established in rural areas, away from cities like Lyons where male preindustrial silk weavers had a centuries-long history of guild organization (and of unrest). Given that information, can you discern why the mill's location was chosen and why a female workforce was sought? What attractions did the mill, with its long workday, offer unmarried rural women who otherwise would have been reluctant to seek industrial employment away from home?

The testimony of William Cooper to the Sadler Committee of the British Parliament (Source 8) provides dramatic evidence about the conditions of industrial labor in early textile mills. What effect did mill labor have on Cooper? What were the hours of work? How did overseers enforce punctuality and a faster work pace on young workers? Were conditions within the mills conducive to good health? Compare his height to that of his father. What could have accounted for Cooper's shorter stature? When he had health problems and was unable to work, what recourse did Cooper have?

Source 9 also describes the condition of labor in the textile industry, but it records the lot of women fifty or more years after William Cooper's experiences in the mills. Had working conditions improved very much since Cooper's day? How long was the workday? Did the work demand exceptional energy or skill from the workers? How did management impose discipline in such matters as punctuality?

With the selections brought together as Source 10, you will once more analyze the records of English parliamentary inquiries, but this time the committees examined coal mine labor in the 1840s. Read first the testimony of Joseph Staley. Note his position in the mine. How might this have affected his conclusion about his miners' health? How many boys did he employ and what ages were they? What sort of labor did the boys do? What were their hours? Analyze the testimony of William Jagger. What age was he? How long had he worked in the mine? What were his hours? What do his testimony and the comment by the investigator following that testimony tell you about work conditions and mine safety?

With the testimony of Patience Kershaw we have a record of women's labor in the mines. What sort of

Chapter 5

Labor Old

and New:

The Impact of

the Industrial

Revolution

labor did Kershaw do? What weight of coal did she move daily? What health effects did such labor have on women like Kershaw and her sisters? What impression did she make on the parliamentary investigator, as indicated in his comment following her testimony?

Industrialization transformed the Western world in many ways, and we will examine aspects of its consequences in other chapters of this book as well (see especially Chapters 7 and 14). Your analysis of the evidence presented here should aid you in understanding one aspect of that transformation: the emergence of a new world of industrial labor and how it affected men and women of the eighteenth and nineteenth centuries.

THE EVIDENCE

THE OLD LABOR

Source 1 from Alain Lottin, Chavatte, ouvrier lillois. Un contemporain de Louis XIV *(Paris: Flammarion, 1979), pp. 323–324.*

1. The Work Year in 17th-century Lille, France

Holidays in Seventeenth-Century Lille

January	Monday following Epiphany (January 6)
22 January	Feast of St. Vincent
25 January	Feast of St. Paul's Conversion
February	Ash Wednesday
22 February	Feast of the Chair of St. Peter
March or April	Tuesday of Holy Week until the Thursday after Easter (eight working days)
3 May	Feast of the Finding of the True Cross
9 May	Feast of St. Nicholas
May or June	Feast of Pentecost (seventh Sunday after Easter): Pentecost eve through the following Thursday (five days)
5 June	Corpus Christi
9 June or second Sunday in June	Municipal procession accompanied by banquets
11 June	Feast of St. Barnabas
June	Thursday after municipal procession is a holiday
2 July	Feast of the visitation of the Virgin
1 August	Feast of St. Peter in Chains
3 August	Feast of St. Stephen
29 August	Feast of the Beheading of St. John the Baptist, followed by five days off

1 October	Feast of St. Remy
18 October	Feast of St. Luke
1 November	All Saints Day
24–31 December	Christmas (eight days)

This represents a total of forty-four days off, in addition to Sundays.

Sources 2 and 3 from Sidney Pollard and Colin Holmes, editors, Documents in European Economic History, *vol. 1,* The Process of Industrialization, 1750–1870 *(New York: St. Martin's, 1968), pp. 45–48, pp. 91–92.*

2. Guild Regulations in the Prussian Woolen Industry, 1797

§ 760

Although it is laid down in the General Privilege (8 Nov. 1734) that it shall not be necessary to produce a masterpiece in order to gain the master's freedom; yet it was ruled afterwards: that anyone aspiring to the freedom of the gild, shall (22 November 1772) apart from being examined by the Inspector of Manufactures and the Gild Master whether he be properly experienced in sorting and fulling, wool shearing and preparing and threading the looms, also weave a piece of cloth of mixed colour from wool dyed by himself.

§ 765–§ 771

The woollen weavers may sell by retail and cutting-up home produced cloths and baizes[1] on condition that they and their fellow gild members may not only sell in their own town the goods made locally, but may also offer them for sale at fairs and annual markets. The latter, however, is limited to this extent (1772 and 1791): that a gild member may not take part in any market or fair unless he has at least 12 pieces of cloth for sale, though it is permissible (18 December 1791) for two of them to enter a fair and to offer cloth for sale if they have at least 12 pieces of cloth between them; at the same time, this privilege is extended also to weavers (1772) who are no longer practising their trade themselves.

The woollen weavers of Salzwedel, however, may not sell the cloths produced by themselves, by retail and cutting-up, even in their own town, because the local cloth cutters' and tailors' gild enjoys, according to its old privilege (1233, 1323 and last confirmed on 26 January 1715) the sole right of

---

1. **baize:** a soft woolen fabric.

Chapter 5

Labor Old

and New:

The Impact of

the Industrial

Revolution

cutting up woollen and similar cloth for sale, so that neither the local merchants, nor the mercers, nor the woollen weavers of the town, whose rights were recently confirmed, have the right to cut up woollen cloth for sale.

Woollen weavers may not trade in woollen cloths made outside their own town, unless they have been specially granted this right, because this would infringe the privileges granted to the merchants . . . .

Neither finishers nor croppers,[2] dyers or other craftsmen (1772) are permitted to trade in woollen cloths or undertake putting-out agencies on pain of losing their craft privileges.

In the countryside (28 August 1723, 14 November 1793) neither linen (?) weavers, nor vergers[3] or schoolmasters, nor husbandmen themselves, are permitted to manufacture woollen or worsted cloth not even for their own use. Neither are town linen weavers permitted to make goods wholly of wool.

Woollen weavers are permitted to dye their own cloths, but neither they nor the merchants are permitted to have the cloths made in the Electoral Mark finished or dyed in foreign towns, on pain of confiscation of the goods. While the export of unfinished and undyed cloths is permissible (1772), merchants and woollen weavers should be persuaded (26 October and 10 November 1791) to export only dyed and finished cloths.

Woollen weavers may not (1772) keep their own tenting frame and stretch their own cloths, but must leave this finishing process to the cloth finishers. They have however the concession (28 October and 11 November 1773) that they may keep 10–12 frames, but on these they may only stretch $\frac{3}{4}$ widths, and twill flannels. . . .

§ 798

On pain of requisition and, for repeated offences, on pain of loss of the freedom of the gild, better yarn may not be used for the ends of pieces of cloth than is used for the middle. No weaver is permitted to keep frames of his own, on pain of loss of his gild freedom, and he is obliged to take his cloths to the master shearmen; tanned wool and wool-fells may not be woven into pieces, but must be made only into rough goods and horse blankets. Finally it is laid down in detail how each type of woollen and worsted cloth shall be manufactured; and weavers have been advised several times to observe closely the detailed rules and regulations of the woollen and worsted order (20 September 1784, 9 September and 8 October 1787). . . .

2. **cropper:** the craftsmen who sheared the nap from woolen cloth.

3. **verger:** a parish official generally charged with care of the interior of a church.

§ 800

It is further laid down as a general rule, that all cloths shall be viewed by sworn aulnagers,[4] of whom eight shall be elected in large companies, six in medium sized ones, and two to four among small ones, and they shall be viewed three times, and sealed accordingly after each time. The first viewing shall determine that the piece is woven with sufficient and satisfactory yarn, woven sufficiently closely and without flaws, and of the correct length and width. The second, held on the frame, shall determine whether the cloth is overstretched, and has wholly pure wool, is fulled cleanly and free of errors in fulling, and the third, held on the frame after dyeing, whether it has suffered by the dyeing.

3. La Rochefoucauld Describes the Putting-Out System in Rouen, France, 1781–1783

I then saw the material called cotton check (*cotonnades*). There are all sorts of cotton manufacture made up at Rouen and in the area 15 leagues[5] around it. The peasant who returns to the plough to work his fields, sits at his cotton frame and makes either *siamoises*[6] or ticking or even white, very fine, cotton cloth. One must admire the activity of the Normans. This activity does not interfere at all with their daily work. Land is very dear and consequently very well cultivated. The farmer works on the land during the day and it is in the evening by the light of the lamp that he starts his other task. His workers and his family have to help. When they have worked all week they come into the town with horses or carts piled up with material. Goods are sold in the Hall, which is all that remains of the palace of the former Dukes of Normandy, on Thursdays. It is a truly wonderful sight. It takes place at a surprising speed. Almost 800,000 francs worth of business is transacted between 6.00 and 9.00 in the morning. Among those who do the buying there are many agents who buy for merchants and then the goods pass to America, Italy and Spain. The majority goes to America. I have seen many pieces destined to become shirts for negroes; but their skin will be seen through the material, since the cloth is thin and almost sufficiently coarse to make ticking. It costs 17, 20 and even 25 francs per aune[7] in the Hall.

---

4. **aulnager:** an official charged with measuring and inspecting woolen cloth.
5. **league:** a league equals 2.764 miles.
6. **siamoises:** common cotton goods.
7. **aune:** an old French measurement unit for textiles; equal to 45 inches.

Chapter 5

Labor Old

and New:

The Impact of

the Industrial

Revolution

Source 4 from James Burnley, The History of Wool and Wool Combing (London: Sampson Low, Marston, Searle and Rivington, Ltd., 1889), pp. 160–163.

"The Clothier's Delight; or, the Rich Men's Joy, and the Poor Men's Sorrow, Wherein Is Exprest the Craftiness and Subtility of Many Clothiers in England by Beatting Down their Workmen's Wages," Song, 18th century

Of all sorts of callings that in England be,
There is none that liveth so gallant as we;
Our trading maintains us as brave as a knight,
We live at our pleasure, and take our delight;
We heapeth up riches and treasure great store,
Which we get by griping and grinding the poor.
    And this is a way for to fill up our purse,
    Although we do get it with many a curse.

Throughout the whole kingdom, in country and town,
There is no danger of our trade going down,
So long as the Comber[8] can work with his comb,
And also the Weaver weave with his lomb;[9]
The Tucker[10] and Spinner[11] that spins all the year,
We will make them to earn their wages full dear.
    And this is the way, &c.

In former ages we us'd to give,
So that our work-folks like farmers did live;
But the times are altered, we will make them know
All we can for to bring them all under our bow;
We will make to work hard for sixpence a day,[12]
Though a shilling they deserve if they had their just pay.
    And this is the way, &c.

8. **comber:** person who performed one of the processes in finishing raw wool, the combing out of the wool.

9. **lomb:** archaic spelling of *loom*.

10. **tucker:** in the processing of wool, person who performs the task of *fulling* the wool, that is, cleaning, shrinking, and thickening the fabric with moisture, heat, and pressure.

11. **spinner:** person who spun the raw wool into thread on a spinning wheel or other device.

12. English coinage mentioned in this and following selections (with the abbreviations for each denomination where appropriate) includes:
    £: pound sterling.
    s.: shilling; 20 shillings to 1 pound sterling.

And first for the Combers, we will bring them down
From eight groats a score unto half a crown.
If at all they murmur, and say 'tis too small,
We bid them choose whether they will work at all:
We'll make them believe that trading is bad;
We care not a pin, though they are ne'er so sad.
   And this is the way, &c.

We'll make the poor Weavers work at a low rate;
We'll find fault where there's no fault, and so we will bate;[13]
If trading grows dead, we will presently show it;
But if it grows good, they shall never know it;
We'll tell them that cloth beyond sea will not go,
We care not whether we keep clothing or no.
   And this is the way, &c.

Then next for the Spinners we shall ensue,
We'll make them spin three pound instead of two;
When they bring home their work unto us, they complain,
And say that their wages will not them maintain;
But if that an ounce of weight they do lack,
Then for to bate threepence we will not be slack.
   And this is the way, &c.

But if it holds weight, then their wages they crave,
We have got no money, and what's that you'd have?
We have bread and bacon and butter that's good,
With oatmeal and salt that is wholesome for food;
We have soap and candles whereby to give light,[14]
That you may work by them so long as you have light.
   And this is the way, &c.

We will make the Tucker and Shereman understand
That they with their wages shall never buy land;
Though heretofore they have been lofty and high
Yet now we will make them submit humbly;

---

d: pence (from Latin *denari*); 12 pence to 1 shilling.
crown: a coin worth 5 shillings.
groat: a coin worth 4 pence.
There were 12 pence to a shilling; hence sixpence represented a 50 percent pay cut. In the next verse, the value of 8 groats was 32 pence; half a crown was worth 30 pence. Thus the song portrays the clothiers as seeking to reduce wages a small and perhaps unnoticed amount, 2 pence.

13. **bate:** to beat back or reduce a worker's wages.

14. This whole verse refers to a practice, theoretically illegal in England after 1701, of paying putting-out workers in textiles with goods, not cash. This practice kept workers dependent on their employers because they lacked hard currency when they were paid in such commodities as bread, bacon, butter, oatmeal, salt, soap, and candles. That the practice endured despite the law is indicated by additional laws directed against it as late as 1779.

[115]

Chapter 5

Labor Old

and New:

The Impact of

the Industrial

Revolution

We will lighten their wages as low as may be,
We will keep them under in every degree.
 And this is the way, &c.

And thus we do gain all our wealth and estate,
By many poor men that work early and late;
If it were not for those that do labour full hard,
We might go and hang ourselves without regard;
The Combers, the Weavers, the Tuckers also,
With the Spinners that work for wages full low.
 By these people's labour we fill up our purse, &c.

Then hey for the Clothing Trade, it goes on brave;
We scorn for to toyl and moyl,[15] nor yet to slave.
Our workmen do work hard, but we live at ease;
We go when we will, and come when we please;
We hoard up our bags of silver and gold;
But conscience and charity with us are cold.
 By poor people's labour, &c.

Source 5 from British Parliamentary Papers: Reports of Special Assistant Poor Law Commissioner on the Employment of Women and Children in Agriculture *(London: William Clowes and Sons for Her Majesty's Stationery Office, 1843), pp. 66–67.*

5. Testimony of an Agricultural Worker's Wife and Former Factory Worker, 1842[16]

Mrs. *Britton*, Wife of _____ *Britton*, of *Calne, Wiltshire*, Farm-labourer, examined.

I am 41 years old; I have lived at Calne all my life. I went to school till I was eight years old, when I went out to look after children. At ten years old I went to work at a factory in Calne, where I was till I was 26. I have been married 15 years. My husband is an agricultural labourer. I have seven children, all boys. The oldest is fourteen, the youngest three-quarters of a year old. My husband is a good workman, and does most of his work by the lump,[17] and earns from 9s. to 10s. a-week pretty constantly, but finds his

15. **toyl and moyl:** archaic spellings of *toil* and *moil*—that is, work and drudgery.

16. This testimony was delivered before a Parliamentary Committee studying the employment of women and children in British agriculture.

17. **by the lump:** Mr. Britton was paid by the job rather than by the hour or day.

own tools,—his wheelbarrow, which cost 1*l.*, pickaxe, which cost 3*s.*, and scoop, which cost 3*s.*

I have worked in the fields, and when I went out I left the children in the care of the eldest boy, and frequently carried the baby with me, as I could not go home to nurse it. I have worked at hay-making and at harvest, and at other times in weeding and keeping the ground clean. I generally work from half-past seven till five, or half-past. When at work in the spring I have received 10*d.* a-day, but that is higher than the wages of women in general; 8*d.* or 9*d.* is more common. My master always paid 10*d.* When working I never had any beer, and I never felt the want of it. I never felt that my health was hurt by the work. Hay-making is hard work, very fatiguing, but it never hurt me. Working in the fields is not such hard work as working in the factory. I am always better when I can get out to work in the fields. I intend to do so next year if I can. Last year I could not go out, owing to the birth of the baby. My eldest boy gets a little to do; he don't earn more than 9*d.* a-week; he has not enough to do. My husband has 40 lugs[18] of land, for which he pays 10*s.* a-year. We grow potatoes and a few cabbages, but not enough for our family; for that we should like to have forty lugs more. We have to buy potatoes. One of the children is a cripple, and the guardians[19] allow us two gallons of bread a-week for him.[20] We buy two gallons more, according as the money is. Nine people can't do with less than four gallons of bread a-week. We could eat much more bread if we could get it; sometimes we can afford only one gallon a-week. We very rarely buy butcher's fresh meat, certainly not oftener than once a-week, and not more than sixpenny worth. I like my husband to have a bit of meat, now he has left off drinking. I buy ½ lb. butter a-week, 1 oz. tea, ½ lb. sugar. The rest of our food is potatoes, with a little fat. The rent of our cottage is 1*s.* 6*d.* a-week; there are two rooms in it. We all sleep in one room, under the tiles. Sometimes we receive private assistance, especially in clothing. Formerly my husband was in the habit of drinking, and everything went bad. He used to beat me. I have often gone to bed, I and my children, without supper, and have had no breakfast the next morning, and frequently no firing.[21] My husband attended a lecture on

18. **lug:** an old English measure of area equal to 49 square yards. The Brittons' 40 lugs would, therefore, have equaled 1,960 square yards, less the half of a full acre, which is 4,840 square yards.

19. **guardian:** Poor Law official.

20. **two gallons of bread:** the gallon as a gauge of wheat and other dry material is an archaic English measure, the weight of which was far from standard in the British Isles. Sources refer to gallons of wheat weighing anywhere from 8 to almost 10 pounds. If we assume a gallon to have been 9 pounds in the case of the Brittons, we find that the family claims to have required a minimum of 36 pounds of bread per week. For this time, in which bread was the basic dietary element of the poor, demographic historians assume an adult to have consumed 2 pounds per day. Even if the family comprised only two adults and the rest children, these were extremely short rations.

21. **firing:** that is, no morning hearth fire for want of the cost of fuel.

Chapter 5

Labor Old

and New:

The Impact of

the Industrial

Revolution

teetotalism one evening about two years ago, and I have reason to bless that evening. My husband has never touched a drop of drink since. He has been better in health, getting stouter, and has behaved like a good husband to me ever since. I have been much more comfortable, and the children happier. He works better than he did. He can mow better, and that is hard work, and he does not mind being laughed at by the other men for not drinking. I send my eldest boy to Sunday school; them that are younger go to the day school. My eldest boy never complains of work hurting him. My husband now goes regularly to church: formerly he could hardly be got there.

THE NEW LABOR

Source 6 from Sidney Pollard and Colin Holmes, editors, Documents in European Economic History, *vol. 1,* The Process of Industrialization, 1750–1870 *(New York: St. Martin's, 1968), pp. 534–536.*

6. Rules for Workers in the Foundry and Engineering Works of the Royal Overseas Trading Company, Berlin, 1844

In every large works, and in the co-ordination of any large number of workmen, good order and harmony must be looked upon as the fundamentals of success, and therefore the following rules shall be strictly observed.

Every man employed in the concern named below shall receive a copy of these rules, so that no one can plead ignorance. Its acceptance shall be deemed to mean consent to submit to its regulations.

(1) The normal working day begins at all seasons at 6 a.m. precisely and ends, after the usual break of half an hour for breakfast, an hour for dinner and half an hour for tea, at 7 p.m., and it shall be strictly observed.

Five minutes before the beginning of the stated hours of work until their actual commencement, a bell shall ring and indicate that every worker employed in the concern has to proceed to his place of work, in order to start as soon as the bell stops.

The doorkeeper shall lock the door punctually at 6 a.m., 8.30 a.m., 1 p.m. and 4.30 p.m.

Workers arriving 2 minutes late shall lose half an hour's wages; whoever is more than 2 minutes late may not start work until after the next break, or at least shall lose his wages until then. Any disputes about the correct time shall be settled by the clock mounted above the gatekeeper's lodge.

These rules are valid both for time- and for piece-workers, and in cases of breaches of these rules, workmen shall be fined in proportion to their earnings. The deductions from the wage shall be entered in the wage-book of the gatekeeper whose duty they are: they shall be unconditionally accepted as it will not be possible to enter into any discussions about them.

(2) When the bell is rung to denote the end of the working day, every workman, both on piece- and on day-wage, shall leave his workshop and the yard, but is not allowed to make preparations for his departure before the bell rings. Every breach of this rule shall lead to a fine of five silver groschen to the sick fund. Only those who have obtained special permission by the overseer may stay on in the workshop in order to work.—If a workman has worked beyond the closing bell, he must give his name to the gatekeeper on leaving, on pain of losing his payment for the overtime.

(3) No workman, whether employed by time or piece, may leave before the end of the working day, without having first received permission from the overseer and having given his name to the gatekeeper. Omission of these two actions shall lead to a fine of ten silver groschen payable to the sick fund.

(4) Repeated irregular arrival at work shall lead to dismissal. This shall also apply to those who are found idling by an official or overseer, and refuse to obey their order to resume work.

(5) Entry to the firm's property by any but the designated gateway, and exit by any prohibited route, e.g., by climbing fences or walls, or by crossing the Spree, shall be punished by a fine of fifteen silver groschen to the sick fund for the first offences, and dismissal for the second.

(6) No worker may leave his place of work otherwise than for reasons connected with his work.

(7) All conversation with fellow-workers is prohibited; if any worker requires information about his work, he must turn to the overseer, or to the particular fellow-worker designated for the purpose.

(8) Smoking in the workshops or in the yard is prohibited during working hours; anyone caught smoking shall be fined five silver groschen for the sick fund for every such offence.

(9) Every worker is responsible for cleaning up his space in the workshop, and if in doubt, he is to turn to his overseer.—All tools must always be kept in good condition, and must be cleaned after use. This applies particularly to the turner, regarding his lathe.

(10) Natural functions must be performed at the appropriate places, and whoever is found soiling walls, fences, squares, etc., and similarly, whoever is found washing his face and hands in the workshop and not in the places assigned for the purpose, shall be fined five silver groschen for the sick fund.

(11) On completion of his piece of work, every workman must hand it over at once to his foreman or superior, in order to receive a fresh piece of work. Pattern makers must on no account hand over their patterns to the foundry without express order of their supervisors. No workman may take over work from his fellow-workman without instruction to that effect by the foreman.

Chapter 5

Labor Old

and New:

The Impact of

the Industrial

Revolution

(12) It goes without saying that all overseers and officials of the firm shall be obeyed without question, and shall be treated with due deference. Disobedience will be punished by dismissal.

(13) Immediate dismissal shall also be the fate of anyone found drunk in any of the workshops.

(14) Untrue allegations against superiors or officials of the concern shall lead to stern reprimand, and may lead to dismissal. The same punishment shall be meted out to those who knowingly allow errors to slip through when supervising or stocktaking.

(15) Every workman is obliged to report to his superiors any acts of dishonesty or embezzlement on the part of his fellow workmen. If he omits to do so, and it is shown after subsequent discovery of a misdemeanour that he knew about it at the time, he shall be liable to be taken to court as an accessory after the fact and the wage due to him shall be retained as punishment. Conversely, anyone denouncing a theft in such a way as to allow conviction of the thief shall receive a reward of two Thaler, and, if necessary, his name shall be kept confidential.—Further, the gatekeeper and the watchman, as well as every official, are entitled to search the baskets, parcels, aprons etc. of the women and children who are taking the dinners into the works, on their departure, as well as search any worker suspected of stealing any article whatever. . . .

(18) Advances shall be granted only to the older workers, and even to them only in exceptional circumstances. As long as he is working by the piece, the workman is entitled merely to his fixed weekly wage as subsistence pay; the extra earnings shall be paid out only on completion of the whole piece contract. If a workman leaves before his piece contract is completed, either of his own free will, or on being dismissed as punishment, or because of illness, the partly completed work shall be valued by the general manager with the help of two overseers, and he will be paid accordingly. There is no appeal against the decision of these experts.

(19) A free copy of these rules is handed to every workman, but whoever loses it and requires a new one, or cannot produce it on leaving, shall be fined $2\frac{1}{2}$ silver groschen, payable to the sick fund.

Moabit, August, 1844.

Source 7 from Erna Olafson Hellerstein, L. P. Hume, and K. M. Offen, editors, Victorian Women: A Documentary Account of Women's Lives in Nineteenth-Century England, France, and the United States *(Stanford, California: Stanford University Press, 1981), pp. 394–396.*

7. Apprenticeship Contract for Young Women Employed in the Silk Mills of Tarare, France, 1850s

MILLING, REELING, AND WARP-PREPARATION OF SILKS

Conditions of Apprenticeship

Art. 1. To be admitted, young women must be between the ages of thirteen and fifteen, of good character and in good health, intelligent and industrious, and must have been vaccinated. They must present their birth certificate, a certificate of vaccination, and a trousseau.

Art. 2. Girls who are accepted by the establishment will be placed in milling, reeling, or warp[22] preparation by the director, according to the needs of the establishment and their intelligence.

Art. 3. During the apprenticeship period, the pupil will be paid wages, fed, lodged, given heat and light, and laundry *for her body linen only*; she will also be furnished with aprons.

Art. 4. The pupil promises to be obedient and submissive to the mistresses charged with her conduct and instruction, as well as to conform to the rules of the establishment.

Art. 5. In case of illness the director will notify the father or guardian of the sick apprentice, and if her state necessitates a leave, it will be granted to her until her recovery.

Art. 6. If the sick pupil remains in the establishment, every care necessitated by her condition will be given to her.

Art. 7. In case of illness or any other serious cause that warrants her leaving, the apprentice who must absent herself from the establishment will be obligated to prolong her apprenticeship during a time equal to that of her absence.

Art. 8. The director alone has the right to authorize or refuse leaves. They will be granted only on the request of the father or guardian of the pupil.

Art. 9. Apprenticeship is for three consecutive years, *not including an obligatory trial month*. In order to encourage the pupil, she will be paid:

```
1st year:   a wage of 40 to 50 francs
2nd year: "      "    "  60 to 75   "
3rd year: "      "    "  80 to 100  "
```

After the apprenticeship the wage will be established according to merit.

---

22. **warp:** in the weaving process, threads placed lengthwise in the loom. They were woven with threads called the *weft* or *woof* placed perpendicularly to them.

Chapter 5

Labor Old

and New:

The Impact of

the Industrial

Revolution

At the end of the apprenticeship, a gratuity of 20 francs will be given to the apprentice to reward her for her exactitude in fulfilling her engagements.

Art. 10. The effective work time is twelve hours. Summer and winter, the day begins at 5 o'clock and ends at 7 : 15.

Breakfast is from 7 : 30 to 8 : 15; lunch is from 12 : 00 to 1 : 00; snack is from 5 : 00 to 5 : 30; supper is at 7 : 15.

After the second year, pupils will receive lessons in reading, writing, and arithmetic. They will be taught to sew and to do a little cooking.

Art. 11. As a measure of encouragement and with no obligation, it is established that at the end of each month the young people will be graded as follows:

```
1st class, gift for the month 1 fr. 50 c.
2nd class                  1  "   —
3rd class                       50 c.
4th class                       —23
```

Each month a new classification will take place, and the young person will rise or fall according to her merit. This classification will be based on an overall evaluation of conduct, quantity and quality of work, docility and diligence, etc.

Art. 12. Wages are not due until the end of the year. They will be paid during the month following their due date. Gifts, incentive pay, and compensation for extra work will be paid each month.

Art. 13. Any apprentice who leaves the establishment before the end of her term, or who has been dismissed for bad conduct, conspiracy, rebellion, laziness, or a serious breach of the rules loses her rights to wages for the current year; beyond this, in such a case, the father or guardian of the pupil agrees to pay the director of the establishment the sum of one hundred francs to indemnify him for the non-fulfillment of the present agreement: half of this sum will be given to the *bureau de bienfaisance*[24] in the pupil's parish.

Art. 14. If, during the first year, apprentice is recognized as unfit, despite the agreement and in the interest of both parties the director reserves the right to send her away without indemnity.

Art. 15. The apprentice who leaves the establishment at the end of the first month under the pretext that she cannot get used to the place, will pay 50 centimes per day toward the costs she has occasioned, as well as her travel expenses.

Art. 16. On her arrival, the apprentice will submit to inspection by the house doctor. Any girl who has a skin disease or who is found to be sickly will not be accepted and will be sent away immediately at her own expense.

23. Abbreviations for French currency.
    fr.: franc.
    c.: centime; 100 centimes to 1 franc.
24. **Bureau de bienfaissance:** Catholic social welfare organization.

Contract

The undersigned _____ the manufacturer, and have made the following contract:

M. _____, having read and understood the conditions of apprenticeship stipulated above in sixteen articles, declares that he accepts them for _____ aged _____, present and consenting, and pledges to execute them and have them executed in all their contents by _____ . M. _____, manufacturer, pledges likewise to execute the above conditions insofar as they concern him.

The present agreement is consented to for *Three years* beginning on

_____ .

Made and signed in duplicate _____

_____   _____
Father or Guardian   Director

P.S. Girls will not be admitted on Sundays or holidays.[25]

Source 8 from British Parliamentary Papers: Reports from Committees, *vol. 15,* Labour of Children in Factories *(London: House of Commons, 1832), pp. 6–13.*

8. Report of the Sadler Committee, 1832[26]

William Cooper, called in; and Examined.

What is your business?—I follow the cloth-dressing at present.

2. What is your age?—I was eight-and-twenty last February.

3. When did you first begin to work in mills or factories?—When I was about 10 years of age.

4. With whom did you first work?—At Mr. Benyon's flax[27] mills, in Meadowland, Leeds.

5. What were your usual hours of working?—We began at five, and gave over at nine; at five o'clock in the morning.

6. And you gave over at nine o'clock?—At nine at night.

7. At what distance might you have lived from the mill?—About a mile and a half.

8. At what time had you to get up in the morning to attend to your labour?—I had to be up soon after four o'clock.

25. That is, girls were not admitted to employment in the mill on Sundays or holidays.

26. **Sadler Committee:** the Committee on the Bill to Regulate the Labour of Children in the Mills and Factories of the United Kingdom.

27. **flax:** a plant whose fiber is manufactured into linen for thread or weaving into fabrics.

Chapter 5

Labor Old

and New:

The Impact of

the Industrial

Revolution

9. Every morning?—Every morning.

10. What intermissions had you for meals?—When we began at five in the morning, we went on until noon, and then we had 40 minutes for dinner.

11. Had you no time for breakfast?—No, we got it as we could, while we were working.

12. Had you any time for an afternoon refreshment, or what is called in Yorkshire your "drinking?"—No; when we began at noon, we went on till night; there was only one stoppage, the 40 minutes for dinner.

13. Then as you had to get your breakfast, and what is called "drinking" in that manner, you had to put it on one side?—Yes, we had to put it on one side; and when we got our frames doffed, we ate two or three mouthfuls, and then put it by again.[28]

14. Is there not considerable dust in a flax mill?—A flax mill is very dusty indeed.

15. Was not your food therefore frequently spoiled?—Yes, at times with the dust; sometimes we could not eat it, when it had got a lot of dust on.

16. What were you when you were ten years old?—What is called a bobbin-doffer; when the frames are quite full, we have to doff them.

17. Then as you lived so far from home, you took your dinner to the mill?—We took all our meals with us, living so far off.

18. During the 40 minutes which you were allowed for dinner, had you ever to employ that time in your turn in cleaning the machinery?—At times we had to stop to clean the machinery, and then we got our dinner as well as we could; they paid us for that.

19. At these times you had no resting at all?—No.

20. How much had you for cleaning the machinery?—I cannot exactly say what they gave us, as I never took any notice of it.

21. Did you ever work even later than the time you have mentioned?—I cannot say that I worked later there: I had a sister who worked up stairs, and she worked till 11 at night, in what they call the card-room.

22. At what time in the morning did she begin to work?—At the same time as myself.

23. And they kept her there till 11 at night?—Till 11 at night.

24. You say that your sister was in the card-room?—Yes.

28. Vocabulary of the textile mill:

   frame: the water frame, an early spinning machine.

   doff: the task, in the industrial spinning process, of removing spindles filled with yarn from the spinning machine.

   bobbin: a reel, cylinder, or spoollike apparatus on which thread is wound.

   card: a tool used to comb out textile fibers (wool, flax, etc.) in preparation for spinning them into thread.

   gigger: person who worked in the gigging process, a step in dressing wool cloth in which loose fibers were drawn off of the fabric and in which the fabric's nap is raised. The process used **teasles,** thistlelike plants that hooked the fabric and raised it.

   boiler: part of the processing of wool involved boiling and scrubbing to remove oils.

   primmer, brusher: workers involved in the final preparation of woolen cloth.

25. Is not that a very dusty department?—Yes, very dusty indeed.

26. She had to be at the mill at five, and was kept at work till eleven at night?—Yes.

27. During the whole time she was there?—During the whole time; there was only 40 minutes allowed at dinner out of that.

28. To keep you at your work for such a length of time, and especially towards the termination of such a day's labour as that, what means were taken to keep you awake and attentive?—They strapped us at times, when we were not quite ready to be doffing the frame when it was full.

29. Were you frequently strapped?—At times we were frequently strapped.

30. What sort of a strap was it?—About this length [*describing it.*]

31. What was it made of?—Of leather.

32. Were you occasionally very considerably hurt with the strap?—Sometimes it hurt us very much, and sometimes they did not lay on so hard as they did at others.

33. Were the girls strapped in that sort of way?—They did not strap what they called the grown-up women.

34. Were any of the female children strapped?—Yes; they were strapped in the same way as the lesser boys. . . .

44. Were your punishments the same in that mill as in the other?—Yes, they used the strap the same there.

45. How long did you work in that mill?—Five years.

46. And how did it agree with your health?—I was sometimes well, and sometimes not very well.

47. Did it affect your breathing at all?—Yes; sometimes we were stuffed.

48. When your hours were so long, you had not any time to attend to a day-school?—We had no time to go to a day-school, only to a Sunday-school,[29] and then with working such long hours we wanted to have a bit of rest, so that I slept till the afternoon, sometimes till dinner, and sometimes after.

49. Did you attend a place of worship?—I should have gone to a place of worship many times, but I was in the habit of falling asleep, and that kept me away; I did not like to go for fear of being asleep.

50. Do you mean that you could not prevent yourself from falling asleep, in consequence of the fatigue of the preceding week?—Yes. . . .

85. After working at a mill to this excess, how did you find your health at last?—I found it very bad indeed; I found illness coming on me a long time before I fell down.

86. Did you at length become so ill as to be unable to pursue your work?—I was obliged to give it up entirely.

87. How long were you ill?—For six months.

---

29. **Sunday school:** churches often ran schools for mill children on their day off (Sunday) to teach the rudiments of reading and writing along with religious instruction.

Chapter 5

Labor Old

and New:

The Impact of

the Industrial

Revolution

88. Who attended?—Mr. Metcalf and Mr. Freeman.

89. What were you told by your medical attendants was the reason of your illness?—Nothing but hard labour, and working long hours; and they gave me up, and said no good could be done for me, that I must go into the country.

90. Did this excessive labour not only weaken you, but destroy your appetite?—It destroyed the appetite, and I became so feeble, that I could not cross the floor unless I had a stick to go with; I was in great pain, and could find ease in no posture.

91. You could drink in the meantime, if you could not eat?—Yes, I could drink.

92. But you found that not improve your health?—No.

93. Has it been remarked that your excessive labour from early life has greatly diminished your growth?—A number of persons have said that such was the case, and that I was the same as if I had been made of iron or stone.

94. What height are you?—About five feet. It is that that has hindered me of my growth.

95. When you were somewhat recovered, did you apply for labour?—I applied for my work again, but the overlooker said I was not fit to work; he was sure of that, and he would not let me have it. I was then obliged to throw myself on the parish.[30]

96. Have you subsisted on the parish ever since?—Yes.

97. Have you been always willing and anxious to work?—I was always willing and anxious to work from my infancy.

98. Have you been on the parish since your severe illness?—Yes.

99. How long is that ago?—Six months. When I was ill I got something from the Society; they relieved me then, but when I became better I received no benefit from it.

100. Yours is not what is called a Friendly Society?—No, it is what we call Odd Fellows.[31]

101. And they do not extend relief after a certain period?—Not after you get better. . . .

124. You say that you had no time to go to school during the week, but that you went on Sunday?—I went on Sunday; I had no time to go to a day-school.

125. Can you read or write?—I can read, but I cannot write.

126. When you were at school, was there any sort of punishment when you did not attend to your lessons?—They used to give us a clout on the side of the head if we did not attend to our lessons.

30. **on the parish:** under existing English laws, poor relief was the responsibility of the local parish.

31. **Friendly Society, Odd Fellows Society:** organizations founded to benefit workers through "self-help." They took up small weekly sums from their members and used the funds thus collected to aid sick or injured members unable to work, or to assist the widows and orphans of members.

127. Did they use any strap in the school?—They used a stick in the school I went to.

128. Did it not hurt you nearly as much as the strap in the factory?—Yes.

129. But you never went to a schoolmaster who paid such attention to your learning, as to keep you forty-four hours to your book?—No; I have many times fallen asleep at the Sunday-school instead of looking at my book.
. . .

142. If you had refused to work over-hours, would they have turned you off altogether?—Yes, they would have turned us off. If one will not do it, another will.

143. At this particular period, when you were thus over-worked, were there not a great number of able-bodied individuals in Leeds totally out of employment?—A great number. A few individuals have it all, and the rest, of course, are obliged to apply to the parish.

144. If you had refused to work the over-work, there were plenty of others willing to undertake it?—That is very true.

145. And they were people able to perform the sort of work you were engaged in?—They were.

146. You of course know your trade?—Yes.

147. Were those people out of work persons who could have undertaken your situation?—They were out of work.

148. At the time that you were working these over-hours were there a great many out of work in Leeds?—Yes.

149. And were they capable of doing your work?—Yes, capable of doing the same work.

150. Do you work anywhere now?—I have not worked anywhere for rather more than a year. I have been constantly out to seek for employment since I have been better.

151. How are you supported?—By the town.

152. Do you mean by the parish?—Yes.

153. Of what place?—Leeds. . . .

180. You attended at the mill at five in the morning; was that both winter and summer?—It has been, for two years back, winter and summer, working at Mr. Brown's.

181. Were you able to be punctual in your attendance at five o'clock?—I was always there at five o'clock; if we were too late they took us off what we call bating; if we were a quarter of an hour too late in the morning they took off a penny.

182. Are they ever turned away for being too late?—If they are what is called "bad comers," they turn them off and get fresh ones.

183. Are they ever strapped for being too late?—They did not strap them at the room that I was in.

184. How did you contrive to be awake so soon in the morning?—My father always used to call me up.

Chapter 5

Labor Old

and New:

The Impact of

the Industrial

Revolution

185. Did he get up so early as that for his own business?—He got up on purpose to call me.

186. How many hours did he work in a day at his own business?—Sometimes from five in the morning till eight at night.

187. You say he was a shoemaker?—Yes.

188. Then, according to this, he worked more hours than you did?—I think not so long.

189. Did your father take his regular intervals for his meals?—I should think so.

190. And walked about to market for his family; had he not many pauses in his labour?—He worked at home, and therefore could do as he pleased.

191. After you worked a month at these long hours, could you not get back into lighter employment?—I do not know whether you could get back or not.

192. You said that you were about 17 when you first went from the flax-spinning mills into the cloth-mills?—Yes.

193. Was that before the Act of Parliament made to regulate the hours?—I know nothing about that.

194. How often did these extra hours come about?—Very often.

195. Describe to us a period in which you have worked the greatest possible number of hours; how many weeks running have you worked?—I have gone on for a year round.

196. Working all the Monday night and Friday night?—Yes; always working long hours.

197. Is your sister older or younger than yourself?—There is a year and a half between us; I am the elder.

198. Has your health improved since you left off working long hours?—I am a deal better than I was; but I believe that if I could have got work, and have had something to support me, I should have recruited my health better. I have been very poorly kept for these last six months, having been out of work. I have only half a crown a week allowed from the parish for my wife and myself.

199. When you were working the long hours, were there any people in the same employment, when you were a gigger, for instance, who were working the short hours?—Yes; some mills were working short hours in the same line; there were none in the same room that worked less hours than I did.

200. That did not depend on your own choice, did it?—They would not let us have it of our own choice; we might either do it or leave it.

201. Suppose it was left to you, would you prefer a moderate degree of labour with lower wages, to high wages with this excessive labor?—I would rather have short hours and moderate wages, than great wages and long hours. I should be a great deal better.

202. Of course you do not mean to say that these long hours have continued in mills and factories when trade has slackened; has not the excessive

labour somewhat abated when there is not such a brisk trade?—It has abated when there was not a brisk trade; when there was, it was again increased for those that were working, who were not willing to lose their employment, and so they submitted, or they must have gone travelling about the streets, and applied to the parish. But if the hours of work had not been then so much increased, more hands would have got employment. There would have been not so many over-worked, and not so many without any thing to do; it would have been share and share alike. . . .

206. When you were working these very long hours in a mill as a gigger and boiler, had you the liberty, if you wished to be away for a day or part of a day, to send another person to do your work?—Yes; if we were poorly, we had liberty to send another person in our place.

207. If you wished to rest for half a day, you could send another man in your place?—I was once poorly, and I sent another workman, and they let me have the job again; now that I have been ill six months, they will not let me have the job again. . . .

217. Do you think you would be able to stand your work?—I should like to try; I cannot bear to go wandering about the streets. . . .

220. Is being a gigger harder than the others?—Yes, gigging is very hard work; the fleeces are so heavy and full of water, and you have to stand in this position [*describing it*] to support them and turn the fleece over; if you are not over strong it makes you rather deformed in your legs.

221. At what age do people generally begin gigging?—Some begin about 15, 16 or 17, and some lads begin when about 14.

222. At what age did your father die?—He was 60 when he died.

223. Have you seen the man lately who is doing your work at Mr. Brown's?—Yes.

224. Is he in good health?—I do not know; I must not say a thing that I do not know; it is a good while since I saw him.

225. Was your father a tall or a short man?—He stood about five feet seven.

226. And you are five feet?—Yes.

227. Have you any brothers or sisters?—Two brothers and a sister.

228. Do they work in the same trade?—I have a brother working now at the same trade; he was seventeen the 14th of last February.

229. Has he good health?—He had not over good health when I came from Leeds.

230. What height were you at fifteen years old; do you know?—I was very little.

231. Have you grown since that time?—I do not know that I have grown any these eight or nine years.

232. Were you little when you were a child?—My parents said that I was not very little when I was about four or five years of age.

233. Did your parents think your excessive working injured you?—Yes.

234. Where does your brother work, who is in the same line?—He is working at the bottom of Park-lane, besides Mr. Chorley's.

Chapter 5

Labor Old

and New:

The Impact of

the Industrial

Revolution

235. What hours does he work?—He goes at six in the morning and works till nine at night.

Source 9 from Sidney Pollard and Colin Holmes, editors, Documents in European Economic History, *vol. 2,* Industrial Power and National Rivalry *(New York: St. Martin's, 1972), pp. 322–323.*

9. Working Conditions of a Female Textile Worker in Germany, 1880s and 1890s

In the weaving sheds the girls work in an atmosphere which, on the third day of my work there, gave me bad lung catarrh; tiny flakes of the twisted wool fill the air, settle on dress and hair, and float into nose and mouth; the machines have to be swept clean every two hours; the dust is breathed in by the girls, since they are not allowed to open the windows. To this has to be added the terrible nerve-racking noise of the rattling machines so that no one can hear himself speak. No communication with one's neighbour is possible except by shouting on the top of one's voice. In consequence, all the girls have screeching, irritating voices: even when the shop has gone quiet, at the end of the working day, on the street, at home, they never converse quietly like other people, their conversation is a constant yelling, which produces the impression among outsiders that they are quarrelling.

It is truly a miracle that so many girls still look fresh and blooming, and that they still feel like singing at work, usually sentimental folk songs. . . .

Many girls work happily, particularly those weaving small carpets or curtains woven as one piece who can observe the building up of the pattern. They love their machines like loving a faithful dog; they polish them, and tie coloured ribbons, little pictures of saints and all sorts of gaudy tinsel given to them by their sweethearts at the summer fairs, to the crossbars.

The girls work hard, very hard, and quite a few told me how they collapsed with the exertion of the first four weeks of work, and how most of them suffer for months with irritations of the lung and throat until they get used to the dust. To this has to be added the poor, miserable food, the short periods of rest in rooms which don't deserve the name of "dwelling"—and yet the girls remain cheerful, healthy, lively and enterprising.

I have always watched this with admiration; I could not have stood this for long. I could not take anything in the morning beside coffee; only in the evening I hurried, totally exhausted, to my hotel, to swallow some nourishing food with great difficulty. . . .

No one would dream of stopping work and taking a rest even when suffering from violent headache or toothache, not even a quarter of an hour of being late was tolerated without a substantial fine at the end of the week. . . .

The work of the carpet weavers should not be underrated, it is anything but monotonous or repetitive. When working the complex Turkish patterns, the weaver has to catch the exact moment for changing the different coloured reels. She has to think and coordinate, calculate and pay attention and concentrate all her thoughts. This work requires far more mental activity and sense of responsibility than the crochet work and needlework done by hundreds of girls of society, year after year, in expectation of the shining knight who would one day come and rescue them.

Most factories start work at half past six, pause for breakfast from 8 to 8.30, dinner 12–1; at 4 there are 20–30 minutes for tea, and work goes on until 7. On Saturdays work ends at 5.30, in order to give time to the workers to clean the machines thoroughly and to oil them by 6; Mondays, work starts half an hour later probably because all the girls have a hangover from Sunday.

Source 10 from British Parliamentary Papers: Reports from Commissioners: Children's Employment (Mines), *vol. 17,* Appendix to the First Report of the Commissioners (Mines) *(London: William Clowes for Her Majesty's Stationery Office, 1842), pp. 39, 103, 107–108.*

10. Report on the Employment of Children in British Mines, 1841–1842

May 14, 1841.

No. 49. Mr. *Joseph Staley*, Managing Partner in Coal-works at Yate Common, in the parish of Yate (Two Pits), carried on under the firm of *Staley* and *Parkers*:

Employ from 30 to 35 hands; not more than five or six boys under 13; the two youngest are from eight to nine years old, who work with their father; perhaps three boys not more than 10 years of age; they assist in cutting and carting out the coal from a one-foot seam; no doorboys employed, because there is sufficient ventilation without being particular about closing them; the carters generally manage the doors as they pass; the boys earn from 6s. to 9s. per week when they get handy at cutting; have not more than three or four under 18; all over 15 are earning nearly men's wages—say 15s. per week; the men earn from 18s. to 20s.; considers two tons a fair day's work; wages paid in money every Saturday; the older boys receive their own; the boys, in carting out the coals from the *googs* [narrow inclined planes up which the coal is pulled by a chain and windlass], when short distances, draw by the *girdle* or *lugger, i.e.* a rope round the waist, with an iron hook depending in front, to which a chain, passing between the legs, is attached; if for longer distances, they use wheeled-carriages on a railway; no horses are employed under ground at present; the smaller boys do not tug more

Chapter 5

Labor Old

and New:

The Impact of

the Industrial

Revolution

than 1 cwt.[32] at a time; the carts generally hold about 2 cwt. each; the thickest vein is two feet six inches, and is worked by the young men; the boys cart through a two feet six inches passageway; the young men have four feet, there being a bed of soft stuff above the coal, to cut away before they come to the roof; the shaft is 45 fathoms,[33] worked by a steam-engine, and strong-plaited rope; thinks rope decidedly safer than chain, as it gives more timely notice of any defect, by a strand or two giving way, whereas a link of iron is sometimes near breaking, a good while before it is discovered, and then separates on a sudden. Has had many years' experience in Staffordshire and Derbyshire, having been brought up a collier; say for 40 years; has been engaged 23 years in this coal-field; the workings are quite dry; a pumping-engine of 60-horse power, is constantly at work when there is water; three or four days a-week is sufficient in summer; hours of work average eight to nine hours a-day; no night-work at present; always employ two sets when it occurs.

Some of the boys and young persons attend the Church Sunday-school, and others the Dissenting Sunday-school; most of them can read a little; look clean and tidy on Sundays; thinks there are no healthier boys in the country.

MESSRS. WILLSON, HOLMES, AND STOCKS, QUARRY-HOUSE PIT.

No. 6. *William Jagger*, aged 11.   May 6:

I am a hurrier[34] for my father, Benjamin Jagger; have been in here four years and upwards; I come to work at seven o'clock, and go home at four, five, and six; I get breakfast afore I come down; I get my dinner down here, I get it about one o'clock; I don't know how long I am taking it; I get it as I can; I go to work directly after; I get currant-cake and buttered cake some-times, never any meat; I get a bit of meat for supper when I go up. I went to day-school often; I comed to work about half a year; I go to Sunday-school now at church; I cannot read or write. I have got to hurry a corve 400 yards; I don't know what weight it is [2½ cwt.]; it runs upon rails; I push the corves; some of the boys push when there is no rail. I do not oft hurt my feet; I never met with an accident. The men serve me out sometimes—they wallop

---

32. **cwt:** hundredweight, i.e., 100 pounds.

33. **fathom:** a fathom equals 6 feet; the shaft of 45 fathoms thus extended 270 feet below the earth's surface.

34. Mining vocabulary:
   hurrier: person who drew a wagon loaded with coal through mine tunnels to the shaft up which the load would be raised to the earth's surface.
   corve: small wagon for carrying coal or ore in a mine.
   getter: person who cut the coal from the seam. Young male hurriers, who often suffered stunted growth because of their excessive labor in moving coal as children, often gradu-ated to the occupation of getter. Short stature was an asset in the restricted spaces of mine tunnels. The mining commission report from which this testimony is drawn notes that getters described themselves as "mashed up."

me; I don't know what for, except 'tis when I don't hurry fast enough; I like my work very well; I would rather hurry than set cards.

The mainway of this pit is 3 feet 6 inches high and 400 yards in length; seams 17 inches thick; gear in good order; shaft not walled up. At the moment of stepping out of the corve at the pit's bottom, a stone weighing from five to seven pounds fell in the water close by my feet from the unlined shaft near the top, or from the bank, a circumstance at once illustrative of the importance of protecting persons in their descent, by walling up the sides of the shaft, and thereby preventing loose measures from falling.

MR. JOSEPH STOCKS, BOOTH TOWN PIT, HALIFAX.

No. 26. *Patience Kershaw*, aged 17.   May 15:

My father has been dead about a year; my mother is living and has ten children, five lads and five lasses; the oldest is about thirty, the youngest is four; three lasses go to mill; all the lads are colliers, two getters and three hurriers; one lives at home and does nothing; mother does nought but look after home.

All my sisters have been hurriers, but three went to the mill, Alice went because her legs swelled from hurrying in cold water when she was hot. I never went to day-school; I go to Sunday-school, but I cannot read or write; I go to pit at five o'clock in the morning and come out at five in the evening; I get my breakfast of porridge and milk first; I take my dinner with me, a cake, and eat it as I go; I do not stop or rest any time for the purpose; I get nothing else until I get home, and then have potatoes and meat, not every day meat. I hurry in the clothes I have now got on, trousers and ragged jacket; the bald place upon my head is made by thrusting the corves; my legs have never swelled, but sisters' did when they went to mill; I hurry the corves a mile and more under ground and back; they weigh 300 cwt.; I hurry 11 a-day; I wear a belt and chain at the workings to get the corves out; the getters that I work for are *naked* except their caps; they pull off all their clothes; I see them at work when I go up; sometimes they beat me, if I am not quick enough, with their hands; they strike me upon my back; the boys take liberties with me sometimes, they pull me about; I am the only girl in the pit; there are about 20 boys and 15 men; all the men are naked; I would rather work in mill than in coal-pit.

This girl is an ignorant, filthy; ragged, and deplorable-looking object, and such a one as the uncivilized natives of the prairies would be shocked to look upon.[35]

35. This comment by the mine commissioners is amplified elsewhere in their report, where they note that Kershaw worked in a mine whose tunnels contained 3 or 4 inches of water at all times and that she moved her corve 1,800 to 2,000 yards on each trip.

Chapter 5

Labor Old

and New:

The Impact of

the Industrial

Revolution

QUESTIONS TO CONSIDER

Let us bring together your findings on the old and new labor of European working men and women. Your goal is to understand the changes affecting them in the late eighteenth and nineteenth centuries and how these changes came about. You may want to review the questions in Sources and Method before continuing your study of the evidence.

First, consider the length of time workers devoted to labor. Was the preindustrial workday much different in length from the early industrial age workday? Note especially the findings of the Sadler Committee on the workdays of William Cooper, employed in industrial labor, and his father, a craftsman of the old school. Next, consider the number of workdays per year. Both old and new labor generally required a six-day work week. But reexamine the holidays at Lille, remembering to punctuate the work year with a liberal number of "holy Mondays." Compare this quantity of work with that demanded of William Cooper. Like many nineteenth-century miners, this textile worker could probably have looked forward to holidays only on Christmas, Easter Monday, and the Monday after Pentecost. What other time off from work could he have expected? What effect did the Industrial Revolution have on the annual quantity of work for many laborers?

Old and new labor varied in quality, pace, and discipline, too. The textile workers in the putting-out system at Rouen doubtlessly worked long and hard, but were there any compensating advantages? Contrast William Cooper's workday with that of his shoemaker father. What differences in the demands of their occupations do you find? Agricultural labor was physically taxing, but why do you think Mrs. Britton preferred it to factory work?

Consider the pace of work. Who set the pace for guild members? Who set the pace in the putting-out system, the factory, and the mine? Notice the discipline of the industrial-era workplace, too. What sort of punishments and incentives prodded employees to work quickly? Considering conditions of preindustrial labor, why do you think the specific regulations in Source 6 were necessary? Recall the statement by Andrew Ure that opened this chapter. What were management's goals in imposing this kind of discipline?

Other changes in labor also accompanied the Industrial Revolution. What do the testimonies from the coal miners and the records of French and German textile workers tell us about the labor of women in the industrial age? Reexamine Mrs. Britton's testimony. In what setting did she labor after her marriage? What effect might female and child industrial labor have had on the family? What educational opportunities existed for boys and girls in industrial labor?

Finally, let us consider the health and safety of workers under both the old and the new systems. Which style of labor do you think Mrs. Britton and William Cooper would have considered more healthful? What hazards awaited textile workers like Cooper and miners like William Jagger and Patience Kershaw?

In other ways, old and new labor were not quite so different. Ideally, any job should provide some security of continuing employment. How did the Prussian guild regulations seek to protect the markets and incomes of the textile workers? Did any other workers, old or new, benefit from such efforts to protect job security? Consider the problems of Mr. Britton, the effect of cycles of economic prosperity and depression on William Cooper and his fellow textile workers, and the experiences of putting-out workers described in the song. Did any of them have hopes of continuing employment opportunity?

Consider, too, the problems all these workers confronted when illness, injury, or economic conditions denied them employment. What recourse did Mrs. Britton and her family have in the face of poverty? Did William Cooper have any additional resources to draw on when illness struck? Were they sufficient for his needs?

Your comparative analysis of this chapter's sources provides one more insight into the industrialization of Western Europe. Economic historians speak of *proto-industrialization*, a process that paved the way for industrialization by organizing production into larger units employing traditional technologies. Industrial capitalists later combined experience in such organization with new machines to produce the Industrial Revolution. To understand this process, consider what the factory system meant: large units of production, controlled by capitalists prepared to organize labor and resources for a profit, and competition among producers who sought worldwide markets. What evidence of modern industrial organization do you find in the putting-out system? In what ways did it occupy a transitional role? Were its methods of production old or new? Was its organization of production old or new? How were its labor-management relations similar to those of the industrial age? Compare the discipline Andrew Ure advocated for industrial managers with the alleged goal of the clothiers in the popular song. What significance do you attach to the putting-out workers' complaint that they could no longer buy land? Would you say they were slipping into a work status like that of later industrial workers?

Now you are ready to provide detailed answers to the main questions of this chapter: What was the nature of the new labor? How did it evolve? How did it differ from the old labor? Be sure to base your responses on the evidence you have assessed.

Chapter 5

Labor Old

and New:

The Impact of

the Industrial

Revolution

EPILOGUE

A combination of developments served to improve conditions for later generations of workers. Early industrial workers won such improvements in their lot only slowly and with considerable struggle, however. The right to take part in government by voting was one common demand of nineteenth-century workers in a Europe that accorded a political voice, if at all, only to the wealthy and privileged. Workers in England began to win the vote only in 1867 after considerable agitation; a revolution in France in 1848 established the right of universal suffrage for men. Elsewhere the vote came more slowly, and Russian workers lacked voting rights until the Revolution of 1917.

In the more democratic Western European nations, a widened right to vote in the nineteenth century made political institutions more responsive to workers' needs. During that century legislation passed by several European parliaments sought to regulate working conditions for women and children, to establish minimum safety standards, and to begin to provide the accident, health, and old age insurance plans that protect modern workers. Real improvements, however, often lagged behind such legislation. Early wage, hour, and safety regulations ran counter to an important political philosophy of the nineteenth century, liberalism (see Chapter 6), which viewed such legislation as interference in freedom of management. Early regulations thus frequently lacked enough officials to enforce them by comprehensive factory inspections. If you refer to William Cooper's testimony, you will find him completely unaware of a parliamentary act to regulate work hours, eloquent proof of this early lack of enforcement. Governments were slow to create the machinery necessary to enforce these rules.

The nineteenth century also witnessed an often bitter struggle by workers to form their own organizations promoting their common welfare. Because unions and strikes, as we have seen, were illegal in many countries, the first worker organizations of the early nineteenth century often were self-help groups such as the one that aided William Cooper. Only after much struggle did governments in countries like England and France legalize labor unions and the right to strike.

The legalization of unions, however, allowed industrial workers to take collective action in strikes to win better wages and conditions. Early strikes often produced bloody conflict between labor on one side and management, sometimes backed by police or the army in the name of keeping order, on the other. The first major victory for a noncraft union, however, occurred in the London dockworkers' strike of 1889. Twentieth-century developments have improved the lot of workers in other ways, especially through increased leisure time realized in the forty-hour work week and paid vacations.

Improvements in wages and working conditions, however, did not change the basic nature of modern factory labor. In the industrial workplace, the pace of work continued to be set by machines, granting little independence to the individual worker, who remained a human cog in the greater modern industrial machine. Though most workers adjusted to this kind of labor, manifestations of their discontent have not disappeared entirely. In 1968, for example, millions of French workers went on strike and occupied their factories. One of their chief demands was for a concept they called *autogestion*, that is, some voice in the workplace decisions that governed their lives on the job.

Such demands by employees have not gone entirely unheeded by management. There have been efforts to reintroduce some worker input in the production process through such practices as quality circles, in which workers engaged in the same phases of production meet periodically to discuss their jobs and to make suggestions for improving the production process. Other experiments in such industries as automobile assembly have sought to involve individual workers in several phases of the production process as a way of mitigating the monotony of assembly-line work. Nevertheless, for the majority of Western workers today the basic nature of industrial employment, as symbolized by the production line, remains unchanged.

CHAPTER SIX

TWO PROGRAMS FOR
SOCIAL AND POLITICAL
CHANGE: LIBERALISM
AND SOCIALISM

THE PROBLEM

"Workingmen of all countries unite!" proclaimed Karl Marx and Friedrich Engels in *The Communist Manifesto* of 1848, urging working people to overthrow the capitalist system and end the working conditions of the early Industrial Revolution, which we explored in Chapter 5. Marx and Engels were partisans in a nineteenth-century ideological clash in which they and other proponents of socialism opposed liberalism, the dominant doctrine among the rising class of factory owners and managers. Nineteenth-century liberals and socialists differed greatly in their views on such issues as the definition of freedom and democracy, the role of government, and their visions of the future.

We must be careful in this chapter to understand liberalism in its nineteenth- and not its twentieth-century

sense. "Freedom" was the key word for nineteenth-century liberals. But for them this meant individual freedom. In a political sense, nineteenth-century liberals saw in the French Revolution the essential victory they sought to win all over Europe. In destroying the Old Regime with its absolute monarchy and privilege for the aristocratic few, the Revolution had created a new political order based on individual freedom. Everywhere, liberals sought to draft constitutions that would limit royal authority and ensure basic individual rights. The citizen was to be safe from arbitrary arrest and was to enjoy freedom of speech, assembly, religion, and the press.

For the early or classical liberals, individual freedom did not, however, mean political democracy, a voice for all in government. The constitutional arrangements created by liberals usually included some sort of property qualification to vote. Most liberals were members of the middle classes and believed that, to exercise the right to vote, a citizen had to have some stake in the existing social and economic order in the form of property. The majority lacked sufficient wealth to vote in all early and mid-nineteenth-century countries under liberal rule. But one liberal French minister, François Guizot, noted that the poor possessed full freedom to increase their wealth so that they could acquire property and participate in political life! Extreme as this view may seem to us, it does express the liberal faith that peaceful political change was possible. The key for the success of such a system of government was the establishment of a society of laws protecting individual freedoms.

Liberal economic thought was also a doctrine of absolute freedom. Liberals opposed the guild and aristocratic privileges that had limited career opportunities in Old Regime Europe. Thus individual economic opportunity, embodied in the opening of all careers to citizens on the basis of their talents, not their titles, became the central liberal economic tenet. But liberals' faith in economic freedom had far greater implications.

Liberals believed that immutable natural laws, like supply and demand, regulated economic life. Government interference in economic life, they believed, not only violated these laws but individual freedom as well. Based in large part on the writings of such classical liberal economists as the Englishmen Adam Smith (1723–1790), Thomas Malthus (1766–1834), and David Ricardo (1772–1823), liberal economic thought defended the right of early industrial employers to be free of government regulation. Their doctrine was summed up in the French phrase *laissez faire* (literally, "leave it alone").

Socialists differed from liberals in seeing the French Revolution of 1789 as simply the first step in revamping Europe's old order. The Revolution had established individual freedom but not political democracy. More important for socialists, the Revolution had not brought social democracy. To achieve this goal, they advocated a more equitable distribution of society's wealth. Their message, as you might imagine, had considerable appeal to those workers employed in the mills, factories, and mines of the early Industrial Revolution whose lot we explored in Chapter 5.

Some early socialist thinkers expressed the view that economic equality could be realized by peaceful evolutionary change. Karl Marx applied the label "utopian" to those thinkers because of the impracticality, in his view, of their schemes. Charles Fourier (1771–1837) advocated a restructuring of society around essentially agricultural communities that represented an attempt to turn the clock back to a preindustrial economy. Louis Blanc (1811–1882) advocated state assistance in the creation of worker-owned units of production that was difficult to imagine in a Europe dominated by the liberal ideology of government noninterference in economic life. But some utopian socialists, notably Robert Owen (1771–1858), who created a model industrial town around his

Chapter 6

Two Programs

for Social

and Political

Change:

Liberalism

and Socialism

textile mills in New Lanark, Scotland, achieved real improvements for working people.

Utopian socialism did not transform society. Some of its ideas, however, did influence other socialist thinkers, including Karl Marx, who advocated a revolutionary transformation of society. Indeed, revolutionary socialism gained large numbers of working-class followers and by the middle and late nineteenth century threatened Western Europe's liberal political leaders with the possibility of a complete overhaul of so-

ciety in the name of political and social democracy.

Nineteenth-century liberalism and socialism both produced important thinkers who analyzed the ills of their society and advanced not only plans for change but critiques of the opposing ideology. What visions of the future did liberals and socialists propose? How did they hope to realize their ideals? How did their ideologies differ? Your task in this chapter is to answer these questions by examining the ideas of two nineteenth-century political and social theorists.

SOURCES AND METHOD

Your sources in this chapter are the writings of the liberal Alexis de Tocqueville and the revolutionary socialist Karl Marx. These two thinkers have been selected because they expressed strikingly different views on similar subjects: the historical development of the West, the nature of democracy, and the role of revolution. Tocqueville and Marx also analyzed the French Revolution of 1848, a topic you may wish to review in your textbook. Their contrasting views on the same issues will provide the basis for your answers to the general questions on liberalism and socialism.

In analyzing the works of Tocqueville and Marx, you must understand that these works were polemical in character—that is, that they were written to advocate the causes espoused by their authors. All such works may be expected to emphasize

their authors' viewpoints and summarily to dismiss opposing points of view that may have considerable validity. Because each theorist was an eloquent advocate of his cause, some examination of their separate backgrounds and viewpoints is necessary to permit you to analyze their ideas fruitfully.

Alexis Charles Henri Clerel de Tocqueville was born in 1805, the son of an aristocratic father who hoped for the restoration of the French monarchy destroyed by the Revolution of 1789. When Napoleon's fall from power finally brought a restored monarchy, the Tocquevilles rose to positions of importance in government. Alexis de Tocqueville's talents gained early recognition with his appointment as a judge at the youthful age of twenty-one. It was not as a jurist, however, that Tocqueville gained fame but rather as a liberal political theorist and as an early student of what we would call today sociology and political science.

In 1831 Tocqueville and his long-time friend, Gustave de Beaumont, undertook a fact-finding tour in the United States to study that country's pioneering penitentiary system. For nine months Tocqueville and Beaumont traveled through the United States, observing prisons and much more. The fruit of their trip was a study of prisons written largely by Beaumont and Tocqueville's observations on American society and government, published as *Democracy in America* (1835–1840). Tocqueville's keen analysis of American society in the latter work gained him immediate international recognition, and he received an honor unusual for a person of his age: election to the French Academy in 1841.[1]

In 1839 Tocqueville had already won election to the French Chamber of Deputies, which permitted him an active role in French politics. He joined the opposition to the government of King Louis Philippe and rejected especially the monarchy's restriction of the right to vote to wealthy Frenchmen. As a deputy, Tocqueville wrote a report on slavery that contributed to its abolition in France's colonies. Further, in a speech to the Chamber of Deputies in January 1848 during a period of political calm, his analysis of social conditions led him to predict the imminence of revolution. Indeed, it broke out less than four weeks later.

Despite his opposition to Louis Philippe, Tocqueville long had criticized revolution, perceiving a danger that individual liberty could be lost in revolutionary enthusiasm. Nevertheless, he gained election to the legislature of the new Second Republic created by the Revolution of 1848 and took part in the drafting of its constitution, arguing unsuccessfully against a directly elected president. He correctly foresaw the possibility that an ambitious demogogue could sway the people to gain election and threaten democracy. In December 1848, the victor in the presidential elections was Louis-Napoleon Bonaparte. This nephew of Emperor Napoleon I destroyed the republic in favor of an authoritarian empire, naming himself Emperor Napoleon III.[2] Tocqueville retired permanently from public life after Bonaparte's seizure of power, unable to support the new, undemocratic regime.

Returning to writing, Tocqueville produced two more important works before his death from tuberculosis in 1859. The first was his *Recollections* of the Revolution of 1848 and the Second Republic, based on his experiences in Paris in 1848 and 1849; the

1. **French Academy**: an association of scholars, writers, and intellectual leaders founded in 1635 to maintain the purity of the French language and establish standards of correct usage. The Academy has only forty members, called the "immortals," who vote to fill vacancies in their ranks caused by deaths of members. The dignity of such election is usually confined to persons of advanced years and long-proven merit.

2. **Emperor Napoleon III**: Bonapartists recognize the son of Emperor Napoleon I (ruled 1804–1814, 1815) as Napoleon II. But Napoleon II never actually ruled France. Aged three years when his father abdicated, he was taken to Vienna by his maternal grandfather, the Emperor of Austria, and spent his brief life there until his death in 1832.

Chapter 6

Two Programs

for Social

and Political

Change:

Liberalism

and Socialism

second was a study of the French Revolution of 1789, *The Old Regime and the Revolution*. Both works demonstrate again Tocqueville's liberal ideology and political astuteness.

In reading the selections by Tocqueville, you should ascertain the nature of his liberal thought. In Source l, what does Tocqueville identify as the main trend in historical development? What implications did this trend, which he found strong in America, have for Europe's existing class structure? What problems does Tocqueville in Source 2 find accompanying American democracy? What threatened the individual? What danger did centralized authority pose? In Source 3 Tocqueville treats revolution. Why does he see the danger of revolution diminishing with the advance of political democracy? Does he find revolution justified at times?

Sources 3 and 4 provide you with summations of Tocqueville's political thought and his view of the future. Under what sort of government had he spent his youth? What did it contribute to his political thought?

Born in Germany in 1818, thirteen years after Tocqueville, Karl Marx was the advocate of a very different political order, one of socialist revolution. The son of a successful attorney, Marx enjoyed an excellent education. He studied law first and then philosophy, a field in which he completed the doctoral degree that normally would have led to an academic career. Young Marx, however, was an advocate of political and economic democracy whose growing radicalism and atheism precluded such a career. When he turned instead to journalism, his ideas quickly offended the Prussian censors, who suppressed his newspaper.

Marx left Germany in 1843 for Paris, a city in which there was considerable discussion of utopian socialist ideas. Perhaps the greatest single event in Marx's two-year stay in Paris was his meeting with the young businessman, Friedrich Engels, with whom he was to enjoy a lifelong friendship. Engels shared Marx's socialist ideas, gave him intellectual support, and provided financial aid that allowed Marx to devote his life to writing.

French authorities expelled Marx for his radical political ideas in 1845. He moved to Brussels, Belgium, where he and Engels wrote *The Communist Manifesto*, an abstract declaration of war between the working class and their capitalist exploiters. Belgian authorities ultimately also expelled Marx. Back in Paris by March 1848, Marx, like Tocqueville, based his writings on some firsthand experience of the French Revolution of 1848. He also returned to Germany during 1848 before settling in England in 1849, where he spent the rest of his life.

Marx's poor command of spoken English and his illegible handwriting precluded his employment in white-collar jobs, and he and his family often lived in poverty when there were delays in Engels' generosity. In England Marx drew on his own excellent education, his knowledge of French socialist thought from his Paris days, and his daily research in the British Museum Library to refine his views on socialist revolution. He wrote studies of contemporary events, including *Class Struggles in*

France and *The Eighteenth Brumaire of Louis Bonaparte*, which dealt with the French Revolution of 1848 and its aftermath. The final product of his labors was the first volume of *Capital* (1867), a work Engels completed after Marx's death in 1883.

Marx was not to witness the implementation of his ideals during his life. His chief attempt at revolutionary organization, the International Workingmen's Association founded in 1864, broke up as a result of ideological disputes in 1876. After his death, of course, Marx's work became the basis for the international socialist movement.

As you read the selections by Marx, you should answer a number of questions to aid you in formulating your responses to the central problems of this chapter. Marx, like Tocqueville, had a definite view of history. Examine Source 5, a selection from *The Communist Manifesto*. What basic event, according to Marx, has characterized and shaped all histori-

cal development? Why does Marx find the latest phase of history, modern middle-class ("bourgeois") capitalism, particularly oppressive? What is Marx's view of the free economy advocated by nineteenth-century liberals?

In Source 6 Marx deals with the French Revolution of 1848. That revolution, of course, failed to bring the working classes to power. Who did it bring to power in France? In Source 7 we have Marx's statement of his ideals in government. Marx proclaims that he advocates democracy. How does that democracy differ from the kind of democracy acceptable to liberals like Tocqueville?

Now you are ready to read the selections with an eye to answering the main questions of this chapter: What were Tocqueville's and Marx's separate political visions? How did they hope to see their visions realized? How did these two thinkers and their liberal and socialist ideologies differ?

THE EVIDENCE

ALEXIS DE TOCQUEVILLE

Sources 1 and 2 from Alexis de Tocqueville, Democracy in America, *edited by J. P. Mayer and Max Lerner, translated by George Lawrence (New York: Harper & Row, 1965), pp. 3–5, 610–611, 613, 618; pp. 231–233, 665, 667–669.*

1. Tocqueville's View of History

No novelty in the United States struck me more vividly during my stay there than the equality of conditions. It was easy to see the immense influence of this basic fact on the whole course of society. It gives a particular turn to

Chapter 6

Two Programs

for Social

and Political

Change:

Liberalism

and Socialism

public opinion and a particular twist to the laws, new maxims to those who govern and particular habits to the governed.

I soon realized that the influence of this fact extends far beyond political mores and laws, exercising dominion over civil society as much as over the government; it creates opinions, gives birth to feelings, suggests customs, and modifies whatever it does not create.

So the more I studied American society, the more clearly I saw equality of conditions as the creative element from which each particular fact derived, and all my observations constantly returned to this nodal point.

Later, when I came to consider our own side of the Atlantic, I thought I could detect something analogous to what I had noticed in the New World. I saw an equality of conditions which, though it had not reached the extreme limits found in the United States, was daily drawing closer thereto; and that same democracy which prevailed over the societies of America seemed to me to be advancing rapidly toward power in Europe. . . .

A great democratic revolution is taking place in our midst; everybody sees it, but by no means everybody judges it in the same way. Some think it a new thing and, supposing it an accident, hope that they can still check it; others think it irresistible, because it seems to them the most continuous, ancient, and permanent tendency known to history. . . .

Running through the pages of our history, there is hardly an important event in the last seven hundred years which has not turned out to be advantageous for equality.

The Crusades and the English wars decimated the nobles and divided up their lands. Municipal institutions introduced democratic liberty into the heart of the feudal monarchy; the invention of firearms made villein and noble equal on the field of battle; printing offered equal resources to their minds; the post brought enlightenment to hovel and palace alike; Protestantism maintained that all men are equally able to find the path to heaven. America, once discovered, opened a thousand new roads to fortune and gave any obscure adventurer the chance of wealth and power.

If, beginning at the eleventh century, one takes stock of what was happening in France at fifty-year intervals, one finds each time that a double revolution has taken place in the state of society. The noble has gone down in the social scale, and the commoner gone up; as the one falls, the other rises. Each half century brings them closer, and soon they will touch.

And that is not something peculiar to France. Wherever one looks one finds the same revolution taking place throughout the Christian world.

WHY GREAT REVOLUTIONS WILL BECOME RARE

When a people has lived for centuries under a system of castes and classes, it can only reach a democratic state of society through a long series of more or less painful transformations. These must involve violent efforts and many vicissitudes, in the course of which property, opinions, and power are all subject to swift changes.

Even when this great revolution has come to an end, the revolutionary habits created thereby and by the profound disturbances thereon ensuing will long endure.

As all this takes place just at the time when social conditions are being leveled, the conclusion has been drawn that there must be a hidden connection and secret link between equality itself and revolutions, so that neither can occur without the other.

On this point reason and experience seem agreed.

Among a people where ranks are more or less equal, there is no apparent connection between men to hold them firmly in place. None of them has any permanent right or power to give commands, and none is bound by his social condition to obey. Each man, having some education and some resources, can choose his own road and go along separately from all the rest.

The same causes which make the citizens independent of each other daily prompt new and restless longings and constantly goad them on.

It therefore seems natural to suppose that in a democratic society ideas, things, and men must eternally be changing shape and position and that ages of democracy must be times of swift and constant transformation.

But is this in fact so? Does equality of social conditions habitually and permanently drive men toward revolutions? Does it contain some disturbing principle which prevents society from settling down and inclines the citizens constantly to change their laws, principles, and mores? I do not think so. The subject is important, and I ask the reader to follow my argument closely.

Almost every revolution which has changed the shape of nations has been made to consolidate or destroy inequality. Disregarding the secondary causes which have had some effect on the great convulsions in the world, you will almost always find that equality was at the heart of the matter. Either the poor were bent on snatching the property of the rich, or the rich were trying to hold the poor down. So, then, if you could establish a state of society in which each man had something to keep and little to snatch, you would have done much for the peace of the world. . . .

Such men are the natural enemies of violent commotion; their immobility keeps all above and below them quiet, and assures the stability of the body social.

I am not suggesting that they are themselves satisfied with their actual position or that they would feel any natural abhorrence toward a revolution if they could share the plunder without suffering the calamities; on the contrary, their eagerness to get rich is unparalleled, but their trouble is to know whom to despoil. The same social condition which prompts their longings restrains them within necessary limits. It gives men both greater freedom to change and less interest in doing so.

Not only do men in democracies feel no natural inclination for revolutions, but they are afraid of them.

Chapter 6

Two Programs

for Social

and Political

Change:

Liberalism

and Socialism

Any revolution is more or less a threat to property. Most inhabitants of a democracy have property. And not only have they got property, but they live in the conditions in which men attach most value to property. . . .

Therefore the more widely personal property is distributed and increased and the greater the number of those enjoying it, the less is a nation inclined to revolution.

Moreover, whatever a man's calling and whatever type of property he owns, one characteristic is common to all.

No one is fully satisfied with his present fortune, and all are constantly trying a thousand various ways to improve it. Consider any individual at any period of his life, and you will always find him preoccupied with fresh plans to increase his comfort. Do not talk to him about the interests and rights of the human race; that little private business of his for the moment absorbs all his thoughts, and he hopes that public disturbances can be put off to some other time.

This not only prevents them from causing revolutions but also deters them from wanting them. Violent political passions have little hold on men whose whole thoughts are bent on the pursuit of well-being. Their excitement about small matters makes them calm about great ones. . . .

There are also other, and even stronger, reasons which prevent any great change in the doctrines of a democratic people coming about easily. I have already indicated them at the beginning of this book.

Whereas, in such a nation, the influence of individuals is weak and almost nonexistent, the power of the mass over each individual mind is very great. . . .

Whenever conditions are equal, public opinion brings immense weight to bear on every individual. It surrounds, directs, and oppresses him. The basic constitution of society has more to do with this than any political laws. The more alike men are, the weaker each feels in the face of all. Finding nothing that raises him above their level and distinguishes him, he loses his self-confidence when he comes into collision with them. Not only does he mistrust his own strength, but even comes to doubt his own judgment, and he is brought very near to recognizing that he must be wrong when the majority hold the opposite view. There is no need for the majority to compel him; it convinces him.

Therefore, however powers within a democracy are organized and weighted, it will always be very difficult for a man to believe what the mass rejects and to profess what it condemns.

This circumstance is wonderfully favorable to the stability of beliefs.

2. Tocqueville on the Problems of Democracy

TYRANNY OF THE MAJORITY

I regard it as an impious and detestable maxim that in matters of government the majority of a people has the right to do everything, and nevertheless I place the origin of all powers in the will of the majority. Am I in contradiction with myself?

There is one law which has been made, or at least adopted, not by the majority of this or that people, but by the majority of all men. That law is justice.

Justice therefore forms the boundary to each people's right.

A nation is like a jury entrusted to represent universal society and to apply the justice which is its law. Should the jury representing society have greater power than that very society whose laws it applies?

Consequently, when I refuse to obey an unjust law, I by no means deny the majority's right to give orders; I only appeal from the sovereignty of the people to the sovereignty of the human race. . . .

Omnipotence in itself seems a bad and dangerous thing. I think that its exercise is beyond man's strength, whoever he be, and that only God can be omnipotent without danger because His wisdom and justice are always equal to His power. So there is no power on earth in itself so worthy of respect or vested with such a sacred right that I would wish to let it act without control and dominate without obstacles. So when I see the right and capacity to do all given to any authority whatsoever, whether it be called people or king, democracy or aristocracy, and whether the scene of action is a monarchy or a republic, I say: the germ of tyranny is there, and I will go look for other laws under which to live.

My greatest complaint against democratic government as organized in the United States is not, as many Europeans make out, its weakness, but rather its irresistible strength. What I find most repulsive in America is not the extreme freedom reigning there but the shortage of guarantees against tyranny.

When a man or a party suffers an injustice in the United States, to whom can he turn? To public opinion? That is what forms the majority. To the legislative body? It represents the majority and obeys it blindly. To the executive power? It is appointed by the majority and serves as its passive instrument. To the police? They are nothing but the majority under arms. A jury? The jury is the majority vested with the right to pronounce judgment; even the judges in certain states are elected by the majority. So, however iniquitous or unreasonable the measure which hurts you, you must submit.[3]

---

3. [Tocqueville's note:] At Baltimore during the War of 1812 there was a striking example of the excesses to which despotism of the majority may lead. At that time the war was very popular

[147]

Chapter 6

Two Programs

for Social

and Political

Change:

Liberalism

and Socialism

But suppose you were to have a legislative body so composed that it represented the majority without being necessarily the slave of its passions, an executive power having a strength of its own, and a judicial power independent of the other two authorities; then you would still have a democratic government, but there would be hardly any remaining risk of tyranny.

WHAT SORT OF DESPOTISM
DEMOCRATIC NATIONS HAVE TO FEAR

I noticed during my stay in the United States that a democratic state of society similar to that found there could lay itself peculiarly open to the establishment of a despotism. And on my return to Europe I saw how far most of our princes had made use of the ideas, feelings, and needs engendered by such a state of society to enlarge the sphere of their power. . . .

Our contemporaries are ever a prey to two conflicting passions: they feel the need of guidance, and they long to stay free. Unable to wipe out these two contradictory instincts, they try to satisfy them both together. Their imagination conceives a government which is unitary, protective, and all-powerful, but elected by the people. Centralization is combined with the sovereignty of the people. That gives them a chance to relax. They console themselves for being under schoolmasters by thinking that they have chosen them themselves. Each individual lets them put the collar on, for he sees that it is not a person, or a class of persons, but society itself which holds the end of the chain.

---

at Baltimore. A newspaper which came out in strong opposition to it aroused the indignation of the inhabitants. The people assembled, broke the presses, and attacked the house of the editors. An attempt was made to summon the militia, but it did not answer the appeal. Finally, to save the lives of these wretched men threatened by the fury of the public, they were taken to prison like criminals. This precaution was useless. During the night the people assembled again; the magistrates having failed to bring up the militia, the prison was broken open; one of the journalists was killed on the spot and the others left for dead; the guilty were brought before a jury and acquitted.

I once said to a Pennsylvanian: "Please explain to me why in a state founded by Quakers and renowned for its tolerance, freed Negroes are not allowed to use their rights as citizens? They pay taxes; is it not right that they should vote?"

"Do not insult us," he replied, "by supposing that our legislators would commit an act of such gross injustice and intolerance."

"So, with you, Negroes do have the right to vote?"

"Certainly."

"Then how was it that at the electoral college this morning I did not see a single one of them in the meeting?"

"That is not the fault of the law," said the American. "It is true that Negroes have the right to be present at elections, but they voluntarily abstain from appearing."

"That is extraordinarily modest of them."

"Oh! It is not that they are reluctant to go there, but they are afraid they may be maltreated. With us it sometimes happens that the law lacks force when the majority does not support it. Now, the majority is filled with the strongest prejudices against Negroes, and the magistrates do not feel strong enough to guarantee the rights granted to them by the lawmakers."

"What! The majority, privileged to make the law, wishes also to have the privilege of disobeying the law?"

Under this system the citizens quit their state of dependence just long enough to choose their masters and then fall back into it.

A great many people nowadays very easily fall in with this brand of compromise between administrative despotism and the sovereignty of the people. They think they have done enough to guarantee personal freedom when it is to the government of the state that they have handed it over. That is not good enough for me. I am much less interested in the question who my master is than in the fact of obedience. . . .

Subjection in petty affairs is manifest daily and touches all citizens indiscriminately. It never drives men to despair, but continually thwarts them and leads them to give up using their free will. It slowly stifles their spirits and enervates their souls, whereas obedience demanded only occasionally in matters of great moment brings servitude into play only from time to time, and its weight falls only on certain people. It does little good to summon those very citizens who have been made so dependent on the central power to choose the representatives of that power from time to time. However important, this brief and occasional exercise of free will will not prevent them from gradually losing the faculty of thinking, feeling, and acting for themselves, so that they will slowly fall below the level of humanity.

I must add that they will soon become incapable of using the one great privilege left to them. Those democratic peoples which have introduced freedom into the sphere of politics, while allowing despotism to grow in the administrative sphere, have been led into the strangest paradoxes. For the conduct of small affairs, where plain common sense is enough, they hold that the citizens are not up to the job. But they give these citizens immense prerogatives where the government of the whole state is concerned. They are turned alternatively into the playthings of the sovereign and into his masters, being either greater than kings or less than men. When they have tried all the different systems of election without finding one to suit them, they look surprised and go on seeking for another, as if the ills they see did not belong much more to the constitution of the country itself than to that of the electoral body.

It really is difficult to imagine how people who have entirely given up managing their own affairs could make a wise choice of those who are to do that for them. One should never expect a liberal, energetic, and wise government to originate in the votes of a people of servants.

Chapter 6

Two Programs

for Social

and Political

Change:

Liberalism

and Socialism

Source 3 from Alexis de Tocqueville, Democracy in America, *edited by J. P. Mayer and Max Lerner, translated by George Lawrence (New York: Harper & Row, 1965), pp. 674–675 (first part); and J. P. Mayer, editor, Alexander Teixeira De Mattos, translator,* The Recollections of Alexis de Tocqueville *(New York: Meridian, 1959), pp. 63, 68–71 (second part).*

3. Tocqueville on Revolution

[*The general danger of revolution*]

There are some habits, some ideas, and some vices which are peculiar to a state of revolution and which any prolonged revolution cannot fail to engender and spread, whatever may be in other respects its character, object, and field of action.

When in a brief space of time any nation has repeatedly changed its leaders, opinions, and laws, the men of that nation will in the end acquire a taste for change and grow accustomed to see all changes quickly brought about by the use of force. Then they will naturally conceive a scorn for those formalities of whose impotence they have been daily witnesses, and they will be impatient to tolerate the sway of rules which they have so often seen infringed.

As ordinary ideas of equity and morality are no longer enough to explain and justify all the innovations daily introduced by revolution, men fall back on the principle of social utility, political necessity is turned into a dogma, and men lose all scruples about freely sacrificing particular interests and trampling private rights beneath their feet in order more quickly to attain the public aim envisaged.

Such habits and ideas, which I call revolutionary since all revolutions give rise to them, are seen as much in aristocracies as among democratic peoples. But in the former case they are often less powerful and always less permanent, because there they come up against habits, ideas, faults, and eccentricities which are opposed to them. They therefore vanish of their own accord when the revolution is at an end and the nation recovers its former political ways. However, that is not always the case in democratic countries, for in them there is always a danger that revolutionary instincts will mellow and assume more regular shape without entirely disappearing, but will gradually be transformed into mores of government and administrative habits.

Hence, I know of no country in which revolutions are more dangerous than in a democracy, because apart from the accidental and ephemeral ills which they are ever bound to entail, there is always a danger of their becoming permanent, and one may almost say, eternal.

I think that resistance is sometimes justified and that rebellion can be legitimate. I cannot therefore lay it down as an absolute rule that men living in times of democracy should never make a revolution. But I think that they, more than others, have reason to hesitate before they embark on such an enterprise and that it is far better to put up with many inconveniences in their present state than to turn to so dangerous a remedy.

[150]

[*Tocqueville on the Revolution of 1848 in France*]

My Explanation of the 24th of February and My Thoughts as to Its Effects upon the Future[4]

And so the Monarchy of July[5] was fallen, fallen without a struggle, and before rather than beneath the blows of the victors, who were as astonished at their triumph as were the vanquished at their defeat. . . .

I had spent the best days of my youth amid a society which seemed to increase in greatness and prosperity as it increased in liberty; I had conceived the idea of a balanced, regulated liberty, held in check by religion, custom and law; the attractions of this liberty had touched me; it had become the passion of my life; I felt that I could never be consoled for its loss, and that I must renounce all hope of its recovery.

I had gained too much experience of men to be able to content myself with empty words; I knew that, if one great revolution is able to establish liberty in a country, a number of succeeding revolutions make all regular liberty impossible for very many years.

I could not yet know what would issue from this last revolution, but I was already convinced that it could give birth to nothing that would satisfy me; and I foresaw that, whatever might be the lot reserved for our posterity, our own fate was to drag on our lives miserably amid alternate reactions of licence and oppression. . . .

I spent the rest of the day with Ampère, who was my colleague at the Institute,[6] and one of my best friends. He came to discover what had become of me in the affray, and to ask himself to dinner. I wished at first to relieve myself by making him share my vexation. . . .

I saw that he not only did not enter into my view, but that he was disposed to take quite an opposite one. Seeing this, I was suddenly impelled to turn against Ampère all the feelings of indignation, grief and anger that had been accumulating in my heart since the morning; and I spoke to him with a violence of language which I have often since recalled with a certain shame, and which none but a friendship so sincere as his could have excused. I remember saying to him, *inter alia*.[7]

"You understand nothing of what is happening; you are judging like a poet or a Paris cockney.[8] You call this the triumph of liberty, when it is its

---

4. On Thursday, February 24, 1848, King Louis Philippe abdicated the throne in the face of the Paris revolution and fled the capital for England.

5. **July Monarchy**: the term often used for the regime of King Louis Philippe because that government came to power in July 1830.

6. **Institute**: Institut de France, the cultural institution including the French Academy, of which Tocqueville was a member. **Jean-Jacques Ampère**: (1800–1864), a philologist and professor of French literature.

7. **Inter alia**: Latin, among other things.

8. **Cockney**: generally, a person of the lower classes born in London's East End. In this context it refers to someone from that same class in Paris.

Chapter 6

Two Programs

for Social

and Political

Change:

Liberalism

and Socialism

final defeat. I tell you that the people which you so artlessly admire has just succeeded in proving that it is unfit and unworthy to live a life of freedom. Show me what experience has taught it! Where are the new virtues it has gained, the old vices it has laid aside? No, I tell you, it is always the same, as impatient, as thoughtless, as contemptuous of law and order, as easily led and as cowardly in the presence of danger as its fathers were before it. Time has altered it in no way, and has left it as frivolous in serious matters as it used to be in trifles."

After much vociferation we both ended by appealing to the future, that enlightened and upright judge who always, alas! arrives too late.

Source 4 from Roger Boesche, editor, James Toupin and Roger Boesche, translators, Alexis de Tocqueville: Selected Letters on Politics and Society *(Berkeley: University of California Press, 1985), pp. 112–113.*

4. Tocqueville's Ideals of Government (letter to Eugène Stoffels)[9]

I do not think that in France there is a man who is less revolutionary than I, nor one who has a more profound hatred for what is called the revolutionary spirit (a spirit which, parenthetically, is very easily combined with the love of an absolute government). What am I then? And what do I want? Let us distinguish, in order to understand each other better, between the end and the means. What is the end? What I want is not a republic, but a hereditary monarchy. I would even prefer it to be legitimate rather than elected like the one we have, because it would be stronger, especially externally. What I want is a central government energetic in its own sphere of action. Energy from the central government is even more necessary among a democratic people in whom the social force is more diffused than in an aristocracy. Besides our situation in Europe lays down as imperative law for us in what should be a thing of choice. But I wish that this central power had a clearly delineated sphere, that it were involved with what is a necessary part of its functions and not with everything in general, and that it were forever subordinated, in its tendency, to public opinion and to the legislative power that represents this public opinion. I believe that the central power can be invested with very great prerogatives, can be energetic and powerful in its sphere, and that at the same time provincial liberties can be well developed. I think that a government of this kind can exist, and that at the same time the majority of the nation itself can be involved with its own

9. **Eugène Stoffels (1805–1852):** an official in Metz, France and a friend of Tocqueville from their days together in secondary school.

affairs, that political life can be spread almost everywhere, the direct or indirect exercise of political rights can be quite extensive. I wish that the general principles of government were liberal, that the largest possible part were left to the action of individuals, to personal initiative. I believe that all these things are compatible; even more, I am profoundly convinced that there will never be order and tranquility except when they are successfully combined.

As for the means: with all those who admit that we must make our way gradually toward this goal, I am very much in accord. I am the first to admit that it is necessary to proceed slowly, with precaution, with legality. My conviction is that our current institutions are sufficient for reaching the result I have in view. Far, then, from wanting people to violate the laws, I profess an almost superstitious respect for the laws. But I wish that the laws would tend little and gradually toward the goal I have just indicated, instead of making powerless and dangerous efforts to turn back. I wish that the government would itself prepare mores and practices so that people would do without it in many cases in which its intervention is still necessary or invoked without necessity. I wish that citizens were introduced into public life to the extent that they are believed capable of being useful in it, instead of seeking to keep them away from it at all costs. I wish finally that people knew where they wanted to go, and that they advanced toward it prudently instead of proceeding aimlessly as they have been doing almost constantly for twenty years.

KARL MARX

Source 5 from Karl Marx and Friedrich Engels, The Communist Manifesto, *translated by Samuel Moore (New York: Penguin, 1977), pp. 79–83, 85–92, 95–96.*

5. Marx's View of History

1

BOURGEOIS AND PROLETARIANS[10]

The history of all hitherto existing society is the history of class struggles.

Freeman and slave, patrician and plebeian, lord and serf, guild-master[11] and journeyman, in a word, oppressor and oppressed, stood in constant opposition to one another, carried on an uninterrupted, now hidden, now

10. **bourgeois, proletarian**: "By bourgeoisie is meant the class of modern Capitalist, owners of the means of social production and employers of wage labour. By proletariat, the class of modern wage-labourers who, having no means of production of their own, are reduced to selling their labour power in order to live." (note by Engels to the English edition, 1888)

11. **guild-master**: "that is, a full member of a guild, a master within, not a head of a guild" (note by Engels to the English edition, 1888).

Chapter 6
Two Programs
for Social
and Political
Change:
Liberalism
and Socialism

open fight, a fight that each time ended, either in a revolutionary reconstitution of society at large, or in the common ruin of the contending classes.

In the earlier epochs of history, we find almost everywhere a complicated arrangement of society into various orders, a manifold gradation of social rank. In ancient Rome we have patricians, knights, plebeians, slaves; in the Middle Ages, feudal lords, vassals, guild-masters, journeymen, apprentices, serfs; in almost all of these classes, again, subordinate gradations.

The modern bourgeois society that has sprouted from the ruins of feudal society has not done away with class antagonisms. It has but established new classes, new conditions of oppression, new forms of struggle in place of the old ones.

Our epoch, the epoch of the bourgeoisie, possesses, however, this distinctive feature: it has simplified the class antagonisms. Society as a whole is more and more splitting up into two great hostile camps, into two great classes directly facing each other: Bourgeoisie and Proletariat.

From the serfs of the Middle Ages sprang the chartered burghers of the earliest towns. From these burgesses the first elements of the bourgeoisie were developed.

The discovery of America, the rounding of the Cape, opened up fresh ground for the rising bourgeoisie. The East-Indian and Chinese markets, the colonization of America, trade with the colonies, the increase in the means of exchange and in commodities generally, gave to commerce, to navigation, to industry, an impulse never before known, and thereby, to the revolutionary element in the tottering feudal society, a rapid development.

The feudal system of industry, under which industrial production was monopolized by closed guilds, now no longer sufficed for the growing wants of the new markets. The manufacturing system took its place. The guild-masters were pushed on one side by the manufacturing middle class; division of labour between the different corporate guilds vanished in the face of division of labour in each single workshop.

Meantime the markets kept ever growing, the demand ever rising. Even manufacture no longer sufficed. Thereupon, steam and machinery revolutionized industrial production. The place of manufacture was taken by the giant, Modern Industry, the place of the industrial middle class, by industrial millionaires, the leaders of whole industrial armies, the modern bourgeois.

Modern industry has established the world market, for which the discovery of America paved the way. This market has given an immense development to commerce, to navigation, to communication by land. This development has, in its turn, reacted on the extension of industry; and in proportion as industry, commerce, navigation, railways extended, in the same proportion the bourgeoisie developed, increased its capital, and pushed into the background every class handed down from the Middle Ages.

We see, therefore, how the modern bourgeoisie is itself the product of a long course of development, of a series of revolutions in the modes of production and of exchange.

[154]

Each step in the development of the bourgeoisie was accompanied by a corresponding political advance of that class. An oppressed class under the sway of the feudal nobility, an armed and self-governing association in the medieval commune;[12] here independent urban republic (as in Italy and Germany), there taxable "third estate" of the monarchy (as in France), afterwards, in the period of manufacture proper, serving either the semi-feudal or the absolute monarchy as a counterpoise against the nobility, and, in fact, corner-stone of the great monarchies in general, the bourgeoisie has at last, since the establishment of Modern Industry and of the world market, conquered for itself, in the modern representative State, exclusive political sway. The executive of the modern State is but a committee for managing the common affairs of the whole bourgeoisie.

The bourgeoisie, historically, has played a most revolutionary part.

The bourgeoisie, wherever it has got the upper hand, has put an end to all feudal, patriarchal, idyllic relations. It has pitilessly torn asunder the motley feudal ties that bound man to his "natural superiors," and has left remaining no other nexus between man and man than naked self-interest, than callous "cash payment." It has drowned the most heavenly ecstasies of religious fervour, of chivalrous enthusiasm, of philistine sentimentalism, in the icy water of egotistical calculation. It has resolved personal worth into exchange value, and in place of the numberless indefeasible chartered freedoms, has set up that single, unconscionable freedom—Free Trade. In one word, for exploitation, veiled by religious and political illusions, it has substituted naked, shameless, direct, brutal exploitation.

The bourgeoisie has stripped of its halo every occupation hitherto honoured and looked up to with reverent awe. It has converted the physician, the lawyer, the priest, the poet, the man of science, into its paid wage-labourers.

The bourgeoisie has torn away from the family its sentimental veil, and has reduced the family relation to a mere money relation. . . .

The bourgeoisie cannot exist without constantly revolutionizing the instruments of production, and thereby the relations of production, and with them the whole relations of society. Conservation of the old modes of production in unaltered form, was, on the contrary, the first condition of existence for all earlier industrial classes. Constant revolutionizing of production, uninterrupted disturbance of all social conditions, everlasting uncertainty and agitation distinguish the bourgeois epoch from all earlier ones. All fixed, fast-frozen relations, with their train of ancient and venerable prejudices and

12. **commune**: "the name taken, in France, by the nascent towns even before they had conquered from their feudal lords and masters local self-government and political rights as the 'Third Estate.' Generally speaking, for the economical development of the bourgeoisie, England is here taken as the typical country; for its political development, France" (note by Engels to the English edition, 1888). "This was the name given their urban communities by the townsmen of Italy and France, after they had purchased or wrested their initial rights of self-government from their feudal lords" (note by Engels to the German edition, 1890).

Chapter 6

Two Programs

for Social

and Political

Change:

Liberalism

and Socialism

opinions are swept away, all new-formed ones become antiquated before they can ossify. All that is solid melts into air, all that is holy is profaned, and man is at last compelled to face with sober senses, his real conditions of life, and his relations with his kind.

The need of a constantly expanding market for its products chases the bourgeoisie over the whole surface of the globe. It must nestle everywhere, settle everywhere, establish connexions everywhere. . . .

Modern bourgeois society with its relations of production, of exchange and of property, a society that has conjured up such gigantic means of production and of exchange, is like the sorcerer, who is no longer able to control the powers of the nether world whom he has called up by his spells. For many a decade past the history of industry and commerce is but the history of the revolt of modern productive forces against modern conditions of production, against the property relations that are the conditions for the existence of the bourgeoisie and of its rule. It is enough to mention the commercial crises that by their periodical return put on its trial, each time more threateningly, the existence of the entire bourgeois society. In these crises a great part not only of the existing products, but also of the previously created productive forces, are periodically destroyed. In these crises there breaks out an epidemic that, in all earlier epochs, would have seemed an absurdity—the epidemic of over-production. . . .

And how does the bourgeoisie get over these crises? On the one hand by enforced destruction of a mass of productive forces; on the other, by the conquest of new markets, and by the more thorough exploitation of the old ones. That is to say, by paving the way for more extensive and more destructive crises, and by diminishing the means whereby crises are prevented.

The weapons with which the bourgeoisie felled feudalism to the ground are now turned against the bourgeoisie itself.

But not only has the bourgeoisie forged the weapons that bring death to itself; it has also called into existence the men who are to wield those weapons—the modern working class—the proletarians.

In proportion as the bourgeoisie, i.e., capital, is developed, in the same proportion is the proletariat, the modern working class, developed—a class of labourers, who live only so long as they find work, and who find work only so long as their labour increases capital. These labourers, who must sell themselves piecemeal, are a commodity, like every other article of commerce, and are consequently exposed to all the vicissitudes of competition, to all the fluctuations of the market.

Owing to the extensive use of machinery and to division of labour, the work of the proletarians has lost all individual character, and, consequently, all charm for the workman. He becomes an appendage of the machine, and it is only the most simple, most monotonous, and most easily acquired knack, that is required of him. Hence, the cost of production of a workman is restricted, almost entirely, to the means of subsistence that he requires for his maintenance, and for the propagation of his race. . . .

Modern industry has converted the little workshop of the patriarchal master into the great factory of the industrial capitalist. Masses of labourers, crowded into the factory, are organized like soldiers. As privates of the industrial army they are placed under the command of a perfect hierarchy of officers and sergeants. Not only are they slaves of the bourgeois class, and of the bourgeois State; they are daily and hourly enslaved by the machine, by the overlooker, and, above all, by the individual bourgeois manufacturer himself. The more openly this despotism proclaims gain to be its end and aim, the more petty, the more hateful and the more embittering it is. . . .

The proletariat goes through various stages of development. With its birth begins its struggle with the bourgeoisie. At first the contest is carried on by individual labourers, then by the work-people of a factory, then by the operatives of one trade, in one locality, against the individual bourgeois who directly exploits them. They direct their attacks not against the bourgeois conditions of production, but against the instruments of production themselves; they destroy imported wares that compete with their labour, they smash to pieces machinery, they set factories ablaze, they seek to restore by force the vanished status of the workman of the Middle Ages.

At this stage the labourers still form an incoherent mass scattered over the whole country, and broken up by their mutual competition. If anywhere they unite to form more compact bodies, this is not yet the consequence of their own active union, but of the union of the bourgeoisie, which class, in order to attain its own political ends, is compelled to set the whole proletariat in motion, and is moreover yet, for a time, able to do so. At this stage, therefore, the proletarians do not fight their enemies, but the enemies of their enemies, the remnants of absolute monarchy, the landowners, the non-industrial bourgeois, the petty bourgeoisie. Thus the whole historical movement is concentrated in the hands of the bourgeoisie; every victory so obtained is a victory for the bourgeoisie.

But with the development of industry the proletariat not only increases in number; it becomes concentrated in greater masses, its strength grows, and it feels that strength more. The various interests and conditions of life within the ranks of the proletariat are more and more equalized, in proportion as machinery obliterates all distinctions of labour, and nearly everywhere reduces wages to the same low level. The growing competition among the bourgeois, and the resulting commercial crises, make the wages of the workers ever more fluctuating. The unceasing improvement of machinery, ever more rapidly developing, makes their livelihood more and more precarious; the collisions between individual workmen and individual bourgeois take more and more the character of collisions between two classes. Thereupon the workers begin to form combinations (Trades Unions) against the bourgeois; they club together in order to keep up the rate of wages; they found permanent associations in order to make provision beforehand for these occasional revolts. Here and there the contest breaks out into riots.

[157]

Chapter 6

Two Programs

for Social

and Political

Change:

Liberalism

and Socialism

Now and then the workers are victorious, but only for a time. The real fruit of their battles lies, not in the immediate result, but in the ever-expanding union of the workers. This union is helped on by the improved means of communication that are created by modern industry and that place the workers of different localities in contact with one another. It was just this contact that was needed to centralize the numerous local struggles, all of the same character, into one national struggle between classes. But every class struggle is a political struggle. And that union, to attain which the burghers of the Middle Ages, with their miserable highways, required centuries, the modern proletarians, thanks to railways, achieve in a few years. . . .

Of all the classes that stand face to face with the bourgeoisie today, the proletariat alone is a really revolutionary class. The other classes decay and finally disappear in the face of modern industry; the proletariat is its special and essential product.

The lower middle class, the small manufacturer, the shopkeeper, the artisan, the peasant, all these fight against the bourgeoisie, to save from extinction their existence as fractions of the middle class. They are therefore not revolutionary, but conservative. Nay more, they are reactionary, for they try to roll back the wheel of history. . . .

In the conditions of the proletariat, those of old society at large are already virtually swamped. The proletarian is without property; his relation to his wife and children has no longer anything in common with the bourgeois family relations; modern industrial labour, modern subjection to capital, the same in England as in France, in America as in Germany, has stripped him of every trace of national character. Law, morality, religion, are to him so many bourgeois prejudices, behind which lurk in ambush just as many bourgeois interests.

All the preceding classes that got the upper hand sought to fortify their already acquired status by subjecting society at large to their conditions of appropriation. The proletarians cannot become masters of the productive forces of society, except by abolishing their own previous mode of appropriation, and thereby also every other previous mode of appropriation. They have nothing of their own to secure and to fortify; their mission is to destroy all previous securities for, and insurances of, individual property.

All previous historical movements were movements of minorities, or in the interest of minorities. The proletarian movement is the self-conscious, independent movement of the immense majority, in the interest of the immense majority. The proletariat, the lowest stratum of our present society, cannot stir, cannot raise itself up, without the whole superincumbent strata of official society being sprung into the air.

2
PROLETARIANS AND COMMUNISTS

In what relation do the Communists stand to the proletarians as a whole?

The Communists do not form a separate party opposed to other working-class parties.

They have no interests separate and apart from those of the proletariat as a whole.

They do not set up any sectarian principles of their own, by which to shape and mould the proletarian movement.

The Communists are distinguished from the other working-class parties by this only: 1. In the national struggles of the proletarians of the different countries, they point out and bring to the front the common interests of the entire proletariat, independently of all nationality. 2. In the various stages of development which the struggle of the working class against the bourgeoisie has to pass through, they always and everywhere represent the interests of the movement as a whole.

The Communists, therefore, are on the one hand, practically, the most advanced and resolute section of the working-class parties of every country, that section which pushes forward all others; on the other hand, theoretically, they have over the great mass of the proletariat the advantage of clearly understanding the line of march, the conditions, and the ultimate general results of the proletarian movement.

The immediate aim of the Communists is the same as that of all the other proletarian parties: formation of the proletariat into a class, overthrow of the bourgeois supremacy, conquest of political power by the proletariat.

The theoretical conclusions of the Communists are in no way based on ideas or principles that have been invented, or discovered, by this or that would-be universal reformer.

They merely express, in general terms, actual relations springing from an existing class struggle, from a historical movement going on under our very eyes. The abolition of existing property relations is not at all a distinctive feature of Communism.

All property relations in the past have continually been subject to historical change consequent upon the change in historical conditions.

The French Revolution, for example, abolished feudal property in favour of bourgeois property.

The distinguishing feature of Communism is not the abolition of property generally, but the abolition of bourgeois property. But modern bourgeois private property is the final and most complete expression of the system of producing and appropriating products, that is based on class antagonisms, on the exploitation of the many by the few.

In this sense, the theory of the Communists may be summed up in the single sentence: Abolition of private property.

Chapter 6

Two Programs

for Social

and Political

Change:

Liberalism

and Socialism

Source 6 from Karl Marx, The Class Struggles in France (1848–1850), *edited by E. P. Dutt (New York: International Publishers, 1964), pp. 33–34, 39–40, 50–52, 55, 56, 58–59.*

6. Marx on the Revolution of 1848 in Paris

1
FROM FEBRUARY TO JUNE 1848

With the exception of a few short chapters, every important part of the annals of the revolution from 1848 to 1849 carries the heading: Defeat of the revolution!

But what succumbed in these defeats was not the revolution. It was the pre-revolutionary traditional appendages, results of social relationships, which had not yet come to the point of sharp class antagonisms—persons, illusions, conceptions, projects, from which the revolutionary party before the February Revolution was not free, from which it could be freed, not by the victory of February, but only by a series of defeats.

In a word: revolutionary advance made headway not by its immediate tragi-comic achievements, but on the contrary by the creation of a powerful, united counter-revolution, by the creation of an opponent, by fighting whom the party of revolt first ripened into a real revolutionary party.

To prove this is the task of the following pages.

I. THE DEFEAT OF JUNE 1848

After the July Revolution, when the Liberal banker, Laffitte, led his godfather, the Duke of Orleans, in triumph to the Hôtel de Ville,[13] he let fall the words: "From now on the bankers will rule." Laffitte had betrayed the secret of the revolution. . . .

It was not the French bourgeoisie that ruled under Louis Philippe, but a fraction of it, bankers, Stock Exchange kings, railway kings, owners of coal and iron works and forests, a section of landed proprietors that rallied around them—the so-called finance aristocracy. It sat on the throne, it dictated laws in the Chambers, it conferred political posts from cabinet portfolios to the tobacco bureau.

The real industrial bourgeoisie formed part of the official opposition, *i.e.,* it was represented only as a minority in the Chambers. . . .

The petty bourgeoisie of all degrees, and the peasantry also, were completely excluded from political power. Finally, in the official opposition or

13. **Hôtel de Ville**: City Hall. The Duke of Orleans emerged from the July Revolution as King Louis Philippe.

entirely outside the *pays légal*,[14] there were the ideological representatives and spokesmen of the above classes, their savants, lawyers, doctors, etc., in a word: their so-called talents. . . .

The Provisional Government which emerged from the February barricades, necessarily mirrored in its composition the different parties which shared in the victory.[15] It could not be anything but a compromise between the different classes which together had overturned the July throne, but whose interests were mutually antagonistic. A large majority of its members consisted of representatives of the bourgeoisie. . . . The working class had only two representatives, Louis Blanc and Albert. . . .

Up to noon on February 25, the republic had not yet been proclaimed; on the other hand, the whole of the Ministries had already been divided among the bourgeois elements of the Provisional Government and among the generals, bankers and lawyers of the *National*. But the workers were this time determined not to put up with any swindling like that of July 1830. They were ready to take up the fight anew and to enforce the republic by force of arms. With this message, Raspail betook himself to the Hôtel de Ville. In the name of the Parisian proletariat he commanded the Provisional Government to proclaim the republic; if this order of the people were not fulfilled within two hours, he would return at the head of 200,000 men. The bodies of the fallen were scarcely cold, the barricades were not yet cleared away, the workers not yet disarmed, and the only force which could be opposed to them was the National Guard. Under these circumstances the prudent state doubts and juristic scruples of conscience of the Provisional Government suddenly vanished. The interval of two hours had not expired before all the walls of Paris were resplendent with the tremendous historical words:

République française! Liberté, Egalité, Fraternité![16] . . .

The proletariat, by dictating the republic to the Provisional Government and through the Provisional Government to the whole of France, stepped into the foreground forthwith as an independent party, but at the same time

14. **Pays legal**: literally, "legal country." Here Marx refers to the fact that the monarchy established by the July Revolution created a very limited right to vote. One had to possess a substantial amount of property to qualify for the right to vote, with the result that only 170,000 men, out of a population of about 30,000,000, qualified to vote for the Chamber of Deputies in the 1830s.

15. In his work, *The Eighteenth of Brumaire of Louis Bonaparte* (New York: International Publishers, 1935), p. 101, Marx referred to the participation of a broad spectrum of social groups in the February Revolution as the "Universal brotherhood swindle." This means that, in his view, the lower classes were seduced into revolutionary action by unfilled bourgeois promises of democracy in the postrevolutionary government.

16. **Republique française: Liberté, Egalité, Fraternité**: "The French Republic: Liberty, Equality, Fraternity," the motto of the Revolution of 1789.

Chapter 6

Two Programs

for Social

and Political

Change:

Liberalism

and Socialism

challenged the whole of bourgeois France to enter the lists against it. What it won was the terrain for the fight for its revolutionary emancipation, but in no way this emancipation itself! . . .

A hundred thousand workers thrown on the streets through the crisis and the revolution were enrolled by the Minister Marie in so-called National *Ateliers*![17] Under this grand name was hidden nothing but the employment of the workers on tedious, monotonous, unproductive earthworks at a wage of 23 sous.[18] English *workhouses* in the open—that is what these National *Ateliers* were. . . .

All the discontent, all the ill humour of the petty bourgeois was simultaneously directed against these National *Ateliers*, the common target. With real fury they reckoned up the sums that the proletarian loafers swallowed, while their own situation became daily more unbearable. A state pension for sham labour, that is socialism! they growled to themselves. They sought the basis of their misery in the National *Ateliers*, the declarations of the Luxembourg,[19] the marches of the workers through Paris. And no one was more fantastic about the alleged machinations of the Communists than the petty bourgeoisie who hovered hopelessly on the brink of bankruptcy[20]. . . .

In the National Assembly all France sat in judgment on the Paris proletariat. It broke immediately with the social illusions of the February Revolution; it roundly proclaimed the bourgeois republic, nothing but the bourgeois republic. It at once excluded the representatives of the proletariat, Louis Blanc and Albert, from the Executive Commission appointed by it; it threw out the proposal of a special Labour Ministry,[21] and received with stormy applause the statement of the Minister Trélat: "The question is merely one of bringing labour back to its old conditions."

17. **Atelier**: workshop. The National Ateliers were government-funded projects to provide work to the unemployed.

18. **23 sous**: The sou was a French coin worth 5 centimes (100 centimes to 1 franc). Thus Marx cites a wage of a little over 1 **franc** per day for the labor. Initially, wages in the workshops were 2 francs per day for laborers and 1 franc per day for those unemployed for whom labor could not be found. Even 2 francs per day was less than the usual wage for skilled artisans like tailors and shoemakers.

19. **The Luxembourg**: the revolutionary government established a commission to study labor problems; chaired by the socialist Louis Blanc and composed of representatives of various trades, it was headquartered in the Luxembourg Palace. The commission secured the government's enactment of a ten-hour workday in Paris and a twelve-hour workday in the provinces. This reform would have reduced most workers' hours of labor had it been enforced by government supervision.

20. One of the causes of the Revolution of 1848 was a general European economic crisis in 1846–1848 that had its origins in agricultural problems. Potato harvests were disastrously deficient in Ireland and other countries in 1845–1848 because of a blight. Weather factors conspired to reduce wheat harvests in these same years, creating rising food prices and general distress in the economies of most European countries.

21. The National Assembly, elected by universal manhood suffrage in April 1848, had a moderate to conservative majority: of the 900 members, about 500 were moderate republicans and 300 were monarchists. In such a chamber, proposals for a Ministry of Labor and for a guaranteed right to work proposed by Louis Blanc gained little support.

But all this was not enough. The February republic was won by the workers with the passive support of the bourgeoisie. The proletarians regarded themselves, and rightly, as the victors of February, and they made the proud claims of victors. They had to be vanquished on the streets, they had to be shown that they were worsted as soon as they fought, not with the bourgeoisie, but against the bourgeoisie. Just as the February republic, with its socialist concessions, required a battle of the proletariat, united with the bourgeoisie, against monarchy, so a second battle was necessary in order to sever the republic from the socialist concessions, in order to officially work out the bourgeois republic as dominant. The bourgeoisie had to refute the demands of the proletariat with arms in its hands. And the real birthplace of the bourgeois republic is not the February victory; it is the June defeat. . . .

The Executive Commission began by making entry into the National *Ateliers* more difficult, by turning the day wage into a piece wage, by banishing workers not born in Paris to Sologne, ostensibly for the construction of earthworks. These earthworks were only a rhetorical formula with which to gloss over their expulsion, as the workers, returning disillusioned, announced to their comrades. Finally, on June 21, a decree appeared in the *Moniteur*,[22] which ordered the forcible expulsion of all unmarried workers from the National *Ateliers*, or their enrolment in the army.

The workers were left no choice: they had to starve or start to fight. They answered on June 22 with the tremendous insurrection in which the first great battle was joined between the two classes that split modern society. It was a fight for the preservation or annihilation of the bourgeois order. The veil that shrouded the republic was torn to pieces.

It is well known how the workers, with unexampled bravery and talent, without chiefs, without a common plan, without means and, for the most part, lacking weapons, held in check for five days the army, the Mobile Guard, the Parisian National Guard, and the National Guard that streamed in from the provinces. It is well known how the bourgeoisie compensated itself for the mortal anguish it underwent by unheard of brutality, and massacred over 3,000 prisoners.[23] . . .

By making its burial place the birth place of the bourgeois republic, the proletariat compelled the latter to come out forthwith in its pure form as the state whose admitted object is to perpetuate the rule of capital, the slavery of labour. With constant regard to the scarred, irreconcilable, unconquerable enemy—unconquerable because its existence is the condition of its own life—bourgeois rule, freed from all fetters, was bound to turn immediately into bourgeois terrorism. With the proletariat removed for the time being from

---

22. **Moniteur**: a journal that published parliamentary debate and government decrees.

23. Marx does not wildly exaggerate the losses here. Casualties in the actual fighting and in the retribution following it were high.

Chapter 6

Two Programs

for Social

and Political

Change:

Liberalism

and Socialism

the stage and bourgeois dictatorship recognised officially, the middle sections, in the mass, had more and more to side with the proletariat as their position became more unbearable and their antagonism to the bourgeoisie became more acute. Just as earlier in its upsurge, so now they had to find in its defeat the cause of their misery. . . .

Only through the defeat of June, therefore, were all the conditions created under which France can seize the initiative of the European revolution. Only after baptism in the blood of the June insurgents did the tricolour[24] become the flag of the European revolution—the red flag.

And we cry: *The revolution is dead!—Long live the revolution!*

Source 7 from Karl Marx and Friedrich Engels, The Communist Manifesto, *translated by Samuel Moore (New York: Penguin, 1977), pp. 104–105.*

7. Marx's Ideals of Government and Economy

We have seen above, that the first step in the revolution by the working class, is to raise the proletariat to the position of ruling class, to win the battle of democracy.

The proletariat will use its political supremacy to wrest, by degrees, all capital from the bourgeoisie, to centralize all instruments of production in the hands of the State, i.e., of the proletariat organized as the ruling class; and to increase the total of productive forces as rapidly as possible.

Of course, in the beginning, this cannot be effected except by means of despotic inroads on the rights of property, and on the conditions of bourgeois production; by means of measures, therefore, which appear economically insufficient and untenable, but which, in the course of the movement, outstrip themselves, necessitate further inroads upon the old social order, and are unavoidable as a means of entirely revolutionizing the mode of production.

These measures will of course be different in different countries.

Nevertheless, in the most advanced countries, the following will be pretty generally applicable:

1. Abolition of property in land and application of all rents of land to public purposes.

2. A heavy progressive or graduated income tax.

3. Abolition of all right of inheritance.

4. Confiscation of the property of all emigrants and rebels.

5. Centralization of credit in the hands of the State, by means of a national bank with State capital and an exclusive monopoly.

24. **tricolor**: the three-colored flag, composed of vertical stripes of blue, white, and red, adopted in the 1789 Revolution and today the flag of France.

6. Centralization of the means of communication and transport in the hands of the State.

7. Extension of factories and instruments of production owned by the State; the bringing into cultivation of wastelands, and the improvement of the soil generally in accordance with a common plan.

8. Equal liability of all to labour. Establishment of industrial armies, especially for agriculture.

9. Combination of agriculture with manufacturing industries; gradual abolition of the distinction between town and country, by a more equable distribution of the population over the country.

10. Free education for all children in public schools. Abolition of children's factory labour in its present form. Combination of education with industrial production, &c., &c.

When, in the course of development, class distinctions have disappeared, and all production has been concentrated in the whole nation, the public power will lose its political character. Political power, properly so called, is merely the organized power of one class for oppressing another. If the proletariat during its contest with the bourgeoisie is compelled, by the force of circumstances, to organize itself as a class, if, by means of a revolution, it makes itself the ruling class, and, as such, sweeps away by force the old conditions of production, then it will, along with these conditions, have swept away the conditions for the existence of class antagonisms and of classes generally, and will thereby have abolished its own supremacy as a class.

In place of the old bourgeois society, with its classes and class antagonisms, we shall have an association, in which the free development of each is the condition for the free development of all.

QUESTIONS TO CONSIDER

Tocqueville and Marx pose different responses to many of the same issues in the selections presented in this chapter. Your basic task in answering the main questions of this chapter is to compare their ideas.

Central to the thought of both men is a certain vision of historical evolution. Indeed, Marx called himself a "scientific socialist" because, in his view, he had discovered the immutable course of historical development. What was this historical process for Marx? What patterns of history did Tocqueville identify? As you continue your study of modern Western history in this course, consider which of these thinkers' ideas seem most adequately to have predicted the political and economic development of the West.

Both Marx and Tocqueville address the problem of revolution in the selections that you have read. First consider Tocqueville. What threats to democracy did he see emerging in the West? Why did he believe that revo-

Chapter 6

Two Programs

for Social

and Political

Change:

Liberalism

and Socialism

lution was not likely to be a threat to democracy? What dangers, according to Tocqueville, did revolution pose when it did erupt? Do Tocqueville's liberal principles admit any circumstances under which society should resort to revolution as a means of change? Recall Tocqueville's attitude toward the government of King Louis Philippe in Source 3. Why did Tocqueville oppose the Revolution of 1848 despite this view?

Let us now analyze Marx's ideas on revolution. Examine the historical role for revolution that Marx believed he had found. Why does Marx see the middle class, those who owned the factories and embraced liberal ideas, as revolutionary? In what ways, according to Marx, was capitalism sowing the seeds of its destruction? What class would challenge the factory owners in revolution? What vision of the future did that class have, according to Marx? Did they want the political democracy Tocqueville was prepared to accept or a broader reorganization of society? How did Marx and Tocqueville differ in their views of the desirability of revolution?

Both authors also wrote on the same revolution, the French uprising of 1848, providing us a further opportunity to contrast their views. As your study of the 1848 revolutions no doubt has demonstrated, it is impossible to consider the uprisings of that year a success. Whether revolutionaries' goals were nationalist or liberal, the revolutions ended everywhere in defeat. This was certainly the case in France, where the conflict of June 1848 between the govern-

ment of the Second Republic and the Parisian unemployed created the political climate for the election of Louis-Napoleon Bonaparte.

How did each author view the revolution of 1848? What guiding emotion do you detect in Tocqueville's *Recollections* of February 24, 1848? What was its source? In formulating your answer, consult the selection in which Tocqueville discusses general aspects of revolution and expresses his ideals in government. What is Marx's view of the failure of the June 1848 revolt? Why was the victory that emerged in 1848 an essential step for Marx toward the final revolution?

Finally, let us compare the political and economic ideals advocated by the liberal Tocqueville and the socialist Marx. Your task here is made more challenging by the assertion of both these political thinkers that they advocated democracy. To understand the differences between them, review their writings to determine how each defined "democracy." Is Tocqueville's conception of democracy expressed primarily in terms of political participation? Is there any room in his thought for social democracy, that is, a more egalitarian distribution of society's wealth? How does Tocqueville characterize his political thought in Source 4? Recall France's history of recurring revolution. Why might he accept a monarch in Europe and an elected head of government in America?

Sources 5 through 7 express especially clearly Marx's democratic philosophy. Did Marx believe in political democracy? How is he concerned with social democracy? Who would control property, credit, and the means of production in his ideal society? What answers does Marx have to such abuses of industrialization as child labor? What impact would his system have on the lives of its citizens?

Finally, consider the two thinkers' views on the role of government. What role does Tocqueville assign to the government in the lives of its citizens? How does that view mark him as a nineteenth-century liberal? What sort of post-revolutionary government does Marx envision? How does it differ from Tocqueville's ideal? Are there areas where Marx and Tocqueville might agree?

With answers to these fairly specific questions in mind, you are now ready to answer the general questions presented earlier in this chapter: What visions of the future did liberals and socialists propose? How did they hope to realize their ideals? How did their ideologies differ?

EPILOGUE

The selections in this chapter present two contrasting nineteenth-century visions of Western society. Most of what you have read appeared around the middle of the nineteenth century, much of it in the midst of the West's last general outbreak of revolution in 1848. Because both authors wrote about that event and had a definite view of revolution, perhaps it is appropriate to examine briefly how their predictions fared after 1848.

The events of 1848 shook Tocqueville's faith in the growth of democracy founded on limited government and increasing equality of property as well as in political stability and evolutionary change based on respect for the rule of law. Indeed, he wrote to his friend Eugène Stoffels of events in France with considerable despair in 1850:

What is clear to me is that for sixty years we have fooled ourselves by be-lieving that we could see the end of revolution. The revolution was thought to have finished at 18 *brumaire*, the same was thought in 1814; I thought myself in 1830 that it could well be at an end . . . I was wrong. It is clear today . . . not only that we have not seen the end of the immense revolution which started before our time, but that today's child will probably not see it.[25]

If Tocqueville died in 1859 questioning his vision of the future and Marx lived on to 1883 confidently predicting communist revolution, subsequent events would have surprised both men. Political change in

25. Tocqueville to Eugène Stoffels, quoted in Jack Lively, *The Social and Political Thought of Alexis de Tocqueville* (Oxford: Clarendon Press, 1962), p. 211. The radical leaders of the French Revolution of 1789–1799 had sought to break with the traditional Western calendar and its Christian observances. Thus they created a new calendar devoid of Christian holidays and with renamed months. The date 18 *brumaire* was the day in 1799 that marked Napoleon's seizure of power in France; 1814 was the year of the restoration of the French monarchy after Napoleon's fall; 1830, of course, was the year King Louis Philippe came to power.

Chapter 6

Two Programs

for Social

and Political

Change:

Liberalism

and Socialism

much of Europe proved to be far more evolutionary than revolutionary in the years after 1848, thanks to several developments predicted neither by Tocqueville nor by Marx.

The liberal ideology represented by Tocqueville became less and less a narrow doctrine of individual economic freedom. Later liberals, like the Englishman John Stuart Mill (1806–1873), emphasized that economic liberty reached its limits when it allowed employers to abuse their employees with the low wages and poor working conditions we examined in Chapter 5. Consequently they supported legislation to rectify many of the worst abuses of industrial employment. Such liberals also believed in political democracy and won extended franchises in countries like England and Italy.

Many of the predictions of Marx's scientific socialism were correct. He rightly predicted, for example, that industrial capital would become increasingly consolidated in a few major production units that would dominate each industry. But he proved incorrect in assuming that such concentration would lead to increasing working-class misery and revolution. Communist revolution has succeeded in parts of the Western world—but in the least industrialized, not the most industrialized, countries. At the time of its 1917 Revolution, Russia, for example, was only at the threshold of industrialization.

In much of the industrialized West the widened right to vote, in fact, engendered a new kind of evolutionary socialism quite distinct from Marx's revolutionary socialism. The German Eduard Bernstein (1850–1932) was among the first to recognize that working-class voting rights eliminated the need for Marx's class warfare and revolution. Armed with the vote, Bernstein emphasized, workers could elect parliaments favoring their needs and peacefully win a better life through legislation. The need for revolution was at an end.

In the twentieth century, socialist parties committed to democratic processes have been instrumental in bringing greater social equality for working people in much of Western Europe. In modern England, France, Italy, West Germany, and other nations, legislation improving working conditions and wages as well as establishing the protection of health and unemployment insurance and old age pensions stands as monument to the widened vote created by liberals and the use of that vote by democratic socialists. The consequent improvement in working-class conditions ultimately resulted in the decline in broad popular appeal experienced by Marxian revolutionary socialists in much of the West.

CHAPTER SEVEN

THE CREATION

OF MODERN URBAN LIFE,

1850–1914

If you contemplate from the summit of Montmartre, or any other hill in the neighborhood, the congestion of houses piled up at every point of a vast horizon, what do you observe? Above, a sky that is always overcast, even on the finest day. Clouds of smoke, like a vast floating curtain, hide it from view. A forest of chimneys with black or yellowish chimneypots renders the sight singularly monotonous. . . . Looking at it, one is tempted to wonder whether this is Paris; and, seized with sudden fear, one is reluctant to venture into this vast maze, in which a million beings jostle each other, where the air, vitiated by unhealthy effluvia, rising in a poisonous cloud, almost obscures the sun. Most of the streets in this wonderful Paris are nothing but filthy alleys forever damp from a reeking flood. Hemmed in between two rows of tall houses, they never get the sun; it reaches only the tops of the chimneys dominating them. To catch a glimpse of the sky you have to look straight up above your head. A haggard and sickly crowd perpetually throngs these streets, their feet in the gutter, their noses in infection, their eyes outraged by the most repulsive garbage at every street corner. The best-paid workmen live in these streets. There are alleys, too, in which two cannot walk abreast, sewers of ordure and mud, in which the stunted dwellers daily inhale death. These are the streets of old Paris, still intact.[1]

This was how one French author characterized Paris in 1848. His description of the French capital might have been applied just as effectively to any great European city of the mid-nineteenth century. As your text has shown, the Industrial Revolution

1. H. Lecouturier, *Paris incompatible avec la République, plan d'un nouveau Paris où les révolutions seront impossibles* (Paris: 1848), quoted in Louis Chevalier, *Laboring Classes and Dangerous Classes in Paris During the First Half of the Nineteenth Century*, trans. Frank Jellinek (Princeton: Princeton University Press, 1981), p. 155. Montmartre is the highest point in Paris.

greatly accelerated the urbanization of the West, producing greatly expanded cities that drew increasing numbers of Europeans. The following table illustrates the rapidity of that growth for four major cities, showing their populations for 1800–1801 and their rates of growth during the nineteenth century.[2]

	Population (% increase)		
City	*1800–1801*	*1850–1851*	*1910–1911*
Berlin	172,000	419,000 (244%)	2,071,000 (1200%)
London	1,117,000	2,685,000 (240%)	7,256,000 (650%)
Paris	547,000	1,053,000 (192%)	2,888,000 (528%)
Vienna	247,000	444,000 (180%)	2,031,000 (822%)

Rapid population growth overwhelmed the capacity of early-nineteenth-century municipal governments to provide for the needs of their new citizens. Consequently, the conditions described in the quotation above were almost universal. Housing was a particular problem. Many cities in Continental Europe remained hemmed in by medieval or early modern fortifications designed to protect much smaller populations from military attack. Even without this obstacle to expansion, however, urban spread was limited by the almost complete absence of cheap, public transportation. People had to live close to their jobs because they walked to them, and housing generally retained the essentially medieval pattern that we examined in Chapter 4. Craftsmen and merchants dwelled behind or above their places of business, while poorer persons occupied the upper floors of the same buildings.

The growing urban population led to an increasingly dense pattern of residence. Landlords added more floors to existing buildings, cut up once spacious apartments into many smaller living units, erected inferior dwellings in courtyards and other open spaces, and rented basement and attic rooms. Sunlight and fresh air disappeared as building heights increased along narrow, medieval streets. Basements formed particularly unhealthy dwellings; they often leaked and seldom received light or ventilation. With little but musty, stale air available to them, it was customary for their residents to resort to "airings" out of doors.

Simple movement of people created a problem in the streets of such cities. Lacking sidewalks, pedestrians competed with horsedrawn vehicles for the opportunity to move through cramped streets wet with household waste water and soiled by horse droppings. A trip across central London or Paris, today a matter

2. B. R. Mitchell, *European Historical Statistics 1750–1970*, abridged ed. (New York: Columbia University Press, 1978), pp. 12–15. The population figures for London represent Greater London. This is the source of all population statistics through 1970 provided in this chapter.

of minutes by subway, consumed considerably more time in 1848. Many cities were almost strangled by such transportation difficulties within their old walls.

Rapid population growth in the limited spaces of many cities produced serious health and social problems. Extremely primitive methods for disposal of human wastes often polluted water supplies, and in the first decades of the nineteenth century, sewers in London, Paris, and other cities emptied into the very rivers that were the main sources of municipal water. Under such conditions disease spread rapidly, and life could be short. Epidemics of cholera, a disease often transmitted through polluted drinking water, struck many cities in 1832 and 1846. Indeed, well into the nineteenth century most cities retained an age-old urban demographic pattern in which death rates among their citizens exceeded birth rates. Such urban population growth as did occur before approximately 1850 was almost entirely the result of immigration to the cities from rural areas.

A rapidly rising crime rate was probably the most vexing social consequence of urban growth. Urban life often plunged unskilled immigrants of rural origin into deep poverty. Though crime sometimes stemmed from poverty, certain features of urban life encouraged it. The social controls of rural village life largely were absent in the cities, where the anonymity of the individual in the urban mass facilitated lawbreaking. Police resources for controlling such behavior were limited or nonexistent during the first half of the nineteenth century, too. The pioneering effort in urban crime control, the London Metropolitan Police Force, was not created until 1829 and imitated widely only after 1850.

In fact, only after about 1850 can we find Western society systematically attempting to solve the real problems of urban life. Collectively these responses transformed city life and produced our modern pattern of urban life. Several nineteenth-century developments made possible this transformation. We should note first that the century everywhere witnessed the growing power of central governments. The state's ability to command resources in the form of taxes financed many improvements. Its growing bureaucracy also provided the personnel to undertake the first projects of modern urban planning.

The Industrial Revolution played a major role in the urban transformation, too. It produced new technologies whose application to city life would improve conditions, and it created wealth, increasingly shared by more and more persons, that would finance private projects of urban building and improvement. Industrialization also sustained a new consumer-oriented economy characterized by the mass distribution of the products of the Industrial Revolution's factories to large urban markets. Modern science contributed to urban development as well. The work of Louis Pasteur (1822–1895) and other scientists made possible such public health improvements as purer water and food.

The combination of these nineteenth-century developments would transform the Western city by 1914. Your problem in this chapter is to examine the physical expressions and social consequences of this transformation in the four major cities whose rapid population growth we observed earlier: Berlin, London, Paris, and Vienna. How were these cities physically reshaped in response to early nineteenth-century problems? How did this physical transformation affect the lifestyle of urban dwellers?

SOURCES AND METHOD

Four of nineteenth-century Europe's great cities provide this chapter's evidence. London, Paris, Vienna, and Berlin all were political capitals and industrial centers that early felt the effects of rapid population growth. In order for you to analyze the evidence, some background on these cities is necessary.

London, as the population statistics in this chapter demonstrate, was the West's first great modern city. As such, it was also the first to experience—and aim to solve—many of the problems of urbanization.

Several important factors influenced London's response to these problems. Nineteenth-century London was the world's wealthiest city, with abundant capital available to finance private initiatives for change. Governmental authority at all levels cooperated with private interests to improve the city. At the national level, acts of Parliament provided authority for private development such as street construction by, for example, condemning slums. At the local level, a London County Council, (LCC) created in 1888 coordinated major public works projects that affected a large metropolitan area containing many units of municipal government.

Also important to London's development was the city's natural security. The English Channel protected England from Continental attackers, and London early abandoned its confining fortifications as the city expanded.

Across the English Channel, Paris traditionally had been confined by fortifications against attackers and by barriers erected to enforce the collection of taxes on goods entering the city. Within those confines the city described at the beginning of this chapter developed. Only in the 1850s did major improvements of the central city begin. But Paris had an advantage over London in that the central government administered the French capital through its prefect of the Seine department.[3] Change in Paris could occur rapidly as a result, because the financial resources of

3. In 1791 the Legislative Assembly divided France into eighty-three departments for administrative purposes. Paris formed the department of the Seine until twentieth-century reformers subdivided the metropolitan area into a number of new departments to increase efficiency. Napoleon I instituted the office of the prefect to administer in each department the central government's programs.

the national government could be brought to the process. Eager for the prestige that a handsome capital would confer, France's monarch took full advantage of his power.

After 1852 Emperor Napoleon III governed France. The emperor personally drafted detailed plans for the improvement of Paris, which he entrusted to his energetic prefect of the Seine, Baron Georges Eugène Haussmann (1809–1891). Like those in London, Haussmann's projects combined government initiative and money with private capital; his results, however, were sweeping and rapid. The improvements continued after Haussmann left office in 1870 and after the fall of Napoleon III later that year.

Vienna, like Paris, sustained a rapid and planned transformation from a walled city to a modern metropolis. As in Paris the initiative came from the central government. In December 1857, Emperor Francis Joseph ordered the destruction of Vienna's fortifications and the implementation of a plan for his capital's expansion into the area of the old walls and the open spaces surrounding them. In that space public buildings rose alongside privately financed residences. Other dramatic alterations soon followed.

The Prussian capital of Berlin became the capital of a unified Germany in 1871, but its development and growth predated the German Empire. Fortifications hampered the expansion of the city until the 1860s, however, and multistory apartment buildings to accommodate its growing population already were numer-

ous in the 1820s. During Berlin's subsequent growth as an industrial and administrative center, apartment houses increased rapidly in number, as did public buildings necessary to the government of a world power.

Now let us consider the evidence using this information about London, Paris, Vienna, and Berlin. The sources presented in this chapter are of two chief types. First you encounter pictorial evidence, a type of historical source that you have analyzed in earlier chapters. Here you will wish to examine this evidence to discern the solutions to urban problems that it illustrates. The pictures also reveal various architectural answers to the problems of living in the city. You should observe these solutions carefully, for architecture is an important historical source. Architects do not design for themselves but for their customers. As a result, their work generally reflects the needs and values of their employers.

This chapter presents a second kind of evidence, one that so far in this volume you have not analyzed extensively—drawings in the form of maps and city plans. Maps are important records of human activity that often are underused in historical study. Many historians employ maps only to illustrate their narratives, as a military historian frequently does when presenting a battle plan to support his or her description of a battle. Other social scientists, like sociologists and human geographers, make more extensive use of maps. Their study of maps as primary sources allows them to discover basic elements of human activity, such as residential patterns. It is in this fashion that you should view the maps offered here. You will want to examine those concerning public transportation facilities, for example, to determine why people lived where they did.

Let us now apply these general guidelines to analysis of specific pieces of evidence. To help you in this task, the worksheet that follows the sources allows you to gather your conclusions about each city's approach to urban development. Its organization follows that of the evidence, arranged to reflect trends in land use and the social consequences thereof.

In Source 1 you find a picture of the Quadrant on Regent Street in London. Observe the picture closely, recalling our description of early modern cities in The Problem. Why do you suppose the private developers of Regent Street, authorized by Parliament, laid out a street of this width? What advantages do you think accrued to London from Regent Street and others like it? Notice the buildings at the right of the picture. What land use do they suggest developers would favor in the central city? How much residential space appears in this picture?

In Sources 2 and 3, you turn to evidence on Paris. The map in Source 2 is particularly rich in detail on the city improvements wrought by Baron Haussmann during the Second French Empire. How has Haussmann changed Parisian streets? What other developments in transportation can you observe from the map? Consider, too, the impact of Haussmann's work on the quality of life for

Parisians. How did Haussmann attempt to solve the problem of public health?

Source 3 presents an engraving of one of the boulevards created under Haussmann, the Boulevard Richard-Lenoir. Built as a virtual roof for the St. Martin Canal, this boulevard is 231 feet wide. Beneath the street barges still sail into the center of Paris, while wheeled traffic moves along the boulevard. Why do you think Haussmann laid out such wide boulevards? Did such development offer health benefits? Compare Source 3 with the photograph in Chapter 4 (Source 3) of a street characteristic of Paris prior to Haussmann. How would a street such as rue du Fer-à-Moulin favor rebellious Parisians had the government attempted to retake Paris with force after July 14, 1789? What advantages would Haussmann's new boulevards offer the army of a government confronted by a belligerent Paris? Consider, too, the land use along such boulevards. What sort of buildings flank the Boulevard Richard-Lenoir?

Sources 4 and 5 present Vienna, the capital of Austria-Hungary. The map in Source 4 shows the city after the construction of ring boulevards along the line of former city fortifications. What development occurred along the ring? Note the location of the Prater, an extensive park laid out during the second half of the nineteenth century. How do the ring boulevards (see Source 5) compare with Haussmann's projects? What benefits might they offer? Why do you think that Austrian army commanders argued for streets broader than the 82-foot-wide boulevards?

Source 6 is a map of central Berlin in the late nineteenth and early twentieth centuries. The city originated on the island in Spree River identified as "Museum Island" and on the riverbanks opposite it. Berlin's main boulevard, the Unter den Linden, was constructed in the late seventeenth century. Along this boulevard and in the city center, the government of a unified Germany after 1871 endeavored to erect the symbols of great power status: the Reichstag or Parliament building, the Victory Column surrounded by statues of Germany's rulers, a new cathedral, new museums, the Chancellery, the army general staff headquarters, and other structures. What effect do you think the urban core's development as the capital of an empire had on residential patterns?

Now that you have examined trends in land use during the late nineteenth century, consider carefully their impact. With Sources 2 and 7 through 10 we can discern the extent and some of the effects of physical growth in the cases of Paris and London. Observe Sources 2 and 7. During what periods did London and Paris experience their greatest outward expansion? Pay close attention to the road system visible in Source 7 and the railways shown in Source 8. What relationship do you find between population movement and transportation facilities? What role do you think the Industrial Revolution played in such urban expansion?

Source 9 illustrates the population of the City, the one-square-mile core of central London. Recall Source 1 and the land use patterns you identified there. What do the population figures for the City and the map in Source 7 suggest was occurring in the urban core of London? Observe Source 10 for population trends in Paris in the early twentieth century. What relationship do you notice between areas of dense settlement and railroad lines? Where were many people in outlying areas employed? What similarities to London do these trends suggest?

If Sources 2 and 7 through 10 suggest the extent and physical results of urban growth, Sources 11 through 18 permit you to understand the nature of that growth and the social effects of urban change. Source 11 is an engraving of a typical building that rose to line Haussmann's new boulevards in Paris. Such structures commonly had shops facing the street on the ground floor with apartments on upper floors. Residents usually gained access to their homes through a large double door (at lower left in the picture) leading past the lodging of a *concièrge*, who controlled entrance to the building and who kept it clean, to an inner courtyard.

Source 12 illustrates an architect's plan for another such apartment building. We analyzed a simplified house plan in Chapter 4. Source 12 presents a much more detailed one. Such plans, showing the building literally as it would appear if you removed its roof and looked down into it, are easy to read when you know a few rules; on this plan the openings in the dark outline of the building represent doorways and the white gaps in the outline indicate windows. The remaining features of the building are identified in the keys.

Remember that architects design buildings with a definite clientele in mind. Examine the two apartments located on the ground floor and the three apartments found on each of the first, second, and third floors. How many rooms do these apartments contain? What features of the floor plans suggest to you the types of residents expected for these apartments? Notice the exterior decoration of the Viennese apartment building in Source 13. For what class of resident do you think the architect designed this building?

In Source 14 you find an aerial photograph of a nineteenth-century housing development in the Kreuzberg borough of Berlin. Germans called such structures *Mietskasernen*, or "rent barracks," because of the conditions experienced by the workers who lived in them. These buildings, an outgrowth of the city's rapid nineteenth-century population growth, represented the efforts of real estate speculators to profit from the vastly increased demand for housing by providing apartments on a minimum amount of increasingly expensive urban land. Flaws in city regulations encouraged such building practices. Building codes specified minimum dimensions for apartments, but they placed no limits on either the height of buildings or the percentage of the building lot that an apartment house might occupy. The result was a large number of high tenements, each occupying its full building lot. The consequent dense

concentration of population was not eased by Berlin's first city planning efforts. The development plan operative from 1862 to 1919 provided new sections of the city with broad boulevards resembling those in Paris and Vienna but separated by very large blocks of land ideal for more *Mietskasernen*.

Observe the details of these "rent barracks" in Source 14. What sort of living conditions were the lot of Berlin workers? How many floors did many of these buildings have? What degree of residential density did such multi-story construction produce? Many of these blocks rose in suburbs like Moabit (see Source 6); do you see any evidence of recreational space nearby?

Sources 15 and 16 illustrate the nature of English urban expansion. Observe Herne Hill and Orchard Road. What architectural features suggest to you the class of buyer expected to purchase a home in Herne Hill? In Orchard Road? What class of person seemed likely to reside in the outlying areas of Paris, according to Source 17? How does Source 18 amplify your early impressions of Berlin housing?

As you examine the evidence in this chapter, record your answers to these questions on your worksheet. By noting the significance of each source, you should be well on your way to formulating replies to this chapter's main questions. How were cities physically reshaped in response to the problems of the early nineteenth century? How did this physical transformation affect the lifestyle of urban dwellers?

THE EVIDENCE

CHANGES IN THE URBAN CORE

Source 1 from the Guildhall Library, City of London. Photo Godfrey.

1. The Quadrant on Regent Street, London, early 19th century

Source 2 from John P. McKay, Bennett D. Hill, and John Buckler, A History of Western Society, *3rd ed. (Boston: Houghton Mifflin, 1987), p. 769.*

2. Paris, 1850–1870

City walls

① Wall of Philippe Auguste (1180–1210)

② Tollhouse Wall (1784–1791), razed by Haussmann to rebuild as boulevards

③ Fortress Wall (1841–1845)

Paris before 1860

Expanded city limits established in 1860

Streets constructed by Haussmann

Other streets

Railway system created by Haussmann during Second Empire

Public parks opened during Second Empire

0   1 Km.

0   1 Mi.

Source: *Encyclopaedia Universalis*

Source 3 from Sigfried Giedion, Space, Time and Architecture (Cambridge, Mass.: Harvard University Press, 1962).

3. **The Boulevard Richard-Lenoir, Paris, Constructed 1861–1863**

Source 4 from Royal Institute of British Architects.

4. Vienna, 1887

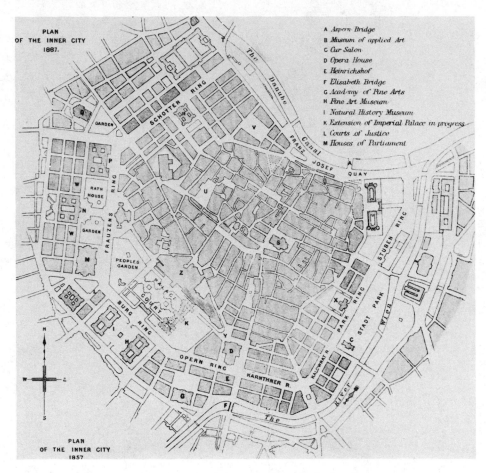

5. Vienna, late 19th century: View of the Houses of Parliament (foreground), City Hall (spired building at upper left), and University (domed structure at upper right)

OUTWARD GROWTH

Source 6 from F. Roy Willis, Western Civilization, *vol. II,* From the Seventeenth Century to the Contemporary Age, *4th ed. (Lexington, Mass.: D. C. Heath, 1985), p. 319.*

6. Central Berlin, 1871–1914

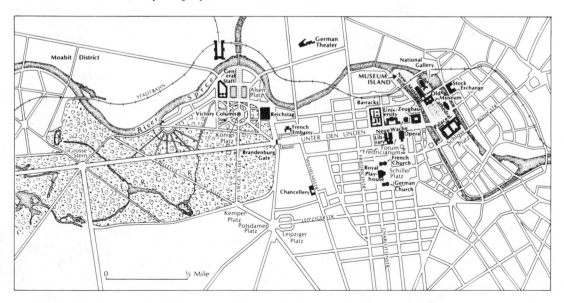

7. The Growth of London, 1600–1900

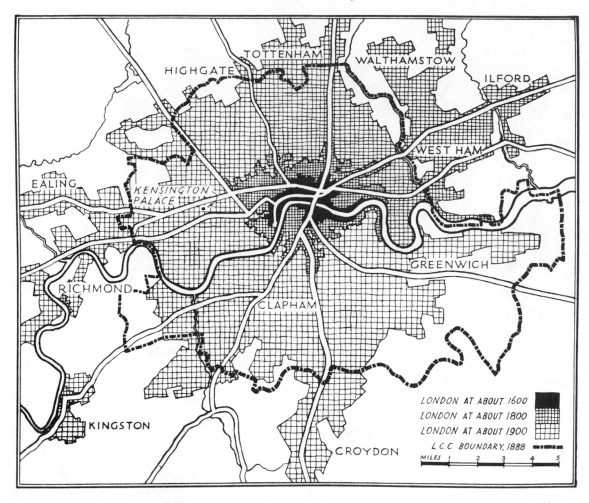

LONDON AT ABOUT 1600
LONDON AT ABOUT 1800
LONDON AT ABOUT 1900
L.C.C. BOUNDARY, 1888

MILES 1 2 3 4 5

HIGHGATE
TOTTENHAM
WALTHAMSTOW
ILFORD
EALING
KENSINGTON PALACE
WEST HAM
RICHMOND
GREENWICH
CLAPHAM
KINGSTON
CROYDON

Source 8 from Donald J. Olsen, The Growth of Victorian London *(New York: Holmes and Meier Publishers, 1976), p. 309.*

8. London Railways in 1895

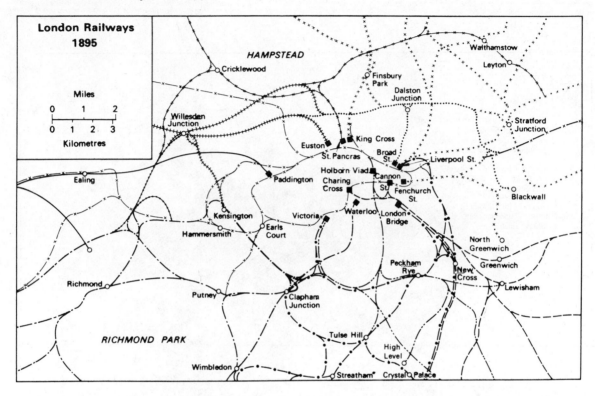

Source 9 from Gavin Weightman and Steve Humphries, The Making of Modern London *(London: Sidgwick and Jackson, 1983), p. 16.*

9. Approximate Population of the City, London

Year	Population
ca 1850	130,000
1900	27,000
1980	5,000

Source 10 adapted from R. Crozier, La Gare du Nord *(Paris, 1941), p. 253.*

10. Greater Paris, early 20th century

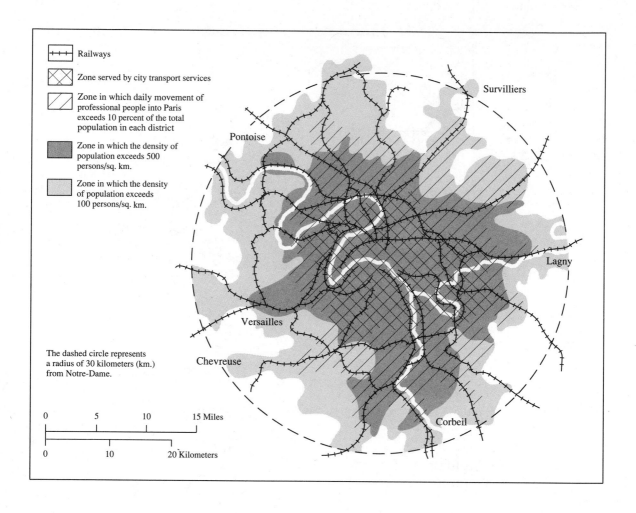

Railways

Zone served by city transport services

Zone in which daily movement of
professional people into Paris
exceeds 10 percent of the total
population in each district

Zone in which the density of
population exceeds 500
persons/sq. km.

Zone in which the density
of population exceeds
100 persons/sq. km.

The dashed circle represents
a radius of 30 kilometers (km.)
from Notre-Dame.

Survilliers

Pontoise

Lagny

Versailles

Chevreuse

Corbeil

0   5   10   15 Miles

0   10   20 Kilometers

RESIDENTIAL FORMS AND PATTERNS

Source 11 from The Builder *(London), vol. XVI (March 6, 1858), p. 159.*

11. A Paris Apartment House, late 19th century

Source 12 from Revue générale d'architecture, *vol. XVIII (1860), p. 41.*

12. Floor Plans (left, ground floor; right, floors 1–3) of the Apartment Building at 39, Rue Neueve des Mathurins, Paris

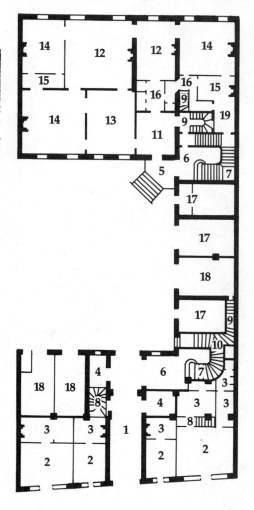

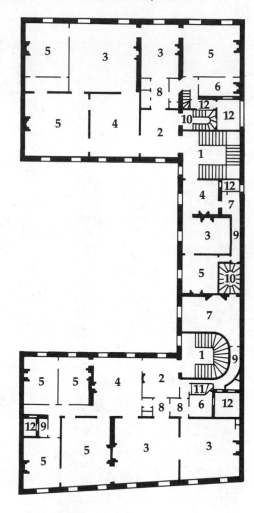

1 Passage from carriage entrance to courtyard
2 Shop
3 Shop backroom
4 Residence and kitchen of concièrge
5 Entry steps
6 Vestibule of grand staircase
7 Grand staircase

8–10 Service staircase
11 Antechamber
12 Parlor
13 Dining room
14 Bedroom
15 Bathroom
16 Cloakroom
17 Stable
18 Coach house
19 Light/air shaft

1 Grand staircase
2 Antechamber
3 Parlor
4 Dining room
5 Bedroom
6 Bathroom
7 Kitchen
8 Cloakroom
9 Corridor
10, 11 Service staircase
12 Light/air shaft

Source 13 from Johanna Fiegl.

13. Vienna Apartment Building, Constructed 1870

Source 14 from the German Information Center.

14. Workers' Tenements or *Mietskasernen* in the Berlin Borough of Kreuzberg, mid-19th century

15. An Early London Suburb: Herne Hill, Camberwell, ca 1830

16. A Later London Suburb: Orchard Road, Plumstead, 1910

17. Paris Beyond the Peripheral Boulevards: Rue Champlain, ca 1860

18. A One-Room Berlin Apartment, ca 1914

WORKSHEET

City	Changes in Urban Core		Outward Growth		Residential Patterns	
	Physical form	*Social consequences*	*Physical form*	*Social consequences*	*Physical form*	*Social consequences*
London						
Paris						
Vienna						
Berlin						

QUESTIONS TO CONSIDER

In the previous two sections of this chapter, we have considered each city individually. To answer the central questions we now need to study the cities jointly, drawing from their individual experiences general trends in urban development. Your worksheet comparing urban developments in London, Paris, Vienna, and Berlin should help you in this task.

Consider first the core of the cities. Notice the street patterns, and recall the problems that faced early-nineteenth-century cities. What common approaches to street construction do you find in London, Paris, Vienna, and Berlin? Why did city and national governments lay out such streets? What facilities for recreation do you find incorporated in the cities? What is the significance of the parks of Haussmann in Paris, the Prater in Vienna, and the Tiergarten in Berlin? Consult especially the maps of Paris, Vienna, and Berlin. How do you think a Parisian or Viennese of 1800 would have reacted to his or her city in 1900? Why?

Improvements in the urban core of cities benefited all to some extent. Let us look more deeply into these physical improvements, however, to discern if one class gained more than others from private and government initiatives for municipal improvements. Consult the sources to determine the kinds of buildings that rose in the central cities during the late nineteenth century. For what purposes do you find the center of London, for example, being used? What social group's interests seem served by such developments? Paris and Vienna continued to reserve a large part of their central cores for residential use. What classes seem to have occupied the new buildings constructed along Haussmann's boulevards and the ring boulevards in Vienna? Who, according to Source 14, largely populated the outskirts of Paris? Consider, too, the residential models of London and Berlin. Do you detect an economically segregated housing pattern? How do transportation developments support your conclusion?

Reflect also on the buildings erected at public expense in the second half of the ninteenth century, remembering that widespread, free public education became a reality only during the late nineteenth or early twentieth centuries in most countries. The Opera (Source 2) in Paris, completed in 1875, typifies such buildings, as do the museums and libraries built in London at roughly the same time. What evidence of similar construction do you find in Vienna and Berlin? What social groups do you think benefited most from such institutions? What does this tell you about the groups influential in late-nineteenth-century politics? Do you agree with those historians who call the nineteenth the "century of the middle class"?

After considering the sources as a unit, you should be ready to formulate answers to the chapter's main questions. How were cities physically reshaped in response to the problems of the early nineteenth century? How did this physical transformation affect the lifestyle of urban dwellers?

Two of our cities, Vienna and Berlin, experienced very changed circumstances after 1914 and therefore do not lend themselves to general statements on urban development during the years following the outbreak of World War One. The Empire of Austria-Hungary fought on the losing side in that war, and as a result the peace treaties of 1919 broke the old empire into two independent and very small states, Austria and Hungary. Vienna was the capital of a truncated Austria, a city with the buildings for imperial glory but without the old empire's territory and population. Indeed, post-World War One Vienna's population represented about 28 percent of the population of the new Austrian republic established by the peace treaties. Vienna's growth ended with the empire, and the city's population shrank. The 1910–1911 census figure of 2,031,000 people was never again achieved; the city's population in 1981 was 1,504,200.

Unlike Vienna, Berlin continued to grow after World War One in patterns we have identified. Its northern and eastern suburbs remained distinctly grim, working-class enclaves, and its population reached its greatest extent by about 1940 with 4,332,000 persons. World War Two, however, fundamentally changed Berlin. Bombings by the air forces of the United States and Great Britain destroyed ten square miles of central Berlin and one-third of its buildings. Much of what remained standing was destroyed in the Russian artillery shelling of the city in 1945. By the spring of 1945, Berlin lay in physical ruin.

Moreover, its traditional role as the capital of a great power disappeared. Defeated Germany was divided into Russian, British, French, and U.S. occupational zones, with Berlin located one hundred miles within the Russian zone. Under the terms of wartime agreements, the city continues to be occupied by Russian, British, French, and U.S. forces, even though the U.S., British, and French zones of Germany were united into the Federal Republic of Germany (West Germany) and the Russian zone became the German Democratic Republic in 1949 (see Chapter 13). West Germany's capital is Bonn; East Berlin is the capital of the small Democratic Republic.

Berlin has largely been rebuilt since 1945, yet it is still divided by the events of World War Two and by the wall that passes just east of the Brandenburg Gate, erected by Communist authorities to prevent refugees fleeing the Democratic Republic for the Western-occupied zones of Berlin. The city divided by that wall is much smaller (1971 population of both East and West Berlin was 3,208,000 persons) than it was previous to World War Two.

London and Paris better illustrate trends in urban life, because twentieth-century warfare less seriously affected these cities. Both continue to offer cultural advantages and technological improvements to their residents; twentieth-century ecological developments like air pollution from large concentrations of motor vehicles are posing new problems for solution, however. London and Paris also continued to grow in population until the middle of the twentieth century. Peaking in 1938 at 8,700,000, the population of greater London (present-day Europe's largest urban area) now approximates 6,756,000 (1984 estimate). Paris's population reached its greatest extent about 1950 at 2,850,000 persons and is now 2,188,918.

Urban growth in these and many other cities has ceased during the late twentieth century. It has been replaced by a suburbanization far more widespread than that of the nineteenth century, a trend that extends one we have identified. Suburbanization has continued to follow transportation routes. In the nineteenth century, as we have seen, growth followed the roads, railroads, and, later, subways. In the twentieth century, limited-access highways have also abetted suburban sprawl. Suburbanization patterns also reflect nineteenth-century residential trends. Railroads offering cheap fares to workers opened up London's northern and eastern suburbs to working-class residents, while the middle and upper classes went west. In Paris, which continues to rank a greater portion of its population among economically and professionally higher status groups than the rest of France, transportation carried the working classes to the communities surrounding the capital. That residential pattern persists to the present. The often drab working-class outer districts of Paris and its suburban communities reflect their social composition at election time. Modern French politics traditionally have been polarized by a heavily Marxist working class and a more conservative middle and upper class. In such a political system, the social composition of Paris's outlying districts is underscored by their nickname, "the Red Belt."

In fact, suburbanization has become so extensive that modern urban planners in Western Europe have started to direct its course, much like nineteenth-century planners tried to shape urban development. During the past few decades French planners, for example, have begun to lay out large population centers on the distant periphery of Paris. Such centers, like Cergy-Pontoise northeast of Paris, are suburban in both their location and access to the city by train and highway but are almost urban in their population density. The modern city thus continues as the locus of Western civilization, but it is now a smaller city influencing a much broader area.

CHAPTER EIGHT

EXPANSION AND PUBLIC

OPINION: ADVOCATES OF

THE "NEW IMPERIALISM"

THE PROBLEM

From the 1870s until around 1905, Western nations engaged in a brief but extremely intense period of imperial expansion. In one sense, of course, this was not entirely a new phenomenon. From the sixteenth through the eighteenth centuries, the emerging nations of Western Europe had struggled over possession of the New World. Between roughly 1815 and 1871, the West, beset with internal problems, had engaged in only limited attempts at colonialism, but some nations, principally England, nevertheless had sought to expand their economic spheres of influence. In some ways, then, the "new imperialism" of the late nineteenth century was not dramatically different from the old.

Yet to many living at the time (as well as to a number of later historians), the imperialism of the late nineteenth and early twentieth centuries was markedly different from earlier forms of territorial expansion. For one thing, the number of contestants for empire had increased with the addition of the newly formed nations of Germany and Italy. Indeed, even the United States, itself a nation composed of former European colonies, joined in the headlong scramble for new territories. The increased number of empire-seeking nations probably contributed to the speed with which unclaimed areas were brought under Western control.

Another factor that made the colonial expansion of the late nineteenth and early twentieth centuries appear "new" was that many people believed this was their nation's last opportunity to build or enlarge an empire. Only Africa and parts of Asia remained vulnerable to imperialistic ventures. Awareness of this fact filled the nations of the West with a sense of urgency: if a nation did not acquire colonies quickly, other nations would do so. This feeling of urgency doubtless contributed to the speed of empire building as well as to the heightened sense of national competition for greatness. So great was this sentiment that by the turn of the century almost all of Africa and parts of Asia had fallen under Western control and the West, accurately or not, could boast of itself as the master of much of the world.

No historical trend such as the new imperialism takes place in a vacuum, unaffected by other trends and events that precede and parallel it and, in some cases, help to cause it. In the West, several important developments in the second half of the nineteenth century not only acted to create the new imperialism but also helped impart to that movement its particular shape and character.

One of the most important occurrences in the West preceding and paralleling the new imperialism was that of rapid population growth. Between 1850 and 1900, the population of Europe (including Russia) increased 54 percent, from approximately 274 million to 423 million. Germany's population jumped over 62 percent, Great Britain's 41 percent, Italy's around 41 percent, and Belgium's 48 percent. This population boom was primarily the result of falling death rates, in turn caused by the controlling of epidemic diseases, increased food production, and improvements in transportation that allowed food supplies to reach cities and regions of local famines. In the United States, where massive immigration from Europe supplemented large natural increase, the population increased an astounding 227 percent.[1]

This dramatic jump in population, especially in the cities of Europe, created a serious need for jobs, especially in the nonagricultural sector. The pressure for greater employment in turn increased Europe's demand for raw materials for industrial production and markets for those manufactured goods. Moreover, in some areas of Europe (notably Italy), the rise in rural population put a heavy strain on land and agricultural resources, which resulted in increased emigration. It is easy to imagine how these problems, caused by population pressures, might be linked to calls for expansionism.

A second important trend during this time was the spread and apparent peaking of the Industrial Revolution. By the latter part of the nineteenth century, much of the West had joined in the Industrial Revolution and thus (as noted earlier) needed raw materials and, equally important, markets for manufactured goods. A severe depression, which struck Europe and the United States in 1873 and lasted into the 1890s, made it impossible for the West to consume all the manufactured goods it could produce. Unless industries were to shut down, bringing on massive unemployment, new markets would have to be found. With most of the Western countries erecting protective tariff barriers to keep out foreign goods, these new markets

1. Between 1846 and 1900, the number of emigrants from Europe to the United States and Latin America probably exceeded 30 million.

Chapter 8

Expansion and

Public Opinion:

Advocates of

The "New

Imperialism"

would have to be found outside the West, in areas that could be exploited almost at will.

The Industrial Revolution not only provided an incentive for a new upsurge of imperialism, it also gave the West the means to accomplish this expansion. Technological improvements, especially in transportation and communications, allowed Western mercantile and financial houses gradually to draw much of the world into an integrated global market dominated by Western merchants and financiers. As English economist Stanley Jevons boasted in 1866:

> The several quarters of the globe are our willing tributaries. The plains of North America and Russia are our cornfields; Chicago and Odessa our granaries; Canada and the Baltic our forests; Australia contains our sheep farms, and in South America are our herds of oxen . . . the Chinese grow tea for us; and coffee, sugar and spice arrive from East Indian plantations. Spain and France are our vineyards, and the Mediterranean our fruit garden.[2]

Advances in medicine and in weapons technology made it further possible for Westerners to subdue non-Western peoples and live for extended periods in non-Western climates. Great Britain, for example, acquired the Upper Nile River area in 1898, but only after slaughtering 20,000 tribesmen at Omdurman,

2. Quoted in R. R. Palmer and Joel Colton, *A History of the Modern World* (New York: Alfred A. Knopf, 1965), pp. 574–575.

thanks to the newly invented machine gun.

A third important trend that contributed to late nineteenth-century imperialism was that of intensified competition among Western nations. It was obvious at the time to many people that Western nations did not have to seize non-Western territories in order to dominate them economically. Moreover, some of the territories that Western nations colonized could offer no immediate profits to their conquerors. Yet in this era of intensified rivalry, colonies were widely regarded as assets that could be exploited in the increased competition among Western nations and also as potential military bases to protect the extraction of raw materials and the maintenance of trade lanes. Safe harbors and coaling stations for a modern steam-powered navy were seen as critically important to each Western nation's power and survival. At the same time, no single country could be allowed to gain an advantage over others in the rush for colonies and the establishment of national "greatness." Thus U.S. President William McKinley justified taking the Philippine Islands partly to keep them out of the hands of any other national competitor seeking to exploit Asia and the Pacific. Truly, heightened national competition, along with other trends, helped renew the spirit of imperialism in the West. With the new nations of Germany and Italy and the newly imperialistic United States added to the race, the scramble for colonies at times seemed almost frantic.

In addition to the more pragmatic reasons, many Westerners justified this renewed imperialistic impulse in two interesting and, in some cases, rather contradictory ways. The latter part of the nineteenth century witnessed the rapid spread throughout the West of the doctrine of Social Darwinism. An application of the theories of biological evolution to human affairs, Social Darwinism taught that peoples, like species, were engaged in a life-or-death struggle to determine the "survival of the fittest." Those classes or nations that emerged triumphant in this struggle were considered the most fit, hence best suited to carry on the evolution of the human race. Therefore the subjugation of weak peoples by strong ones was not only in accordance with the laws of nature, it was bound to result in a more highly civilized world as well. Most celebrated among the Social Darwinists was the Englishman Herbert Spencer, a diminutive and eccentric writer who became a worldwide celebrity through his writings. (A letter was once addressed to him, "Herbert Spencer. England. And if the postman doesn't know the address, he ought to." It was delivered.)

Although Spencer himself disapproved of imperialism, it is easy to see how his writings could be used as a justification for empire building. One reflection of the West's belief in its own "fitness," as opposed to the "unfitness" of the non-West, is English writer and poet Rudyard Kipling's poem "Arithmetic on the Frontier," the last verse of which follows:

With home-bred hordes the hill-side
   teem,
The troop-ships bring us one by one,
At vast expense of time and steam,
To slay Afridis where they run.
The "captives of our bow and spear"
Are cheap, alas! as we are dear.[3]

Paralleling this notion of struggle for survival between the "fittest" and the "unfit" (a doctrine with strong racist overtones) was the concept of the "White Man's burden." This concept held that it was the duty of the "fittest" not so much to destroy the "unfit" as to "civilize" them; white people, according to this view, had a responsibility to educate the rest of the world to the norms of Western society. As racist as Social Darwinism, the belief in the White Man's burden downplayed the idea of a struggle for survival between peoples and emphasized the "humanitarian" notion of bringing the benefits of "civilization" to the "uncivilized." Using this argument, many in the West justified imperialism as an obligation, a sacrifice that God had charged the "fittest" to make. Though the doctrine differs in tone from that of Social Darwinism, one can see that its practical results might well be the same.

Thus, a number of important trends preceded and paralleled the rising imperialist tide in the West. Yet by the late nineteenth century no

3. From Rudyard Kipling, *Departmental Ditties and Ballads and Barrack Room Ballads*, p. 95. Reprinted by permission of Doubleday & Company, Inc.

Chapter 8
Expansion and
Public Opinion:
Advocates of
The "New
Imperialism"

Western nation could undertake such ventures without the support of public opinion. Although none of the Western nations could be called a pure democracy at this time, political and social reforms in France, Great Britain, Germany, and the United States tended to enhance the notion that extension of the suffrage and public assent were important components of a strong nation, an attitude given more weight by the various working people's movements in Europe and the United States. Moreover, the mass circulation of newspapers, increased educational opportunities, and the adoption of modern political campaign techniques had given Westerners of all classes an increased awareness of issues and governmental policies. In such an atmosphere, the "people" might not rule, but they had to be heeded. The few remaining autocrats, like the stubborn Nicholas II of Russia, ignored this impulse at their peril . . . and ultimate destruction.

Your task in this chapter is to analyze the speeches and writings of advocates of imperialism from five of the Western nations (Great Britain, the United States, Germany, Italy, and Belgium) that were among the most active in pursuing imperialist policies. What were the main arguments used by each spokesman in favor of colonial expansion? How did each attempt to appeal to public opinion? Finally, how can their speeches and writings help us identify the principal motives and justifications for the "new imperialism"?

SOURCES AND METHOD

Before the late eighteenth century, public opinion was not considered a crucial factor when monarchs or bodies representing a limited electorate decided what policies their respective governments should pursue. To be sure, certain interest groups had to be consulted or appealed to, but public opinion as a whole was rarely heeded. As noted, however, the expansion of the electorate, increased educational opportunities and literacy, the corresponding mass circulation of newspapers, and the evolution of modern political campaign techniques to appeal to the expanded electorate all served to make people more aware of their national government's policies and even to have a limited voice in the shaping of those policies. Hence, supporters or defenders of particular policies were obliged to appeal to—and, in some cases, manipulate—public opinion. So it was with the advocates of the new imperialism. Probably not representing a majority of the population, these people nevertheless were able to link their causes to the dominant trends and ideas of the period, thereby appearing to be prophets of a new age of Western greatness and glory.

The first four pieces of evidence are selections from speeches that in turn were either transcribed or summarized in the press. Source 1 is a speech made by Joseph Chamberlain (1836–1914), a wealthy manufacturer and member of the British Parliament since 1876, to a city relief association. Chamberlain, a former mayor of Birmingham (1873–1875) who was an advocate of social reforms to aid the working classes, was invited to speak at the meeting, which was called to discuss widespread unemployment and hard times in Birmingham.

Source 2 is a speech delivered by U.S. Senator Albert Beveridge (1862–1927) on the Senate floor, January 9, 1900. From a poor farm background, Beveridge worked his way through college, was admitted to the bar in 1887, and became a freshman Republican Senator in 1899. Beveridge's speech was part of a debate over a Senate resolution that the Philippine Islands belonged to the United States and that it was the right of the United States to retain them and to "establish and maintain such governmental control . . . as the situation may demand." At the time this speech was made, the United States was in the process of crushing a revolt for independence in the Philippines.

The third speech was made by Kaiser Wilhelm II (Emperor William II) of Germany (1859–1941) on the occasion of his dispatching of part of the German fleet to China in retaliation for the killing of German missionaries in 1897. The ships were to be commanded by the Kaiser's brother, Prince Henry. Acceding to the throne of a unified Germany in 1888, Wilhelm sought to launch the new nation in imperial ventures that would rival those of other Western nations, principally England and

France, and make Germany a world power.

Source 4 is taken from a welcoming speech that King Leopold II of Belgium (1835–1909) addressed to an international conference of geographers in Brussels, September 12, 1876. Coming to the throne in 1865, Leopold was interested in involving Belgium in imperialistic expansion in Africa. The conference was called by Leopold himself to discuss the future exploration and "civilizing" of Africa. Later that year he told his cousin, Queen Victoria of Great Britain, "I have sought to meet those most interested in bringing civilization to Africa. There is an important task to be undertaken there, to which I would feel honored to contribute."

The fifth piece of evidence is taken from a book that gained wide circulation in Italy, *Cose africane* (*Concerning Africa*) (Milan, 1897), by Ferdinando Martini. Martini (1841–1928) was a well-known author, playwright, theater producer, and government official (he was governor of the Italian colony Eritrea from 1897 to 1900). *Cose africane* was written in the wake of the Italian defeat by Ethiopia when Italy attempted to seize that African nation. This was a major humiliation for Italy.

All the pieces of evidence presented here were designed to influence or sway public opinion on imperialistic ventures. To help you answer the central questions in this chapter, you will want to examine each piece of evidence for the following points: (1) Does the author identify a problem or problems which he thinks imperialism can solve? What

[199]

Chapter 8

Expansion and

Public Opinion:

Advocates of

The "New

Imperialism"

are they? If more than one, which is the most important? How will imperialism solve it? (2) How (if at all) does the author regard the "host populations" in the regions to be colonized? What adjectives, if any, are used to describe them? Does the author mention what effect Western imperialism will have on the "host populations"? (3) How does the author deal (if at all) with opponents of imperialism? How are they characterized? (4) How (if at all) does the author connect imperialism with one or more of the parallel trends and events? (5) In what other ways does the author attempt to influence public opinion?

Remember that each piece of evidence may include more than one reason to undertake imperialistic ventures. It would be helpful to take notes as you examine the evidence.

Keep the central questions in mind: What were the main arguments used by the five advocates of imperialism in favor of colonial expansion? How did each spokesman attempt to appeal to public opinion? How can these selections aid in identifying the principal motives and justifications for the "new imperialism"?

THE EVIDENCE

Source 1 from Joseph Chamberlain, M. P., Foreign & Colonial Speeches *(London: George Routledge & Sons, 1897), pp. 131–139.*

1. Joseph Chamberlain, Speech to the West Birmingham Relief Association, January 22, 1894

We must look this matter in the face, and must recognise that in order that we may have more employment to give we must create more demand. (Hear, hear.) Give me the demand for more goods and then I will undertake to give plenty of employment in making the goods; and the only thing, in my opinion, that the Government can do in order to meet this great difficulty that we are considering, is so to arrange its policy that every inducement shall be given to the demand; that new markets shall be created, and that old markets shall be effectually developed. (Cheers.) You are aware that some of my opponents please themselves occasionally by finding names for me—(laughter)—and among other names lately they have been calling me a Jingo.[4] (Laughter.) I am no more a Jingo than you are. (Hear, hear.) But for the reasons and arguments I have put before you tonight I am convinced

4. **Jingo:** a belligerent patriot; a chauvinist.

that it is a necessity as well as a duty for us to uphold the dominion and empire which we now possess. (Loud cheers.) For these reasons, among others, I would never lose the hold which we now have over our great Indian dependency—(hear, hear)—by far the greatest and most valuable of all the customers we have or ever shall have in this country. For the same reasons I approve of the continued occupation of Egypt; and for the same reasons I have urged upon this Government, and upon previous Governments, the necessity for using every legitimate opportunity to extend our influence and control in that great African continent which is now being opened up to civilisation and to commerce; and, lastly, it is for the same reasons that I hold that our navy should be strengthened—(loud cheers)—until its supremacy is so assured that we cannot be shaken in any of the possessions which we hold or may hold hereafter.

Believe me, if in any one of the places to which I have referred any change took place which deprived us of that control and influence of which I have been speaking, the first to suffer would be the working-men of this country. Then, indeed, we should see a distress which would not be temporary, but which would be chronic, and we should find that England was entirely unable to support the enormous population which is now maintained by the aid of her foreign trade. If the working-men of this country understand, as I believe they do—I am one of those who have had good reason through my life to rely upon their intelligence and shrewdness—if they understand their own interests, they will never lend any countenance to the doctrines of those politicians who never lose an opportunity of pouring contempt and abuse upon the brave Englishmen, who, even at this moment, in all parts of the world are carving out new dominions for Britain, and are opening up fresh markets for British commerce, and laying out fresh fields for British labour. (Applause.) If the Little Englanders[5] had their way, not only would they refrain from taking the legitimate opportunities which offer for extending the empire and for securing for us new markets, but I doubt whether they would even take the pains which are necessary to preserve the great heritage which has come down to us from our ancestors. (Applause.)

When you are told that the British pioneers of civilisation in Africa are filibusters,[6] and when you are asked to call them back, and to leave this great continent to the barbarism and superstition in which it has been steeped for centuries, or to hand over to foreign countries the duty which you are unwilling to undertake, I ask you to consider what would have happened if 100 or 150 years ago your ancestors had taken similar views of their responsibility? Where would be the empire on which now your livelihood depends? We should have been the United Kingdom of Great Britain and Ireland; but those vast dependencies, those hundreds of millions with whom we keep

5. **Little** Englanders: Britain's anti-imperialists.
6. **filibuster:** a person engaged in a private military action against a foreign government.

Chapter 8

Expansion and

Public Opinion:

Advocates of

The "New

Imperialism"

up a mutually beneficial relationship and commerce would have been the subjects of other nations, who would not have been slow to profit by our neglect of our opportunities and obligations. (Applause.)

Let me give you one practical illustration, in order to show what ought to be done, and may be done, in order to secure employment for our people. I will take the case of a country called Uganda, of which, perhaps, you have recently heard a good deal. A few years ago Uganda was only known to us by the reports of certain enterprising and most venturesome travellers, or by the accounts which were given by those self-denying missionaries who have gone through all these wild and savage lands, endeavouring to carry to the people inhabiting them the blessings of Christianity and civilisation. (Applause.) But within very recent times English authority has been established in Uganda, and an English sphere of influence has been declared. Uganda is a most fertile country. It contains every variety of climate; in a large portion of it European colonisation is perfectly feasible; the products are of the utmost richness; there is hardly anything which is of value or use to us in our commerce which cannot be grown there; but in spite of these natural advantages, during the past generation the country has been desolated by civil strife and by the barbarities of its rulers, barbarities so great that they would be almost incredible if they did not come to us on the authority of thoroughly trustworthy eye-witnesses.

All that is wanted to restore this country to a state of prosperity, to a commercial position which it has never attained before, is settled peace and order. (Hear, hear.) That peace and order which we have maintained for so long in India we could secure by a comparatively slight exertion in Uganda, and, when this is proposed to us, the politicians to whom I have referred would repudiate responsibility and throw back the country into the state of anarchy from which it has only just emerged; or they would allow it to become an appendage or dependency of some other European nation, which would at once step in if we were to leave the ground free to them. I am opposed to such a craven policy as this. (Applause.) I do not believe it is right. I do not believe it is worthy of Great Britain; and, on the contrary, I hold it to be our duty to the people for whom at all events we have for the time accepted responsibility, as well as to our own people, even at some cost of life, some cost of treasure, to maintain our rule and to establish settled order, which is the only foundation for permanent prosperity. When I talk of the cost of life, bear in mind that any cost of life which might result from undertaking this duty would be a mere drop in the ocean to the bloodshed which has gone on for generations in that country before we ever took any interest in it.

But I will go further than that. This rich country should be developed. It is at the present time 800 miles from the sea, and unless we can reach a country by the sea we cannot obtain its products in a form or at a cost which would be likely to be of any use to us, nor can we get our products to them.

Therefore what is wanted for Uganda is what Birmingham has got—an improvement scheme. (Laughter.) What we want is to give to this country the means of communication by a railway from the coast which would bring to that population—which is more intelligent than the ordinary populations in the heart of Africa—our iron, and our cloths, and our cotton, and even our jewelry, because I believe that savages are not at all insensible to the delights of personal adornment. (Laughter.) It would bring to these people the goods which they want and which they cannot manufacture, and it would bring to us the raw materials, of which we should be able to make further use.

Now, it is said that this is the business of private individuals. Private individuals will not make that railway for fifty years to come, and for the good reason that private individuals who go into investments like railways want to see an immediate prospect of a return. They cannot afford to go for ten or twenty years without interest on their money, and accordingly you will find that in undeveloped countries no railway has ever been made by private exertion, but has always been made by the prudence and foresight and wisdom of a government. . . .

Ladies and gentlemen, I ought to make an apology for having strayed so far from the direct object of the meeting, but my excuse must be that I do not see too much of my constituents, and that when I have such an opportunity as this, I may be justified in looking a little beyond the mere palliatives for distress such as those which in this association we are to the best of our ability endeavouring to provide, and may seek beyond them if haply we may trace the causes for this distress, and if haply we may find some permanent and effectual remedy. (Loud applause.)

Source 2 from U.S. Congressional Record, *vol. 23, part 1 (January 9, 1900), pp. 704–712.*

2. Albert Beveridge, Speech to the U.S. Senate, January 9, 1900

Mr. President, the times call for candor. The Philippines are ours forever, "territory belonging to the United States," as the Constitution calls them. And just beyond the Philippines are China's illimitable markets. We will not retreat from either. We will not repudiate our duty in the archipelago. We will not abandon our opportunity in the Orient. We will not renounce our part in the mission of our race, trustee, under God, of the civilization of the world. And we will move forward to our work, not howling out regrets like slaves whipped to their burdens, but with gratitude for a task worthy of our strength, and thanksgiving to Almighty God that He has marked us as His chosen people, henceforth to lead in the regeneration of the world.

Chapter 8

Expansion and

Public Opinion:

Advocates of

The "New

Imperialism"

This island empire is the last land left in all the oceans. If it should prove a mistake to abandon it, the blunder once made would be irretrievable. If it proves a mistake to hold it, the error can be corrected when we will. Every other progressive nation stands ready to relieve us.

But to hold it will be no mistake. Our largest trade henceforth must be with Asia. The Pacific is our ocean. More and more Europe will manufacture the most it needs, secure from its colonies the most it consumes. Where shall we turn for consumers of our surplus? Geography answers the question. China is our natural customer. She is nearer to us than to England, Germany, or Russia, the commercial powers of the present and the future. They have moved nearer to China by securing permanent bases on her borders. The Philippines give us a base at the door of all the East.

Lines of navigation from our ports to the Orient and Australia; from the Isthmian Canal to Asia; from all Oriental ports to Australia, converge at and separate from the Philippines. They are a self-supporting, dividend-paying fleet, permanently anchored at a spot selected by the strategy of Providence, commanding the Pacific. And the Pacific is the ocean of the commerce of the future. Most future wars will be conflicts for commerce. The power that rules the Pacific, therefore, is the power that rules the world. And, with the Philippines, that power is and will forever be the American Republic.

China's trade is the mightiest commercial fact in our future. Her foreign commerce was $285,738,300 in 1897, of which we, her neighbor, had less than 9 per cent, of which only a little more than half was merchandise sold to China by us. We ought to have 50 per cent, and we will. And China's foreign commerce is only beginning. Her resources, her possibilities, her wants, all are undeveloped. She has only 840 miles of railway. I have seen trains loaded with natives and all the activities of modern life already appearing along the line. But she needs, and in fifty years will have, 20,000 miles of railway.

Who can estimate her commerce, then? That statesman commits a crime against American trade—against the American grower of cotton and wheat and tobacco, the American manufacturer of machinery and clothing—who fails to put America where she may command that trade. Germany's Chinese trade is increasing like magic. She has established ship lines and secured a tangible foothold on China's very soil. Russia's Chinese trade is growing beyond belief. She is spending the revenues of the Empire to finish her railroad into Pekin itself, and she is in physical possession of the imperial province of Manchuria. Japan's Chinese trade is multiplying in volume and value. She is bending her energy to her merchant marine, and is located along China's very coast; but Manila is nearer China than Yokohama is. The Philippines command the commercial situation of the entire East. . . .

But if they did not command China, India, the Orient, the whole Pacific for purposes of offense, defense, and trade, the Philippines are so valuable in themselves that we should hold them. I have cruised more than 2,000 miles through the archipelago, every moment a surprise at its loveliness and wealth. I have ridden hundreds of miles on the islands, every foot of the way a revelation of vegetable and mineral riches.

No land in America surpasses in fertility the plains and valleys of Luzon. Rice and coffee, sugar and cocoanuts, hemp and tobacco, and many products of the temperate as well as the tropic zone grow in various sections of the archipelago. I have seen hundreds of bushels of Indian corn lying in a road fringed with banana trees. The forests of Negros, Mindanao, Mindora, Paluan, and parts of Luzon are invaluable and intact. The wood of the Philippines can supply the furniture of the world for a century to come. At Cebu the best informed man in the island told me that 40 miles of Cebu's mountain chain are practically mountains of coal. Pablo Majia, one of the most reliable men on the islands, confirmed the statement. Some declare that the coal is only lignite; but ship captains who have used it told me that it is better steamer fuel than the best coal of Japan.

I have a nugget of pure gold picked up in its present form on the banks of a Philippine creek. I have gold dust washed out by crude processes of careless natives from the sands of a Philippine stream. Both indicate great deposits at the source from which they come. In one of the islands great deposits of copper exist untouched. The mineral wealth of this empire of the ocean will one day surprise the world. I base this statement partly on personal observation, but chiefly on the testimony of foreign merchants in the Philippines, who have practically investigated the subject, and upon the unanimous opinion of natives and priests. And the mineral wealth is but a small fraction of the agricultural wealth of these islands.

And the wood, hemp, copra, and other products of the Philippines supply what we need and can not ourselves produce. And the markets they will themselves afford will be immense. Spain's export and import trade, with the islands undeveloped, was $11,534,731 annually. Our trade with the islands developed will be $125,000,000 annually, for who believes that we can not do ten times as well as Spain? Consider their imperial dimensions. Luzon is larger and richer than New York, Pennsylvania, Illinois, or Ohio. Mindanao is larger and richer than all New England, exclusive of Maine. Manila, as a port of call and exchange, will, in the time of men now living, far surpass Liverpool. Behold the exhaustless markets they command. It is as if a half dozen of our States were set down between Oceania and the Orient, and those States themselves undeveloped and unspoiled of their primitive wealth and resources. . . .

At the outbreak of the last insurrection, in August, 1896, Spain had only 1,500 Spanish soldiers in all the Philippines, and 700 of these were in Manila. In November of that year she had only 10,000 men. The generals in command of these were criticised and assailed in Spain. It is characteristic of Spain that the people at home do not support, but criticise their generals in the field. The Spanish method has always been a mixed policy of peace and war, a

Chapter 8

Expansion and

Public Opinion:

Advocates of

The "New

Imperialism"

contradiction of terms, an impossible combination, rendering war ineffective and peace impossible. This was Compo's plan. It was Blanco's plan. Those who would make it our plan will inherit Blanco's fate and failure.

Mr. President, that must not be our plan. This war is like all other wars. It needs to be finished before it is stopped. I am prepared to vote either to make our work thorough or even now to abandon it. A lasting peace can be secured only by overwhelming forces in ceaseless action until universal and absolutely final defeat is inflicted on the enemy. To halt before every armed force, every guerrilla band, opposing us is dispersed or exterminated will prolong hostilities and leave alive the seeds of perpetual insurrection.

Even then we should not treat. To treat at all is to admit that we are wrong. And any quiet so secured will be delusive and fleeting. And a false peace will betray us; a sham truce will curse us. It is not to serve the purposes of the hour, it is not to salve a present situation, that peace should be established. It is for the tranquillity of the archipelago forever. It is for an orderly government for the Filipinos for all the future. It is to give this problem to posterity solved and settled; not vexed and involved. It is to establish the supremacy of the American Republic over the Pacific and throughout the East till the end of time.

It has been charged that our conduct of the war has been cruel. Senators, it has been the reverse. I have been in our hospitals and seen the Filipino wounded as carefully, tenderly cared for as our own. Within our lines they may plow and sow and reap and go about the affairs of peace with absolute liberty. And yet all this kindness was misunderstood, or rather not understood. Senators must remember that we are not dealing with Americans or Europeans. We are dealing with Orientals. We are dealing with Orientals who are Malays. We are dealing with Malays instructed in Spanish methods. They mistake kindness for weakness, forbearance for fear. It could not be otherwise unless you could erase hundreds of years of savagery, other hundreds of years of orientalism, and still other hundreds of years of Spanish character and custom.

Our mistake has not been cruelty; it has been kindness. It has been the application to Spanish Malays of methods appropriate to New England. Every device of mercy, every method of conciliation, has been employed by the peace-loving President of the American Republic, to the amazement of nations experienced in oriental revolt. Before the outbreak[7] our general in command appointed a commission to make some arrangement with the natives mutually agreeable. I know the members of the commission well—General Hughes, Colonel Crowder, and General Smith—moderate, kindly, tactful men of the world; an ideal body for such negotiation. It was treated with contempt.

We smiled at intolerable insult and insolence until the lips of every native in Manila were curling in ridicule for the cowardly Americans. We refrained

7. **outbreak:** Beveridge is referring to the outbreak of the Filipino revolt against the United States.

from all violence until their armed bravos crossed the lines in violation of agreement. Then our sentry shot the offender, and he should have been court-martialed had he failed to shoot. That shot was the most fortunate of the war. For there is every reason to believe that Aguinaldo[8] had planned the attack upon us for some nights later. Our sentry's shot brought this attack prematurely on. He arranged for an uprising in Manila to massacre all Americans, the plans for which, in a responsible officer's handwriting, are in our possession. This shot and its results made that awful scheme impossible. We did not strike till they attacked us in force, without provocation. This left us no alternative but war or evacuation. . . .

The news that 60,000 American soldiers have crossed the Pacific; that, if necessary, the American Congress will make it 100,000 or 200,000 men; that, at any cost, we will establish peace and govern the islands, will do more to end the war than the soldiers themselves. But the report that we even discuss the withdrawal of a single soldier at the present time and that we even debate the possibility of not administering government throughout the archipelago ourselves will be misunderstood and misrepresented and will blow into a flame once more the fires our soldiers' blood has almost quenched.

Mr. President, reluctantly and only from a sense of duty am I forced to say that American opposition to the war has been the chief factor in prolonging it. Had Aguinaldo not understood that in America, even in the American Congress, even here in the Senate, he and his cause were supported; had he not known that it was proclaimed on the stump and in the press of a faction in the United States that every shot his misguided followers fired into the breasts of American soldiers was like the volleys fired by Washington's men against the soldiers of King George his insurrection would have dissolved before it entirely crystallized.

The utterances of American opponents of the war are read to the ignorant soldiers of Aguinaldo and repeated in exaggerated form among the common people. Attempts have been made by wretches claiming American citizenship to ship arms and ammunition from Asiatic ports to the Filipinos, and these acts of infamy were coupled by the Malays with American assaults on our Government at home. The Filipinos do not understand free speech, and therefore our tolerance of American assaults on the American President and the American Government means to them that our President is in the minority or he would not permit what appears to them such treasonable criticism. It is believed and stated in Luzon, Panay, and Cebu that the Filipinos have only to fight, harass, retreat, break up into small parties, if necessary, as they are doing now, but by any means hold out until the next Presidential election, and our forces will be withdrawn.

All this has aided the enemy more than climate, arms, and battle. Senators, I have heard these reports myself; I have talked with the people; I have seen our mangled boys in the hospital and field; I have stood on the firing line

---

8. **Emilio Aguinaldo:** leader of the Filipino independence movement, at first against Spain and then against the United States.

Chapter 8

Expansion and

Public Opinion:

Advocates of

The "New

Imperialism"

and beheld our dead soldiers, their faces turned to the pitiless southern sky, and in sorrow rather than anger I say to those whose voices in America have cheered those misguided natives on to shoot our soldiers down, that the blood of those dead and wounded boys of ours is on their hands, and the flood of all the years can never wash that stain away. In sorrow rather than anger I say these words, for I earnestly believe that our brothers knew not what they did.

But, Senators, it would be better to abandon this combined garden and Gibraltar of the Pacific, and count our blood and treasure already spent a profitable loss, than to apply any academic arrangement of self-government to these children. They are not capable of self-government. How could they be? They are not of a self-governing race. They are Orientals, Malays, instructed by Spaniards in the latter's worst estate.

They know nothing of practical government except as they have witnessed the weak, corrupt, cruel, and capricious rule of Spain. What magic will anyone employ to dissolve in their minds and characters those impressions of governors and governed which three centuries of misrule has created? What alchemy will change the oriental quality of their blood and set the self-governing currents of the American pouring through their Malay veins? How shall they, in the twinkling of an eye, be exalted to the heights of self-governing peoples which required a thousand years for us to reach, Anglo-Saxon though we are?

Let men beware how they employ the term "self-government." It is a sacred term. It is the watchword at the door of the inner temple of liberty, for liberty does not always mean self-government. Self-government is a method of liberty—the highest, simplest, best—and it is acquired only after centuries of study and struggle and experiment and instruction and all the elements of the progress of man. Self-government is no base and common thing, to be bestowed on the merely audacious. It is the degree which crowns the graduate of liberty, not the name of liberty's infant class, who have not yet mastered the alphabet of freedom. Savage blood, oriental blood, Malay blood, Spanish example—are these the elements of self-government?

We must act on the situation as it exists, not as we would wish it. I have talked with hundreds of these people, getting their views as to the practical workings of self-government. The great majority simply do not understand any participation in any government whatever. The most enlightened among them declare that self-government will succeed because the employers of labor will compel their employees to vote as their employer wills and that this will insure intelligent voting. I was assured that we could depend upon good men always being in office because the officials who constitute the government will nominate their successors, choose those among the people who will do the voting, and determine how and where elections will be held.

The most ardent advocate of self-government that I met was anxious that I should know that such a government would be tranquil because, as he said, if anyone criticised it, the government would shoot the offender. A few of them have a sort of verbal understanding of the democratic theory, but the above are the examples of the ideas of the practical workings of self-government entertained by the aristocracy, the rich planters and traders, and heavy employers of labor, the men who would run the government.

Example for decades will be necessary to instruct them in American ideas and methods of administration. Example, example; always example—this alone will teach them. As a race, their general ability is not excellent. Educators, both men and women, to whom I have talked in Cebu and Luzon, were unanimous in the opinion that in all solid and useful education they are, as a people, dull and stupid. In showy things, like carving and painting or embroidery or music, they have apparent aptitude, but even this is superficial and never thorough. They have facility of speech, too.

The three best educators on the island at different times made to me the same comparison, that the common people in their stupidity are like their caribou bulls. They are not even good agriculturists. Their waste of cane is inexcusable. Their destruction of hemp fiber is childish. They are incurably indolent. They have no continuity or thoroughness of industry. They will quit work without notice and amuse themselves until the money they have earned is spent. They are like children playing at men's work. . . .

Administration of good government is not denial of liberty. For what is liberty? It is not savagery. It is not the exercise of individual will. It is not dictatorship. It involves government, but not necessarily self-government. It means law. First of all, it is a common rule of action, applying equally to all within its limits. Liberty means protection of property and life without price, free speech without intimidation, justice without purchase or delay, government without favor or favorites. What will best give all this to the people of the Philippines—American administration, developing them gradually toward self-government, or self-government by a people before they know what self-government means?

The Declaration of Independence does not forbid us to do our part in the regeneration of the world. If it did, the Declaration would be wrong, just as the Articles of Confederation, drafted by the very same men who signed the Declaration, was found to be wrong. The Declaration has no application to the present situation. It was written by self-governing men for self-governing men.

It was written by men who, for a century and a half, had been experimenting in self-government on this continent, and whose ancestors for hundreds of years before had been gradually developing toward that high and holy estate. The Declaration applies only to people capable of self-government. How dare any man prostitute this expression of the very elect of self-governing peoples to a race of Malay children of barbarism, schooled in Spanish methods and ideas? And you, who say the Declaration applies to all men, how dare you deny its application to the American Indian? And if

Chapter 8

Expansion and

Public Opinion:

Advocates of

The "New

Imperialism"

you deny it to the Indian at home, how dare you grant it to the Malay abroad?

The Declaration does not contemplate that all government must have the consent of the governed. It announces that man's "inalienable rights are life, liberty, and the pursuit of happiness; that to secure these rights governments are established among men deriving their just powers from the consent of the governed; that when any form of government becomes destructive of those rights, it is the right of the people to alter or abolish it." "Life, liberty, and the pursuit of happiness" are the important things; "consent of the governed" is one of the means to those ends. . . .

Blind indeed is he who sees not the hand of God in events so vast, so harmonious, so benign. Reactionary indeed is the mind that perceives not that this vital people is the strongest of the saving forces of the world; that our place, therefore, is at the head of the constructing and redeeming nations of the earth; and that to stand aside while events march on is a surrender of our interests, a betrayal of our duty as blind as it is base. Craven indeed is the heart that fears to perform a work so golden and so noble; that dares not win a glory so immortal. . . .

Pray God that spirit never fails. Pray God the time may never come when Mammon and the love of ease shall so debase our blood that we will fear to shed it for the flag and its imperial destiny. Pray God the time may never come when American heroism is but a legend like the story of the Cid.[9] American faith in our mission and our might a dream dissolved, and the glory of our mighty race departed.

And that time will never come. We will renew our youth at the fountain of new and glorious deeds. We will exalt our reverence for the flag by carrying it to a noble future as well as by remembering its ineffable past. Its immortality will not pass, because everywhere and always we will acknowledge and discharge the solemn responsibilities our sacred flag, in its deepest meaning, puts upon us. And so, Senators, with reverent hearts, where dwells the fear of God, the American people move forward to the future of their hope and the doing of His work.

Mr. President and Senators, adopt the resolution offered, that peace may quickly come and that we may begin our saving, regenerating, and uplifting work. Adopt it, and this bloodshed will cease when these deluded children of our islands learn that this is the final word of the representatives of the American people in Congress assembled. Reject it, and the world, history, and the American people will know where to forever fix the awful responsibility for the consequences that will surely follow such failure to do our manifest duty. How dare we delay when our soldiers' blood is flowing? [Applause in the galleries.]

9. **the Cid** (1040–1099): a Castilian named Ruy, or Rodrigo, Diaz de Vivar, whose fighting against the Moors made him a legendary Spanish hero. Here Beveridge may have been referring to what he considered a loss of heroism among the Spanish, whom fellow U.S. Senator Henry Cabot Lodge called "unfit among nations."

The PRESIDENT pro tempore. Applause is not permitted in the United States Senate.[10]

Source 3 from Annual Register: A Review of Public Events at Home and Abroad, for the Year 1897 *(London: Longmans, Green, 1898), pp. 282–284.*

3. Kaiser Wilhelm II, Speech to the German Fleet, 1897

The voyage on which you are starting and the task you have to perform have nothing essentially novel about them. They are the logical consequences of the political labours of my late grandfather and his great Chancellor, and of our noble father's[11] achievements with the sword on the battlefield. They are nothing more than the first effort of the reunited and re-established German Empire to perform its duties across the seas. In the astonishing development of its commercial interests, the empire has attained such dimensions that it is my duty to follow the new German Hansa,[12] and to afford it the protection it has a right to demand from the empire and the Emperor. Our German brethren in holy orders who have gone out to work in peace, and who have not shrunk from risking their lives in order to carry our religion to foreign soil and among foreign nations, have placed themselves under my protection, and we have now to give permanent support and safety to these brethren, who have been repeatedly harassed, and often hard pressed.

For this reason, the enterprise I have entrusted to you, and which you will have to carry out conjointly with the comrades and the ships already on the spot, is essentially of a defensive and not of an offensive nature. Under the protecting banner of our German war-flag, the rights we are justified in claiming are to be secured to German commerce, German merchants, and German ships—the same rights that are accorded by foreigners to all other nations. Our commerce is not new, for the Hansa was, in old times, one of the mightiest enterprises the world has ever seen, and the German towns were able to fit out fleets such as the broad expanse of the sea had hardly ever borne before. The Hansa decayed, however, and could not but decay, for the one condition—*viz.* imperial protection—was wanting. Now things are altered. As the first preliminary condition, the German Empire has been created. As the second preliminary condition, German commerce is flourishing and developing, and it can develop and prosper securely only if it feels

10. The Vice President of the United States presides over the Senate as the President *pro tempore* and is addressed in the Senate as Mr. President.

11. Wilhelm's grandfather was Wilhelm I of Prussia, his father was Frederick III, and the "great Chancellor" was Otto von Bismarck.

12. **Hansa:** The Hanseatic League was a commercial network of northern German cities that dominated Baltic and North Sea trade from the thirteenth through the fifteenth centuries.

Chapter 8

Expansion and

Public Opinion:

Advocates of

The "New

Imperialism"

safe under the power of the empire. Imperial power means naval power, and they are so mutually dependent that the one cannot exist without the other.

As a sign of imperial and of naval power, the squadron, strengthened by your division, will now have to act in close intercourse and good friendship with all the comrades of the foreign fleets out there, for the protection of our home interests against everybody who tries to injure Germany. That is your vocation and your task. May it be clear to every European out there, to the German merchant, and above all, to the foreigner whose soil we may be on, and with whom we shall have to deal, that the German Michael has planted his shield, adorned with the eagle of the empire, firmly on that soil, in order, once for all, to afford protection to those who apply to him for it. May our countrymen abroad, whether priests or merchants, or of any other calling, be firmly convinced that the protection of the German Empire, as represented by the imperial ships, will be constantly afforded them. Should, however, any one attempt to affront us, or to infringe our good rights, then strike out with mailed fist, and if God will, weave round your young brow the laurel which nobody in the whole German Empire will begrudge you.

Source 4 from Henri Brunschwig, French Colonialism, 1871–1914: Myths and Realities *(New York: Praeger, 1966), pp. 35–36.*

4. Leopold II of Belgium, Speech to an International Conference of Geographers, September 12, 1876

The matter which brings us together today is one most deserving the attention of the friends of humanity. For bringing civilisation to the only part of the earth which it has not yet reached and lightening the darkness in which whole peoples are plunged, is, I venture to say, a crusade worthy of this century of progress, and I am glad to find how favourable public opinion is to the accomplishment of this task. We are swimming with the tide. Many of those who have closely studied Africa have come to realise that it would be in the interest of the object they are all seeking to achieve for them to meet and consult together with a view to regulating the course to be taken, combining their efforts and drawing on all available resources in a way which would avoid duplication of effort.

I felt that Belgium, as a centrally situated and neutral state, would be an appropriate place for such a meeting. I was therefore emboldened to invite you all to join me here at this small conference. . . . Need I say that no selfish motives impelled me to invite you to Brussels? Such were not my motives, for, even if Belgium is small, she is happy and satisfied with her lot and my only ambition is to serve her well. But I will not go so far as to say that I should be insensitive to the honour which would accrue to my country if an important step forward in a matter which historians of our time will regard as significant, were dated from Brussels. I should be glad if Brussels became, in some measure, the headquarters of the civilising movement.

Because of this, I permitted myself to think that you might regard it as appropriate, in view of the authority you have, to come here to discuss and reach agreement on what courses to follow and what means to employ, to the end of raising the standard of civilisation in Central Africa. I also felt you might agree on what needs to be done to interest the public in your noble work and how to persuade it to make financial contributions to this task. . . . We must seek mass support and find ways of getting it. What resources should we not have if all those to whom a franc meant nothing, or very little, agreed to pay such a sum into the fund for suppressing the slave trade in the interior of Africa!

Much progress has already been made and the unknown has been attacked from many sides. You whom I am addressing have made most important contributions to scientific knowledge and it would be of the greatest encouragement if you would outline the main tasks to be performed. Among the matters which remain to be discussed, the following may be mentioned:

1. Deciding exactly where to acquire bases for the task in hand . . . on the Zanzibar coast and near the mouth of the Congo, either by means of conventions with chiefs or by purchasing or renting sites from individuals.

2. Deciding on the routes to be successively opened up into the interior, and on the medical, scientific and peace-keeping stations which are to be set up with a view to abolishing slavery, and bringing about good relations between the chiefs by providing them with fair-minded, impartial persons to settle their disputes, and so forth.

3. Setting up—once the task to be done has been clearly defined—a central, international committee with national committees, each to carry out this task in the aspects of it which concern them, to explain the object to the public of all countries, and to appeal to the feeling of charity to which no worthy cause has ever appealed in vain. These are some of the points which seem worthy of your attention. . . . My wish is to serve the great cause for which you have already done so much, in whatever manner you may suggest to me. It is with this object that I put myself at your disposal, and I extend a cordial welcome to you.

Chapter 8

Expansion and

Public Opinion:

Advocates of

The "New

Imperialism"

Source 5 from Ferdinando Martini, Cose affricane: da Saati ad Abba Carmina: discoursi e scritti *(Milan: Fratelli Treves, 1897), pp. 122, 136, 140. Translated by Gina Pashko.*

5. Ferdinando Martini, from *Cose affricane*, 1897

Italy has 108 inhabitants per square kilometer; France has only 73. In proportion to its territory, only three countries in Europe surpass Italy in population density: Belgium, Holland, and Great Britain. If we continue at this rate, Italy will soon take the lead: in the decade of 1871–1881, the birth rate exceeded the death rate by seven percent, and in the following years, by eleven percent. Every year 100,000 farmers and agricultural laborers emigrate from Italy. In spite of this immense exodus, the country witnesses its place in the family of civilized people growing smaller and smaller as it looks on with fear for its political and economic future. In fact, during the last eighty years, the English-speaking population throughout the world has risen from 22 to 90 million; the Russian-speaking population from 50 to 70; and so forth, down to the Spanish-speaking population, who were 18 million and are now 39. On the other hand, the Italian-speaking population has only increased from 20 to 31 million, and most of this growth has taken place within Italy's own geographical borders. This is not very surprising. At first, our emigrants were spreading Italy's name, language, and prestige in foreign countries, but since all, or nearly all, of them went to highly developed areas, their sons and grandsons were surrounded and attracted to the life of the vigorous people of the nations giving them hospitality, and ended up by forgetting the language of their fathers and forefathers. Now they merely increase the population of other nations, like branches that are grafted on a plant of a different species. . . .

Realizing that our stubbornness and our mistakes have cost us so much in the past and continue to cost us today, I believe that, even leaving aside all other considerations and taking into account only expenditures and the chances of success, it is less secure and more expensive to endeavor to cultivate three million hectares of barren land in Italy than to insure the prosperity of a large agricultural colony in Eritrea. . . .

Even the Abyssinian[13] hut lends itself to jokes and laughter. But after the jokes and laughter have subsided, there is good reason to cry when comparing these huts, where our colonial officers continue to live comfortably, to the sandstone caves in which the ploughmen and the reapers of the Roman Campagna sleep; or to the crumbling huts of the Basilicata region, where men, women and children are living on top of each other, and where, according to medical descriptions, it is possible to breathe only because air filters through the cracks in the rotten walls.

13. **Abyssinia:** Ethiopia.

QUESTIONS TO CONSIDER

Begin by examining each piece of evidence separately. Your task is to identify the principal arguments each speaker used to support imperialist ventures by his nation. To help you complete that task, recall the questions in Sources and Method: (1) What problem or problems does the speaker identify that he claims imperialism will solve? (2) How does the speaker regard the "host populations" of the regions to be colonized? (3) How does the speaker treat (if at all) the opponents of imperialism? How does he characterize them? (4) Does the speaker connect imperialism with other important and simultaneous trends and events? If so, how?

Historian Henri Brunschwig claims that Britain's was the most commercially motivated imperialism of all European nations. Does Joseph Chamberlain's speech support Brunschwig's hypothesis? How does Chamberlain attempt to convince the British working classes that imperialism will help them? Is the argument convincing?

Chamberlain barely referred to the "host populations." When he did, however, how did he portray them? On another note, how did Chamberlain characterize British anti-imperialists?

Chamberlain struck a responsive chord (as evidenced by the applause he received) when he referred to "those self-denying missionaries who have gone through all these wild and savage lands." What is the nature of that appeal to the working people of Birmingham? Finally, what principal trends and events does Chamberlain link to imperialism? In what way does he make those connections?

Senator Beveridge's speech was a strong defense of U.S. imperialism in the Philippines. In what ways are his arguments similar to those of Chamberlain? In what ways are they different? Chamberlain, for example, spends a good deal of time justifying British imperialism as beneficial to the working classes; how important is this argument in Beveridge's speech? Do you think that is Beveridge's main reason for advocating U.S. imperialism? Why or why not? If not, what do you think his main reason is?

Opponents of imperialism in the United States claimed that such activities were against the spirit of the Declaration of Independence of 1776. How does Beveridge reply to those critics? What arguments does he use?

Toward the conclusion of his speech, Beveridge claims that the "hand of God" can be seen in the events of the time. To what specifically was he referring? Do you think that this was an important part of Beveridge's argument (even though not much space was devoted to it)? Do you find this argument in Chamberlain's speech?

Kaiser Wilhelm II's 1897 speech contains some of the same arguments used by Chamberlain and Beveridge. Yet in tone it is quite different from the other two speeches. What points did the Kaiser make that were similar to those made by Chamberlain and

Chapter 8

Expansion and

Public Opinion:

Advocates of

The "New

Imperialism"

Beveridge? In what ways is the Kaiser's speech different? For example, both Chamberlain and Beveridge devote considerable attention to economic motives for imperialism. Judging from his speech, how important was the economic factor to the Kaiser? Do you think any other factor was more important to him?

Keep in mind that Germany was a newcomer to the "family" of nations, having been unified as one country only since 1871. Judging from his speech, what effect do you think this fact had on Wilhelm II's thinking? On Germany's urge to establish an empire?

Leopold II's speech stands in marked contrast to those of Chamberlain, Beveridge, and Wilhelm II. In what ways is it different? What points does he make in support of imperialism?

A few years later, Leopold II was able to acquire for himself (not for the Belgian nation) a principality in the Congo, which he proceeded to exploit mercilessly and which made him enormously wealthy. Do you find any clues about this future action in his speech? Indeed, what is Leopold II attempting to accomplish here? Remember that Belgium is a small country and would have needed the consent of larger and more powerful European nations in order to engage in empire building. Could this fact influence the nature of Leopold II's speech?

In contrast, in what ways did Ferdinando Martini see Italy's situation as unique among European nations? How does he see the power and prestige of Italy changing? What accounts for that change? More important, how might building an empire help to solve Italy's problems?

As with the other four advocates of imperialism, Martini deals with the "host population" of what would be Italy's new empire, though only fleetingly. Yet Martini uses that image in quite a different way. What point is he making when he refers to the "Abyssinian hut"? By inference, how would Italian imperialism solve the problem that Martini perceives?

After reading all the selections and answering these questions, look at the five pieces of evidence collectively. What were the most important arguments imperialists used in trying to influence public opinion? How did they view the "host populations"? The anti-imperialists? Did the arguments in favor of imperialism differ significantly from nation to nation? If so, can you explain these differences?

EPILOGUE

The brief imperialistic surge of the late nineteenth and early twentieth centuries profoundly altered the history of the world. Because of it, most of the earth's lands fell under Western political and economic influence.

In 1880 only about 10 percent of Africa was controlled by European nations; by 1900, however, only Ethiopia and Liberia had been able to resist the imperialist onslaught. In Asia, Western nations acquired some territory and effectively dominated the trade of most of the rest of the continent. And when Europe greedily eyed the vulnerable nations of Latin America, the United States—by 1900 itself a colonial power—announced that, in effect, that area fell within its national "sphere of influence." Indeed, by 1905 the nations of the West had come to believe that they were the center of the universe and that the rest of the earth existed to work for, produce profits for, and please the peoples of Europe and the United States. In their arrogance as the self-proclaimed "fittest" peoples in the world, most Westerners believed this dominance was only right and just.

This is not to say, however, that all Westerners approved of empire building. Though a minority, these critics of imperialism were extremely vocal and their criticisms could not be entirely ignored. In England, economist J. A. Hobson attacked colonialism as economically unprofitable to all but a few and morally bankrupting to the West. For his part, Vladimir Ilyich Lenin, soon to be leader of the Bolshevik Revolution, saw imperialism as the last stage of capitalism, which ultimately would lead to war and revolution. In the United States, anti-imperialists counted among their number industrialist Andrew Carnegie, author Mark Twain, philosopher William James, reformer Jane Addams, and political leader William Jennings Bryan. Yet these and other voices, though loud and articulate, for the most part went unheeded amid the almost frantic scramble for colonial possessions.

Armed with hindsight, we can see that these critics of colonialism had much stronger arguments than their contemporaries either realized or ap-

preciated. Acquiring and administering an empire was an enormously expensive process, draining off funds that might have been used for economic and social reforms. Snuffing out resistance to colonial rule required the maintenance of a strong military presence that often responded to anti-Western upsurges with extreme brutality. In China, resistance to imperialism was countered with naval bombardments of cities and wholesale executions of resisters. In the Philippines, the United States used approximately 74,000 troops to crush the movement for independence, resorting to torture, repression, and atrocities in order to "civilize" the Filipinos. In the Congo Free State, agents of Leopold II resorted to forced labor and incredibly brutal treatment, including mutilations, of protestors in order to extract ivory and rubber.[14] In truth, colonialism could be both an exceedingly expensive and a morally reprehensible activity. Moreover, the scramble for empire heightened the rivalry and conflict among Western nations and was one factor leading to World War One in 1914. In 1898 England and France very nearly came to blows at Fashoda (on the upper Nile River) until the French backed down. In 1905 Germany's attempts to intrude into Morocco almost brought it to war with France until the Algeciras Conference of 1906 awarded control of Morocco to the French. In 1904–1905, Russian imperialism in East Asia brought Russia into a war with

14. The situation in the Congo Free State, Leopold's personal possession, became so scandalous that the king was forced to turn over control to the Belgian government in 1908.

[217]

Chapter 8

Expansion and

Public Opinion:

Advocates of

The "New

Imperialism"

Japan in which it suffered a humiliating defeat. As Western nations looked for power vacuums to exploit in Africa, China, and the Balkans, the threat of armed hostilities increased. Indeed, it was Russia's efforts to penetrate the Balkan tinderbox that led directly to war in 1914.

At the same time, the West's control of its newly acquired territories was never strong. Movements for national independence constantly had to be put down. Efforts to "westernize" Africans and Asians were never very successful, except among some of the elites of those regions. Though an increasing number of non-Westerners gradually came to embrace Western technology and political ideas in the twentieth century, they nevertheless insisted that the West should withdraw so they could govern themselves. Thus, later movements for independence often tended to be "anti-Western" as well, to purge those societies of westernized elites, if not of Western technology. Within a half-century, all the empires built by the West in the late nineteenth century would be in shambles. For a very short time, the West lived in an imperialistic sunshine. Yet—to paraphrase Herman Melville—the brighter the sunshine, the greater the resulting shadows.

CHAPTER NINE
A CRISIS IN WESTERN
THOUGHT, 1870–1920

During World War One, a small group of writers and artists came together in Zurich, Switzerland to form the core of a movement they called Dada.[1] They chose the name intentionally, precisely because it is a meaningless, nonsensical word conveying their reaction to a West capable of the carnage of the Great War. Dadaists saw everything in Western civilization as absurd and futile, the products of a world become increasingly mechanistic, and they gave form to their vision in startling literary and artistic innovations designed to mock conventional modes of expression. A Dadaist poet cut words randomly from newspapers, dropped them into a bag and shook them up, then drew them out and assembled them in the order they emerged as a nonsensical poem.[2] A Dadaist artist displayed his version of Leonardo da Vinci's *Mona Lisa*, faithful to the original save for a mustache added, an act that at the time appeared shockingly disrespectful of artistic conventions.[3] In such ways did Dadaists call into question all traditional values and modes of expression.

Although the Dada movement had spent itself by 1924, it was nonetheless a highly significant cultural phenomenon, marking the culmination of a number of developments in Western thought that, taken together, represented for many an intellectual crisis, a real challenge to traditional values and beliefs.

---

1. **Dada**: the precise origin of this term has been explained in various ways. It means "hobbyhorse" in French, and one version of its origin holds that it was selected by a random opening of a French dictionary at the word *dada*. Others explain "Dada" as the "Da, Da," that is "Yes, Yes," of the Romanian conversation of one of its founders. Whatever its actual origins, the term was nonsensical to most Europeans in 1918. The original Dada *Manifesto* issued in Berlin in 1918 is reprinted in Hans Richter, *Dada: Art and Anti-Art*, trans. David Britt (New York: Oxford University Press, 1978), pp. 104–107.

2. Tristan Tzara (1896–1963).

3. Marcel Duchamp (1887–1968).

The traditional values and beliefs of most nineteenth-century Westerners were founded on the tenets of Judeo-Christian religion and the legacy of the eighteenth-century Enlightenment. From the Bible, most Westerners derived their faith in a Creator. From the Enlightenment, they drew a belief in the rational nature of humans and their ability to use their intellectual gifts to understand and master the physical world (see Chapter 2). In the thirty years before the turn of the century, however, the findings of physical and social scientists called traditional values and beliefs into question while failing to advance an alternative faith. At the same time, as we will see, the art of the age reflected an increasing knowledge of the physical world and the diminished authority of old standards of thought and behavior. We will note here only the more important late nineteenth-century developments in Western knowledge that contradicted traditional thought, some aspects of which continue to stir controversy a century later.

Western religious beliefs met challenges on several fronts after 1870. The pioneering English biologist Charles Darwin (1809–1882) had presented his theory of evolution as it applied to animals in his 1859 classic, *On the Origin of Species*. In 1871 Darwin published what was for many a more disturbing work, *Descent of Man*, in which he applied his evolutionary theories to mankind.[4] Edu-

cated Westerners suddenly found that their religious beliefs, grounded on the story of the Creation in the Bible's book of Genesis, conflicted with the rational framework of the natural science in which they also put great stock. The result was a crisis of belief that still manifests itself in parts of the West in struggles over the content of public school biology courses.

At the same time that Darwin's work challenged one basic article of the Judeo-Christian faith, other archeological and biblical studies diminished the uniqueness of the Judeo-Christian heritage. Increasing Western knowledge of ancient Middle Eastern civilization, for example, revealed a great cultural kinship between the Hebrews of the Old Testament and the Babylonians and other ancient peoples. Similarly, scholars of the New Testament period found remarkable parallels to the story of the life of Christ in non-Christian cultures. Was the Judeo-Christian heritage, based on a belief in the Jews as God's chosen people and in a Savior of humankind, as unique as it had previously seemed? The debate still continues between religious fundamentalists and those who accept an increasing body of knowledge founded on scholarship and not faith.

As modern scholarship challenged traditional religious thought, it also raised doubts about the intellectual legacy of the eighteenth century. A central tenet of the Enlightenment held that reason was the supreme and exclusive achievement of humankind. The work by psychological and biological researchers in the late

4. The full titles of these works were *On the Origin of Species by Means of Natural Selection or the Preservation of Favored Races in the Struggle for Life* and *The Descent of Man in Relation to Sex*.

nineteenth and early twentieth centuries, however, cast increasing doubt on the validity of that belief. Wilhelm Wundt (1832–1920) opened the first experimental psychology laboratory at the University of Leipzig in 1870. His purpose was to conduct experiments on animal subjects to demonstrate that the animal mind and the human mind were fundamentally similar. The Russian physiologist Ivan Pavlov (1849–1936), conducting similar laboratory experiments with dogs in the 1890s, determined that certain responses in his subjects could be conditioned—that is, learned and unlearned. The emerging behaviorist school of psychology to which Pavlov's experiments contributed held that most human actions and emotions, like those of the laboratory dogs, could be similarly conditioned. The human mind suddenly seemed quite similar to that of the animal. Such a concept did not accord with the Enlightenment belief in human rationality. Even more destructive of reason as the cornerstone of human behavior was the work of the Austrian physician Sigmund Freud (1856–1939).

Freud began his pioneering work in mental disorders in the 1880s, achieving success with a therapeutic process in which he allowed his patients to talk freely about their childhood memories, their emotions, and their fantasies. The result of his work was the modern school of psychoanalysis and a very unsettling view of the human mind. Freud and other psychological researchers posited the existence of the human unconscious, an irrational and inaccessible portion of the psyche that exerted tremendous influence, through feelings and impulses repressed from consciousness, on human behavior. Indeed, for Freud, the unconscious was a virtual battleground of conflicting inner forces. The *id* embodied base and instinctual drives, such as sex and violence, which demanded immediate, hedonistic gratification. The *superego*, on the other hand, embraced the conventions of society and the strictures of religion that aimed at repressing such impulses. Between these two extremes was the *ego*, the mediating point of consciousness in which some sort of balance between the hedonistic drives of the id and the repressive tendencies of the superego had to be achieved for the well-balanced mind. The goal of Freud's psychoanalysis was to defuse potentially dangerous unconscious impulses by making them conscious, that is, drawing them into the patient's field of awareness, where they could then be examined and treated.

After Freud, reason could no longer be upheld as the motivating principle of human behavior. The optimistic view of progress—that is, that history and human development moved toward better and better forms—also declined as a result of the work of two pioneering sociologists, the Frenchman Emile Durkheim (1858–1917) and the German Max Weber (1864–1920). In examining his society, Durkheim found that modern times in the West were not necessarily an improvement over the past. In medieval and early modern Europe, social station was determined at birth and traditional social values and religious strictures dictated the individual's comportment within his or her station. In the modern Western world, however, the individual enjoyed greater freedom at the same time that the force of traditional religious and social controls waned. Anarchy threatened society, and *anomie*, a loss of personal direction resulting from the collapse of moral guidelines, afflicted the individual and contributed, Durkheim said, to the West's high rate of suicide. Consequently, he believed, the modern world required a new, secular moral order.

Max Weber examined the results of the Enlightenment effort to explain the physical world scientifically and to organize governments rationally around constitutions and bureaucratic procedures. The results had been high scientific accomplishment and stable government won at the cost of the spiritual element. As a consequence, human creativity had suffered and society also faced a threat. Weber understood that the human character had an affective side, too, and that, in times of stress, this aspect of the human psyche could lead citizens to follow the emotional urgings of an irrational but charismatic leader. Progress, it seemed, was a mixed blessing.

Other social theorists advanced a different but equally disturbing view of the world, one marked by strife, violence, and conflict. Marxists, as we found in Chapter 6, found human existence to be dominated by class conflict; other thinkers advanced equally unsettling visions of human conflict. An important tenet of Enlightenment thought was the basic equality of all humans. Yet some nineteenth-century thinkers, in their enthusiasm for the new scientific discoveries of the age, applied Darwin's biological theory of evolution to society as a whole. Emphasizing the struggle for existence that they found in Darwin's work, they claimed that a process of "survival of the fittest" characterized modern human society. All people were not created equal; rather, the stronger or more intelligent had a right to triumph and survive in life's struggle, whereas others did not. Such an application of Darwin's ideas, known as Social Darwinism, could be used, for example, to justify imperialism on the grounds that a "superior" people had a right to rule an "inferior" people (see Chapter 8). According to this view, despite the progressive improvement predicated by Enlightenment thinkers, human beings still were engaged in a primal struggle for existence.

Philosophers, too, joined in the criticism of the Christian tradition, the Enlightenment, and the modern world. Indeed, the German philosopher Friedrich Nietzsche (1844–1900) offered the most thoroughgoing rebuttal of Enlightenment thought and everything associated with it. Nietzsche saw the modern world in decay because its elevation of reason had undermined the capacity to feel passionately, to will, and to be creative. But if he attacked the Enlightenment tradition, Nietzsche was equally hostile to Christianity. An atheist, he proclaimed that "God is dead," people's belief in the supernatural having been effectively destroyed by generations of rational scientific thinking. And yet, Nietzsche maintained, Christianity continued to exert a large and harmful influence, and its moral dictates still inhibited people's will to act spontaneously and creatively. Nietzsche also deplored the growth of democratic government, which in his view subjected the creative few to the authority of the mediocre majority—the common herd. Nietzsche advocated instead the leadership of a few superior persons, of *Übermenschen* ("overmen" or "higher men"), philosopher-rulers whose wills would be unencumbered by the controls of rational thought, Christianity, or democratic rule.

Even the work of the Scientific Revolution, which formed the basis for the Enlightenment (see Chapter 2), came under attack in the half-century from 1870 to 1920. Nineteenth-century science was based on Newtonian physics, which held that the human intellect could discern the basic laws that structured the physical world. With such knowledge, scientists confidently believed that they could ultimately predict the development of the physical world. The result of scientific research in our period, however, has proved instead the existence of a highly unpredictable world.

In Newtonian physics, the atom was considered a solid, indivisible particle and the basis of all matter. In a number of scientific breakthroughs, however, this concept, along with certain laws of Newtonian physics, was disproved. In 1897 Joseph John Thompson (1856–1940), an English physicist, discovered that the atom is not solid but composed of electrons revolving around a nucleus. Niels Bohr (1855–1962), a Danish physicist,

found in 1913 that the electrons do not adhere to Newton's laws of motion. The German physicist Werner Heisenberg (1901–1976) summed up this and other work in modern atomic physics shortly after 1920 in his *uncertainty principle*, which posited that modern physicists could only attempt to describe what occurrences were probable in subatomic matter. Nothing was absolutely certain. Heisenberg's principle prompted one distinguished traditional scientist of the era to exclaim in disbelief, "I refuse to believe that God plays dice with the world!"

The work of Albert Einstein (1879–1955) marked the culmination of research in the physical sciences in our period. Einstein dislodged another cornerstone of traditional science, the notion that time, space, and matter were absolute and measurable phenomena. In Einstein's *relativity theory*, time and space became relative, not absolute concepts. Moreover, energy and matter might be converted into each other. Expressed in the famous equation, E (energy) $= m$ (mass) $\times c^2$ (speed of light squared), this concept was to have literally earth-shattering results when the splitting of the atom allowed the conversion of matter into vast and potentially destructive amounts of energy. Einstein's work brought the world to the threshold of the atomic age while discrediting the long-held tenets of absolute time and space.

The greatest challenge to the world view of nineteenth-century Westerners, however, came not as abstract theory but devastating reality: World War One (see Chapter 10). Many intellectuals and artists initially joined their fellow citizens in welcoming a war that they believed would revitalize the West. In that conflagration, however, every belligerent government harnessed modern science and industry to its war effort. The result was bloodletting on an unprecedented scale that caused intellectuals and artists to despair of traditional values—the mood represented by the Dada movement. As the Dada *Manifesto* declared: "After the carnage, we keep only the hope of a purified humanity."

By the early decades of the twentieth century, then, the patterns of nineteenth-century Western thought seemed under assault on every front. As old ways of thinking fell to the new discoveries in the physical and social sciences, Western artistic expression cast off old norms as well, often with provocative results. To take the example of music, a number of composers of the early twentieth

century abandoned traditional harmonies in their compositions, producing a new dissonant sound. The first performance in 1913 of a ballet, *The Rite of Spring*, by one of these composers, Igor Stravinsky (1882–1971), almost provoked a Paris audience to riot. To composers like Stravinsky, harmony no longer seemed appropriate in a world of discord.

Reflecting the trends of the period 1870 to 1920, another art form, painting, also abandoned traditional conventions during this time of intellectual crisis. Your goal in this chapter is to examine the magnitude of the transformations in Western thought of this period by analyzing the works of a group of major painters. How do the paintings reflect a break with traditional artistic standards? What trends can be traced from each artist's work? How did artists reveal the intellectual currents of the period in their works?

SOURCES AND METHOD

This chapter introduces you to a primary source historians traditionally have used in studying a past era—its art. Analysis of a period's works of art can provide the historian with an excellent entry into the intellectual life of that epoch because art often reflects the thought of its age. But we must be clear about what is and is not part of the analytical process you must carry out with this chapter's evidence.

The evidence should not be the object of your aesthetic analysis, that is,

your attempt to determine which paintings express your individual concept of beauty. We all have opinions and preferences regarding art, especially the modern art this chapter presents. Consequently, you might be inclined simply to dismiss some of the paintings reproduced here as "strange looking" because they do not accord with your individual taste.

You should, however, analyze the paintings in the context of their times. To help focus your analysis, the paintings selected all have a common subject, the human form, to enable you to appreciate the different visions artists brought to the problem of portraying their fellow humans. They also are arranged roughly chronologically to show you both traditional nineteenth-century art before 1870 and some of its main trends over the half-century from 1870 to 1920. You should attempt to assess the impact that these works would have had on their contemporary viewers. Try to imagine yourself as an educated Western European born about 1850 and living until 1920. You would have reached maturity about 1870 and, in the course of your lifetime, would have experienced tremendous change. Materially, you would have been born in an age in which most people traveled by foot or horse and carriage and would have lived to see people traveling by train, automobile, and airplane. Your messages in later life would be carried by telephone and telegraph, and the diseases that threatened your parents would be only a memory by your middle years. In the course of your lifespan of seventy years, then, your material world would have been totally transformed. So, too, would have been your culture's art. Would you have found this transformation unsettling? To supplement your analysis, a brief introduction to the artists whose work this chapter presents is necessary.

Sources 1 and 2, representing two conventional styles of nineteenth-century art, are works whose style would have seemed familiar to their viewers. They are the starting point for your analysis of artistic trends. The French painter Jean-Auguste Dominique Ingres (1780–1867) was an exponent of the Neoclassical style

of painting. Art historians apply the label "Neoclassical" to Ingres and other artists of his period who found much of their inspiration in classical subjects. In the execution of their works these artists sought to duplicate the harmony, balance, and realism they found in Greek and Roman art. The portrait of Louis Bertin (Source 1), one of the most important figures in early nineteenth-century French journalism, embodies the Neoclassical quest for realistic portrayal. What qualities of Bertin does Ingres seek to convey? How does the artist's vision of Bertin reflect the intellectual tradition of the first half of the nineteenth century?

Source 2, *Greece Expiring on the Ruins of Missolonghi*, by Eugène Delacroix (1798–1863), is an example of nineteenth-century Romanticism. Romanticism arose in large part as a reaction to the Enlightenment with its emphasis on a rational interpretation of the human experience. In literature and art, exponents of the Romantic impulse sought to recover the emotion and drama of life. The Greek rebellion of the 1820s against Turkey excited European Romantics because it was the war for independence of the land of Homer and Plato; the English Romantic poet, Lord Byron, died in Greece seeking to join the rebel cause. Delacroix's painting shows a Greek fighter crushed in the ruins of the city of Missolonghi, where the Greek defenders succumbed in 1826 to a long siege by the Turks. (Missolonghi, not inconsequentially, was the site of Byron's death.) The woman's gesture of defenseless resignation reflects Greek martyrdom. What view of the world and the role of human beings in it did Delacroix convey? What view of the individual does the image of "Greece" convey to you? Compare the paintings of Delacroix and Ingres. Certainly the artists reflected two very different philosophies. Nevertheless, what similarities do you find in their portrayal of the human form?

As your analysis moves beyond Source 2, you must be careful to assess the paintings in light of the intellectual breakthroughs we have just examined. Remember, too, that by 1850 the invention of the camera, with its ability to produce accurate images, obliged artists to make a serious reevaluation of the function of their art. What was the purpose of the labor involved in creating the portrait of Bertin when a photograph would capture an even more accurate image?

In Source 3 we encounter the work of an artistic movement that reflected the late nineteenth century's interest in science and the reassessment of the artistic function prompted by the camera. With the Impressionist artists who flourished especially in France in the 1870s and 1880s, we see a reconsideration of the whole function of painting that relegated portraiture to the photographer. We also find a systematic attempt, much in the vein of modern science, to portray the artist's subjects with an accuracy that would convey to the viewer the subtle effects of light and shadow as they actually appeared to the human eye.

Some Impressionists executed their works with large splashes of color. Georges Seurat (1859–1891)

moved beyond this technique to create pictures with intricate arrangements of tiny dots of color, the result of his study of scientific theories of color perception. *A Sunday Afternoon on the Island of La Grande Jatte* shows excursioners on an island in the river Seine near Paris. What was the artist's purpose in this painting? Why did he pay so little apparent attention to developing the individual characteristics of the persons in his painting? How would you characterize the figures in *La Grande Jatte*?

In the 1870s many viewed Impressionism as a dramatic revolt against artistic conventions, but far more was to come.

The Dutchman Vincent van Gogh (1853–1890) also had studied the Impressionists and moved beyond them. He gloried in the use of broad brush strokes to express his excitement and emotions in a picture, distorting images in that quest. His work thus makes him an early exponent of another style of art, Expressionism. A deeply religious man, van Gogh sought to express his personal vision of his subjects while also seeking in them what he called "that something of the eternal which the halo used to symbolize."[5] Source 4, his portrait *La Berceuse* (The Cradle Rocker), employs startling colors: the woman's hair is orange, her dress green, the wallpaper background green and pink flowers, and the floor red. What feelings did the artist seek to express here? Compare *La Berceuse* with the portrait of Bertin. Why did

5. Quoted in H. W. Janson, *History of Art: A Survey of the Major Visual Arts from the Dawn of History to the Present Day* (New York: Harry N. Abrams and Prentice-Hall, 1962), p. 507.

van Gogh engage in such obvious distortions of the human physiognomy?

Paul Gauguin (1848–1903) also emerged from the Impressionists to create a style called Symbolism. Gauguin had two careers, first as a successful Parisian stockbroker, then as an impoverished artist. Indeed, he left his family and business for his art in 1883. In rejecting his middle-class past, he also rejected much of modern industrial society. Gauguin found that Westerners had lost much of life's emotions and mystery in their progress toward the industrial age with its concern for material gain. Western art, he believed, reflected this loss, and he sought to reinfuse the missing emotion into his paintings by studying the art of non-Western peoples. Gauguin spent most of his last years in the South Pacific trying to capture the spirit of non-Western art. A number of artists followed Gauguin's lead, especially after World War One, which convinced them of the bankruptcy of Western culture and values. Indeed, later artists sought non-Western inspiration more widely than Gauguin; many, for example, incorporated African art forms in their work. In Source 5, Gauguin's painting *Manao Tupapau—The Spirit of the Dead Watches*, how has he added non-Western elements in achieving his artistic goal? How did he inject a fantastic element into Western art?

Source 6, *The Dream*, is the work of Frenchman Henri Rousseau (1844–1910). A self-taught artist, Rousseau spent the first half of his adulthood as a government customs inspector, and his paintings reflect his lack of traditional training. *The Dream* is a fantastic, impossible, and highly detailed scene that conveys Rousseau's view of life. What does the choice of a dream as his subject tell you about the artist's outlook? Does the artist present a realistic group of figures in the nude, the lions, and the snake charmer? Why might you think that Rousseau sought to paint the same natural and non-Western settings that Gauguin did?

The work of the Norwegian artist Edvard Munch (1863–1948) reflected the influence of van Gogh, Gauguin, and the philosophical thought of his day. His *The Scream*, Source 7, is an Expressionist work. Even more than van Gogh, however, Munch subordinated detail and character study to a strong message. What sentiments does the central figure convey in *The Scream*? How does the artist's treatment of the background magnify the feelings of the central character? What might the artist be saying about the central figure's relationships with other people?

The work of van Gogh and Gauguin influenced other artists as well. Exhibits of their works in Paris during the first years of the twentieth century inspired a group of young artists to break so much with artistic conventions that their contemporaries called them *les Fauves*, or "The Wild Beasts." Georges Rouault (1871–1958) was one of these Fauvist artists. Almost completely unconcerned with portraying his subjects accurately or with much character study, Rouault was deeply religious and found modern life devoid of spiritual direction. His paintings reflect this sentiment and his hope to play some role in a renewed importance for his Roman Catholic faith.

His *Head of Christ*, Source 8, shocked audiences who felt more comfortable with works like those of Ingres. Do you find much in Christ's face that is realistically human? Why did the artist so abandon convention? What sentiments did the artist express in the brush slashes with which he created this picture? What does the face tell you about the fate of Christ and that of Christianity in the modern world?

A young Spanish artist, Pablo Picasso (1881–1973), moved to Paris in 1900 and immediately reflected in his work the influence of many of the artists we have discussed. Yet Picasso went beyond them in the extent of his break with artistic tradition. Source 9, *Les Demoiselles d'Avignon*, shocked Picasso's audiences in several ways in 1907. First, its subject is a group of prostitutes on Avignon Street in Barcelona. Second, it is an early expression of the Cubist style in art, in which the artist used a variety of wedges and angles to create his picture.

In *Les Demoiselles d'Avignon*, Picasso abandoned traditional rules of perspective as well as any effort to portray the human form accurately. Some found his Cubism almost an attempt to portray his subjects geometrically; others remarked that Picasso's women looked like arrangements of broken pieces of glass. Why do you think Picasso abandoned artistic conventions? Can you discern any parallels between Picasso's art and the physical science of Einstein and others? What trend in modern art is reflected in the two faces on the picture's right?

Picasso was one of a number of Abstract artists at work early in the twentieth century. Abstract art puts primary emphasis on the structure, not the subject, of the picture. Another Abstract artist was the German George Grosz (1893–1959), who joined the Dada movement after World War One. Grosz's works show Cubist influences in a type of collage technique; they also frequently have a social message, as in Source 10, *Germany, A Winter's Tale*. Completed amid the famine and defeat that overtook Germany in the last days of World War One, this painting presents Grosz's views on the war and the society that produced it. The central figure is an "average" German surrounded by a kaleidoscope of Berlin scenes. What do you notice about the plate in front of him? What comment does this make on the Germany of 1918? What social groups do the three figures in the foreground represent? What roles did they play in pre-1918 German society, according to the artist? What vision of German society in 1918 does the background convey?

The final artist whose work appears in our evidence is the Frenchman Marcel Duchamp (1887–1968). Duchamp joined the Dada movement in despair after the First World War. (It was he who painted the mustache on the *Mona Lisa*.) Even before the war, however, his work tended to be fantastic in its portrayals. Source 11, *The Bride*, bears no resemblance to its subject; if anything, it reminds us of equipment for a chemistry laboratory. Why do you think the artist rejected any attempt to portray the human form accurately? What manner of comment on the machine age might this work be making? How and why were artists like Duchamp striving for a new and more subjective reality?

Using this background on the painters, turn now to the evidence.

As you look at the paintings, seek to assess the magnitude of the changes in Western thought in the period 1870–1920. How do the paintings reflect a break with traditional artistic standards? What trends can be traced from each artist's work? How did the artists reveal the intellectual currents of the period in their works?

THE EVIDENCE

Source 1 from the Louvre/Cliché des Musées Nationaux-Paris.

1. Jean-Auguste Dominique Ingres, *Portrait of Louis Bertin*, 1832

Source 2 from the Musée des Beaux Arts, Bordeaux/Cliché des Musées Nationaux-Paris.

2. Eugène Delacroix, *Greece Expiring on the Ruins of Missolonghi*, 1827

[230]

3. Georges Seurat, *A Sunday Afternoon on the Island of La Grande Jatte*, 1884–1886. Oil on canvas, 207.6 × 308.0 cm.

Source 4 from the Rijksmuseum Kröller-Müller, Otterlo.

4. Vincent van Gogh, *La Berceuse*, 1889

5. Paul Gauguin, *Manao Tupapau—The Spirit of the Dead Watches*, 1892. Oil on burlap mounted on canvas, 28½″ × 38⅜″.

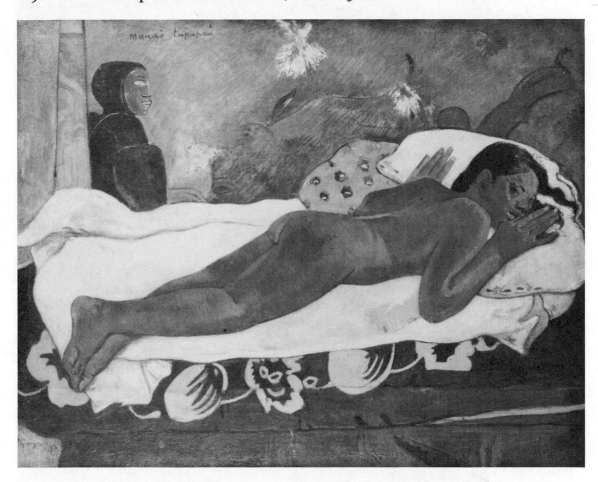

6. Henri Rousseau, *The Dream*, 1910. Oil on canvas, 6′8½″ × 9′9½″.

Source 7 from the Nasjonalgalleriet, Oslo.

7. Edvard Munch, *The Scream*, 1893

Source 8 from The Chrysler Museum, Norfolk, Virginia (Gift of Walter P. Chrysler Jr.).

8. Georges Rouault, *The Head of Christ*, 1905. Oil on canvas mounted on paper, 39″ × 25¼″.

9. Pablo Picasso, *Les Demoiselles d'Avignon*, 1907. Oil on canvas, 8′ × 7′8″.

Source 10 formerly from the Collection Garvens, Hanover, Germany (painting has been lost).

10. George Grosz, Germany, *A Winter's Tale*, 1918

Source 11 from The Philadelphia Museum of Art (Louise and Walter Arensberg Collection).

11. Marcel Duchamp, *The Bride*, 1912

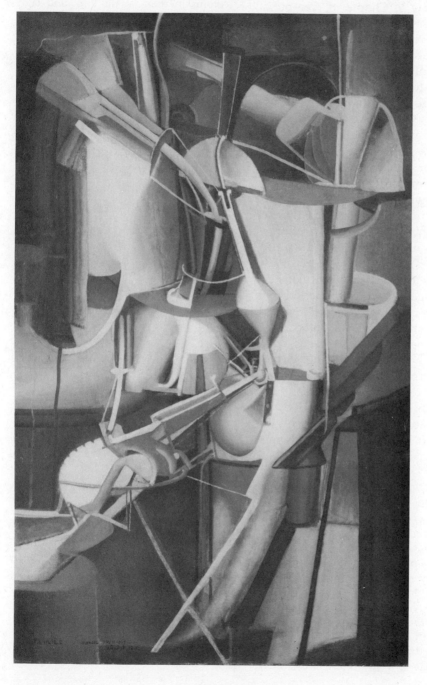

QUESTIONS TO CONSIDER

As we saw in Chapter 8, free public education was becoming more widely available in Western Europe by the late nineteenth century. The number of people with sufficient education to understand intellectual trends grew rapidly in the years before 1920. Consequently, the shifts in thinking we are examining in this chapter were evident to a considerably larger audience than that of the Enlightenment (Chapter 2). Many in this growing educated class must have found the upheavals in the natural sciences, philosophy, and art of their day unpredictable and disturbing.

At the most basic level, consider the changes in art in the period 1870 to 1920. Contrast Sources 1 and 2 with the art that follows. How do you think nineteenth-century audiences would have received the Impressionists' offerings after a steady diet of works like Sources 1 and 2? How would you account for the following reaction in 1876 by one French journalist to an early Impressionist exhibit?

The Rue le Peletier is a road of disasters. After the fire at the Opera, there is now yet another disaster there. An exhibition has just been mounted at Durand-Ruel [gallery] which allegedly contains paintings. I enter and my horrified eyes behold something terrible. Five or six lunatics, among them a woman, have joined together and exhibited their works. I have seen people rock with laughter in front of these pictures, but my heart bled when I saw them. These would-be artists call themselves revolutionaries, "Impressionists." They take a piece of canvas, colour and brush, daub a few patches of colour on them at random, and sign the whole thing with their name. It is a delusion of the same kind as if the inmates of Bedlam picked up stones from the wayside and imagined they had found diamonds.[6]

But the art of the period was the result of an aesthetic impulse far more significant than change for the sake of change, and perhaps all the more significant for that reason. Art reflected a new view of the world and the place of the individual in it. You must now examine the paintings reproduced here in light of the emerging intellectual outlook we examined at the outset of this chapter. How did the Impressionists respond to the great faith in science that characterized their age? Why do you find in the work of the late Impressionist Seurat far less emphasis on the individual than in the work of Ingres and Delacroix? What vision of life does Seurat express? What philosophical changes (and responses by educated persons to those changes) might this diminished importance have represented? How does Seurat's view of the individual contrast with that of later artists like Picasso?

Van Gogh's portrait *La Berceuse* offered its viewers a projected expression of the artist's sentiments. Why was van Gogh expressing his own feelings through the medium of another individual rather than creating

6. Quoted in E. H. Gombrich, *The Story of Art* (New York: Phaidon, 1971), pp. 392–393. **Bedlam:** the early English institution for the insane.

a photolike replica of that person? What developments in nineteenth-century thought did he reflect in this study of his subject?

In the works of Gauguin we find a search for an art with more meaning than that produced by Western civilization, which the artist found sterile. How would those familiar with the work of Nietzsche, Durkheim, Weber, and perhaps Marx have interpreted Gauguin's work? Remember, too, that Gauguin painted during the age of imperialism (see Chapter 8). How does his art stand in relation to his age's avowed belief in the superiority of Western civilization, the rallying point of the Social Darwinists?

Munch's *The Scream* brings together in one work of art many tendencies in late nineteenth- and early twentieth-century thought. Recall the ideas of Durkheim and Weber. Why did Munch portray his subject as a solitary individual? What do you think provoked the agonized scream? Although Munch's work predated most of Freud's great writings, why might you think that Munch and Freud shared a common view of the human psyche?

Georges Rouault's *Head of Christ*, as we have seen, reflects the artist's spiritual search. Why might nineteenth-century intellectual trends have elicited such a search from the pious Rouault? While Rouault reached for answers to conditions in his changing world, George Grosz satirized the world he lived in. Recall particularly the ideas of the pioneering German socialist Max Weber and the sterility he found in an increasingly bureaucratized world. What elements of Weber's thought do you find embodied in Grosz's response to German society?

You may find that Picasso's *Les Demoiselles d'Avignon* reflects several trends in Western thought. What is the significance of mathematical and geometric relationships in the Cubist approach to the human form? What contrasting message is given by the masklike faces on the right of the picture? How do they reflect some of the same influences Gauguin experienced? What effect had the age's ideas had on Picasso?

Consider Rousseau's *The Dream*. In one of his most significant works, *The Interpretation of Dreams* (1900), Freud sought to understand the irrational side of the human psyche, the unconscious, by explaining the psychological meaning of dreams. How does Rousseau's vision of reality coincide with Freud's? What significance might you ascribe to the nude and the powerful lions in the context of Freud's work?

The final painting is Duchamp's *The Bride*. Review our findings on the paintings that precede his chronologically. Why are you probably not surprised to find in his work a painting totally devoid of anything resembling the human form? What trends in art culminate in Duchamp's work? Remember that he eventually became a Dadaist. Can you detect in *The Bride* a message about the machine age and its impact on the individual?

As you answer these questions, you should gain a better understanding of the sweeping intellectual changes that overtook the late nineteenth- and early twentieth-century Western world. The Dadaist outlook on Western civilization, described in the introduction to this chapter, embodied one extreme reaction to those changes, and the art we have studied presents other responses. You should now be able to answer the central questions of this chapter: How did the paintings reflect a break from traditional artistic standards? What trends can be identified in each artist's work? Finally, how did the artists collectively reveal the intellectual currents of the period?

EPILOGUE

In a sense, this chapter presents a turning point in the history of Western civilization. The West after 1920 was in many ways a far less secure place than the West of the eighteenth and nineteenth centuries, when Europe had been equally secure in its world power and its world view. The nineteenth century in particular had produced a standard of living in the West higher than ever before enjoyed by people anywhere. Westerners were convinced of their primacy.

As the nineteenth century drew to a close, however, many Europeans looked to a disturbing future. Certainly the trends in art we have observed here continued. Dadaism gave way to Surrealism, which drew on the artist's unconscious. Later, Abstract Expressionism and other styles would also develop to present viewers with even greater challenges to their interpretive skills. Other undercurrents were even more distressing, however. Intellectually, the authority of the old faiths and tenets that long had guided Westerners eroded, and the consequent questioning of traditional values and practices invaded every area of human endeavor. Internationally, the strength of the European powers was challenged by the rise of non-European nations like the United States and Japan. Politically, the nineteenth-century faith in democracy would be challenged by twentieth-century totalitarian movements that reminded many of the threat Max Weber saw in an irrational but charismatic leader (see Chapter 12). Technologically, humankind's progress meant that it had developed unprecedented ability to destroy life (see Chapter 10). Economically, nineteenth-century bourgeois capitalism faced the challenge of communist revolution (see Chapter 11). The art of the period 1870–1920 reflected all these disturbing developments.

Indeed, the art produced after 1920 by Surrealist, Abstract Expressionist, and other modern artists mirrored the changes in the West that came with accelerating speed after the period we have examined in this chapter. Einstein's work unlocked the destructive possibilities of the atom, and Western science was to create technologies of war far in excess of those employed in World War One. In the giant corporations that came to dominate the Western economy, the individual's significance diminished still further. Using the analytical technique you have mastered in this chapter, you may wish to continue exploring the ideological messages of modern art beyond the period 1870–1920.

CHAPTER TEN

WORLD WAR ONE:

TOTAL WAR

In the first days of August 1914, every major capital city in Europe was the scene of enthusiastic patriotic demonstrations in favor of the declarations of war that began World War One. All confidently predicted victory for their own nation, and all expected a short war. Emperor William II (Kaiser Wilhelm II) told German troops departing for the front, "You will be home before the leaves have fallen from the trees." The war indeed ended in autumn, but it was the autumn of 1918, not 1914. Previous military history did not prepare Europeans in any way for the war they were to undertake in 1914.

Europe's last general war had ended in 1815 with Napoleon's defeat at Waterloo. Subsequent nineteenth-century conflicts never involved all the great powers, and they were invariably short wars. The Prussians, for example, had defeated Austria in six weeks during the Austro-Prussian War of 1866. In the last nineteenth-century conflict involving major powers, the Franco-Prussian

War of 1870–1871, France and Prussia had signed an armistice after a little over twenty-seven weeks of combat.

These nineteenth-century wars after Waterloo were also highly limited conflicts, involving relatively small professional armies whose weapons and tactics differed little from those of the Napoleonic era. Civilian populations seldom felt much impact from such conflicts, although Paris endured a siege of eighteen weeks in the Franco-Prussian War.

The war on which Europeans so enthusiastically embarked in 1914 proved a far different one than the 1870–1871 conflict. The prewar alliance system meant that, for the first time in a century, all the great powers were at war, making the scope of the hostilities greater than in any recent fighting. Moreover, the conflict quickly became a world war as the belligerents fought one another outside Europe and as non-European powers such as Japan and the United States joined the ranks of warring nations.

Even more significant than the number of nations engaged in the conflict, however, was the nature of the war they fought. The Industrial Revolution of the nineteenth century had brought technical changes to warfare that were to transform the 1914 conflict into the Western world's first modern, total war. This would be a war of tremendous cost to both soldiers and civilians, a struggle requiring effort and sacrifice by every citizen of the warring countries.

Modern railroads and motorized transport permitted belligerent nations to bring the full weight of their new industrial strengths to the battlefields of World War One. Both sides for the first time made extensive use of the machine gun as well as new, longer-range heavy artillery. Whole new weapons systems included flame throwers, poison gas, the tank, the airplane, the lighter-than-air dirigible, and the submarine.

Generals trained in an earlier era of warfare failed at first to understand the increased destructive capacity of these new weapons and practiced military tactics of 1870 in fighting the war's first battles. As before, they attacked the enemy with massed infantrymen armed with bayonets fixed, flags flying, drums sounding, and led by officers in dress uniforms complete with white gloves. This was the kind of war Europeans had enthusiastically anticipated in 1914, but because of modern firepower, casualties in such attacks were extremely heavy—indeed, completely unprecedented.

Especially in Western Europe, such losses resulted in increased reliance on what has been called the "infantryman's best friend," the shovel. To avoid the firepower of the new modern weaponry, opposing armies dug into the earth, and by Christmas 1914 they opposed each other in 466 miles of trenches stretching through France from the English Channel to the border of Switzerland. These trenches represented stalemate. They were separated by "No Man's Land," the open space an attacker had to cross to reach the enemy. Swept with machine gun and artillery fire and blocked by barbed wire and other obstacles, "No Man's Land" was an area that an attacking force could cross only with great losses. In such circumstances, neither side could achieve the traditional decisive breakthrough into the enemy's lines. Field Marshal Horatio Kitchener, an experienced commander of the old school of warfare and British Secretary for War until 1916, expressed the frustration of many about such combat: "I don't know what is to be done—this isn't war."

In their efforts to achieve victory, generals and statesmen sought to break the stalemate in a number of ways that extended the impact of World War One. The warring nations mobilized unprecedented numbers of men; over 70 million were called to military service. Never before had so large a part of Europe's population been put in uniform: England mobilized 53 percent of its male population of military age in 1914–1918, and France and Germany called on the service of some 80 percent of their males of draft age.

Each government involved took unprecedented steps to meet its forces' needs for food, material, and ammunition. Governments rationed consumer goods to provide for their armies. England and Germany asserted extraordinary government control over raw materials, privately owned production facilities, and civilian labor in the name of war production.

Civilians felt the war in other ways, too. The stalemate meant a long war, and governments soon recognized they could not maintain their war efforts for the length of time needed if civilian morale broke. Each warring government involved attempted to exert total control over news and public opinion, often at the expense of the rights of their citizens. They censored the press, used propaganda to maintain civilian morale, and placed war critics under surveillance or arrest.

Each nation recognized the equal importance of the home front to their enemies in achieving victory. Thus warring governments made sus-

tained efforts among their enemies' civilian populations to break the will to fight and to slow war production. One favored way to accomplish this goal was to cut off vital imported supplies of food and raw materials.

The First World War not only subjected civilians in warring nations to sacrifice, it also exposed them to physical dangers unusual in previous conflicts as the men at the front died in shocking numbers. This, after all, was the world's first total war; until the outbreak of another such war in 1939, participants remembered it as the "Great War." Your task in this chapter is to assess the all-encompassing nature of modern warfare through several different kinds of sources. Why was World War One different from previous wars? What impact did it have on the soldiers at the front? How did it affect civilians at home?

SOURCES AND METHOD

As we have seen in Chapter 9, artists and intellectuals at first joined other Europeans in welcoming World War One. They believed that the conflict would sweep away a decadent cultural life and replace it with one more vital. Many talented and well-educated men sought to hasten this cultural transformation by volunteering for military service. Front-line combat, however, soon showed these young men that they were caught up in a war unlike any previous strug-

gle. Conscious of the uniqueness of their battlefield experience and aware that their front-line service would leave them forever changed, many made an effort to record their experiences. Letters, diaries, autobiographical works, paintings, and sketches by individual soldiers all supplement the dry official records kept by war ministries of the participating countries and give the historian an excellent sense of battlefield realities and their impact. Your main sources in this chapter comprise creative works, in the form of poetry and fiction, in which a number of talented soldiers sought to convey the experience of modern war and its effect on them.

Literature can be a valuable source for the student of history in understanding the past. We must, however, stay fully aware of its limits as well as its value. The utility of literature as a historical source is somewhat limited by its very nature: as the product of an individual, it reflects personal and social perspectives that must be identified. Most of the authors represented here, for example, came from the middle or upper classes because such individuals, not the sons of the working classes, had the education to write works of enduring significance. With such a social background many served as officers, and the conditions they endured were in some ways better than those of the enlisted men: the war was often significantly worse for a private than for a captain.

Individuals have opinions, too, and opinions often invade war literature. The soldier often portrayed himself as a victim of forces beyond his control: a powerful government, modern technology, or the military authorities. As historians, we must note these opinions because they convey to us the individual's reaction to the war, but we must look beyond them as well to discern the objective wartime conditions the author was recording.

Not all chroniclers of the war were equally well placed to understand the war. We must ask if each work was based on actual front-line experience. If not, we should discount it as his-

torical evidence. We must also ask if an author's work was written in the midst of war, in which case it may reflect the passions of the moment. If the work was written after the war, the author's selective memory for certain facts may have influenced his work. The evidence in this chapter presents works by front-line authors written both at the time of their experiences as well as after the war. Indeed, the great majority of literary works on the war appeared, like the literature on Vietnam, about a decade after the cessation of hostilities. Perhaps a gestation period is necessary for the minds of many to analyze the combat experience. If that is the case, we must recognize the frailty of the human memory and measure the message of postwar literature against those writings composed in the heat of battle.

Once the various viewpoints and perspectives are identified, however, a student of history can obtain an excellent sense of World War One through works of poetry and fiction. These works present the war in human terms far more vividly than do government reports and statistics. To assist your reading, some information on each of the writers presented here is in order.

Rupert Brooke (1887–1915), the author of Source 1, was a graduate of Cambridge University and one of England's most promising young poets when he enlisted in September 1914 as a sublieutenant in the Royal Naval Division, a land force attached to the British Navy. After brief service in Belgium in 1914, his unit was dispatched to the Middle East in 1915 as part of the British and French attack on the Turks at Gallipoli—a strategy designed to open the straits to the Black Sea so that Western supplies could reach Russia. (The attack itself, in which many Australian and New Zealand troops perished, was generally deemed a disaster.) Not quite twenty-eight years of age, Brooke died of blood poisoning en route to Gallipoli and was buried on the island of Skyros, Greece, home of Achilles of the ancient Homeric myths. The selection by Brooke presented here, the poem "Peace," reflects the romanticism characteristic of much prewar English poetry but also expresses Brooke's response to the war. What were his sensations as he watched war engulf Europe? Does he reflect the feeling of many intellectuals that the war offered the possibility of intellectual liberation, of a new, more vital culture?

A remarkable Frenchman, Charles Péguy (1873–1914), wrote Source 2, "Blessed Are." Péguy was a talented poet and essayist, much of whose work expresses his nationalism as well as his concern for the poor and the cause of social justice. His writings also reflect a remarkable spiritual journey. Raised a Catholic, his dislike for the authoritarian character of the Church grew by the time he reached adulthood, and he declared himself an atheist about 1893. In 1908, however, he rediscovered a deep religious faith, though he kept his distance from the institutional Church and probably never participated in its sacramental life. Péguy's later writings bear witness to this religiosity as well as to his continued concern for his fellow man and his French nationalism.

Péguy was forty-one when war broke out in 1914, and he therefore qualified for the army reserve, not front-line duty. Always a man of action, however, he volunteered for active service. Commissioned a lieutenant of infantry, he died leading his men in an attack on September 5, 1914. Remember the details of his life as you read "Blessed Are." What elements of Péguy's thought does the poem combine? What was his view of war?

Source 3, the "Hymn of Hate," is the work of the German poet Ernst Lissauer (1882–1937), who served as a private in the German army. Composed as the war broke out, the poem was soon set to music and became very popular in Germany. To appreciate its significance fully, you may wish to review in your textbook the sections on nineteenth-century nationalism and on the international rivalries that contributed to World War One. Which nation do the Germans see as their archenemy? Why, after consulting your textbook, do you think this country was so hated in Germany?

Novelists also drew on their wartime experiences. Henri Barbusse (1873–1935), the author of *Under Fire*, worked as a French government employee and a journalist before World War One. Politically a socialist, he was swept up by the general surge of patriotism in 1914 and volunteered for military service. He served in the

French army from 1914 through the early days of the great Battle of Verdun in 1916, when he was wounded and left the service. In *Under Fire*, which was written in the trenches, he attempted to portray realistically the physical and psychological impact of modern war. The novel was recognized early as an important work and received France's most prestigious literary award, the Goncourt Prize, in 1916. The excerpt presented as Source 4 describes an attack on the Germans by veteran French infantrymen led by their trusted Corporal Bertrand. How does Barbusse describe modern warfare?

Excerpts from a second novel, *All Quiet on the Western Front* (Source 5), offer us the view of the losing side in the war. Its author, Erich Maria Remarque (1898–1970), grew up the son of a German bookbinder. Drafted at the age of eighteen, he served in the German army from 1916 to the war's end. Remarque had already begun to write before his military service, and his *All Quiet on the Western Front* represented such a realistic picture of the war that many perceived it as an attack on German patriotism. As a consequence, the novel was among the first batch of books burned by the Nazis in 1933. How does Remarque describe the experience of modern warfare? What effect did it have on the many youthful front-line soldiers like the main character, Paul Baumer? What impact did that war have on German civilians?

Two poems conclude our literary evidence on World War One. Source 6, "Dulce et Decorum Est" ("It is sweet and fitting"), is the work of

Wilfred Owen (1893–1918). Owen studied briefly at the University of London before the war, intending a career in the clergy. He enlisted in the British army in 1915, aged twenty-two, and as an infantry lieutenant served in France in the great Battle of the Somme. Owen was wounded three times in 1917 and recuperated in England, where he met Siegfried Sassoon, author of the next selection, who encouraged Owen in his writing. After recovering from his wounds, Owen again served on the western front. He received the Military Cross for bravery in October 1918 and died leading his men in an attack on November 4, 1918, one week before the war's end.

Owen's battlefield experiences shaped his poetry. "Dulce et Decorum Est" is titled with a phrase from the Roman poet Horace, whose work would have been familiar to all upper-class English schoolboys of Owen's day. How would you summarize Owen's view of the war, especially his opinion of those on the home front who blindly supported it?

Siegfried Sassoon (1886–1967), author of "The General" (Source 7), was seven years older than his friend Owen, and his poetic response to the war is the reaction of one with greater experience in life and its problems. A Cambridge graduate like Rupert Brooke, he had written poetry since his boyhood. The war transformed Sassoon from an upper-class young man who enjoyed the hunt to a postwar social activist and socialist. Although he served with great bravery as a front-line officer, he experienced an increasingly bitter sense of the war's futility. Wounded in 1917, he had a long convalescence in England and went through an emotional crisis as he attempted to balance his growing pacifism with his enduring sense of duty and the comradeship he felt with those still on the front line. Sassoon's response was to throw away his Military Cross awarded for bravery and to draft a letter of protest of the war to his commanding officer. Stating that a war undertaken as one of defense had become a war of conquest, he declared, "I can no longer be a party to prolong those sufferings for ends which I believe to be evil and unjust." Such a letter from an officer in wartime would normally have resulted in court martial. Intervention of friends on his behalf led instead to Sassoon's treatment for shell shock, a common psychological problem among frontline troops. It was during his hospitalization for this treatment that Sassoon met Owen. Returning to service in 1918, Sassoon was wounded again but lived to survive the war. His poem, "The General," is very brief, but it reflects Sassoon's attitude toward the war. How does Sassoon view the general?

Participants in the war left other personal records of the conflict in the form of letters and autobiographical works. The letters in Sources 8 and 9 record such remarkable events in the midst of total war that people then, as now, tended to doubt they ever occurred. Nevertheless, the stories of these two anonymous German soldiers can be verified in the writings of their battlefield opponents. How had initial enthusiasm for the war

and hatred of the enemy fared at the front? Why?

World War One was the first conflict to demand great participation from women in the war effort. Yet, oddly, few left extensive written records of the war's effect on them. Source 10, drawn from the Englishwoman Vera Brittain's *The Testament of Youth*, is one of the few works we have by a woman. A student at Oxford when England declared war, Brittain left her studies shortly after for service as a nurse, and her book in part records the war from that vantage point. It also gives us a sense of the war's impact on those at the home front. What kind of warfare does Brittain describe the Germans as practicing? What was their objective in such warfare? What effect did the war have on Brittain?

Sources 11 through 15 are evidence of a nonpersonal nature, reports and statistics amassed by modern governments of the kind we have examined in earlier chapters. Nevertheless, such material will allow you to amplify your understanding of the impact of total warfare. Source 11, taken from the official record compiled by the U.S. Army's forces occupying the Rhineland area of Germany at the war's end, describes the rations for Germany's civilian population during the last days of the war in 1918. These rations reflect the effects of a British naval blockade of the ports of Germany, established to cut the country off from imported food and strategic raw materials. Because prewar Germany was not self-sufficient in food production, the effect of such a blockade was great.

In analyzing this ration information, we must, as students of history, recognize that the supplies shown here may not completely reflect the German dietary situation. Rationing presumes that producers placed all foodstuffs at their government's disposal. In practice they did not, because rationing was based on government-regulated prices that were invariably lower than free market prices in a period of shortage. The result was a lively black market trade in foodstuffs for those who could pay higher prices.

Still, the evidence here does indicate the basic ration for many Germans. Analyze this record. What dietary basics do you find lacking or in short supply? What did German civilians eat a great deal of during the war? What cumulative effect do you think such a diet, imposed by total war, had on German civilians?

The strain of warfare was not only a matter of food and other material restrictions, however. As we noted earlier, warring governments tried to gauge and influence public opinion because they knew that total warfare would become untenable if civilian spirit broke. In Source 12 you will read a report to French police officials from the area of Grenoble in southeastern France in 1917. What does that report show about public opinion? In calling millions of men for military service, total war created tremendous labor shortages and yet another strain on civilians in all countries. Who filled the jobs vacated by men in England, according to Source 13? How did governments pay for modern warfare, according to Source 15?

The ultimate cost of the war can be measured precisely in human lives lost. Official casualty figures, however, present considerable problems of analysis. We must first understand that all such figures are approximate. Deficiencies in wartime record keeping are part of the problem, but governments manipulated figures, too. During the war security considerations led to consistent understatements of losses by each nation involved to prevent the enemy from knowing its manpower resources. At the war's end, some victorious governments allegedly inflated figures as a basis for postwar claims on their defeated enemies.

The figures for military deaths in Source 14 are taken from a recent study attempting to determine the best estimates of war losses from several sources, not just governmental records. Though we still must accept those figures as only approximations, they do allow a good sense of the relative losses of each country. Which suffered the greatest numerical losses? In which armies did a man mobilized for military service have the greatest chance of being killed? What do the high casualty rates of certain Eastern European countries tell you about those nations' capacities to wage modern warfare? Among the great powers, which nation lost the greatest portion of its population?

As you now read the evidence for this chapter, keep all these questions in mind. They should aid you in answering the central questions posed: Why was World War One different from previous wars? What impact did it have on soldiers at the front? How did it affect civilians at home?

THE EVIDENCE

THE FRONT LINES

Source 1 from Geoffrey Keynes, editor, The Poetical Works of Rupert Brooke *(London: Faber and Faber, 1960), p. 19.*

1. Rupert Brooke,
"1914 Sonnet: I. Peace,"
1914

Now, God be thanked Who has matched us with His hour,
  And caught our youth, and wakened us from sleeping,
With hand made sure, clear eye, and sharpened power,
  To turn, as swimmers into cleanness leaping,
Glad from a world grown old and cold and weary,
  Leave the sick hearts that honour could not move,
And half-men, and their dirty songs and dreary,
  And all the little emptiness of love!

Oh! we, who have known shame, we have found release there,
  Where there's no ill, no grief, but sleep has mending,
   Naught broken save this body, lost but breath;
Nothing to shake the laughing heart's long peace there
  But only agony, and that has ending;
   And the worst friend and enemy is but Death.

Source 2 from Charles Péguy, Basic Verities: Prose and Poetry, *translated by Ann and Julian Green (New York: Pantheon, 1943), pp. 275–277.*

2. Charles Péguy, "Blessed
Are," 1914

Blessed are those who died for carnal earth
Provided it was in a just war.
Blessed are those who died for a plot of ground.
Blessed are those who died a solemn death.

Blessed are those who died in great battles,
Stretched out on the ground in the face of God.
Blessed are those who died on a final high place,
Amid all the pomp of grandiose funerals.

Blessed are those who died for carnal cities.
For they are the body of the city of God.
Blessed are those who died for their hearth and their fire,
And the lowly honors of their father's house. . . .

Blessed are those who died, for they have returned
Into primeval clay and primeval earth.
Blessed are those who died in a just war.
Blessed is the wheat that is ripe and the wheat that is gathered in sheaves.

Source 3 from Ernst Lissauer, Jugend *(1914). Translated by Barbara Henderson,* New York Times, *October 15, 1914.*

3. Ernst Lissauer, "Hymn of Hate," 1914

French and Russian they matter not,
A blow for a blow and a shot for a shot;
We love them not, we hate them not,
We hold the Weichsel and Vosges-gate,[1]
We have but one—and only hate,
We love as one, we hate as one,
We have one foe and one alone.

He is known to you all, he is known to you all,
He crouches behind the dark grey flood,
Full of envy, of rage, of craft, of gall,
Cut off by waves that are thicker than blood.
Come, let us stand at the Judgment place,
An oath to swear to, face to face,
An oath of bronze no wind can shake,

An oath for our sons and their sons to take.
Come, hear the word, repeat the word,
Throughout the Fatherland make it heard.
We will never forego our hate,
We have all but a single hate,
We love as one, we hate as one,
We have one foe, and one alone—

ENGLAND!

1. The Germans possessed defensible boundaries against the Russians and the French. In the east, they held the Vistula (*Weichsel*) River in Poland as a barrier to Russian attack. In the west, they blocked the French attack with their possession of the Vosges Mountains.

In the Captain's mess, in the banquet hall,
Sat feasting the officers, one and all,
Like a sabre-blow, like the swing of a sail,
One seized his glass held high to hail;
Sharp-snapped like the stroke of a rudder's play,
Spoke three words only: "To the Day!"[2]
Whose glass this fate?
They had all but a single hate.
Who was thus known?
They had one foe, and one alone—

ENGLAND!

Take you the folk of the Earth in pay,
With bars of gold your ramparts lay,
Bedeck the ocean with bow on bow,
Ye reckon well, but not well enough now.
French and Russian they matter not,
A blow for a blow, a shot for a shot,
We fight the battle with bronze and steel,
And the time that is coming Peace will seal.

You will hate with a lasting hate,
We will never forego our hate,
Hate by water and hate by land,
Hate of the head and hate of the hand,
Hate of the hammer and hate of the crown,
Hate of seventy millions, choking down.
We love as one, we hate as one,
We have one foe, and one alone—

ENGLAND!

Source 4 from Henri Barbusse, Under Fire: The Story of a Squad, *translated by Fitzwater Wray (New York: E. P. Dutton, 1917), pp. 250–259.*

4. From Henri Barbusse, *Under Fire: The Story of a Squad,* 1916

We are ready. The men marshal themselves, still silently, their blankets crosswise, the helmet-strap on the chin, leaning on their rifles. I look at their pale, contracted, and reflective faces. They are not soldiers, they are men.

2. **To the Day!**: in German naval officers' messes before World War One, it was customary to offer a toast to "the Day," that is, the day England would be defeated.

They are not adventurers, or warriors, or made for human slaughter, neither butchers nor cattle. They are laborers and artisans whom one recognizes in their uniforms. They are civilians uprooted, and they are ready. They await the signal for death or murder; but you may see, looking at their faces between the vertical gleams of their bayonets, that they are simply men.

Each one knows that he is going to take his head, his chest, his belly, his whole body, and all naked, up to the rifles pointed forward, to the shells, to the bombs piled and ready, and above all to the methodical and almost infallible machine-guns—to all that is waiting for him yonder and is now so frightfully silent—before he reaches the other soldiers that he must kill. They are not careless of their lives, like brigands, nor blinded by passion like savages. In spite of the doctrines with which they have been cultivated they are not inflamed. They are above instinctive excesses. They are not drunk, either physically or morally. It is in full consciousness, as in full health and full strength, that they are massed there to hurl themselves once more into that sort of madman's part imposed on all men by the madness of the human race. One sees the thought and the fear and the farewell that there is in their silence, their stillness, in the mask of tranquillity which unnaturally grips their faces. They are not the kind of hero one thinks of, but their sacrifice has greater worth than they who have not seen them will ever be able to understand.

They are waiting; a waiting that extends and seems eternal. Now and then one or another starts a little when a bullet, fired from the other side, skims the forward embankment that shields us and plunges into the flabby flesh of the rear wall. . . .

A man arrives running, and speaks to Bertrand, and then Bertrand turns to us—

"Up you go," he says, "it's our turn."

All move at once. We put our feet on the steps made by the sappers, raise ourselves, elbow to elbow, beyond the shelter of the trench, and climb on to the parapet.

Bertrand is out on the sloping ground. He covers us with a quick glance, and when we are all there he says, "*Allons*, forward!"[3]

Our voices have a curious resonance. The start has been made very quickly, unexpectedly almost, as in a dream. There is no whistling sound in the air. Among the vast uproar of the guns we discern very clearly this surprising silence of bullets around us—

We descend over the rough and slippery ground with involuntary gestures, helping ourselves sometimes with the rifle. . . . On all sides the slope is covered by men who, like us, are bent on the descent. On the right the outline is defined of a company that is reaching the ravine by Trench 97—

3. **Allons:** "Let's go!"

an old German work in ruins. We cross our wire by openings. Still no one fires on us. Some awkward ones who have made false steps are getting up again. We form up on the farther side of the entanglements and then set ourselves to topple down the slope rather faster—there is an instinctive acceleration in the movement. Several bullets arrive at last among us. Bertrand shouts to us to reserve our bombs and wait till the last moment.

But the sound of his voice is carried away. Abruptly, across all the width of the opposite slope, lurid flames burst forth that strike the air with terrible detonations. In line from left to right fires emerge from the sky and explosions from the ground. It is a frightful curtain which divides us from the world, which divides us from the past and from the future. We stop, fixed to the ground, stupefied by the sudden host that thunders from every side; then a simultaneous effort uplifts our mass again and throws it swiftly forward. We stumble and impede each other in the great waves of smoke. With harsh crashes and whirlwinds of pulverized earth, towards the profundity into which we hurl ourselves pell-mell, we see craters opened here and there, side by side, and merging in each other. Then one knows no longer where the discharges fall. Volleys are let loose so monstrously resounding that one feels himself annihilated by the mere sound of the downpoured thunder of these great constellations of destruction that form in the sky. One sees and one feels the fragments passing close to one's head with their hiss of red-hot iron plunged in water. The blast of one explosion so burns my hands, that I let my rifle fall. I pick it up again, reeling, and set off in the tawny-gleaming tempest with lowered head, lashed by spirits of dust and soot in a crushing downpour like volcanic lava. The stridor of the bursting shells hurts your ears, beats you on the neck, goes through your temples, and you cannot endure it without a cry. The gusts of death drive us on, lift us up, rock us to and fro. We leap, and do not know whither we go. Our eyes are blinking and weeping and obscured. The view before us is blocked by a flashing avalanche that fills space.

It is the barrage fire. We have to go through that whirlwind of fire and those fearful showers that vertically fall. We are passing through. We are through it, by chance. Here and there I have seen forms that spun round and were lifted up and laid down, illumined by a brief reflection from over yonder. I have glimpsed strange faces that uttered some sort of cry—you could see them without hearing them in the roar of annihilation. A brasier full of red and black masses huge and furious fell about me, excavating the ground, tearing it from under my feet, throwing me aside like a bouncing toy. I remember that I strode over a smoldering corpse, quite black, with a tissue of rosy blood shriveling on him; and I remember, too, that the skirts of the great-coat flying next to me had caught fire, and left a trail of smoke behind. On our right, all along Trench 97, our glances were drawn and dazzled by a rank of frightful flames, closely crowded against each other like men.

Forward!

Now, we are nearly running. I see some who fall solidly flat, face forward, and others who founder meekly, as though they would sit down on the ground. We step aside abruptly to avoid the prostrate dead, quiet and rigid, or else offensive, and also—more perilous snares!—the wounded that hook on to you, struggling.

The International Trench! We are there. The wire entanglements have been torn up into long roots and creepers, thrown afar and coiled up, swept away and piled in great drifts by the guns. Between these big bushes of rain-damped steel the ground is open and free.

The trench is not defended. The Germans have abandoned it, or else a first wave has already passed over it. Its interior bristles with rifles placed against the bank. In the bottom are scattered corpses. From the jumbled litter of the long trench, hands emerge that protrude from gray sleeves with red facings, and booted legs. In places the embankment is destroyed and its woodwork splintered—all the flank of the trench collapsed and fallen into an indescribable mixture. In other places, round pits are yawning. . . .

We have spread out in the trench. The lieutenant, who has jumped to the other side, is stooping and summoning us with signs and shouts—"Don't stay there; forward, foward!"

We climb the wall of the trench with the help of the sacks, of weapons, and of the backs that are piled up there. In the bottom of the ravine the soil is shot-churned, crowded with jetsam, swarming with prostrate bodies. Some are motionless as blocks of wood; others move slowly or convulsively. The barrage fire continues to increase its infernal discharge behind us on the ground that we have crossed. But where we are at the foot of the rise it is a dead point for the artillery.

A short and uncertain calm follows. We are less deafened and look at each other. There is fever in the eyes, and the cheek-bones are blood-red. Our breathing snores and our hearts drum in our bodies.

In haste and confusion we recognize each other, as if we had met again face to face in a nightmare on the uttermost shores of death. Some hurried words are cast upon this glade in hell—"It's you!"—"Where's Cocon?"—"Don't know."—"Have you seen the captain?"—"No."—"Going strong?"—"Yes."

The bottom of the ravine is crossed and the other slope rises opposite. We climb in Indian file by a stairway rough-hewn in the ground: "Look out!" The shout means that a soldier half-way up the steps has been struck in the loins by a shell-fragment; he falls with his arms forward, bareheaded, like the diving swimmer. We can see the shapeless silhouette of the mass as it plunges into the gulf. I can almost see the detail of his blown hair over the black profile of his face.

We debouch upon the height. A great colorless emptiness is outspread before us. At first one can see nothing but a chalky and stony plain, yellow and gray to the limit of sight. No human wave is preceding ours; in front of us there is no living soul, but the ground is peopled with dead—recent corpses that still mimic agony or sleep, and old remains already bleached and scattered to the wind, half assimilated by the earth.

As soon as our pushing and jolted file emerges, two men close to me are hit, two shadows are hurled to the ground and roll under our feet, one with a sharp cry, and the other silently, as a felled ox. Another disappears with the caper of a lunatic, as if he had been snatched away. Instinctively we close up as we hustle forward—always forward—and the wound in our line closes of its own accord. The adjutant stops, raises his sword, lets it fall, and drops to his knees. His kneeling body slopes backward in jerks, his helmet drops on his heels, and he remains there, bareheaded, face to the sky. Hurriedly the rush of the rank has split open to respect his immobility.

But we cannot see the lieutenant. No more leaders, then—— Hesitation checks the wave of humanity that begins to beat on the plateau. Above the trampling one hears the hoarse effort of our lungs. "Forward!" cries some soldier, and then all resume the onward race to perdition with increasing speed.

"Where's Bertrand?" comes the laborious complaint of one of the foremost runners. "There! Here!" He had stooped in passing over a wounded man, but he leaves him quickly, and the man extends his arms toward him and seems to sob.

It is just at the moment when he rejoins us that we hear in front of us, coming from a sort of ground swelling, the crackle of a machine-gun. It is a moment of agony—more serious even than when we were passing through the flaming earthquake of the barrage. That familiar voice speaks to us across the plain, sharp and horrible. But we no longer stop. "Go on, go on!"

Our panting becomes hoarse groaning, yet still we hurl ourselves toward the horizon.

"The Boches![4] I see them!" a man says suddenly.

"Yes—their heads, there—above the trench—it's there, the trench that line. It's close. Ah, the hogs!"

We can indeed make out little round gray caps which rise and then drop on the ground level, fifty yards away, beyond a belt of dark earth, furrowed and humped. Encouraged they spring forward, they who now form the group where I am. So near the goal, so far unscathed, shall we not reach it? Yes, we will reach it! We make great strides and no longer hear anything. Each man plunges straight ahead, fascinated by the terrible trench, bent rigidly forward, almost incapable of turning his head to right or to left. I have a notion that many of us missed their footing and fell to the ground. I

---

4. **Boches**: a derogatory term applied by the French to German soldiers, originating from the French *caboche*, or blockhead.

jump sideways to miss the suddenly erect bayonet of a toppling rifle. Quite close to me, Farfadet jostles me with his face bleeding, throws himself on Volpatte who is beside me and clings to him. Volpatte doubles up without slackening his rush and drags him along some paces, then shakes him off without looking at him and without knowing who he is, and shouts at him in a breaking voice almost choked with exertion: "Let me go, let me go, *nom de Dieu!*[5] They'll pick you up directly—don't worry."

The other man sinks to the ground, and his face, plastered with a scarlet mask and void of all expression, turns in every direction; while Volpatte, already in the distance, automatically repeats between his teeth, "Don't worry," with a steady forward gaze on the line.

A shower of bullets spurts around me, increasing the number of those who suddenly halt, who collapse slowly, defiant and gesticulating, of those who dive forward solidly with all the body's burden, of the shouts, deep, furious, and desperate, and even of that hollow and terrible gasp when a man's life goes bodily forth in a breath. And we who are not yet stricken, we look ahead, we walk and we run, among the frolics of the death that strikes at random into our flesh.

The wire entanglements—and there is one stretch of them intact. We go along to where it has been gutted into a wide and deep opening. This is a colossal funnel-hole, formed of smaller funnels placed together, a fantastic volcanic crater, scooped there by the guns.

The sight of this convulsion is stupefying; truly it seems that it must have come from the center of the earth. Such a rending of virgin strata puts new edge on our attacking fury, and none of us can keep from shouting with a solemn shake of the head—even just now when words are but painfully torn from our throats—"Ah, Christ! Look what hell we've given 'em there! Ah, look!"

Driven as if by the wind, we mount or descend at the will of the hollows and the earthy mounds in the gigantic fissure dug and blackened and burned by furious flames. The soil clings to the feet and we tear them out angrily. The accouterments and stuffs that cover the soft soil, the linen that is scattered about from sundered knapsacks, prevent us from sticking fast in it, and we are careful to plant our feet in this débris when we jump into the holes or climb the hillocks.

Behind us voices urge us—"Forward, boys, forward, *nom de Dieu!*"

"All the regiment is behind us!" they cry. We do not turn round to see, but the assurance electrifies our rush once more.

No more caps are visible behind the embankment of the trench we are nearing. Some German dead are crumbling in front of it, in pinnacled heaps or extended lines. We are there. The parapet takes definite and sinister shape and detail; the loopholes—we are prodigiously, incredibly close!

5. **nom de Dieu**: "Name of God!"

Something falls in front of us. It is a bomb. With a kick Corporal Bertrand returns it so well that it rises and bursts just over the trench.

With that fortunate deed the squad reaches the trench.

Pépin has hurled himself flat on the ground and is involved with a corpse. He reaches the edge and plunges in—the first to enter. Fouillade, with great gestures and shouts, jumps into the pit almost at the same moment that Pépin rolls down it. Indistinctly I see—in the time of the lightning's flash— a whole row of black demons stooping and squatting for the descent, on the ridge of the embankment, on the edge of the dark ambush.

A terrible volley bursts point-blank in our faces, flinging in front of us a sudden row of flames the whole length of the earthen verge. After the stunning shock we shake ourselves and burst into devilish laughter—the discharge has passed too high. And at once, with shouts and roars of salvation, we slide and roll and fall alive into the belly of the trench!

Source 5 from Erich Maria Remarque, All Quiet on the Western Front *(New York: Fawcett Crest, 1969), pp. 167–171, 174–175.*

5. From Erich Maria Remarque, *All Quiet on the Western Front*, 1928

We have been able to bury Müller, but he is not likely to remain long undisturbed. Our lines are falling back. There are too many fresh English and American regiments over there. There's too much corned beef and white wheaten bread. Too many new guns. Too many aeroplanes.

But we are emaciated and starved. Our food is so bad and mixed up with so much substitute stuff that it makes us ill. The factory owners in Germany have grown wealthy;—dysentery dissolves our bowels. The latrine poles are always densely crowded; the people at home ought to be shown these grey, yellow, miserable, wasted faces here, these bent figures from whose bodies the colic wrings out the blood, and who with lips trembling and distorted with pain, grin at one another and say: "It is not much sense pulling up one's trousers again—"

Our artillery is fired out, it has too few shells and the barrels are so worn that they shoot uncertainly, and scatter so widely as even to fall on ourselves. We have too few horses. Our fresh troops are anæmic boys in need of rest, who cannot carry a pack, but merely know how to die. By thousands. They understand nothing about warfare, they simply go on and let themselves be shot down. A single flyer routed two companies of them for a joke, just as they came fresh from the train—before they had ever heard of such a thing as cover.

"Germany ought to be empty soon," says Kat.

We have given up hope that some day an end may come. We never think so far. A man can stop a bullet and be killed; he can get wounded, and then the hospital is his next stop. There, if they do not amputate him, he sooner or later falls into the hands of one of those staff surgeons who, with the War Service Cross in his buttonhole, says to him: "What, one leg a bit short? If you have any pluck you don't need to run at the front. The man is A1.[6] Dismiss!"

Kat tells a story that has travelled the whole length of the front from the Vosges to Flanders;—of the staff surgeon who reads the names on the list, and when a man comes before him, without looking up says: "A1. We need soldiers up there." A fellow with a wooden leg comes up before him, the staff surgeon again says A1—"And then," Kat raises his voice, "the fellow says to him: 'I already have a wooden leg, but when I go back again and they shoot off my head, then I will get a wooden head made and become a staff surgeon.'" This answer tickles us all immensely.

There may be good doctors, and there are, lots of them; all the same, every soldier some time during his hundreds of inspections falls into the clutches of one of these countless hero-grabbers who pride themselves on changing as many C3's and B3's as possible into A1's.

There are many such stories, they are mostly far more bitter. All the same, they have nothing to do with mutiny or lead-swinging. They are merely honest and call a thing by its name; for there is a very great deal of fraud, injustice, and baseness in the army.—Is it nothing that regiment after regiment returns again and again to the ever more hopeless struggle, that attack follows attack along the weakening, retreating, crumbling line?

From a mockery the tanks have become a terrible weapon. Armoured they come rolling on in long lines, and more than anything else embody for us war's horror.

We do not see the guns that bombard us; the attacking lines of the enemy infantry are men like ourselves; but these tanks are machines, their caterpillars run on as endless as the war, they are annihilation, they roll without feeling into the craters, and climb up again without stopping, a fleet of roaring, smoke-belching armour-clads, invulnerable steel beasts squashing the dead and the wounded—we shrivel up in our thin skin before them, against their colossal weight our arms are sticks of straw, and our hand-grenades matches.

Shells, gas clouds, and flotillas of tanks—shattering, starvation, death.

Dysentery, influenza, typhus—murder, burning, death.

Trenches, hospitals, the common grave—there are no other possibilities.

6. **A1**: the highest category of physical fitness, that is, qualified for front-line duty.

In one attack our company commander, Bertinck, falls. He was one of those superb front-line officers who are foremost in every hot place. He was with us for two years without being wounded, so that something had to happen in the end.

We occupy a crater and get surrounded. The stink of petroleum or oil blows across with the fumes of powder. Two fellows with a flame-thrower are seen, one carries the tin on his back, the other has the hose in his hands from which the fire spouts. If they get so near that they can reach us we are done for, we cannot retreat at the moment.

We open fire on them. But they work nearer and things begin to look bad. Bertinck is lying in the hole with us. When he sees that we cannot escape because under the sharp fire we must make the most of this cover, he takes a rifle, crawls out of the hole, and lying down propped on his elbows, he takes aim. He fires—the same moment a bullet smacks into him, they have got him. Still he lies and aims again;—once he shifts and again takes his aim; at last the rifle cracks. Bertinck lets the gun drop and says: "Good," and slips back into the hole. The hindermost of the two flame-throwers is hit, he falls, the hose slips away from the other fellow, the fire squirts about on all sides and the man burns.

Bertinck has a chest wound. After a while a fragment smashes away his chin, and the same fragment has suffcient force to tear open Leer's hip. Leer groans as he supports himself on his arm, he bleeds quickly, no one can help him. Like an emptying tube, after a couple of minutes he collapses.

What use is it to him now that he was such a good mathematician at school?

The months pass by. The summer of 1918 is the most bloody and the most terrible. The days stand like angels in gold and blue, incomprehensible, above the ring of annihilation. Every man here knows that we are losing the war. Not much is said about it, we are falling back, we will not be able to attack again after this big offensive, we have no more men and no more ammunition. . . .

There are so many airmen here, and they are so sure of themselves that they give chase to single individuals, just as though they were hares. For every one German plane there come at least five English and American. For one hungry, wretched German soldier come five of the enemy, fresh and fit. For one German army loaf there are fifty tins of canned beef over there. We are not beaten, for as soldiers we are better and more experienced; we are simply crushed and driven back by overwhelmingly superior forces.

Behind us lie rainy weeks—grey sky, grey fluid earth, grey dying. If we go out, the rain at once soaks through our overcoat and clothing;—and we remain wet all the time we are in the line. We never get dry. Those who still wear high boots tie sand bags round the top so that the mud does not pour in so fast. The rifles are caked, the uniforms caked, everything is fluid and dissolved, the earth one dripping, soaked, oily mass in which lie the yellow pools with red spiral streams of blood and into which the dead, wounded, and survivors slowly sink down.

The storm lashes us, out of the confusion of grey and yellow the hail of splinters whips forth the childlike cries of the wounded, and in the night shattered life groans wearily to the silence.

Our hands are earth, our bodies clay and our eyes pools of rain. We do not know whether we still live. . . .

It is autumn. There are not many of the old hands left. I am the last of the seven fellows from our class.

Everyone talks of peace and armistice. All wait. If it again proves an illusion, then they will break up; hope is high, it cannot be taken away again without an upheaval. If there is not peace, then there will be revolution.

I have fourteen days' rest, because I have swallowed a bit of gas; in a little garden I sit the whole day long in the sun. The armistice is coming soon, I believe it now too. Then we will go home.

Here my thoughts stop and will not go any farther. All that meets me, all that floods over me are but feelings—greed of life, love of home, yearning of the blood, intoxication of deliverance. But no aims.

Had we returned home in 1916, out of the suffering and the strength of our experiences we might have unleashed a storm. Now if we go back we will be weary, broken, burnt out, rootless, and without hope. We will not be able to find our way any more.

And men will not understand us—for the generation that grew up before us, though it has passed these years with us here, already had a home and a calling; now it will return to its old occupations, and the war will be forgotten—and the generation that has grown up after us will be strange to us and push us aside. We will be superfluous even to ourselves, we will grow older, a few will adapt themselves, some others will merely submit, and most will be bewildered;—the years will pass by and in the end we shall fall into ruin.

But perhaps all this that I think is mere melancholy and dismay, which will fly away as the dust, when I stand once again beneath the poplars and listen to the rustling of their leaves. It cannot be that it has gone, the yearning that made our blood unquiet, the unknown, the perplexing, the oncoming things, the thousand faces of the future, the melodies from dreams and from books, the whispers and divinations of women, it cannot be that this has vanished in bombardment, in despair, in brothels.

Here the trees show gay and golden, the berries of the rowan stand red among the leaves, country roads run white out to the sky-line, and the canteens hum like beehives with rumours of peace.

I stand up.

I am very quiet. Let the months and years come, they bring me nothing more, they can bring me nothing more. I am so alone, and so without hope that I can confront them without fear. The life that has borne me through these years is still in my hands and my eyes. Whether I have subdued it, I know not. But so long as it is there it will seek its own way out, heedless of the will that is within me. . . .

He fell in October, 1918, on a day that was so quiet and still on the whole front, that the army report confined itself to the single sentence: All quiet on the Western Front.

He had fallen forward and lay on the earth as though sleeping. Turning him over one saw that he could not have suffered long; his face had an expression of calm, as though almost glad the end had come.

Source 6 from C. Day Lewis, editor, The Collected Poems of Wilfred Owen *(New York: New Directions, 1964), p. 55.*

6. Wilfred Owen, "Dulce et Decorum Est," ca 1917

Bent double, like old beggars under sacks,
Knock-kneed, coughing like hags, we cursed through sludge,
Till on the haunting flares we turned our backs
And towards our distant rest began to trudge.
Men marched asleep. Many had lost their boots
But limped on, blood-shod. All went lame; all blind;
Drunk with fatigue; deaf even to the hoots
Of tired, outstripped Five-Nines[7] that dropped behind.

Gas! GAS! Quick, boys!—An ecstasy of fumbling,
Fitting the clumsy helmets just in time;
But someone still was yelling out and stumbling
And flound'ring like a man in fire or lime . . .
Dim, through the misty panes and thick green light,
As under a green sea, I saw him drowning.

In all my dreams, before my helpless sight,
He lunges at me, guttering, choking, drowning.

7. **Five-Nines**: one of the types of artillery used by the Germans was the 5.9 inch howitzer, which projected a very large shell in a high arc. As the barrels of such guns became worn, their accuracy was impaired.

If in some smothering dreams you too could pace
Behind the wagon that we flung him in,
And watch the white eyes writhing in his face,
His hanging face, like a devil's sick of sin;
If you could hear, at every jolt, the blood
Come gargling from the froth-corrupted lungs,
Obscene as cancer, bitter as the cud
Of vile, incurable sores on innocent tongues,—
My friend, you would not tell with such high zest
To children ardent for some desperate glory,
The old Lie: Dulce et decorum est
Pro patria mori.[8]

Source 7 from Siegfried Sassoon, Collected Poems, 1908–1956 *(London: Faber and Faber, 1961), p. 75.*

7. Siegfried Sassoon, "The General," ca 1917

'Good-morning; good-morning!' the General said
When we met him last week on our way to the line.
Now the soldiers he smiled at are most of 'em dead,
And we're cursing his staff for incompetent swine.
'He's a cheery old card,' grunted Harry to Jack
As they slogged up to Arras with rifle and pack.

But he did for them both by his plan of attack.

Source 8 from Rudolf Hoffman, editor, Der deutscher Soldat: Briefe aus dem Weltkrieg *(Munich: 1937), pp. 297–298. Translated and quoted in Hanna Hafkesbrink,* Unknown Germany: An Inner Chronicle of the First World War Based on Letters and Diaries *(New Haven: Yale University Press, 1948), p. 141.*

8. New Year's Eve, 1914: Letter from a Former German Student Serving in France

On New Year's Eve we called across to tell each other the time and agreed to fire a salvo at 12. It was a cold night. We sang songs, and they clapped (we were only 60–70 yards apart); we played the mouth-organ and they sang

8. From Horace, *Odes*, III, 2,3: "It is sweet and fitting to die for one's country."

and we clapped. Then I asked if they haven't got any musical instruments, and they produced some bagpipes (they are the Scots guards, with the short petticoats and bare legs) and they played some of their beautiful elegies on them, and sang, too. Then at 12 we all fired salvos into the air! . . . It was a real good "Sylvester,"[9] just like in peace-time!

Source 9 from A. F. Wedd, editor and translator, German Students' War Letters, *from the original edition by Philipp Witkop (London: Methuen, 1929), p. 36. Quoted in Hanna Haf-kesbrink,* Unknown Germany: An Inner Chronicle of the First World War Based on Letters and Diaries *(New Haven: Yale University Press, 1948), pp. 141–142.*

9. Christmas Eve, 1916: Letter from a German Soldier Serving in France

There I stood for four hours in the trench on Christmas Eve, up to my ankles in water and slime, and armed with hand grenades and signal shells. My thoughts were far away, my eyes sought the silhouette of the enemy trench. Then suddenly at 12 o'clock there was a solemn pause. From our reserve position came the sound of a quartette singing Christmas carols. Singing in God's out-of-doors as in peacetime, actually only 60 meters[10] away from an embittered enemy. Was this possible? I know of no hour so uplifting and solemn as was this one. Now several Englishmen ventured to sing a lovely song. Yes, this was peace on the battlefield, peace as one had not known it for two and a half years. Neither infantry nor artillery fire disturbed this night of peace. Lost in meditation we stood in the trench and listened to the singing.

THE HOME FRONT

Source 10 from Vera Brittain, The Testament of Youth: An Autobiographical Study of the Years 1900–1925 *(London: Gollancz, 1981), pp. 365–366.*

10. A London Air Raid, June 13, 1917

Although three out of the four persons were gone who had made all the world that I knew,[11] the War seemed no nearer a conclusion than it had been

9. **Sylvester:** Roman Catholics observe December 31 as the feast of Saint Sylvester.

10. **60 meters:** 198 feet.

11. Vera Brittain lost her fiancé and two other male friends in World War One. The fourth person still alive in June 1917, her brother Edward, perished while serving with the British army in Italy later in 1917.

in 1914. It was everywhere now; even before Victor was buried, the daylight air-raid of June 13th "brought it home," as the newspapers remarked, with such force that I perceived danger to be infinitely preferable when I went after it, instead of waiting for it to come after me.

I was just reaching home after a morning's shopping in Kensington High Street when the uproar began, and, looking immediately at the sky, I saw the sinister group of giant mosquitoes sweeping in close formation over London. My mother, whose temperamental fatalism had always enabled her to sleep peacefully through the usual night-time raids, was anxious to watch the show from the roof of the flats, but when I reached the doorway my father had just succeeded in hurrying her down to the basement; he did not share her belief that destiny remained unaffected by caution, and himself derived moral support in air-raids from putting on his collar and patrolling the passages.

The three of us listened glumly to the shrapnel raining down like a thunder-shower upon the park—those quiet trees which on the night of my return from Malta[12] had made death and horror seem so unbelievably remote. As soon as the banging and crashing had given way to the breathless, apprehensive silence which always followed a big raid, I made a complicated journey to the City[13] to see if my uncle had been added to the family's growing collection of casualties.

When at last, after much negociation of the crowds in Cornhill and Bishopsgate, I succeeded in getting to the National Provincial Bank, I found him safe and quite composed, but as pale as a corpse; indeed, the whole staff of men and women resembled a morose consignment of dumb spectres newly transported across the Styx.[14] The streets round the bank were terrifyingly quiet, and in some places so thickly covered with broken glass that I seemed to be wading ankle-deep in huge unmelted hailstones. I saw no dead nor wounded, though numerous police-supervised barricades concealed a variety of gruesome probabilities. Others were only too clearly suggested by a crimson-splashed horse lying indifferently on its side, and by several derelict tradesman's carts bloodily denuded of their drivers.

These things, I concluded, seemed less inappropriate when they happened in France, though no doubt the French thought otherwise.

Source 11 from the American Military Government of Occupied Germany, 1918–1920, Report of the Officer in Charge of Civil Affairs, Third Army and American Forces in Germany *(Washington, D.C.: U.S. Government Printing Office, 1943), pp. 155–156.*

12. Brittain had served as a military nurse on the British island of Malta in the Mediterranean.
13. **the City**: the financial district of London.
14. **Styx**: in Greek mythology, the river that the souls of the dead must cross as they leave the world of the living.

11. German Wartime Civilian Rations, 1918

Conditions on arrival of Third Army.—When the Third Army entered its area of occupation, it found the principal foodstuffs rationed, as had been the case for several years. In brief, the situation may be outlined thus, prior to the war, the average food consumption for the German population, expressed in calories, was about 3500 calories per person per day. According to German figures, this had shrunk to 3000 calories in 1914, 2000 in 1915, 1500 in 1916, and to 1200 in the winter of 1917–1918.

All the principal foodstuffs had been rationed during the war, and, on paper at least, every resource of the Empire in the way of food was entirely under control and carefully distributed.

The ration at the beginning of the occupation was essentially as follows:

Bread	260 grams per head per day[15]
Potatoes	500 grams per head per day

The main reliance for sustenance was placed on the above two foods and, except in the large cities, where the supply was subject to much fluctuation, the amounts indicated, or more, were fairly consistently provided during the whole of the year 1919.

In addition, the following substances constituted a part of the ration in the amounts indicated:

Meat	200 grams per head per week. Frequently reduced in amount, and often not issued at all.
Fat	150–200 grams per head per week. Later became very scarce.
Butter	20 grams per head per week. Practically never issued in the ration.
Sugar	600–750 grams per head per month.
Marmalade	200 grams per head per week. Often unavailable.
Milk	Not issued at all to the population in general, on account of its scarcity. Issued only to children under 6 years of age and, on physician's certificates, to the sick, nursing mothers, pregnant women and the aged. One half to one litre per day.

Fresh vegetables, in general, were not rationed and were fairly plentiful. Additional substances, such as rice, oats, grits, margarine, sausage, "Ersatz" (substitute) coffee, eggs, and additional flour, were added to the ration from time to time when available.

---

15. To convert grams to ounces, multiply grams by 0.035. Thus the German bread ration was a little over 9 ounces per day per person, and the potato ration was 17.5 ounces per person per day.

Source 12 from Jean-Jacques Becker, The Great War and the French People, *translated by Arnold Pomerans (New York: St. Martin's, 1986), pp. 232–234.*

12. Report on French Public Opinion in the Department of the Isère

Grenoble, 17 June 1917

The Prefect[16] of the Department of Isère to the Minister of the Interior[17]
Office of the Sûreté Générale[18]

I have the honour to reply herewith to the questions contained in your confidential telegram circulated on *10 June inst.*:

The inquiry I have myself conducted, or with the help of colleagues, to test the opinion of certain leading personages has shown that the morale of the people of Isère is far from satisfactory and that their exemplary spirit has suffered a general decline during the past two months. Today there is weariness bordering on dejection, a result less of the curtailment of the public diet and supply difficulties than of the disappointment caused by the failure of our armies in April,[19] the feeling that military blunders have been made, that heavy losses have been sustained without any appreciable gains, that all further offensives will be both bloody and in vain. The inactivity of Russia, whose contribution now seems highly doubtful, has accentuated the decline in morale.[20] The remarks of soldiers coming back from the front are the major cause of this decline: these remarks, made in the trains, in the railway stations, in the cafés on the way home, and then in the villages, convey a deplorable picture of the mentality of a great number of servicemen. Each one tells of and amplifies this or that unpleasant incident, this or that error

16. **prefect**: since the Revolution of 1789, France has been divided into departments. The chief administrative officer in each department, since the time of Napoleon, has been the prefect. The prefect, historically, has been an appointee of the central government and thus responsible to it and not to local interests.

17. **Minister of the Interior**: most police services in France are under the control of the central government's Ministry of the Interior.

18. **Sureté Général**: the central police command charged with criminal investigations.

19. In April 1917, the French army had received a new commander, General Nivelle, who launched a massive and costly offensive to break through German lines and end the war. The offensive failed and, coming after great French losses at Verdun in 1916, provoked a mutiny in the army in which soldiers refused orders to attack until August 1917. The mutinies placed the entire French war effort at risk. Order was restored only by a new commander, General Petain, and a new and authoritarian Prime Minister, Georges Clemenceau.

20. Russia's war effort was hampered by the revolution that broke out in March 1917. This, in combination with the French mutiny, Germany's unrestricted submarine warfare against all shipping around England, and the disastrous defeat of the Italian army beginning in October at Caporetto made 1917 the year of crisis for France and its allies.

committed by his commander, this or that useless battle, this or that act of insubordination presented as so many acts of courage and determination. These remarks, listened to with a ready ear by those who are already nervous or depressed enough as it is, are then peddled about and exaggerated with the result that discontent and anxiety are increased further. Each day, incidents in public places, particularly in the large railway stations and on the trains, reflect the most deplorable attitude in the minds of servicemen.

In the countryside, the restive mood is less obvious than it is in the towns; the peasants work, but they do not hide the fact that 'it's been going on too long'; they are tired of their continuous over-exertion in the fields, of the lack of hands and of the very heavy burden of the requisitions. They are growing more and more suspicious and indifferent to the idea of collective effort and mutual solidarity, and to patriotic appeals, and can think only of their immediate interests and their own safety.

Growers increasingly complain about price rises, even though they probably suffer less than others from the cost of living and even though their produce is sold at ever higher prices.

Nevertheless, it is among the rural populations that one finds the greatest composure and resignation.

In the towns, and particularly in the industrial centres, the more impressionable and hence more excitable population—the workers, the ordinary people—are upset about the duration of the struggle, impatient with the increasing cost of living, irritated by the considerable profits being made out of the war by the big industrialists in their neighbourhood, and increasingly taken in by the propagandists of the united Socialist Party and their internationalist ideas. Under the influence of the Russian Revolution they already dream of workers' and soldiers' committees and of social revolution. These sentiments are aired frequently at workers' meetings, called ostensibly to discuss economic or union matters, and in their paper, *Le Droit du Peuple*,[21] which is waging a very skillful anti-war and internationalist campaign.

This attitude, together with the constant rise in the cost of living, has fuelled a widespread demand for wage increases which the employers have quietly met to a large degree. Unfortunately, the calm following these increases has been momentary only. The cost of living keeps rising further and it is painful to watch each wage increase being followed directly by a corresponding increase in the price of food and the cost of board and lodging. Already those workers engaged on national defence contracts are finding that the new wage scales agreed less than two months ago for Grenoble and district have become inadequate; they are presently asking for a cost-of-living allowance of 2 francs a day and have made it quite clear that if their demand is not met there will be trouble in the streets; some of them have even gone so far as to declare that they know where to find the necessary arms, alluding

21. **Le Droit du Peuple**: the *Right of the People*.

to the shell and explosives factories in the suburbs of Grenoble. I know perfectly well that these remarks were presumably made in order to intimidate the citizens, but it is nevertheless symptomatic that they should have been made in the first place. When they lack the courage to speak out themselves, the factory propagandists use the women working beside them who, running smaller risks, are less restrained in their threats. The demands of the reservists in the munitions factories have been forwarded to the ministry of supply and a number of agitators have been sent away—not to the front, which would have been dangerous, but to other factories in various parts of the area. Calm has therefore been restored, but there are fears that the present lull may be temporary.

If working-class militancy were to make itself felt in the munitions factories in Grenoble and in the industrial centres of the department, it would be very difficult and extremely risky to try to control it by force: the local police force would prove inadequate, even if it were reinforced by gendarmes. It is clearly necessary to strengthen the police contingent, but this can only be done through the deferment of professional policemen serving in the territorial army or the reserve. The auxiliary policemen drawn from the ranks of the retired are admittedly men of goodwill, but they are physically and mentally worn out, and their contribution and energy are inadequate. The relocation, or rather the transfer, of some gendarmerie brigades would be very useful, but the consequent changes in domicile would involve cumbersome formalities. . . . It would not be unhelpful if an intelligent, serving special commissioner were put in charge, with particular emphasis on the surveillance of aliens who continue to move about freely in the department and can undermine the morale of our people even as these aliens go about the business of gathering information useful to the enemy.

In conclusion, I believe that the present situation, both in respect of morale and also of social stability, while not giving cause for alarm, is far from satisfactory and that it ought to be considered serious enough to call for precautionary measures, and if necessary for energetic intervention.

What is really needed to lift flagging courage and to restore confidence in the future is a military success by our armies, a major Russian offensive, or just a German retreat.

Source 13 from Report of the War Cabinet Committee on Women in British Industry *(London: His Majesty's Stationery Office, 1919).*

13. Employment of Women in Wartime British Industry

Trades	Est. Number Females Employed in July 1914	Est. Number Females Employed in July 1918	Difference Between Numbers of Females Employed in July 1914 and July 1918	Percentage of Females to Total Number Workpeople Employed		Est. Number Females Directly Replacing Males in Jan. 1918
				July 1914	July 1918	
Metal	170,000	594,000	+424,000	9	25	195,000
Chemical	40,000	104,000	+64,000	20	39	35,000
Textile	863,000	827,000	−36,000	58	67	64,000
Clothing	612,000	568,000	−44,000	68	76	43,000
Food, drink, and tobacco	196,000	235,000	+39,000	35	49	60,000
Paper and printing	147,500	141,500	−6,000	36	48	21,000
Wood	44,000	79,000	+35,000	15	32	23,000
China and earthenware	32,000 ⎫					
Leather	23,100 ⎬ 197,100		+93,000	4	10	62,000
Other	49,000 ⎭					
Government establishments	2,000	225,000	+223,000	3	47	197,000
Total	2,178,600	2,970,600	+792,000	26	37	704,000

Source 14 from J. M. Winter, The Great War and the British People (Cambridge, Mass.: Harvard University Press, 1986), p. 75.

14. Estimated Military Casualties, by Nation

Country	Total Killed or Died	Total Mobilized (in thousands)	Prewar Male Pop. 15–49	Total Prewar Pop.	Total Killed		
					Per 1,000 Mobilized	Per 1,000 Males 15–49	Per 1,000 People
Britain, Ireland	723	6,147	11,540	45,221	118	63	16
Canada	61	629	2,320	8,100	97	26	8
Australia	60	413	1,370	4,900	145	44	12
New Zealand	16	129	320	1,100	124	50	15
South Africa	7	136	1,700	6,300	51	4	1
India	54	953	82,600	321,800	57	1	0
France	1,327	7,891	9,981	39,600	168	133	34
French colonies	71	449	13,200	52,700	158	5	1
Belgium	38	365	1,924	7,600	104	20	5
Italy	578	5,615	7,767	35,900	103	75	16
Portugal	7	100	1,315	6,100	70	5	1
Greece	26	353	1,235	4,900	73	21	5
Serbia	278	750	1,225	4,900	371	227	57
Rumania	250	1,000	1,900	7,600	250	132	33
Russia	1,811	15,798	40,080	167,000	115	45	11
United States	114	4,273	25,541	98,800	27	4	1
Allied Total	5,421	45,001	204,018	812,521	120	27	7
Germany	2,037	13,200	16,316	67,800	154	125	30
Austria-Hungary	1,100	9,000	12,176	58,600	122	90	19
Turkey	804	2,998	5,425	21,700	268	148	37
Bulgaria	88	400	1,100	4,700	220	80	19
Central Powers' Total	4,029	25,598	35,017	152,800	157	115	26
Total Overall	9,450	70,599	239,035	965,321	134	40	10

Source 15 from Felix Gilbert, The End of the European Era, 1890 to the Present, *3rd ed. (New York: Norton, 1984), p. 161.*

15. War Indebtedness to the United States, Through 1918

Great Britain	$3,696,000,000
France	1,970,000,000
Italy	1,031,000,000

QUESTIONS TO CONSIDER

Now that you have read the selections, try to consider them collectively, drawing out the effects of war on the people of Western Europe. First, consider the initial reaction to war. We saw in The Problem that war was universally greeted with patriotic enthusiasm. What forms did that enthusiasm assume in the poems of Brooke, Péguy, and Lissauer? What previous experience had these authors with modern warfare?

Next, assess the experience of front-line service as it is expressed in the literary and other sources. Why do you think the initial ardor for warfare wore off quickly? On whom or what did the writers lay the blame for the horrors of war? How radical was their discontent? Compare their literary reactions to the war with the artistic responses we examined in Chapter 9. Consider again the casualty figures in Source 14 and the descriptions of trench warfare in Sources 4 and 5. Remember that Barbusse wrote during the war and Remarque a decade later. Do their descriptions of modern warfare differ

substantially? What do you think was uppermost in the minds of men subjected to such conditions?

The war inflicted unprecedented battle losses on every belligerent country, but societal groups within the warring countries did not suffer equally. In any combat situation the highest casualty rate affects noncommissioned and junior officers—the sergeants, lieutenants, and captains who lead attacks at the front of their units. What social groups does Remarque's *All Quiet on the Western Front* suggest made up the officer corps of each warring nation? What postwar effect do you think the loss of such men might have?

The front-line experience had costs for those who survived, too. Why might you conclude from the German soldiers' accounts of the holidays in 1914 and 1916 that one of the war's first casualties was patriotic devotion to its cause? As the war wore on, other reactions to combat became widespread among soldiers. Barbusse said that the war created two separate Frances, front-line and civilian. Does the character of Baumer in Remarque's novel reflect a similar division in Germany? Do you think a sense of alienation was a common reaction among veterans? How would it affect adjustment to postwar civilian life? Finally, assess the poems of Wilfred Owen and Siegfried Sassoon. How might you describe the sentiments expressed in those poems? What view of military authority does Sassoon's poem express? How old were Owen and Sassoon when they began military service? Are sentiments such as theirs usual in persons so young? What was the source for these views?

World War One affected civilian populations in ways no previous conflict had. Drawing on the German ration data, how do you think you would have found German wartime conditions? Why do you think Germans suffered nutritional deficiencies? Did such shortages also affect the German military, according to Source 5?

Every belligerent country recognized that the home front was essential to victory. The areas the Germans attacked in the London bombing described by Vera Brittain certainly lacked obvious military value. The Germans also launched long-range artillery attacks on Paris, and one shell fell on a crowded church on Good Friday, 1918, killing or injuring 200 people. What was the goal of such attacks on targets of no military value? Recall the report to the French police on public opinion in the Grenoble area. What ideas were current among civilians? Why were French authorities so concerned about public opinion?

The war had a deep impact on women, too. Source 13 clearly shows a great spurt in the employment of Englishwomen in many industries. In which industries especially did they find employment? How were these jobs probably related to the war effort? Women left certain jobs, too. Which did they abandon? Many of the industries they left traditionally offered low-paying employment for unskilled or semiskilled workers. How did wartime conditions allow women to improve their economic positions in England and, indeed, in all the warring nations? Do you think women's wartime contributions (remember that the nursing efforts of Vera Brittain and other women are not reflected in Source 13) would argue for improved postwar status for women?

The effects of World War One would be felt long after the armistice that ended hostilities in 1918. Refer to the table in Source 14. Notice the total numbers of men mobilized, recalling that in countries like France and Germany 80 percent of the military-age male population was in uniform. What effect on the birth rate do you think the absence of so many young men from their homes had on the birth rate during the years 1914–1918? What enduring impact did the deaths of many of these men have on their countries' birth rates? What implications could all these factors have in future defense considerations? Among the great powers, which country suffered the greatest proportional war losses? What do you predict the public attitudes in this country might be when war threatened again within twenty years of World War One's end? Do you think the costs of war would evoke the same response in other countries?

Finally, consider the economic costs of war. Wartime expenses outstripped tax revenues for all governments. All borrowed to pay for their war efforts. You must understand the figures in Source 15 in terms of the value of dollars during that period. Viewed in this light, the British debt represented almost five times the entire annual expenditure of the U.S. government in the years preceding the war's outbreak. From whom did the British and their allies borrow? What effect would this new creditor status have on the lender? How would such vast indebtedness affect European countries?

And what of Germany and Austria-Hungary, who lost the war, or Italy, who was on the winning side but failed to achieve all of its wartime goals? These countries made sacrifices comparable to those of the winning side. How would they view their war costs?

Your examination of all these issues should now allow you to answer the main questions of this chapter: Why was World War One different from previous wars? What impact did it have on the soldiers at the front? How did it affect civilians at home?

EPILOGUE

Europe and the world felt the effects of the first modern, total war for years after the armistice of 1918. Much more than a generation of young men died in the trenches. The war permanently transformed the power structure of Europe. The stress of modern warfare meant that no government survived politically when its war effort ended in defeat. Revolutions overthrew monarchs in Germany, Austria-Hungary, Bulgaria, and Turkey, and Austria-Hungary and Turkey broke up as their subject peoples asserted political independence of their old rulers. Russia's tsarist regime fell to communist revolution.

The war changed Europe economically, too. The financial needs of total warfare forced every government to borrow. The most obvious change was that the United States emerged from the war as the greatest creditor nation, but other economic changes occurred as well. As warring nations purchased raw materials and manufactured goods in the Americas and Asia during the conflict, the West's wealth began to shift out of Europe. In addition, Western European nations, particularly France, faced tremendous war-related property damage whose repair would consume funds for years to come.

Another cost of the war both in economic and human terms was found among its victims. The injured and crippled had to be treated, rehabilitated, and paid pensions. The situation of England illustrates the extent of the problem. When the government finalized its pension rolls in 1929, 2,424,000 men were receiving some sort of disability pension, about 40 percent of all the soldiers who had served in the British army in the war.

The war transformed Western society. Women's labor in war industries, their work in nursing, and their participation in uniformed auxiliary services of the armed forces sustained the prewar demands of women for a political voice. In most Western countries, women gained the right to vote after World War One, a major step in attaining a status equal to that of males.

The war's unhappiest result, however, was that it did not become what U.S. President Woodrow Wilson called "a war to end all wars." Rather, seeds for the next conflict were sown by the events and consequences of World War One. Total war created the desire for total victory, and the peace treaties reflected animosities produced by four years of bloody conflict. The Treaty of Versailles presented Germany with a settlement that would produce a desire for revision of the peace terms and even revenge. At the same time, the great losses of life in World War One engendered in many people in victorious nations a "never again" attitude that would lead them to seek to avoid another war at all costs. This attitude would in part result in efforts to appease a resurgent and vengeful Germany under Adolf Hitler (see Chapter 12) in the 1930s.

The alienation of former soldiers from civilian life led many to search out civilian opportunities for renewing the comradeship of the front, such as veterans' groups and paramilitary organizations. Especially in the defeated countries or in those victorious countries disappointed with their gains, this impulse had dangerous consequences. In Italy and Germany, veterans enlisted in great numbers in the ranks of uniformed, right-wing organizations that became the power base for the brutal armed supporters of the dictators Mussolini and Hitler (see Chapter 12). Pledged to winning back the losses in their nations' real and imagined defeats in World War One, such leaders as Hitler and Mussolini seized political power by exploiting postwar problems and resentments. Their policies were to breed a second global conflict.

CHAPTER ELEVEN
WOMEN IN
RUSSIAN REVOLUTIONARY
MOVEMENTS

During the last half of the nineteenth century and the first decades of the twentieth, women throughout Europe became involved in a wide range of movements advocating political change. Inspired by liberal reform efforts to improve conditions in prisons and mental hospitals, expand educational opportunities, and broaden the suffrage, women in Europe and America began to call for the extension of women's legal rights, availability of higher education to women, and the right to vote. They formed national and international organizations to agitate for these changes. Gradually, married women were granted the right to own property, a scattering of colleges and universities allowed women to enroll in some courses, and a few countries, such as Norway, New Zealand, and Australia, allowed women the right to vote. Despite increasingly militant tactics by advocates of women's suffrage, most European coun-

tries did not grant women the right to vote until after World War One (France did not extend this right until after World War Two).

The nineteenth-century women's rights movement was largely made up of middle-class women, for whom changes such as greater access to education were extremely important, but working-class women also saw a need for reforms. Like working-class men, women laborers wanted the workday reduced from twelve hours to ten; safety conditions improved in mines, mills and factories; an end to child labor; and the right to organize without losing their jobs. Working-class women also had specific concerns because they were women. They were often harassed sexually by their employers and fired when they became pregnant. Women's wages were always lower than men's, even when they performed the same tasks. Because their wages were low, women returned to work very soon after giving birth, a practice that was detrimental to their own health and that of their infants. Though both women and men worked the same long hours in mills and factories, the actual workday for women was even longer because they generally did most or all of the cooking, housework, and child care.

A number of working-class women sought to improve conditions for all workers, especially women, through organizing and political action. Some joined labor unions and socialist political parties; in Germany women formed a separate socialist women's organization. These actions were not always supported by the men who made up the vast majority of labor unions and socialist groups. Many working-class men viewed women workers with hostility because women were used as strikebreakers or to force wages down. Often these men did not want their own wives and daughters speaking out in public or acting as organizers. Their own low wages dictated that their wives and daughters worked, but many had internalized the middle-class notion that the woman's proper place was the home and so were unwilling to accept women joining them in the fight for workers' rights or better conditions.

In addition, some leaders of the socialist movement viewed separate women's organizations as harmful to working-class solidarity. Though Marx and Engels had both clearly advocated women's political equality and most socialist parties included votes for women as part of their platforms, working-class women were urged to work first for the overthrow of capitalism or for more gradual improvements in the status of the entire

working class. Male socialist theorists argued that class solidarity should always take precedence over gender solidarity, and many prominent women socialists agreed with them.

The middle-class women's rights movement and the socialist movement began in Western Europe, but both quickly found advocates in Russia, which boasted the most autocratic and repressive government in all of Europe. By the mid-nineteenth century, Russian women had already joined men in calling for the abolition of serfdom and introduction of some representative institutions. A small middle-class women's movement advocated higher education for women and the right for women to leave home without their fathers' permission. Advocates of women's rights wrote articles about what was termed the "woman question," discussing the consequences of expanding women's educational and employment opportunities and legal rights. They viewed women's rights as an important part of any political reform, noting that the absolute power of the tsar was simply an extension of the absolute power of the father in Russian families. (The word *tsar*, in fact, means "little father.")

A small number of women from all social classes felt the reformist aims of the women's rights movement were much too mild and gradual, and these women joined groups that advocated revolutionary change and the violent overthrow of the tsar. Because their actions often made political radicalism and women's emancipation seem like two sides of the same coin in the minds of many Russian officials, periods of general political repression also brought increasing restrictions on the rights of women.

Tsar Alexander II freed the serfs in 1861 and began a brief period of reform that also produced some alterations in the status of women. Women were allowed to attend selected classes at the universities, and local representative assemblies, called *zemstvos*, were established. A woman who owned enough property could even nominate a man of her choice as her proxy in the *zemstvo*, though she could not attend herself. These reforms led to growing calls for more radical changes and an increasingly active terrorist movement. Alexander II reverted to a policy of repression that only increased the ardor of revolutionary groups; in 1881, one of them, the People's Will, succeeded in its attempts to assassinate him. The assassination was led by a woman, Sofia Perovskaia, who a month later became the first female in Russian history to be executed for a political crime: she was hung along with four male compatriots. Another female conspirator, Gesia Gelfman, was also sentenced, but her hanging was deferred because she was pregnant; she died in prison after childbirth. Perovskaia and Gelfman were not the only female revolutionaries; about 30 percent of the members of the People's Will were women, as were about 15 percent of all those arrested for political crimes in the 1870s, a much higher proportion of female membership than in any other contemporary European socialist or radical movement.

The assassination of Alexander II was followed by a period of repressive reaction under the tsar's successors. Women as well as men were arrested and exiled to Siberia, but this did not stop their activities. During the 1890s, Russia began to industrialize heavily and socialist organizers joined the workforce of the new factories to convince workers of the need to organize for better working conditions, improved wages, and the right to form unions and political parties. Female organizers went to work in factories where large numbers of women were employed, spreading ideas about rights for both workers and women. Because workers' and socialist groups were illegal, joining one could lead to dismissal, imprisonment, or exile, but these groups still began to grow slowly. Women workers were more hesitant to join than men, probably because many worried more about the economic consequences of such an action for their families and less about abstract political rights. The organizers who were most successful in recruiting women were generally females themselves who addressed the specific concerns of working women such as sexual harassment, maternity leave, and women's lower wages.

Dissatisfaction among both peasants and workers came to a head during Russia's disastrous war with Japan. In January of 1905, soldiers fired on a crowd of workers who were marching peacefully to the tsar's palace to petition for reforms, an incident that sparked a series of riots, strikes, assassinations, naval mutinies, and peasant revolts. Workers in

St. Petersburg and elsewhere spontaneously organized bodies advocating various reforms and set up their own councils, called *soviets*. The tsar was forced to allow the establishment of a national representative assembly, the *Duma*, to be elected by almost universal male suffrage.

The 1905 revolution was followed by a period of reaction. Under the Fundamental Law establishing the Duma, the tsar retained considerable power, including the right to dismiss this body and call for new elections. In 1907 voting rights were increasingly restricted so that landowners and wealthier urban voters had the most seats; the last two Dumas put up little objection to the tsar's policies before World War I.

None of the underlying political and economic problems had been solved, however, and they re-emerged dramatically when Russia entered the war against Germany in 1914. Huge numbers of ill-equipped soldiers were killed in the first year of the war, and Nicholas II provided no leadership in solving problems of how to mobilize the country for an all-out war effort. The tsar decided to act as his ancestors always had, by assuming personal command at the front, leaving the government largely in the hands of his wife. As a firm believer in absolutism and autocracy, the tsarina, Alexandra, refused to yield to the Duma's and other groups' demands for change.

During the winter of 1916–1917, food supplies became increasingly scarce and women were desperate to feed their families. In February 1917, as part of an observance of International Women's Day, women in Pe-

trograd (formerly St. Petersburg) organized a strike for food and better working conditions. Male union leaders tried to prevent the strike, asserting that a separate action by women was harmful to the solidarity of the workers' movement, but the women were not to be dissuaded. The strike proved extremely effective because the soldiers in the city refused to fire on the women, leading male union leaders finally to show their support. This strike led to sympathy strikes in the factories and public demonstrations of over 300,000 people. Soldiers joined the demonstrators, the Duma declared a Provisional Government, and Nicholas II was forced to abdicate.

The February Revolution was welcomed throughout the country, and the new government quickly advocated a program of liberal and democratic reforms, meanwhile deferring many actual reforms to concentrate on the war effort. Exiled radicals, among them V. I. Lenin, returned to the country and urged the Petrograd Soviet to push for more dramatic changes, including Russia's withdrawal from the war and the takeover of farms and factories by peasants and workers. In October 1917, Lenin's political party, the Bolsheviks, led the Petrograd Soviet in a revolution against the Provisional Government and succeeded in taking over the city. Four months later, they signed a treaty with the Germans that ended Russian involvement in the war, though civil war would persist for the next decade.

Continuing the radical movement tradition of the nineteenth century, women were involved and active in both the 1905 and 1917 revolutions. Your task in this chapter will be to analyze that involvement, using memoirs, political pamphlets, and histories to answer the following questions: What changes did those women involved in Russian revolu-tionary movements want to bring about, and what actions did they take to implement these changes? Did women's concerns, strategies, and objections differ from those of men, and if so, how?

SOURCES AND METHOD

The questions posed in this chapter, particularly the second one, ask you to make distinctions between the historical experience of women and men—in other words, to assess how gender affected people's experiences. Though it seems quite obvious that gender shapes an individual life to a great degree, only recently have historians begun to differentiate the historical past of females from that of males.

This awareness of gender is a result of the relatively new field of women's history, which arose in conjunction with the feminist movement of the 1960s. As historians studied the social history of women, they discovered that periods of advance for men, such as the Renaissance or the Enlightenment, did not bring corresponding advances for women. A timeline of great events in women's history would be very different from a timeline of great events in men's history (or what had until that point been called "human" history).

Once historians began exploring the history of women, they realized that because the male experience alone had most often been identified as the human experience, only rarely had men in the past been studied as men. This led to the recognition that whereas throughout human history *sex* has been determined biologically, *gender*, or what it means cognitively to be male or female, is a social construct that has changed over time. Men and women have always had different roles, rights, opportunities, and expectations, but these have been created by the society they lived in and are not the result of natural sex differences. Sophisticated analysts of any historical change now investigate the differing roles played by men and women and the way in which that change affected gender relations and the relative position of women and men.

Studying the history of women has led historians not only to add gender as an essential category of historical analysis and to ask new questions of all historical events but also to look for new types of sources. Both intentionally and unintentionally, traditional sources often exclude the experience and activities of women. Most written records have come from the hands of men, who have either ignored women's experiences or viewed them as less important than those of men. Even newspapers and journals that purport to offer objective accounts were until very recently

[281]

owned and run exclusively by men, which means that they, too, are gender biased. Discovering the history of women in any period thus involves creative sleuthing and the use of less traditional sources, such as private letters and diaries.

Studying the history of women in Russian revolutionary movements poses additional problems. After the Soviet state was established, "official" histories of the revolution played up the ideas and activities of leaders such as Lenin, excluding the activities of lesser figures, both male and female. Especially under the rule of Stalin, individuals and groups whose ideas this leader disagreed with were totally excluded from Russian and Soviet history, and many of these same individuals were executed or exiled for life. Western historians' exclusion of women has been generally less intentional, emerging as it did from their emphasis on the theorists behind the movements, who were usually men, rather than on the organizers attempting to put theory into practice, who were often women as well as men.

For a balanced view of the actions of both men and women, we need to turn from official sources to the writings of women themselves. All the sources for this chapter either were written by women or directly report women's words. Simply locating women's writings is not always easy. Many of the women revolutionaries took very little time to write, and much of what revolutionaries of both sexes did write was destroyed by authorities. Before 1917, tsarist officials confiscated and destroyed not only many political pamphlets and propaganda but also private letters and journals. After 1917, Bolshevik officials destroyed documents written by those who did not agree with them—moderates, anarchists, Mensheviks, Socialist Revolutionaries, or Bolsheviks who had fallen out of favor with the party leadership. As noted, women's writings that actually reached print were often forgotten or ignored in later histories of these movements. Many of the sources here have been rediscovered and translated only in the past ten or fifteen years by scholars interested in the history of women who have combined archives and libraries for neglected material.

To realize how discovering and integrating material on women and adding gender as a category of analysis can change your understanding of events, first read (or reread) the section in your text that deals with nineteenth-century Russia and the Bolshevik Revolution. Which women are mentioned by name? What actions by women are described, and how are these integrated into the general narrative of events? Do the descriptions of various revolutionary movements make it clear that both men and women were involved? Are their experiences ever compared or differentiated by gender? Now read the sources in this chapter; when you have finished, you may discover that your text is in need of some revision.

The first three sources are excerpts from the memoirs of Russian women revolutionaries in the late nineteenth century. As you read these, make a list of the changes each author wished to bring about in Russian society and the actions she took to bring about these changes. (As you read the selections, keep your text handy as a reference to political developments and to well-known radicals whose ideas influenced the authors.)

Elizaveta Kovalskaia, the author of the first selection, was born to a serf mother and nobleman father, though her father later used his influence to have both Kovalskaia and her mother declared free citizens. The actions she describes here led to her arrest in 1880; she was sent to Siberia for twenty-three years. Source 2 is by Olga Liubatovich, the daughter of an engineer, who grew up in Moscow and first came into contact with radical ideas in Zurich, where she had gone to study medicine. In 1875 she began organizing factory workers as a member of the Pan-Russian Social Revolutionary Organization, an activity for which she was imprisoned in Siberia. Kovalskaia escaped three years later, resumed her revolutionary activities, and began to write her memoirs, from which these selections are taken. Source 3, by Praskovia Ivanovskaia, the daughter of a poor provincial village priest, describes her political activities in 1876. Later she became a member of the People's Will, the group that assassinated Alexander II, and was exiled to Siberia for twenty years for her involvement in the plot. Ivanovskaia escaped and played a very active role in the revolution of 1905.

What activities did these three women see as most important in bringing about fundamental social changes? What tactics did they rec-

ommend? How did their tactics change as the political circumstances changed? How did their tactics change as their own ideas matured and developed? What specific concerns of women did the authors address? In Source 2, what special problems did Gesia Gelfman face because she was female? How was she treated differently because of her sex? How were the problems facing working-class Russian women different from those facing middle-class women?

Source 4 is an excerpt from the memoirs of Eva Broido, who grew up in a moderately prosperous Jewish family and entered the revolutionary movement by organizing workers in St. Petersburg in 1899. Exiled to Siberia for running a secret printing press, she escaped and continued organizing. After the 1905 revolution, she became a Menshevik and carried out the activities she describes here. After the Bolshevik Revolution she was forced to leave Russia, but she returned in 1927 and probably died in the Stalinist purges of the 1930s. What role did Broido ascribe to workers' clubs? Why were these clubs especially important to women?

The fifth and sixth selections describe the actions of women during the 1905 revolution. Source 5 is taken from a history of the working women's movement in Russia written in 1920 by Alexandra Kollontai. Kollontai, the daughter of a prominent army officer, was the most important woman within the leadership of the Bolshevik party; after the October Revolution she became the commissar of social welfare and head of the women's department within the party, called the *Zhenotdel*. She wrote on a wide range of subjects, including many of special interest to women, such as marriage and the family. As you read this selection, add Kollontai's aims and actions to your list and also pay attention to the general tone of the piece. How does she portray women workers and peasants? How does she portray middle-class women? Source 6 is a petition brought by peasant women to the Duma established after the 1905 revolution. How had the changes brought about by this first revolution affected them differently from peasant men? Does this petition fit with the actions Kollontai describes in her history?

Source 7 is also a petition by women, this one brought to the Provisional Government after the February Revolution of 1917. Again, notice both content and tone. How had the February Revolution affected women's political status? How would you compare this with the 1905 petition?

The last two selections were also written by Alexandra Kollontai. Source 8 is an article from *Pravda*, the Bolshevik party newspaper, which appeared in May 1917, months before the Bolshevik Revolution, under the headline "In the Front Line of Fire." What actions does Kollontai suggest to the reader? Source 9 is taken from a pamphlet titled "Working Woman and Mother," written in 1914, which contains ideas Kollontai later tried to put into practice when

she became the commissar of public welfare. What special problems of working women does she identify, and how does she propose to solve them?

Look over your list of each author's aims and actions. What aims did all share? Did any of their aims and tactics appear to contradict each other? Which authors make clear distinctions between the problems facing middle-class women and those facing women peasants and workers? Which authors believe the concerns of workers in general take precedence over those of women?

You should not let contradictions in the goals and beliefs of these women revolutionaries surprise you. It is as misleading to generalize about all women as it is to generalize about all men, though the first investigators of the history of women tended to do just this. Generalizations overlook the fact that because women make up half of every social class and economic category, their experiences are often much more similar to those of the men of their class than to women of other classes. Generalizations along class lines (e.g., "middle-class women think . . . ") can also be misleading, because class background alone is not enough to explain the diversity of opinion among women, just as it is not enough to explain the diversity of opinion among men. Viewing "middle-class women" or "working-class women" as an undifferentiated group ignores the fact that women develop their own ideas individually, just as men do.

Sources 1 through 3 from Barbara Alpern Engel and Clifford N. Rosenthal, editors and translators, Five Sisters: Women Against the Tsar *(New York: Knopf, 1975), pp. 210–212, 217–218, 226, 233-234; pp. 185–187, 194; pp. 103–105.*

1. From the *Memoirs* of Elizaveta Kovalskaia, Moscow, 1926

The emancipation of the serfs in 1861 had given rise to the women's movement. Like a huge wave, the movement to liberate women swept over all the urban centers of Russia. I, too, was caught up in it. My father had died soon after I finished school, leaving me a large inheritance. In one of the houses he left me, I organized free courses for women seeking higher education. Iakov Kovalskii, whom I later married, worked with me on this. There were so many auditors for the courses that we had trouble squeezing them all into the house. Kovalskii gave lectures on physics, chemistry, and cosmography; de la Rue, an assistant professor, taught the natural sciences; and we used university students for political economy, history, and higher mathematics.

At the same time, I belonged to the Kharkov Society for the Promotion of Literacy. At the Sunday schools where I worked, I picked out the most capable of the women laborers and invited them to my house on holidays. Gradually, a school for women workers was formed. I read them fragments of Russian fiction and recounted episodes from Russian history; I told them about the French Revolution; but mainly, I conducted propaganda on the woman question.

A men's study circle devoted to social questions met in my house; its orientation was radical, although not revolutionary. Parallel to this group, I organized one exclusively for women who were interested in socialism. A male comrade who had a good grasp of French, as well as access to the university library, made excerpts from source works to help me in compiling papers on Fourier, Saint-Simon, Owen, and other utopian socialists.

On holidays, some village schoolteachers who were friends of Kovalskii came to visit us. We provided them with books and organized small conferences on pedagogy, in the course of which we also dealt with political topics. During one of these conferences, a police officer and his entourage appeared in our house. When he saw the maps and visual displays spread out on the desks, he was taken aback. "All this is fine," he declared; "you're doing useful work and I see nothing illegal in it. But according to the orders from my superiors, all your meetings must cease, and if they don't, I'll have to arrest you all."

We had to stop everything.

Dmitrii Tolstoi, the minister of education, was supposed to visit Kharkov around that time, and we agitated for the right to present a petition to him: we wanted permission for women to enroll in the universities. Meetings were held constantly; I was chosen to the committee that drew up the petition, and also as a delegate to present it. But as it turned out, Tolstoi was very hostile to us: he declared that he would never allow women into the universities. . . .

[Kovalskaia then went to St. Petersburg, where she organized discussion circles for women, but was ordered by her doctor to go south for health reasons.]

I soon went south, as I had been ordered. When I got there, I started to revive the circles I had organized earlier, but my doctors quickly packed me off to Zurich.

In Zurich I came into contact with various revolutionary currents, especially Lavrism and Bakuninism. I was attracted to Bakuninism,[1] and when my health had improved somewhat, I returned to Russia in order to "go to the people."

Because of my physical weakness, I was absolutely unsuited for the role of a manual laborer. Instead, I took a position as a schoolteacher in the district of Tsarskoe Selo, close to the Kolpino factory, where the young people of the village worked. I quickly came under surveillance for conducting propaganda and illegally distributing revolutionary pamphlets among the factory workers. One day, the *zemstvo* school inspector came to warn me that I was about to be arrested.

I escaped to St. Petersburg, where I got to know some workers and began providing them with illegal literature. My status was semi-illegal, but I managed to avoid arrest by dividing my time between St. Petersburg and Kharkov. Then, during the demonstration that followed Vera Zasulich's acquittal[2] [March 31, 1878, in St. Petersburg], I was severely beaten by the police. I had to spend almost a year in bed back in Kharkov.

After I recovered, I organized several groups—two circles of metalworkers from the factories and a third one composed of young people. . . .

1. **Bakuninism:** the anarchist philosophy of the Russian nobleman Mikhail Bakunin, who believed that revolution should rise from locally controlled, grassroots movements of many social classes, in contrast to Marx's emphasis on the industrial proletariat.

2. Vera Zasulich had shot General Trepov, the governor of St. Petersburg because he had ordered the whipping of a political prisoner who had refused to remove his cap in Trepov's presence. The jury acquitted her, but the tsar refused to accept the acquittal and ordered her arrested again. Friends smuggled her out of Russia to Switzerland, where she spent most of the next twenty-five years. She returned to Russia after the 1905 revolution, and was viewed by many groups as a great hero.

I presented the program Shchedrin[3] and I had developed, which later served as the basis for the Union of Russian Workers of the South. It was essentially this: the goal was to transform the existing order into a socialist system. This was possible only by means of a *popular revolution*. The preconditions for such a revolution existed in Russia: the *obshchina*, or peasant land commune, and the propensity of the Russian people for workers' cooperatives and self-government. If there was to be a revolution in Russia, it could only be a socialist one, because the people would rise in rebellion only for the land; political demands made little sense to them. Any revolution that did not involve the participation of the people—even one carried out by a socialist party—would inevitably be *merely political*: that is, it would bring the country freedom similar to that enjoyed in Western Europe without changing the economic situation of the working people at all. It would simply make it easier for the bourgeoisie to organize itself and thus become a more formidable enemy of the workers.

Now, the peasants and workers of Russia were dissatisfied with their situation, but they lacked faith in their own ability to overthrow the established order, and this prevented them from rebelling. The people had to be instilled with the necessary confidence. Political terror directed at the center of the system was too remote for them to comprehend. *Economic terror* (we called it "democratic terror" then) defended their immediate interests. It involved the murder of the police officials and administrators of all sorts who were in closest contact with the people; its meaning would be clear to the people, and it would involve fewer sacrifices than the strike or local popular uprising. Only this kind of terror could increase the people's faith in *their own* ability to struggle, to organize and overthrow the existing structure themselves. It was virtually impossible for the intelligentsia to do political work in the countryside. It was easier among city workers. As these workers returned to their villages, they would be able to implement a program of action among the peasantry. . . .

We succeeded in organizing about seven hundred workers. We divided them into groups and met with a different one every night, seeing each only once a week. There were rarely fewer than a hundred people at a meeting— an enormous number for those times. We had no specific agenda for the discussions; our theoretical positions simply emerged as we talked about one or another current social ill. There was no need to dwell on how terrible things were in general for workers and peasants; people were already well aware of this. All we had to do was make the connections between this misery and the workings of the established order as a whole, then go back and integrate each specific instance of discontent.

Despite the organization's success, the struggle against the passivity instilled over the centuries was a difficult one. Often workers would listen

3. **Shchedrin:** Nicolai Shchedrin, her comrade and friend.

attentively and then proceed to tell us that things would somehow get done without them. Everyone had his own version of this, depending on his degree of political development. The most sophisticated believed that some revolutionary committee would take the land away from the landlords for the peasants. Others said that the tsar had abolished serfdom and was now fighting the gentry in order to take away their lands and distribute them among the people. Those who had heard about the Chigirin affair[4] believed that the "tsar's commissars" were genuine, and that the nobles had captured and murdered them. There were some, too, who "knew for a fact" that foreign powers (they didn't know which ones in particular) were doing things to better the situation of the Russian common folk. The least sophisticated workers—even the young people—spoke with profound conviction of how "visions had begun," how the Virgin had appeared to their priest, saying: "Pray, for the day of rejoicing will soon be upon you." They believed in the elders who indicated definite dates on which "everything will be turned upside down and all the poor will be exalted."

Our main task, then, in organizing the workers was to stimulate their initiative so that they would take up their cause themselves.

2. From the *Memoirs* of Olga Liubatovich, Moscow, 1906

[Liubatovich describes her first meeting with Gesia Gelfman, one of those arrested for assassinating Tsar Alexander II.]

She told me her whole life story. She had grown up in Mozyr (Minsk province). Her father, a prosperous but fanatical Jew, gave her no education whatsoever; Gesia owed everything she had become to her own energy. When she reached the age of seventeen, her father decided—without consulting her—to marry her off. A dowry was prepared. The eve of her wedding came—time for the older women to perform on Gesia the repulsive rituals dictated by ancient Jewish custom. But Gesia's sense of modesty made her rebel, and she resolved to leave home. She grabbed her jewelry and escaped by night to the home of a Russian girlfriend who had promised to help her. Gesia moved to Kiev, where she enrolled in the courses in midwifery[5] so as to be able to make an honest living. She made friends among the progressive youth of Kiev, getting to know Alexandra Khorzhevskaia, one of the Fritsche,[6] in 1875. It was at this time that I met her.

4. **Chigirin affair:** during 1876–77, radicals circulated fictitious tsarist orders, calling on the peasants of the Chigirin area to form armies to seize the nobility's land and redistribute it to people. Tsarist officials discovered this conspiracy and arrested all involved.

5. These were the only courses available to women in Kiev at the time.

6. **Fritsche:** a study group formed by thirteen female emigre Russian students in Zurich in 1872. The group read the works of socialists and revolutionaries and resolved to return to Russia to carry out revolutionary activities.

Gesia was arrested in September 1875. Two years later, at the Trial of the Fifty,[7] she was convicted of serving as an intermediary for our organization, which had been engaged in propagandizing and organizing among the youth and workers of various cities of the Russian Empire. She could claim no legal privileges by virtue of her social status,[8] and so she was incarcerated in a St. Petersburg workhouse. In August 1878, when I reached St. Petersburg after escaping from Siberia, Gesia was still languishing in the workhouse. I corresponded with her, and once, after she was transferred to the Litovskii fortress, walked down the street beneath her window. It made her happy to see me free.

In the summer of 1879, Gesia was sent off under police guard to finish out her sentence at Staraia Russa (Novgorod province). Later that year she escaped, and we saw each other for the first time since our sentencing. She told me that she felt extremely weary after her prolonged confinement, that she wanted to rest. But those were times of feverish activity, and Gesia, like the rest of us, got swept up in the intense struggle. She was a very sensitive person, and her life was one of continuous sacrifice; she had the ability to love.

Now, at what proved to be my last meeting with Gesia, she was sad and looked rather ill, but she buried her personal grief amid the endless concerns imposed by her life as a revolutionary. For that matter, there were few cheerful people in revolutionary circles at the time: every day someone else was snatched away by the police, and the survivors, depressed by these losses, were straining every nerve for a final assault on the regime. Gesia seemed to have a foreboding that she was living out the last days of her freedom, the freedom she had enjoyed so briefly.

The apartment Gesia shared with Nikolai Sablin was used for briefings by the people who participated in the assassination of the tsar on March 1. On March 3 the place was raided by the police: Sablin killed himself, and Gelfman was arrested. A few weeks later, she was sentenced to death. Her pregnancy delayed the execution—dooming her instead to another, more horrible fate. She languished under the threat of execution for five months; finally her sentence was commuted, just before she was to deliver. At the hands of the authorities, the terrible act of childbirth became a case of torture unprecedented in human history. For the delivery, they transferred her to the House of Detention. They gave her a fairly large cell, but in it they posted round-the-clock sentries—a device that had driven other women, women who weren't pregnant, insane. The torments suffered by poor Gesia Gelfman exceeded those dreamed up by the executioners of the Middle Ages; but

---

7. **Trial of the Fifty:** a mass trial conducted in Moscow in March 1877. The government arrested fifty members of a revolutionary group, the Pan-Russian Social Revolutionary Organization, who had been organizing among workers. It hoped to brand them as criminals; instead, people viewed the radicals as idealists.

8. Russian criminal law exempted certain social categories of people (especially the nobility) from various forms of punishment.

Gesia didn't go mad—her constitution was too strong. The child was born live, and she was even able to nurse it. Under Russian law, Gesia's rights as a mother were protected, even though she was a convict; no one could take her baby away. But at that time, who would have considered being guided by the law? One night shortly after the child was born, the authorities came in and took her away from Gesia. In the morning, they brought her to a foundling home, where they abandoned her without taking a receipt or having her tagged—this despite the fact that many people (myself included) had offered to raise the child. The mother could not endure this final blow, and she soon died.

Thus ended the life of Gesia Gelfman, who fled from her father's house, filled with indignation at ancient custom, filled with indignation at the tramping of women's rights—only to perish as the victim of unprecedented violence against her sensibilities as a woman, a human being, and a mother.

> [*Liubatovich then returns to
> her own story.*]

The next day, as I was getting ready to leave for St. Petersburg, a comrade from the Executive Committee (Vera Figner, as I recall) came over to tell me that Sofia Bardina's husband, Shakhov, was in Moscow and wanted to see me.

How my heart started to beat when I heard that! Sofia and I might be able to reinvigorate the revolutionary movement. We had been comrades in the Pan-Russian Social Revolutionary Organization, a group that had developed considerable strength through its great ideological and moral unity. Back in 1875, we had laid the foundations for revolutionary workers' associations in Moscow and other cities. Our program reflected in embryo the course of the revolutionary movement in the seventies: from peaceful propaganda to armed resistance and disorganization of the government by means of terror. Many people subsequently told me that the solidarity we had achieved served as a model for the revolutionary organizations that came after us, particularly Land and Liberty. Our group didn't produce a single traitor, thanks to the principle on which it was based: the complete freedom and equality of all its members. Everyone—worker or member of the intelligentsia, man or woman—took a turn at carrying out administrative duties, which were both an obligation and a right. There were no elections. No one was anxious to enter the administration. The administrators had no power; they were intermediaries, and nothing more. But even apart from that, all of us placed a very high value on working directly among the people and doing ordinary manual labor. Although our period of activity was brief—less than a year—our propaganda left very perceptible traces among the people, and our legacy was put to use by those who came after us.

3. From the *Memoirs* of Praskovia Ivanovskaia, Moscow, 1925

I decided to spend the time in Odessa, where I could find factory work without showing my identity papers, which marked me as a member of the intelligentsia. . . .

I got up very early that first Monday morning, so early that the street was still deserted by the time I reached the factory gates. The factory buildings themselves were invisible from the street, blocked by the long, high stone walls—gray, ugly, mottled with obscene graffiti. The factory hadn't come to life yet: I found no one at the gate, which resembled that of a prison. Then the workingmen began to approach, sleepy and sullen, singly and in groups. The wicket gate opened to swallow them up and then slammed shut again, as if of its own volition. Finally, the women workers arrived—late, hurrying, adjusting their clothing on the run. They dived behind the gate, and once more the street was utterly deserted.

I knocked timidly. An eye appeared at a small window in the gate, and a voice shouted: "What do you want? A job? Come in." With no formalities whatsoever, I was led to the lower level of the factory, which reminded me of an enormous shed. It was crammed full of coils of rope, old and new, around which clusters of young girls and old women were bustling. Some insignificant character took my name, and I was led to a group of workers sitting cross-legged on the floor, surrounded on all sides by old rope.

The air was dense throughout the lower level, where old ropes were untwisted and pulled apart and new ropes were covered with canvas. Sometimes we were sent up to the second floor, where wagons carried us swiftly around outstetched ropes, which we lubricated with soap and resin. There was no dawdling here—the slightest carelessness could end in tragedy: I myself saw a youth lose three fingers in an instant. We workers ate and drank our tea sitting on dirty coils of rope; after dinner, we curled up on them like kittens and slept. No one brought dinner to the factory: we simply bought hunks of lard or olives and white bread at the factory gate for five kopecks and took turns bringing boiling water from the tavern.

The air in the building was thick with resin and soap, and the resin quickly saturated all your clothing: within two or three days, every new worker had acquired the factory's distinctive odor, and within a week, there was no way you could get rid of it. The local landladies didn't like to rent rooms to rope workers—they spread their stench through the whole house.

The women were paid twenty-five kopecks a day; the men, as I recall, got thirty or forty. Most of the women workers were totally rootless: as many of them told me, they had nowhere else to go but the streets. Some had come to work there so as not to burden their families. In short, women were driven to the rope factory by the most pressing need, by the cruelest misfortune.

Only women in this situation would put up with the ubiquitous rudeness, the men's disrespectful treatment of them, the pinches and searches as they entered or left the factory.

All the women workers were illiterate. They would have been eager to learn, but when was there time to teach them? After a brief dinner, they caught up on the hours of sleep they'd missed in the morning by curling up on the filthy ropes. By the time we went home, the sun was the thinnest of crescents, sinking into the sea. On holidays, the women couldn't study in their quarters even if they'd wanted to. How, then, could I conduct propaganda among these women, who were so cut off from everyone and everything? Perhaps if I'd remained at the factory longer than two or three months, I might have been able to get something going: a few girls were becoming interested in reading and had begun to drop in at my apartment, and in time I might have been able to propagandize and organize them. But I found conditions at the factory too difficult and depressing to continue working there.

Source 4 from Eva Broido, Memoirs of a Revolutionary, *edited and translated by Vera Broido (Oxford: Oxford University Press, 1967), pp. 133–135.*

4. From the *Memoirs* of Eva Broido, Berlin, 1926

The most important centres of party work were our clubs. In them we concentrated all our propaganda activities: our propaganda was distributed from them, and there the workers came to hear lectures on current affairs. There, too, our members in the Duma came to report to us on their work. Virtually all the organizational work was centred on these clubs—general and special party meetings were held there, party publications were distributed from there, these were the "addresses" of the local district and sub-district branches, there all local news was collected, from there speakers were sent to factory meetings. And these were also the places where enlightened workers—men and women—could meet for friendly exchange of ideas and to read books and newspapers. All clubs aimed above all at having good libraries. And eventually they also encouraged art, there were music and song groups and the like.

At first clubs were exclusively political, but soon their character changed. Propaganda meetings gave place to lectures and discussions of a more general nature, the clubs become "colleges" of Marxism. Representatives of all club committees combined to work out systematic courses of lectures, to provide and distribute the necessary books and to supply book catalogues. Soon, groups of workers asked for courses on scientific subjects. And already in the winter of 1906–7 the programmes included physics, mathematics and technology alongside economics, historical materialism and the history of socialism and the labour movement.

In addition to the clubs there were many "evening schools"; they grew in number as the clubs attracted the attention of the police and were often closed down. These evening schools included some courses for the illiterate, and these were often attended by working-class men and women who were already playing influential roles in the movement.

Apart from their educational functions—varied and important as these were—the clubs provided the workers with their first training grounds in practical politics. This was their main value for the future and for the historical development of the Russian proletariat. But from the very start on democratic principles, the clubs taught the workers the techniques of elections— how to elect and be elected, to accept and exercise responsibility, to organize and lead the movement. It was in the clubs and in the trade unions that the elite of the Russian proletariat was trained. But the trade unions, which sprang up at the same time as the clubs, were more exposed to attacks by the Government and to harassment from the police. They dragged out a precarious, semi-legal existence right up to the outbreak of the World War, when they were practically wiped out.

All in all, the clubs can fairly be described as the pioneers of the new proletarian culture. In the past, after a century under the yoke of absolutism, workers had no place to meet in their leisure hours except the tavern. But now new and better ways of life were being created in the clubs, and this explains the devotion that the workers brought to them.

For the working woman the clubs were of the greatest importance. In earlier days they had even less opportunity than the men to meet outside the home or the factory. Now they loved to come to the clubs; and many of them, too, went on from there to play an important part in the movement. Characteristic of the times is the history of the first "women's club" in St. Petersburg. It was the brain-child of a group of intellectual women and was intended to give the working women a place of their own, where they could discuss their problems unhampered by the presence of men. But the idea of a separate club for women did not go down well with either men or women. It was considered utterly unfair: "Why should women exclude men from their clubs, when they have been enjoying equal rights in the other clubs? We have fought together for equality—now they talk of special rights for women, double rights!"—"If you want equal rights with us, give us equal rights in your women's club!" The indignation was so strong and the opposition so energetic that within a month men were allowed into the "women's club" and soon outnumbered the women—both as members and on the committee—until the club was discovered by the police and closed down. I had no part in the original creation of this club, but in due course I organized several debates there, which were attended by women workers from various factories. I wanted to find out the characteristic traits of life and work of the St. Petersburg working woman and I succeeded in learning a great deal during our informal talks. I assembled much of this material in a booklet, "The Russian Working Woman," which was later published by the party.

Source 5 from Alix Holt, editor and translator, Selected Writings of Alexandra Kollontai *(London: Allison and Busby, 1977), pp. 42–48.*

5. From Alexandra Kollontai, *Towards a History of the Working Women's Movement in Russia,* 1920

The revolutionary year of 1905 had a profound effect on the working masses. For the first time the Russian worker sensed his strength and understood that the well-being of the nation rested on his shoulders. In the revolutionary years of 1905 and 1906 the woman worker also became aware of the world around her. She was everywhere. If we wanted to give a record of how women participated in that movement, to list the instances of their active protest and struggle, to give full justice to the self-sacrifice of the proletarian women and their loyalty to the ideals of socialism, we would have to describe the events of the revolution scene by scene. . . .

During the October days, exhausted by their working conditions and their harsh hungry existence, women would leave their machines and bravely deprive their children of the last crust of bread in the name of the common cause. The working woman would call on her male comrades to stop work. Her words were simple, compelling and straight from the heart. She kept up morale and imparted a renewed vigour to the demoralised. The working woman fought on tirelessly and selflessly; the more involved she became in action, the quicker the process of her mental awakening. The working woman gradually came to understand the world she was living in and the injustice of the capitalist system, she began to feel more bitter at all the suffering and all the difficulties women experienced. The voices of the working class began to ring out more clearly and forcefully for the recognition not only of general class demands but of the specific needs and demands of working women. In March 1905 the exclusion of women from the elections of workers' delegates to the Shidlovskii commission[9] aroused deep dissatisfaction; the hardships the men and women had been through together had brought them closer to each other, and it seemed particularly unjust to emphasize woman's

9. **Shidlovskii commission:** a commission, with elected workers' representatives, which the government instituted during the first weeks of the 1905 revolution to deal with the demands of the movement.

[294]

inferior status at a time when she had shown herself an able fighter and a worthy citizen. When the woman chosen by the Sampsonevskaya factory as one of their seven delegates was ruled by the Shidlovskii commission to be ineligible for such office, indignant women workers from several different factories got together to present the commission with the following protest:

> The working women deputies are not being allowed to take part in the commission of which you are chairman. This decision is unjust. At the factories and places of manufacture in St. Petersburg there are more women workers than men. In the textile industry the number of women workers increases every year. The men transfer to factories where the wages are higher. The workload of women workers is heavier. The employers take advantage of our helplessness and lack of rights; we get worse treatment than our comrades and we get less pay. When the commission was announced our hearts beat with hope: at last the time has come, we thought, when the women workers of St. Petersburg can speak out to all Russia, and make known in the name of their sister workers the oppression, insults and humiliations we suffer, about which the male workers know nothing. Then, when we had already chosen our representatives, we were told that only men could be deputies. But we hope that this decision is not final. The government ukase,[10] at any rate, does not distinguish between women workers and the working class as a whole.

Deprived of representation, women workers were shut off from political life at the moment when through the first state Duma the population had its first opportunity to direct the affairs of the country. This seemed a glaringly unjust move against the women who had borne the brunt of the struggle for freedom. Working women frequently attended the meetings held in connection with the elections to the first and second Dumas, noisily expressing their dissatisfaction with a law that prevented their voting over such an important matter as the selection of delegates to the Russian parliament. There were instances in Moscow, for example, where working women broke up meetings with their demonstrations of protest.

The majority of the forty thousand persons who signed the petitions sent to the first and second Dumas demanding that the franchise be extended to women were working women. . . . Women's meetings were especially numerous during 1905 and 1906. Working women attended them willingly; they listened attentively to the bourgeois feminists but did not respond with much enthusiasm, since the speakers gave no suggestion as to how the urgent problems of those enslaved by capital might be solved. The women of the working class suffered from the harsh conditions at work, from hunger and insecurity. Their most urgent demands were: a shorter working day, higher wages, more human treatment from the factory authorities, less police supervision and more scope for "independent action." Such needs were foreign

---

10. **ukase:** a decree issued by the tsar.

to the bourgeois feminists, who came to the working women with their narrow concerns and exclusively "women's demands."

The political awakening of women was not limited to the urban poor alone. For the first time the Russian peasant woman began to think in a stubborn and resolute way about herself. During the closing months of 1904 and all through 1905 there were continual "women's riots" in the countryside. The Japanese war gave impetus to this movement. The peasant woman, as wife and mother, felt all the horror and hardship, all the social and economic consequences of this ill-fated war. Though her shoulders were already weighed down by a double workload and a double anxiety, she had to answer the call for more food supplies. She, who had always been incapable of standing alone and afraid of everything outside her immediate family circle, was suddenly forced to come face to face with the hostile world of which she had been ignorant. She was made to feel all the humiliation of her inferior status; she experienced all the bitterness of undeserved insults. For the first time the peasant women left their homes and their passivity and ignorance behind, and hurried to the towns to tread the corridors of government institutions in the hope of news of a husband, a son or a father, to make a fuss about allowances or to fight for various other rights. The women saw clearly and with their own eyes the ugliness of reality: they had no rights, and the existing social system was based on falsehood and injustice. They returned to their villages in a sober and hardened mood, their hearts full of bitterness, hatred and anger. In the south, during the summer of 1905, there was a series of "peasant women's riots." With an anger and boldness not usually expected from women the peasant women threatened the troops and the police and frequently gave the requisitioners a beating. Armed with rakes, forks and brooms, the peasant women drove the soldiers out of the villages. This was how they protested against the war. They were, of course, arrested, taken to court and harshly sentenced, but the unrest did not abate. These disturbances were in defence of general peasant interests and of specific women's interests—the two were so closely intertwined that it is impossible to separate them or to see the unrest as part of the "feminist" movement.

Besides the political protests there were others motivated by economic necessity. It was a time of general peasant unrest and strike activity over agricultural matters. The peasant women often took part, urging on their men or sometimes initiating activity. On occasion, when the men were reluctant to make a move, the women would go alone to the landlord's estate with their demands. And armed with what they could lay their hands on, they went out ahead of the village men to face the expeditionary forces. The peasant women, downtrodden by centuries of oppression, found themselves unexpectedly active and indispensable participants in the political drama. Over the period of the revolution they fought, in close unity with their men, in defence of the common peasant interests, and with amazing tact they brought up their own women's needs only when this did not threaten to harm the peasant cause as a whole.

This did not mean that the peasant women remained indifferent to or ignored their own needs as women. On the contrary, the mass entry of peasant women into the general political arena and their participation in the general struggle strengthened and developed their awareness of their position. In 1905 peasant women from Voronezh province sent two delegates to a peasant conference to demand "political rights" and "freedom" for men as well as women. Then there is the historic letter sent by peasant women from the Voronezh and Tver' provinces to the first Duma. And the telegram from Nogatkino to the deputy Alad'in:

> In this great moment of struggle for rights we, the peasant women of the village of Nogatkino, greet those elected representatives who express their distrust of the government by demanding that the ministry resign. We hope that the representatives will support the people, give them land and freedom, open the doors of the prisons to liberate the fighters for the people's freedom and the people's happiness. We hope that the representatives obtain civil and political rights for themselves and for us Russian women, who are unfairly treated and without rights even within our families. Remember that a slave cannot be the mother of a free citizen. (Authorised by the seventy-five women of Nogatkino.)

The peasant women of the Caucasus were particularly militant in the fight for their rights. In Kutaisi province they brought forward resolutions at peasant meetings demanding that they be given equal political rights with men. There were women among the deputies to a meeting held in Tiflis province, where representatives from both the urban and the rural areas gathered to discuss the question of introducing the *zemstvo* system into the Caucasus, and these women were insistent on the need for women's rights.

Alongside the demands for political equality, peasant women everywhere were naturally vocal in defence of their economic interests; the question of the allocation of land was as much a cause of concern for the peasant women as for their men. In some areas the peasant women warmly supported the idea of confiscating privately-owned land, but lost their enthusiasm when it seemed that women might not benefit directly from the redistribution. "If they take the land from the landowners and give it only to the men, that will mean absolute enslavement for us women," was their reaction. "At the moment we at least earn our own kopeks, but if they divide up the land like that we would be simply working for the men instead of the landowner." However, the fears of the peasant women were completely unfounded, because out of purely economic considerations the peasants were forced to demand land for the "female souls" too. The agrarian interests of the peasant men and peasant women are so closely entwined that in struggling for the abolition of the existing oppressive land relations the peasants were fighting

[297]

for the economic interests of their women. And at the same time the peasant women, while fighting for the economic and political interests of the peasantry as a whole, learned to fight for the special needs and demands of women. This was also true of the working women who fought unflaggingly in the general liberation movement, and who did even more than their country sisters to prepare public opinion to accept the principle of the equality of women. The realisation of civil equality for women in Soviet Russia was made possible by the spontaneous struggle of the masses of working and peasant women that came with the first Russian revolution in 1905.

Source 6 from Gail Warshofsky Lapidus, Women in Soviet Society: Equality, Development and Social Change *(Berkeley: University of California Press, 1978), p. 33.*

6. Petition to the Duma, 1905

We, peasant women of Tver gubernia, address ourselves to the honourable members of the State Duma elected from our gubernia. We are dissatisfied with our status. Our husbands and lads are glad to go out with us, but as far as the talk that is going on just now about the land and new laws is concerned, they simply will not talk sense to us. There was a time when, although our men might beat us now and then, we nevertheless decided our affairs together. Now they tell us: "You are not fit company for us. We shall go to the State Duma and take part in the government, perhaps not ourselves, but we will elect members. If the law had made us equal with you, then we would have asked your opinion." So now it happens that women and girls are pushed aside as people of no consequence, and are unable to decide anything about their own lives. This law is wrong; it leads to discord between women and men, and even enmity. . . . We lived in misery together, but when it got so far that everyone may live according to the law, we found we are not needed. . . . And they, the men, do not understand our women's needs. We are able to discuss things no worse than they. We have a common interest in all our affairs, so allow the women to take a hand in deciding them.

Source 7 from Linda Harriet Edmondson, Feminism in Russia, 1900–1917 *(London: Heinemann, 1984), p. 166.*

7. Petition to the Provisional Government, 1917

We have come here to remind you that women were your faithful comrades in the gigantic struggle for the freedom of the Russian people; that they also have been filling up the prisons, and boldly marched to the galleys. The best of us looked into the eyes of death without fear. Here at my side stands V. N. Figner,[11] who has been struggling all her life for what has now been obtained.

We declare that the Constituent Assembly[12] in which only one half of the population will be represented can in no wise be regarded as expressing the will of the whole people, but only half of it.

We want no more promises of good will. We have had enough of them! We demand an official and clear answer—that the women will have votes in the Constituent Assembly.

Sources 8 and 9 from Alix Holt, editor and translator, Selected Writings of Alexandra Kollontai *(London: Allison and Busby, 1977), pp. 123–124; pp. 132–139.*

8. Alexandra Kollontai, "In the Front Line of Fire," *Pravda*, May 7, 1917

"If we close down, you'll suffer—you'll be walking the streets without work." That's how the owners of the laundries try to frighten their women workers. This is the usual method used by the employers to scare their hired slaves. But the laundresses have no need to fear such threats. Just because the owners shut down, seeking more profitable investment for their capital, this does not mean that the demand for laundries disappears. Laundry workers are still needed and that means there is a way out of the situation, particularly now that the "New Russia" is being built.

The town itself must shoulder the responsibility of organising municipal laundries in all areas, and of organising them in such a way that the work is made easier by machines and technology, the working day does not exceed eight hours, wages are established by agreement between the municipality and the laundresses' union, a special cloakroom is provided where the working women can change into dry clothes after work, and much else besides is done to lighten the hard labour of the laundry workers.

During the elections to the regional and central town dumas the laundresses and all class-conscious, organised workers must express their support for these demands. This would be a clear and practical reply to the threat of

11. **V. N. Figner:** Vera Figner was one of the members of the People's Will, the group that assassinated the czar in 1881. She was arrested in 1883 and spent the next twenty years in prison.

12. **Constituent Assembly:** the provisional Government promised that it would soon call for elections to a Constituent Assembly, which would write a constitution for Russia.

redundancy and unemployment with which the employers attempt to intimidate the women on strike. It would then be the employers and [not] the laundresses who would be forced to swallow their pride and make concessions.

At the present moment the strike continues, but the employers are using all means at their disposal to break the firm stand of the three thousand women workers organised in the union. The employers are acting in the most outrageous and insolent manner. They are trying to set up their own employers' union of strike-breakers, and when the organised women come to call out these women, who through their lack of understanding of their class interests are jeopardising the common cause, they are not only met with threats and foul language; there was one instance where a woman agitator had boiling water thrown at her, and in one enterprise the proprietress tried to use a revolver.

The employers do not let slip any opportunity to use violence and slander. The working women have only one method of self-defence—*organisation and unity*. By fighting for better working conditions in the laundries, for an eight-hour day and for a minimum wage of four rubles a day, the women are fighting not only for themselves but for all working people. The men and women working in other sections of the economy must understand this. The victory of the laundresses will be a fresh victory for the whole proletariat. But in order to guarantee victory a flow of aid is necessary; money is needed. We cannot, we must not deny our material and moral support to those who are fighting for the workers' cause and are bearing the hardships of strike-action.

Every gathering or meeting of working men and women should express its solidarity with the firm struggle waged by the laundry women and should make a collection for these women strikers. The Soviet of Workers' and Solders' Deputies[13] should declare their solidarity with the working women, for the women are fighting to force the employers to accede to demands passed by the Soviet. The refusal of the employers to fulfil these demands is thus a *direct challenge to the Soviet*. Comrades, let us hasten to the aid of those who now stand in the trenches, defending the workers' cause; let us support those who are now in the "line of fire," facing the attacks of the capitalist employers.

13. **Soviet of Workers and Soldiers:** the council formed in Petrograd to demand rights for workers.

9. Alexandra Kollontai, from the Pamphlet "Working Woman and Mother," 1914

Children are dying. The children of working men and women die like flies. One million graves. One million sorrowing mothers. But whose children die? When death goes harvesting spring flowers, whose children fall to the scythe? As one would imagine, death gathers the poorest harvest amongst the wealthy families where the children live in warmth and comfort and are suckled on the milk of their mother or wet-nurse. In the families of royalty, only six or seven of every hundred new-born children die. In the workers' families, from thirty to forty-five die. . . . Death makes a firm place for itself in the homes of working-class families because such families are poor, their homes are overcrowded and damp, and the sunlight does not reach the basement; because where there are too many people, it is usually dirty; and because the working-class mother does not have the opportunity to care for her children properly. Science has established that artificial feeding is the worst enemy of the child: five times more children fed on cow's milk and fifteen times more children fed with other foods die than those who are breast-fed. But how is the woman who works outside the home, at the factory or in a workshop to breast-feed her child? She is lucky if the money stretches to buying cow's milk; that does not happen all the time. And what sort of milk do the tradesmen sell to working mothers anyway? Chalk mixed with water. Consequently, 60% of the babies that die, die from diseases of the stomach. Many others die from what the doctors like to call "the inability to live": the mother worn out by her hard physical labour gives birth prematurely, or the child is poisoned by the factory fumes while still in the womb. How can the woman of the working class possibly fulfil her maternal obligations? . . .

Is there a solution to the problem?

If children are to be stillborn, born crippled or born to die like flies, is there any point in the working woman becoming pregnant? Are all the trials of childbirth worthwhile if the working woman has to abandon her children to the winds of chance when they are still so tiny? However much she wants to bring her child up properly, she does not have the time to look after it and care for it. Since this is the case, is it not better simply to avoid maternity?

Many working women are beginning to think twice about having children. They have not got the strength to bear the cross. Is there a solution to the problem? Do working women have to deprive themselves of the last joy that is left them in life? Life has hurt her, poverty gives her no peace, and the factory drains her strength; does this mean that the working woman must give up the right to the joys of having children? Give up without a fight? Without trying to win the right which nature has given every living creature and every dumb animal? Is there an alternative? Of course there is, but not every working woman is yet aware of it. . . .

How can the law help?

The first thing that can be done and the first thing that working men and women are doing in every country is to see that the law defends the working mother. Since poverty and insecurity are forcing women to take up work, and since the number of women out working is increasing every year, the very least that can be done is to make sure that hired labour does not become the "grave of maternity." The law must intervene to help women to combine work and maternity.

Men and women workers everywhere are demanding a complete ban on night work for women and young people, an eight-hour day for all workers, and a ban on the employment of children under sixteen years of age. They are demanding that young girls and boys over sixteen years of age be allowed to work only half the day. This is important, especially from the point of view of the future mother, since between the years of sixteen and eighteen the girl is growing and developing into a woman. If her strength is undermined during these years her chances of healthy motherhood are lost forever.

The law should state categorically that working conditions and the whole work situation must not threaten a woman's health; harmful methods of production should be replaced by safe methods or completely done away with; heavy work with weights or foot-propelled machines etc. should be mechanised; workrooms should be kept clean and there should be no extremes of temperature; toilets, washrooms and dining rooms should be provided, etc. These demands can be won—they have already been encountered in the model factories—but the factory-owners do not usually like to fork out the money. All adjustments and improvements are expensive, and human life is so cheap.

A law to the effect that women should sit wherever possible is very important. It is also vital that substantial and not merely nominal fines are levied against factory owners who infringe the law. The job of seeing that the law is carried out should be entrusted not only to the factory inspectors but also to representatives elected by the workers.

The workers' party in every country demands that there should be maternity insurance schemes that cover all women irrespective of the nature of their job, no matter whether a woman is a servant, a factory worker, a craftswoman or a poor peasant woman. Benefits must be provided before and after birth, for a period of sixteen weeks. A woman should continue receiving benefits if the doctor finds that she has not sufficiently recovered or that the child is not sufficiently strong. . . .

Responsibility for ensuring that the law is observed and that the woman in childbirth receives everything to which she is entitled must lie with delegates elected from among the working women. Pregnant and nursing mothers must have the legal right to receive free milk and, where necessary, clothes for the new baby at the expense of the town or village. The workers' party also demands that the town, *zemstvo* or insurance bureau build creches for young children at each factory. The money for this should be supplied by the factory owner, the town or the *zemstvo*. These creches must be organised so that each nursing mother can easily visit and feed her baby in the breaks from work that the law allows. The creche must be run not by philanthropic ladies but by the working mothers themselves.

These measures must not be stamped with the bitter label of "philanthropy." Every member of society—and that means every working woman and every citizen, male and female—has the right to demand that the state and community concern itself with the welfare of all. Why do people form a state, if not for this purpose? At the moment there is no government anywhere in the world that cares for its children. Working men and women in all countries are fighting for a society and government that will really become a big happy family, where all children will be equal and the family will care equally for all. Then maternity will be a different experience, and death will cease to gather such an abundant harvest among the new-born.

What must every working woman do?

How are all these demands to be won? What action must be taken? Every working-class woman, every woman who reads this pamphlet must throw off her indifference and begin to support the working-class movement, which is fighting for these demands and is shaping the old world into a better future where mothers will no longer weep bitter tears and where the cross of maternity will become a great joy and a great pride. We must say to ourselves, "There is strength in unity"; the more of us working women join the working-class movement, the greater will be our strength and the quicker we will get what we want. Our happiness and the life and future of our children are at stake.

QUESTIONS TO CONSIDER

As with any historical source, in evaluating the material in this chapter you must consider why a specific piece was written. Sources 1 through 4 are memoirs, written after the fact by authors describing their personal experiences. Recall your study in Chapter 1 of the memorist St.-Simon. Why might a person choose to write memoirs? How might the fact that the author was looking back at the events alter his or her perspective? Eva Broido wrote her memoirs after the Bolshevik Revolution, when she was in exile in England. How might this have affected what she wrote? Alexandra Kollontai's description of women's actions in the 1905 revolution (Source 5) was written in the early 1920s, also after the fact and after the Bolshevik Revolution, though she was a prominent member of the party leadership rather than an exile when it was published. How might these circumstances have affected the way her history was written?

Sources 6 and 7 simply quote petitions brought by women, but the last two pieces by Kollontai were again written with very specific purposes in mind. What does the author hope these writings will do? Alexandra Kollontai was the only prominent woman among the Bolshevik leadership other than Lenin's wife, Nadezhda Krupskaya, and she was largely responsible for persuading the party to address women's issues. How might Kollontai's unique position have affected what or the way she wrote? Would you expect the new Soviet government to accept the changes she proposes?

The aims of the women revolutionaries were not static but changed over time as the political situation changed. Do you see any changes in aims or tactics within Sources 1 through 4? How would you compare the aims of the authors of Sources 1 through 4 with those of Kollontai?

Though class background alone is not enough to explain an author's ideas, her family background, level of education and occupation certainly shape her ideas and interpretation of events to some degree. Look again at the short description of each author. How might her family background have affected her ideas and actions?

Why do you think so many women revolutionaries and advocates of workers' rights came from the middle rather than working classes?

Our primary task in this chapter is to assess the role of gender rather than class or education in shaping women's lives. Looking at your list and considering what you have read, what aims did women revolutionaries share with their male comrades? What objectives did some of them have that might have differed from those of the men in their movements? What special problems did women revolutionaries face and how might these have affected their ideas?

You are now ready not only to answer the questions posed in this chapter but also to rewrite the narrative of the Russian revolutionary movements presented in your text. Are there any names or groups or issues that should be added? How might the language of the text be changed to incorporate what you have learned here? Think about other sections of the text—for example, descriptions of the socialist movements of Western Europe. Would you expect that similar revisions might be necessary?

EPILOGUE

The women involved in the revolutionary movements of the 1870s—Elizaveta Kovalskaia, Olga Liubatovich, Praskovia Ivanovskaia, and others—were all arrested around the time of the tsar's assassination and spent long years in prison or in exile in Siberia. The groups to which they belonged, such as the People's Will, fell apart, and later revolutionary movements in Russia generally did not involve so large a proportion of women. Though their actions did not accomplish their aims, women revolutionaries were highly praised by their male comrades and survived Siberian exile more successfully than male revolutionaries because they took better care of each other. Many of them lived to see the revolutions of 1917, returning from Siberia once the tsarist government had been abolished. Many women revolutionaries who had been in voluntary exile abroad also returned to Russia in 1917, just as Lenin did.

The 1905 revolution did bring about some political changes, but none that proved especially beneficial to women. In fact, women's political status declined compared to that of men: before the 1905 revolution only a small group—the tsar and his advisors—held any real political power, whereas after the revolution some groups of men did. Gender became an important determinant in dividing those with a political voice from those without one, in the same way that it had after the American and French revolutions.

Women received the right to vote after the February Revolution of 1917, largely because of petitions like the one you read here, and they supported some of the moves of the new Provisional Government. Other policies of the new government, such as continuing the war effort and not carrying out land reforms, were opposed by large numbers of women and men, who lent their support to the Bolsheviks in their efforts to abolish the Provisional Government.

When the Bolsheviks took over after the October Revolution, they made sweeping changes in women's legal and economic status. Marriage became a civil ceremony; women workers were to receive equal pay for equal work, maternity leave, and breaks during the workday to nurse their infants. In 1918 a new Family Code was passed that tried to equalize relations between spouses. Wives could keep their own earnings and their own names as well as retain greater control over their children; divorce by either spouse was made much easier. Arguing that women workers could never achieve equality so long as they had the extra burden of housework and child care, Alexandra Kollontai and a few others pushed for the opening of communal kitchens, laundries, nurseries, and daycare centers.

Some of the Bolshevik leadership (all of whom were male) accepted Kollontai's ideas in principle, but their primary concern was fighting the civil war, modernizing the economy, and establishing a socialist system. Money and resources were scarce, so daycare centers and similar programs never received much funding; there was considerable resistance or indifference to such programs anyway. The dislocation caused by the war meant many women and children were homeless, and their wages never rose enough to allow women to provide for themselves easily. Simplified divorce led many men to abandon their wives and children, and a large number of women turned to prostitution to support themselves. In 1926 the Family Code was revised, making men again financially responsible for their children and declaring that any couple living together was to be considered legally married. In the short run, this alteration in the law served to benefit women because it eased the worst problems; in the long run, however, it harmed the women's movement by making the support of women and children an individual, rather than a collective, matter. Because of war deaths, women greatly outnumbered men. The many women who consequently never married needed to support themselves, a fact often overlooked by Soviet leadership, who chose to view the new Family Code as the solution to all women's problems. Women's rights lost their most powerful proponent when Lenin removed Kollontai from her position as head of the women's bureau. She was later appointed ambassador to Norway, which further lessened her influence.

Passing laws, in fact, proved easier than implementing them and changing attitudes. The equality between men and women envisioned by Kollontai was never achieved, and the Stalinist period brought further restrictions. Interested in women as workers and mothers of future workers, Soviet leadership worried about the falling birth rate; it consequently restricted divorce, outlawed abortion (the only form of birth control available to most women), and championed motherhood as of supreme importance to the state. These changes were not accompanied by adequate practical assistance for working mothers, who continued to do double duty in the factory and at home.

As a consequence, a smaller percentage of women continued in school or received promotions. In addition, the Stalinist emphasis on heavy industry meant crowded housing, few consumer goods, and a hard life for most people, especially working women, who carried the burden of household tasks and shopping.

Since Stalin's death social restrictions have eased somewhat in Russia. Divorce has been made easier, and abortion was legalized again in 1955. Women are guaranteed paid maternity leave and, in theory, the opportunity to resume their previous jobs (in this the Soviet Union is ahead of the United States). A large share of the professional class consists of women. Soviet women are still not politically or economically equal to men, however. Very few women attain the upper levels of the political hierarchy (about the same percentage as in the United States), and women still do almost all domestic work. Shortages of consumer goods and inadequate day care are persistent problems. Some younger women are demanding improvements at a faster pace, and protests against the government generally include a significant number of women. Thus, at least a portion of contemporary Soviet women are following in the long tradition of protest and action begun by their great-grandmothers over one hundred years ago.

CHAPTER TWELVE

SELLING A

TOTALITARIAN SYSTEM

Hitler's dictatorship differed in one fundamental point from all its predecessors in history. His was the first dictatorship in the present period of modern technical development, a dictatorship which made complete use of all technical means for the domination of its own country.

Through technical devices like the radio and the loud-speaker, eighty million people were deprived of independent thought. It was thereby possible to subject them to the will of one man. . . .

Earlier dictators needed highly qualified assistants, even at the lowest level, men who could think and act independently. The totalitarian system in the period of modern technical development can dispense with them; the means of communication alone make it possible to mechanize the lower leadership. As a result of this there arises the new type of the uncritical recipient of orders. . . . Another result was the far-reaching supervision of the citizens of the State and the maintenance of a high degree of secrecy for criminal acts.

The nightmare of many a man that one day nations could be dominated by technical means was all but realized in Hitler's totalitarian system.[1]

This was how Albert Speer, once one of Hitler's most trusted subordinates, sought to answer the question that every student of the Nazi phenomenon must ultimately ask: "How could it have happened?"[2] Because your textbook examines the roots and development of Hitler's doctrines, we

1. Final statement by Albert Speer to the International Military Tribunal for major war criminals at Nuremberg, 1946. Quoted in Alan Bullock, *Hitler: A Study in Tyranny*, rev. ed. (New York: Harper & Row, 1964), p. 380. An architect by training, Speer (1905–1981) first attracted Hitler's attention because of his expertise in that field and talent for orchestrating party rallies. He testified at Nuremberg, "If Hitler had had any friends, I would certainly have been one of his close friends." (*Inside the Third Reich: Memoirs by Albert Speer*, translated by Richard and Clara Winston [New York: Macmillan, 1970], p. 609). Hitler promoted Speer to Minister of Armaments during World War Two, and in that capacity, Speer's efforts maintained German war production despite Allied bombing. As it became clear, however, that the war was lost and that Hitler was determined to fight on regardless of the cost to Germany, Speer made an attempt to assassinate the dictator.

2. See, for example, Richard F. Hamilton, *Who Voted for Hitler?* (Princeton, N.J.: Princeton University Press, 1982), p. 3.

will not focus in this chapter on the horrific ideology of the Nazi movement. Rather, we will examine the question that Speer addressed, for in the political history of the West, the Nazi party was the first totalitarian movement to make full use of modern media to gain and maintain power.

In their use of modern media and campaign techniques to achieve power, Hitler and his followers built on a number of developments in Western politics, technology, and intellectual life. As we observed in Chapter 8, the nature of politics in the West had begun to change in the late nineteenth century. The right to vote in the more advanced European countries expanded to include all men and, after World War One, women as well. The increased electorate demanded new political techniques. No longer could gentlemen politicians gain power by winning the support of a small, male, socially privileged electorate. A mass audience had to be addressed. Although many politicians at first refused to degrade themselves by appealing for support to such an audience, we can see emerging in late-nineteenth-century campaigns the modern political objective—and the requirement—of swaying large numbers of voters.

In 1879 and 1880, the British statesman William E. Gladstone (1809–1898) won election to Parliament from Midlothian County, Scotland following a campaign that became the model for modern ones, especially after Gladstone built his victory into his second term as prime minister. In Midlothian Gladstone deliv-

ered numerous public speeches. He presented many of these from the platform of his campaign train at a variety of locations, the first "whistle-stop campaign." Gladstone's campaign style found imitators in other democracies, although they did not always achieve his success. In the U.S. presidential campaign of 1896, the Democratic candidate, William Jennings Bryan (1860–1925), traveled about 18,000 miles and gave more than 600 speeches in an unsuccessful campaign against the Republican candidate, William McKinley (1843–1901). McKinley, who epitomized the old-style campaigner, simply received visitors from the press and public at the front porch of his Ohio home. Other candidates in many democracies would follow the example of Gladstone and Bryan.

Technological advances aided political leaders in their appeals for mass support. By the 1890s, developments like the linotype machine, which mechanized typesetting, greatly reduced the price of newspapers and other printed materials for an increasingly literate public. Mass-circulation daily newspapers had tremendous potential for shaping public opinion. Political leaders also used other technological developments in delivering their messages. By 1920 the motion picture, phonograph, radio, and microphone and public address system all represented new media through which to influence the public.

At the same time that new media became available to political leaders, a greater understanding of how to influence public opinion was emerging in the early-twentieth-century West. During World War One, many belligerent countries employed increasingly sophisticated propaganda techniques to sustain the morale of their own citizens or to erode the will to fight among enemy populations. The lessons learned on influencing public opinion were not forgotten, as we will see.[3]

Industrial mass production required mass markets, and in the United States modern advertising techniques developed to stimulate the consumption necessary to sustain production. Advertising had political applications as well. One advertising strategy is to generate interest in a new product by creating suspense about it. When the Nazis launched a new Berlin newspaper, *Der Angriff* (*The Attack*) in 1927, a poster campaign was launched to heighten interest in it. The first posters issued simply stated, "The Attack?" The next group of posters proclaimed, "The Attack takes place on July 4!" The last set of posters was informational, alerting readers that the paper would appear on Mondays, that its motto was "For the Suppressed against the Exploiters," and that "Every German man and every German woman will read 'The Attack' and subscribe to it!"[4]

Even science, particularly psychology, contributed to the understanding of human thought essential to those who sought to shape opinion. The French social psychologist Gustave Le Bon (1841–1931), for example, affected Hitler's political technique. Le Bon's ideas, although doubted today, were highly influential in the early twentieth century. A student of mass psychology, Le Bon claimed that the mind of the crowd was most suceptible to sentiment and emotion, not reason.[5]

The rapid pace of technological development and the equally swift emergence of techniques for molding public opinion meant that, by the 1920s, there existed an incompletely understood, underused, but nonetheless formidable arsenal for the politically ambitious to employ in attaining power. Forces prepared to exploit these technological and methodological developments emerged in the politically unstable environment of much of the West following World War One.

Arising from national defeat, frustration in World War One, or the postwar economic debacle of the Great Depression beginning in 1929, totalitarian movements emerged in many European countries. None of these movements proved more dangerous to traditional Western values than a German party that began insignificantly in 1919 as one of a multitude of right-wing, nationalist parties founded in response to the

3. Hitler in *Mein Kampf* (translated by Ralph Manheim [Boston: Houghton Mifflin, 1943], pp. 176–186) wrote of the lessons he had drawn from Allied propaganda during World War One.

4. Described in Ernest K. Bramsted, *Goebbels and National Socialist Propaganda, 1925–1945* (East Lansing, Mich.: Michigan State University Press, 1965), p. 30.

5. Le Bon's great work was *The Crowd: A Study of the Popular Mind*, originally published in 1897 and available in German.

German defeat in the Great War. The party came to be known as the National Socialist German Workers' Party (Nazi), and Adolf Hitler quickly emerged not only as its leader but as a master of the new style of politics, including political propaganda.

The successful propagandist must correcty identify the fears and hopes of the people he or she wishes to influence. In Germany after World War One, Nazi propaganda had a great number of fears and hopes to exploit. All Germans rejected the Treaty of Versailles that ended the war. Humiliated by the treaty's assignment of war guilt to Germany, they were angered in turn by the huge reparations their country was forced to pay the victorious allies. German nationalists especially rejected the unilateral disarmament the treaty sought to impose on Germany. All Germans hoped for some revision of the Treaty of Versailles.

Some Germans blamed the nation's defeat on internal enemies, not on battlefield disasters. These persons, mostly conservative, identified two chief groups on which to place responsibility for the internal dissent at the war's end that had brought the overthrow of Emperor William II (Kaiser Wilhelm II) and armistice. The first groups condemned for the defeat were the parties of the left, the socialists and communists, who had participated in the Revolution of 1918 that created the Weimar Republic. To many, the communists seemed the greatest threat because that party had attempted to seize power for a Marxist state by force in the Spartacist Revolt of 1919. The communist threat,

moreover, persisted after 1919. The party's voting bloc grew as the economic problems of the Great Depression intensified, and many feared that the communists might gain power through election.

The other group on whom some Germans sought to fix the blame of their defeat was the country's small Jewish minority. Such Germans drew on nineteenth-century nationalist prejudices to allege some Jewish involvement in Germany's defeat. Certain political leaders of the early German republic, the men whose government signed the Versailles Treaty, were Jews. One prominent Jewish official, Walter Rathenau (1867–1922), died at the hands of a nationalist fanatic.

The Great Depression also increased Germans' fears after 1929. The Depression hit Germany particularly hard, threatening economic ruin to many. Many parties and movements identified those fears and hopes of postwar Germans and sought to address them by rejecting the Treaty of Versailles, by portraying themselves as anticommunist or anti-Semitic, and by proposing solutions to the Depression. But, as we will see, it was the skill of Hitler and the Nazis in the new politics and propaganda that allowed them to exploit most effectively Germans' fears and hopes to gain power.

It was Hitler who transformed a party that essentially had been little more than a collection of malcontents in the back room of a Munich beer hall into a movement with a considerable following in the 1920s. It was Hitler who gave the party a visual identity by adopting its symbol, the swastika, and by creating its banners. It was also Hitler who exploited the alienation of many war veterans by drawing them into the S.A. (*Sturmabteilung*), the Storm Troopers or uniformed, paramilitary branch of the party, which was prepared to use violence and intimidation against communists and socialists. And it was Hitler who launched an abortive attempt in 1923 to seize power forcibly for his party.

Hitler's failed revolution resulted in his brief imprisonment, during which he wrote *Mein Kampf* (*My Struggle*), the political statement of his movement. On his release Hitler resolved to seek power within the political system—that is, to win power through the electoral system of the German republic. To his quest for power Hitler brought the Nazi party apparatus and symbols, his excellent oratorical ability, and, most dangerously, a keen understanding of the uses of political propaganda and modern media to mold public opinion. Aiding him in presenting his party to German voters was Joseph Goebbels (1897–1945), a man whose speaking abilities, understanding of propaganda and modern media, and political unscrupulousness rivaled Hitler's own.

In his quest for power after 1923, Hitler led the Nazis through a number of electoral campaigns. The first results of Nazi appeals to German voters disappointed many of Hitler's followers. Indeed, in elections to the Reichstag, Germany's parliament, the party's vote actually declined during the 1920s. In the elections of May 1924, it captured 6.5 percent of the vote; that total declined to 3.0 percent in December 1924 and 2.6 percent in May 1928. The party's electoral breakthrough of 1930, however, reversed this trend as the Nazis increased their share of the Reichstag vote to 18.3 percent. Certainly, in achieving their victory, the Nazis' extreme nationalist message capitalized on the Young Plan of 1929, which had failed to reduce the war reparation payments to the Allies so deeply resented by many Germans. The growing severity of the Great Depression after 1929 also encouraged many Germans to look to the strong leadership Hitler claimed to offer. As party membership and dues grew, and as Hitler secured some limited financial aid from a few wealthy opponents of the Young Plan such as Alfred Hugenberg,[6] for the first time the Nazis had sufficient funds to exploit the modern media thoroughly.

The Nazi share of the vote increased rapidly after 1930. The party especially demonstrated its media skills in 1932, when Hitler ran for president of Germany against the

6. **Alfred Hugenberg** (1865–1951): leader of the Nationalist Party and a bigoted conservative ultranationalist with tremendous wealth based in industry and great influence founded on his control of a number of newspapers and Germany's largest film and newsreel firm. His newsreels, shown regularly in German theaters, and his newspapers gave the Nazis considerable coverage. Like other conservatives, Hugenberg made the mistake of classifying Hitler with other politicians. Hitler quickly excluded Hugenberg from the government once the Nazis had gained power.

incumbent, the octogenarian war hero Field Marshal Paul von Hindenburg. Although Hindenburg won the election with 53 percent of the vote to Hitler's 36.8 percent, the campaign built momentum for the Nazis and helped them to perfect their campaign style. In the Reichstag elections held in July 1932, the Nazis won 37.4 percent of the vote to become the largest single party in parliament, a distinction they retained despite a diminished Nazi 33.1 percent of the vote in Reichstag elections in November 1932. On the basis of these victories, which gave the Nazis control of the largest single bloc of seats in the Reichstag, conservative associates of President von Hindenburg finally convinced him to name Hitler chancellor or prime minister on January 30, 1933. The Nazis had gained control of the government, and German democracy was their first victim: by the end of the year the country was a one-party, totalitarian state.

To achieve power, the Nazis had persuaded substantial numbers of German voters to support their candidates. Certainly in the aftermath of Germany's defeat in 1918, the party's extreme nationalism attracted support, as did its anti-Semitism, which blamed the country's economic and political woes on its tiny Jewish minority. But other German parties in the 1920s offered similar ideologies. Your objective in this chapter is to determine how Nazi use of modern media and techniques, such as propaganda for molding public opinion, allowed Hitler's party to draw the German voter's attention. As you assess the evidence that follows, you should ask yourself what kind of image the Nazis projected. Why did it appeal to German voters? How did the Nazis use media to aid their rise to power? As a result of your analysis, you should be able to answer in some form that most disturbing question, "How could it have happened?"

SOURCES AND METHOD

This chapter presents a variety of evidence: theoretical writings on Nazi political strategy, visual propaganda used by Nazis to publicize their cause, and observations on the public reception of Hitler's media campaign. Through individual and comparative study of these sources, you should be able to determine the nature of the attraction of the Nazis for German voters.

The evidence opens with two selections by Hitler on the means for gaining power. Sources 1 and 2 are taken from Hitler's *Mein Kampf*, which he wrote during his imprisonment in 1923–1924. In this work, often ignored in his early days, Hitler stated much of his future program, including his rabidly anti-Jewish and anti-Marxist policies and his plans to expand Germany eastward. In the evidence presented in this chapter, you will read Hitler's ideas on the use of propaganda and other tactics for coming to power. How were the ideas for seizing power that he expressed in 1924 to be realized within a decade? How would you assess his understanding of human psychology?

When you finish the Hitler materials, you will find an assortment of evidence selected to further your analysis of how the Nazis sought to win support for their party. You will be examining, in effect, a thoroughly modern public relations effort, complete with slogans. In Source 3, assess the nature of the Nazi propaganda effort as defined by its director, Joseph Goebbels. Why do you think Goebbels so closely controlled the party's propaganda?

Consider next the S.A., remembering, of course, that orders like that in Source 4 are not always rigidly obeyed by subordinates in any organization. Examine the pictorial evidence on the S.A. in Sources 5 and 6. The banners express Nazi slogans; the Regensburg S.A. banner proclaims, "Everything for the Fatherland." Nazi meetings always opened with solemn processions of such banners. What impression did the marching men seek to convey to their audience on the streets of Spandau?

Next read Source 7, the report of the brawl in the Pharus Hall in 1927. You should understand that this brawl was no accident; Goebbels deliberately scheduled the meeting to take place in a hall used by the Nazis' enemies, the communist and socialist political and labor groups. The hall, moreover, was in the heart of a left-wing, working-class district of Berlin. What could Goebbels have hoped to gain from the fight that was bound to ensue from his provocative action in selecting such a meeting site?

The next evidence consists of posters produced by the Nazis. The poster, a traditional political medium, was used extensively by the Nazis. They relied especially on posters in their early days, before they secured the funds necessary to exploit more novel media. The poster in Source 8 was part of one of the Nazis' earliest propaganda campaigns in 1924. Analyze it to ascertain what sentiments the Nazis appealed to in post–World War One Germany and to which classes they looked for support. What group did the "String-puller" represent (notice his watch chain)? What message did his identity convey to Germans?

The second poster, Source 9, conveys much about Germany in the 1920s. Why might the Nazis address females? Of what problems did this poster, issued in the midst of the Depression, remind Germans? What did it promise them? The third poster, Source 10, was the work of a skilled propaganda artist, "Mjolnir" ("Hammer"), who drew cartoons extensively for the Berlin newspaper *Der Angriff*, edited by Goebbels. Analyze the artist's message by examining the faces of the Storm Troopers. What sentiment do you find there? What sort of message does this poster convey about the party and its solutions for Germany?

Another Nazi political device was the public mass meeting designed to convey the impression of vast support for the party. It was a technique Hitler learned early while observing Social Democratic demonstrations as a youth in Vienna. He wrote in *Mein Kampf*:

> With what changed feeling I now gazed at the endless columns of a mass demonstration of Viennese workers that took place one day as they marched past four abreast! For nearly two hours I stood there watching with bated breath the gigantic human dragon slowly winding by.

As their resources increased, the Nazis perfected the mass meeting. Source 11 shows one such rally in Berlin's Sports Palace, a favored site because it seated 12,000 persons. Events like this were always carefully staged: the aisles are lined with the party faithful, ready for the entry of the speakers, accompanied by a uniformed S.A. guard unit and party banners. Why would such an elaborate spectacle have been important to the party cause?

The Nazis also employed music as propaganda to win support. The person whose name the song bears in Source 12, Horst Wessel, was a young Nazi who wrote the words to the song as a poem. The words eventually were set to a traditional stirring tune, but Horst Wessel himself drifted away from the party in pursuit of a female prostitute. He took up residence with her and was fatally shot by her procurer, who coincidentally was a communist, in February 1930. In Goebbels's hands, Horst Wessel's misspent life was transformed into that of a hero martyred

in the Nazis' cause by their communist enemies. His song became Germany's second national anthem after *Deutschland über Alles (Germany Above All)* in the Nazi era. In reading the song's words, identify the problems it identifies. What benefits do the song claim the party offered Germans?

Also part of Nazi political propaganda was the creation of what Goebbels himself called the "Führer (Leader) Myth." This myth, which Goebbels regarded as one of his great propaganda accomplishments, attempted to convince Germans that a strong, courageous, and brilliant Hitler personified a Germany restored from its defeat. In its more extreme manifestations, the myth almost deified Hitler, appealing to many Germans accustomed to strong rulers during the monarchy and therefore unhappy with what they believed to be the weak government of the republic. Source 13 is drawn from an elementary school textbook published shortly after the Nazis gained power, but it describes Hitler's campaign for power. What qualities did the party's propaganda apparatus wish the young to believe Hitler possessed?

The Nazis did not come to power solely through conveying a positive image for their party and leader, however. They also used propaganda to exploit fears, employed violence to intimidate voters, and used new technologies to sway the thinking of their fellow Germans. Source 14 is a pamphlet, issued, you must remember, in the midst of the economic collapse of the early 1930s. Recall the events of Germany's past as you read it, and analyze its appeal.

The violence of the Hitler movement can best be viewed on the local level. The graph in Source 15 presents the rhythm of political life in the German town of Northeim. The number of political meetings, to which the Nazis contributed more than their share, increased sharply at election times. What else increased?

Source 16 presents the political beliefs of Dr. Joseph Goebbels, a fervent Nazi and a master of political propaganda. Convinced of his own historical importance, Goebbels kept a diary from his earliest days in politics to give future generations a record of his thought and activities. He was still making entries in 1945 as the war ended. When Russian armies closed in on Berlin, Goebbels committed suicide. His diary, like any diary, must be used with caution, because most writers tend to put their own behavior and motivations in the best light. Nonetheless, it does offer an important perspective on Goebbels's propaganda work. Assess his command of his job as you read the selection. What new technologies did he employ in winning popular support for the Nazis?

The evidence in this chapter concludes with two observations on the impact of Nazi efforts to win support among Germans. The first is a report by a German Protestant leader noting membership losses from the Protestant youth movement to the Nazis. The second is by the American correspondent, William L. Shirer (born 1904), who covered events in Germany from 1934 to 1941. A perceptive observer of the Hitler movement, Shirer was able to assess the kind of appeal it had been building in Germany during the years before he arrived. What appeal to Germans do these two very different persons note in the Nazi movement?

Now turn to the evidence. You should read it with the foregoing considerations in mind, seeking to answer the central questions of this chapter: What image did the Nazis convey to German voters? Why did they appeal to German voters? How did the Nazis use media to aid their rise to power?

THE EVIDENCE

FUNDAMENTAL POLITICAL STRATEGIES OF THE NAZI PARTY

Sources 1 and 2 from Adolf Hitler, Mein Kampf, *translated by Ralph Mannheim (Boston: Houghton Mifflin, 1943), pp. 178–184, 343, 582; pp. 42–44.*

1. Hitler on the Nature and Purpose of Propaganda

The goal of a political reform movement will never be reached by enlightenment work or by influencing ruling circles, but only by the achievement of political power. Every world-moving idea has not only the right, but also the duty, of securing, those means which make possible the execution of its ideas. Success is the one earthly judge concerning the right or wrong of such an effort, and under success we must not understand, as in the year 1918, the achievement of power in itself, but an exercise of that power that will benefit the nation. Thus, a coup d'état must not be regarded as successful if, as senseless state's attorneys in Germany think today, the revolutionaries have succeeded in possessing themselves of the state power, but only if, by the realization of the purposes and aims underlying such a revolutionary action, more benefit accrues to the nation than under the past régime. Something which cannot very well be claimed for the German revolution, as the gangster job of autumn, 1918, calls itself.[7] . . .

The victory of an idea will be possible the sooner, the more comprehensively propaganda has prepared people as a whole and the more exclusive, rigid, and firm the organization which carries out the fight in practice. . . .

To whom should propaganda be addressed? To the scientifically trained intelligentsia or to the less educated masses?

It must be addressed always and exclusively to the masses.

What the intelligentsia—or those who today unfortunately often go by that name—what they need is not propaganda but scientific instruction. The content of propaganda is not science any more than the object represented in a poster is art. The art of the poster lies in the designer's ability to attract the attention of the crowd by form and color. A poster advertising an art exhibit must direct the attention of the public to the art being exhibited; the

---

7. **the gangster job of Autumn 1918:** the revolution of October and November 1918 that overthrew Emperor William II and established the Weimar Republic. Hitler, like many of the German right, believed that revolution to have been the work of socialists, communists, and Jews who, by toppling the old government, had "stabbed in the back" the German army at the front in World War One and made defeat in that conflict inevitable.

better it succeeds in this, the greater is the art of the poster itself. The poster should give the masses an idea of the significance of the exhibition, it should not be a substitute for the art on display. Anyone who wants to concern himself with the art itself must do more than study the poster; and it will not be enough for him just to saunter through the exhibition. We may expect him to examine and immerse himself in the individual works, and thus little by little form a fair opinion.

A similar situation prevails with what we today call propaganda.

The function of propaganda does not lie in the scientific training of the individual, but in calling the masses' attention to certain facts, processes, necessities, etc., whose significance is thus for the first time placed within their field of vision.

The whole art consists in doing this so skillfully that everyone will be convinced that the fact is real, the process necessary, the necessity correct, etc. But since propaganda is not and cannot be the necessity in itself, since its function, like the poster, consists in attracting the attention of the crowd, and not in educating those who are already educated or who are striving after education and knowledge, its effect for the most part must be aimed at the emotions and only to a very limited degree at the so-called intellect.

All propaganda must be popular and its intellectual level must be adjusted to the most limited intelligence among those it is addressed to. Consequently, the greater the mass it is intended to reach, the lower its purely intellectual level will have to be. But if, as in propaganda for sticking out a war, the aim is to influence a whole people, we must avoid excessive intellectual demands on our public, and too much caution cannot be exerted in this direction.

The more modest its intellectual ballast, the more exclusively it takes into consideration the emotions of the masses, the more effective it will be. And this is the best proof of the soundness or unsoundness of a propaganda campaign, and not success in pleasing a few scholars or young aesthetes.

The art of propaganda lies in understanding the emotional ideas of the great masses and finding, through a psychologically correct form, the way to the attention and thence to the heart of the broad masses. The fact that our bright boys do not understand this merely shows how mentally lazy and conceited they are.

Once we understand how necessary it is for propaganda to be adjusted to the broad mass, the following rule results:

It is a mistake to make propaganda many-sided, like scientific instruction, for instance.

The receptivity of the great masses is very limited, their intelligence is small, but their power of forgetting is enormous. In consequence of these facts, all effective propaganda must be limited to a very few points and must harp on these in slogans until the last member of the public understands what you want him to understand by your slogan. As soon as you sacrifice this slogan and try to be many-sided, the effect will piddle away, for the crowd can neither digest nor retain the material offered. In this way the result is weakened and in the end entirely cancelled out.

Thus we see that propaganda must follow a simple line and correspondingly the basic tactics must be psychologically sound. . . .

But the most brilliant propagandist techniques will yield no success unless one fundamental principle is borne in mind constantly and with unflagging attention. It must confine itself to a few points and repeat them over and over. Here, as so often in this world, persistence is the first and most important requirement for success.

2. Hitler on Terror in Politics

Like the woman, whose psychic state is determined less by grounds of abstract reason than by an indefinable emotional longing for a force which will complement her nature, and who, consequently, would rather bow to a strong man than dominate a weakling, likewise the masses love a commander more than a petitioner and feel inwardly more satisfied by a doctrine, tolerating no other beside itself, than by the granting of liberalistic freedom with which, as a rule, they can do little, and are prone to feel that they have been abandoned. They are equally unaware of their shameless spiritual terrorization and the hideous abuse of their human freedom, for they absolutely fail to suspect the inner insanity of the whole doctrine. All they see is the ruthless force and brutality of its calculated manifestations, to which they always submit in the end. . . .

I achieved an equal understanding of the importance of physical terror toward the individual and the masses.

Here, too, the psychological effect can be calculated with precision.

Terror at the place of employment, in the factory, in the meeting hall, and on the occasion of mass demonstrations will always be successful unless opposed by equal terror.

NAZI TECHNIQUES FOR PUBLICIZING THEIR CAUSE

Sources 3 and 4 from Jeremy Noakes and Geoffrey Pridham, editors, Documents on Nazism, 1919–1945 *(New York: Viking, 1975), pp. 103–104; pp. 163–164.*

3. Joseph Goebbels, Directives for the Presidential Campaign of 1932

(1) Reich Propaganda Department to all *Gaue*[8] and all *Gau* Propaganda Departments.

8. **Gaue:** the administrative divisions of Germany set up by the Nazi party.

. . . A striking slogan:

> Those who want everything to stay as it is vote for Hindenburg. Those who
> want everything changed vote for Hitler. . . .

(2) Reich Propaganda Department to all *Gaue* and all *Gau* Propaganda
Departments.
. . . Hitler Poster. The Hitler poster depicts a fascinating Hitler head on a
completely black background. Subtitle: white on black—"Hitler." In accordance with the Führer's wish this poster is to be put up only during the final
days [of the campaign]. Since experience shows that during the final days
there is a variety of coloured posters, this poster with its completely black
background will contrast with all the others and will produce a tremendous
effect on the masses. . . .

(3) Reich Propaganda Department
Instructions for the National Socialist Press for the election of the Reich President

1. From Easter Tuesday 29 March until Sunday 10 April inclusive, all
National Socialist papers, both daily and weekly, must appear in an enlarged
edition with a tripled circulation. Two-thirds of this tripled circulation must
be made available, without charge, to the *Gau* leadership responsible for its
area of distribution for propaganda purposes. . . .

2. From Easter Tuesday 29 March until Sunday 3 April inclusive, a special
topic must be dealt with every day on the first page of all our papers in a
big spread. Tuesday 29 March: Hitler as a man. Wednesday 30 March: Hitler
as a fighter (gigantic achievements through his willpower, etc.). Friday 1
April: Hitler as a statesman—plenty of photos. . . .

3. On Sunday 3 April, at noon (end of an Easter truce), the great propaganda journey of the Führer through Germany will start, through which
about a million people are to be reached directly through our Führer's
speeches. . . . The press organization is planned so that four press centres
will be set up in Germany, which in turn will pass on immediately any
telephone calls to the other papers of their area, whose names have been
given them.

4. S.A. Order 111 of Adolf Hitler, 1926

1. The SA will appear in public only in closed formation. This is at the
same time one of the most powerful forms of propaganda. The sight of a
large number of men inwardly and outwardly uniform and disciplined,

whose total commitment to fighting is clearly visible or can be sensed, makes the deepest impression on every German and speaks a more convincing and inspiring language to his heart than speech, logic, or the written word is ever capable of doing.

Calm composure and natural behaviour underline the impression of strength—the strength of marching columns and the strength of the cause for which they are marching.

The inner strength of the cause makes the German conclude instinctively that it is right: "for only what is right, honest and good can release real strength." Where whole crowds purposefully risk life and limb and their livelihood for a cause (not in the upsurge of sudden mass suggestion), the cause must be great and true!

Here lies the task of the SA from the point of view of propaganda and recruiting. The SA leaders must gear the details and forms of their appearances to a common line.

2. This instinctive "proof of truth" is not underlined but disturbed and dissipated by the addition of logical arguments and propaganda. The following should be avoided: cheers and heckling, posters about day-to-day controversies, abuse, accompanying speeches, leaflets, festivals, public amusements.

3. It is inappropriate for the SA to work in one way one day and differently the next, according to circumstances. The SA must always and on principle refrain from all actual political propaganda and agitation. This should remain the task of the political leadership alone. However, each SA man is also a member of the Party and as such of course must cooperate as much as he can in the propaganda of the political leadership. But not the SA as such. Not the SA men on duty and in uniform.

The SA man is the holy freedom fighter. The member of the Party is the clever propagandist and skilled agitator. Political propaganda tries to enlighten the opponent, to argue with him, to understand his point of view, to enter into his thoughts, to agree with him to a certain extent. But when the SA arrives on the scene, this stops. It makes no concessions. It goes all out. It only recognizes the motto (metaphorically): Kill or be killed!

4. It is forbidden for an SA to appeal to the public (or its opponents) orally or in writing, either through proclamations, announcements, leaflets, press "corrections," letters, advertisements, invitations to festivals or meetings, or in any other way.

Public consecrations of the colours and sports competitions must take place within the framework of an event organized by a local branch, which alone issues the invitations or announcements for it.

Sources 5 and 6 from Bundesarchiv, Koblenz.

6. S.A. Propaganda Rally in Spandau, 1932

5. Banners of the Regensburg S.A.: "Everything for the Fatherland, 1923"

Source 7 from Jeremy Noakes and Geoffrey Pridham, editors, Documents on Nazism, 1919–1945 *(New York: Viking, 1975), pp. 83–84.*

7. Report of a Nazi Meeting Held in a Heavily Communist Quarter of Berlin, February 1927

On the 11th of this month the Party held a public mass meeting in the "Pharus [Beer] Halls" in Wedding, the real working-class quarter, with the subject: "The Collapse of the Bourgeois Class State." Comrade Dr Goebbels was the speaker. It was quite clear to us what that meant. It had to be visibly shown that National Socialism is determined to reach the workers. We succeeded once before in getting a foothold in Wedding. There were huge crowds at the meeting. More than 1,000 people filled the hall whose political composition was four-fifths SA to one-fifth KPD.[9] But the latter had gathered their main forces in the street. When the meeting was opened by Comrade Daluege, the SA leader, there were, as was expected, provocative shouts of "On a point of order!" After the KPD members had been told that *we*, not they, decided points of order, and that they would have the right to ask questions after the talk by Comrade Dr Goebbels, the first scuffling broke out. Peace seemed to be restored until there was renewed heckling. When the chairman announced that the hecklers would be sent out if the interruptions continued, the KPD worked themselves into a frenzy. Meanwhile, the SA had gradually surrounded the centre of the disturbance, and the Communists, sensing the danger, suddenly became aggressive. What followed all happened within three or four minutes. Within seconds both sides had picked up chairs, beer mugs, even tables, and a savage fight began. The Communists were gradually pushed under the gallery which we had taken care to occupy and soon chairs and glasses came hurtling down from there also. The fight was quickly decided: the KPD left with 85 wounded, more or less: that is to say, they could not get down the stairs as fast as they had calmly and "innocently" climbed them. On our side we counted 3 badly wounded and about 10–12 slightly. When the police appeared the fight was already over. Marxist terrorism had been bloodily suppressed.

9. **Kommunistische Partei Deutschlands:** the German Communist Party.

Source 8 from Ansclage: Ebenhausen: hangwieche/Brand Verlag.

8. Poster: "The String-Puller. White Collar and Manual Laborers: Vote for the National List," 1924

10. Poster: "National Socialism: The Organized Will of the People," 1932

9. Poster: "Women! Millions of Men Are Without Work. Millions of Children Are Without a Future. Save the German Family! Vote for Adolf Hitler!," 1932

Source 11 from Bundesarchiv, Koblenz.

11. A National Socialist Rally in the Berlin Sports Palace, September 1930

Source 12 from Liederbuch der Nationalsozialistischen Deutschen Arbeiterpartei *(Munich: Zentralverlag der NSDAP, 1938). Selection translated by Julius R. Ruff.*

12. "The Horst Wessel Song,"
ca 1930

Raise high the banner! Close the serried ranks!
S.A. marches on with calm, firm stride.
Comrades killed by the Red Front and the Reaction[10]
March in spirit in our ranks.

Clear the streets for the brown battalions![11]
Clear the streets for the Storm Troopers!
The swastika gives hope to millions.
The day of freedom and bread is breaking.

The roll call is heard for the last time!
We all stand ready for the struggle!
Soon Hitler's banner will fly over every street
And Germany's bondage will soon end.

10. **Red Front:** the *Rot Frontkämpfer Bund* or Red Fighters League, the communist opposition to the Storm Troopers. The more traditional right, the Nationalist Party that sought a restoration of a monarchy and is here called the **Reaction**, had an armed force, too, uniformed in green.

11. The S.A. uniform was brown.

[325]

Source 13 from George L. Mosse, editor, Nazi Culture: Intellectual, Cultural, and Social Life in the Third Reich (New York: Grosset and Dunlap, 1966), pp. 291–293. Selection translated by the editor.

13. Otto Dietrich, Description of Hitler's Campaign by Airplane, 1932

On April 8, 1932, a severe storm, beyond all imagining, raged over Germany. Hail rattled down from dark clouds. Flash floods devastated fields and gardens. Muddy foam washed over streets and railroad tracks, and the hurricane uprooted even the oldest and biggest trees.

We are driving to the Mannheim Airport. Today no one would dare expose an airplane to the fury of the elements. The German Lufthansa has suspended all air traffic.

In the teeming rain stands the solid mass of the most undaunted of our followers. They want to be present, they want to see for themselves when the Führer entrusts himself to an airplane in this raging storm.

Without a moment's hesitation the Führer orders that we take off at once. We have an itinerary to keep, for in western Germany hundreds of thousands are waiting.

It is only with the greatest difficulty that the ground crew and the SA troopers, with long poles in their strong fists, manage to hold on to the wings of the plane, so that the gale does not hurl it into the air and wreck it. The giant motors begin to turn over. Impatient with its fetters, the plane begins to buck and shake, eager for the takeoff on the open runway.

One more short rearing up and our wild steed sweeps across the greensward. A few perilous jumps, one last short touch with earth, and presto we are riding through the air straight into the witches' broth.

This is no longer flying, this is a whirling dance which today we remember only as a faraway dream. Now we jump across the aerial downdrafts, now we whip our way through tattered clouds, again a whirlpool threatens to drag us down, and then it seems that a giant catapult hurls us into steep heights.

And yet, what a feeling of security is in us in the face of this fury of the elements! The Führer's absolute serenity transmits itself to all of us. In every hour of danger he is ruled by his granite-like faith in his world-historical mission, the unshakable certainty that Providence will keep him from danger for the accomplishment of his great task.

Even here he remained the pre-eminent man, who masters danger because in his innermost being he has risen far above it. In this ruthless contest between man and machine the Führer attentively follows the heroic battle of our Master Pilot Bauer as he steers straight through the gale, or quickly jumps across a whole storm field, and then again narrowly avoids a threatening cloud wall, while the radio operator on board zealously catches the signals sent by the airfields.

Source 14 from Jeremy Noakes and Geoffrey Pridham, editors, Documents on Nazism, 1919–
1945 (New York: Viking, 1975), p. 106.

14. Nazi Pamphlet, ca 1932

Attention! Gravediggers at work!

Middle-class citizens! Retailers! Craftsmen! Tradesmen!

A new blow aimed at your ruin is being prepared and carried out in Hanover!

The present system enables the gigantic concern

WOOLWORTH (America)

supported by finance capital, to build a new vampire business in the centre of the city in the Georgstrasse to expose you to complete ruin. This is the wish and aim of the black-red[12] system as expressed in the following remarks of Marxist leaders.

The Marxist Engels declared in May 1890: "If capital destroys the small artisans and retailers it does a good thing. . . ."

That is the black-red system of today!

Put an end to this system and its abettors! Defend yourself, middle-class citizen! Join the mighty organization that alone is in a position to conquer your arch-enemies. Fight with us in the Section for Craftsmen and Retail Traders within the great freedom movement of Adolf Hitler!

Put an end to the system!

Mittelstand, vote for List 8![13]

12. Prussia was governed by a coalition of the Catholic Center Party and the Social Democrats. Because of its association with the church, the Center was labeled "Black"; the leftist Socialists were labeled "Red."

13. **Mittelstand:** middle class.

Source 15 adapted from William Sheridan Allen, The Nazi Seizure of Power: The Experience of a Single German Town, 1922–1945, *revised ed. (New York: Franklin Watts, 1984), p. 321.*

15. Political Violence in Northeim, Germany, 1930–1932

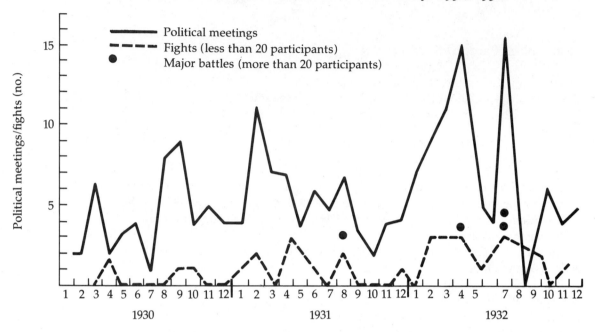

Source 16 from Joseph Goebbels, My Part in Germany's Fight, *translated by Kurt Fielder (New York: Howard Fertig, 1979), pp. 44, 47–48, 55, 66, 145–146, 214.*

16. Joseph Goebbels, *My Part in Germany's Fight*, 1934

February 29th, 1932.

Our propaganda is working at high pressure.

The clerical work is finished. Now the technical side of the fight begins. What enormous preparations are necessary to organize such a vast distribution!

Reported to the Leader (Hitler) at noon. I gave him details as to the measures we are taking. The election campaign is chiefly to be fought by means of placards and addresses. We have not much capital, but as the Party is working gratuitously a little money goes a long way.

Fifty thousand gramophone records have been made, which are so small they can be slipped into an ordinary envelope. The supporters of the Government will be astonished when they place these miniature records on the gramophone!

In Berlin everything is going well.

A film (of me) is being made and I speak a few words in it for about ten minutes. It is to be shown in all public gardens and squares of the larger cities. . . .

March 8th, 1932.

Dictate two articles and heaps of handbills. The placard war has reached its climax. Up till now we lead in the race.

Interview with the *Popolo d'Italia*. I describe our methods and means of propaganda. The representative of this influential Italian paper is positively dumbfounded. "The vastest and most up-to-date propaganda of Europe." . . .

March 18th, 1932.

A critical innovation: the Leader will conduct this next campaign by plane. By this means he will be able to speak three or four times a day at various places as opportunity serves, and address about one and a half millions of people in spite of the time being so short.

April 14th, 1932.

The Leader is planning a new plane campaign for the Prussian elections. He intends to start on Sunday. His perseverance is admirable, and it is amazing how he stands the continual strain.

At work again organizing his great 'plane trips. Now we have quite a lot of experience in these matters.

An important problem is how to make use of the Leader's propaganda flights for the Press. Everything has to be minutely prepared and organized beforehand.

October 4th, 1932.

Monday: Berlin. Prepared for the Leader's meeting at Munich. Dashed off designs for seven huge placards. Things knocked off quickly and enthusiastically are always good.

It is difficult to adapt men used to editorial work to the necessities of electioneering. They are too accurate and slow. . . .

January 18th, 1933.

In the evening we go to see the film "Rebel," by Luis Trencker. A first-class production of an artistic film. Thus I could imagine the film of the future, revolutionary in character, with grand mass-scenes, composed with enormous vital energy. In one scene, in which a gigantic crucifix is carried out of a small church by the revolutionaries, the audience is deeply moved.

[329]

Here you really see what can be done with the film as an artistic medium, when it is really understood. We are all much impressed.

February 10th, 1933.

The Sportpalast (Sports Palace) is already packed by six o'clock in the evening. All the squares in the city swarm with people waiting to hear the Leader's speech. In the whole Reich twenty to thirty millions more are listening in to it.

Drag myself to the Sportpalast, still weak with the illness from which I have not yet fully recovered. On the platform first I address the Press, and then for twenty minutes at the microphone speak to the audience in the Sportpalast. It goes better than I had thought. It is a strange experience suddenly to be faced with an inanimate microphone when one is used to addressing a living crowd, to be uplifted by the atmosphere of it, and to read the effect of one's speech in the expression on the faces of one's hearers.

The Leader is greeted by frantic cheering. He delivers a fine address containing an outspoken declaration of war against Marxism. Towards the end he strikes a wonderful, incredibly solemn note, and closes with the word "Amen"! It is uttered so naturally that all are deeply moved and affected by it. It is filled with so much strength and belief, is so novel and courageous, that it is not to be compared to anything that has gone beforehand.

This address will be received with enthusiasm throughout Germany. The nation will be ours almost without a struggle.

The masses at the Sportpalast are beside themselves with delight. Now the German Revolution has truly begun.

'Phone calls from different parts of the country report on the fine effect the speech has made even over the Radio. As an instrument for propaganda on a large scale the efficacy of the Radio has not yet been sufficiently appreciated. In any case our adversaries did not recognize its value. All the better, we shall have to explore its possibilities.

THE IMPACT OF NAZI
METHODS

Source 17 from Jeremy Noakes and Geoffrey Pridham, editors, Documents on Nazism, 1919–1945 *(New York: Viking, 1975), p. 100.*

17. Report on the Problem of Stemming the Spread of Nazi Ideas in the Protestant Youth Movement, 1931

The cause which at the moment is most closely associated with the name of National Socialism and with which, at a moderate estimate, certainly 70 per cent of our young people, often lacking knowledge of the facts, are in ardent sympathy, must be regarded, as far as our ranks are concerned, more as an ethical than a political matter. Our young people show little political interest. Fifth-formers[14] are not really much concerned with the study of Hitler's thoughts; it is simply something irrational, something infectious that makes the blood pulse through one's veins and conveys an impression that something great is under way, the roaring of a stream which one does not wish to escape: "If you can't feel it you will never grasp it. . . ."

All this must be taken into account when we see the ardour and fire of this movement reflected in our ranks. A pedantic and nagging approach seems to me useless, and so do all attempts, however well-intentioned, by the leader to refute the policy of National Socialism in detail. The majority of the young fight against this with a strange instinct. We must, in keeping with our responsibility, though it is difficult in individual cases, try first to influence the ethos, and in this we must maintain an attitude above parties. We must educate in such a way that this enthusiasm is duly tempered by deeper understanding and by disenchantment, that words like "national honour and dignity" do not become slogans but arouse individual responsibility so that no brash demagogues grow up among us.

Source 18 from William L. Shirer, Berlin Diary, The Journal of a Foreign Correspondent, *1934–1941 (New York: Knopf, 1941), pp. 18, 19, 21, 22, 23.*

18. William L. Shirer, Reactions to the Nazi Party Rally at Nuremberg, 1934

NUREMBERG, *September 5*

I'm beginning to comprehend, I think, some of the reasons for Hitler's astounding success. Borrowing a chapter from the Roman church, he is restoring pageantry and colour and mysticism to the drab lives of twentieth-century Germans. This morning's opening meeting in the Luitpold Hall on the outskirts of Nuremberg was more than a gorgeous show; it also had something of the mysticism and religious fervour of an Easter or Christmas Mass in a great Gothic cathedral. The hall was a sea of brightly coloured flags. Even Hitler's arrival was made dramatic. The band stopped playing. There was a hush over the thirty thousand people packed in the hall. Then the band struck up the *Badenweiler March*, a very catchy tune, and used only, I'm told, when Hitler makes his big entries. Hitler appeared in the back of the auditorium, and followed by his aides, Göring, Goebbels, Hess, Himmler, and the others, he strode slowly down the long centre aisle while thirty thousand hands were raised in salute. It is a ritual, the old-timers say, which

14. **fifth form:** a grade achieved by British secondary school students at the age of fifteen or sixteen.

is always followed. Then an immense symphony orchestra played Beethoven's *Egmont* Overture. Great Klieg lights played on the stage, where Hitler sat surrounded by a hundred party officials and officers of the army and navy. Behind them the "blood flag," the one carried down the streets of Munich in the ill-fated putsch. Behind this, four or five hundred S.A. standards. When the music was over, Rudolf Hess, Hitler's closest confidant, rose and slowly read the names of the Nazi "martyrs"—brown-shirts who had been killed in the struggle for power—a roll-call of the dead, and the thirty thousand seemed very moved.

In such an atmosphere no wonder, then, that every word dropped by Hitler seemed like an inspired Word from on high. Man's—or at least the German's—critical faculty is swept away at such moments, and every lie pronounced is accepted as high truth itself.

NUREMBERG, *September 7*

Another great pageant tonight. Two hundred thousand party officials packed in the Zeppelin Wiese with their twenty-one thousand flags unfurled in the searchlights like a forest of weird trees. "We are strong and will get stronger," Hitler shouted at them through the microphone, his words echoing across the hushed field from the loud-speakers. And there, in the flood-lit night, jammed together like sardines, in one mass formation, the little men of Germany who have made Nazism possible achieved the highest state of being the Germanic man knows: the shedding of their individual souls and minds—with the personal responsibilities and doubts and problems—until under the mystic lights and at the sound of the magic words of the Austrian they were merged completely in the Germanic herd. Later they recovered enough—fifteen thousand of them—to stage a torchlight parade through Nuremberg's ancient streets, Hitler taking the salute in front of the station across from our hotel.

NUREMBERG, *September 10*

(Later)—After seven days of almost ceaseless goose-stepping, speech-making, and pageantry, the party rally came to an end tonight. And though dead tired and rapidly developing a bad case of crowd-phobia, I'm glad I came. You have to go through one of these to understand Hitler's hold on the people, to feel the dynamic in the movement he's unleashed and the sheer, disciplined strength the Germans possess. And now—as Hitler told the correspondents yesterday in explaining his technique—the half-million men who've been here during the week will go back to their towns and villages and preach the new gospel with new fanaticism. Shall sleep late tomorrow and take the night train back to Berlin.

QUESTIONS TO CONSIDER

This chapter posed three basic questions: What image did the Nazis convey to German voters? Why did they appeal to German voters? How did the Nazis use media to aid their rise to power?

First examine the image the party conveyed to Germans in the 1920s and early 1930s. Start by considering the highly visible uniformed wing of the party, the S.A. Why did the S.A. Order 111 (Source 4) place such emphasis on how the S.A. appeared in public? What was the Storm Trooper supposed to epitomize? How was that visual effect designed to build a certain image for the party? How might columns of marching men and political banners contribute to this image? Reflect, too, on the mass meetings so carefully mounted by the party. What impression might they have conveyed to the average man or woman on the street? How did the Leader myth contribute to a certain image for the party? Remember that Hitler was relatively young, forty-three years of age, when he gained power. How do you think many Germans viewed a young party leader whose use of airplanes made him seem omnipresent?

With your concept of the party's image now clearly in mind, assess the Nazi appeal to voters. You may wish to review the numerous problems facing Germany in the 1920s and early 1930s that we examined in the introduction. What did the Nazis propose as solutions to the Versailles Treaty, the threat of communist take-over, and the ills of the Depression? Did the Nazis convey an image that would lead Germans to believe the party could solve the country's problems? Consider the S.A. and the Leader myth. How did they reinforce a promise to restore German power?

What groups did the Nazis specifically appeal to in our evidence, and what were their specific problems? What were the alleged conditions of the workers in Source 8, the poster of "The String-Puller"? Who was threatened by the proposed Woolworth's store in Hanover (Source 14)? How did the Nazis win support in these groups?

Beyond its proposed answers to Germany's problems and its specific appeal to certain groups, the Nazi party also had a more general appeal. Reflect for a moment on the anomie that Durkheim identified as part of modern urban life (see Chapter 9). In what ways do you think participation in mass meetings might combat this feeling? What sorts of positive feelings might it seem to provide? The twentieth century, as we saw in Chapter 9, has witnessed for many a weakening of both the ritual and authority of traditional religion. How do the photographs of the banners and rally (Sources 5 and 6) and Shirer's account (Source 18) indicate a conscious attempt by the Nazis to exploit this development? Why would you not be surprised to find German religious youth movements losing members to the Nazis? Why are you perhaps shocked but probably not surprised at the conclusion of Hitler's speech of February 10, 1933 (Source 16)?

Finally, consider the Nazis' techniques, their use of media and propaganda in achieving their goal of power. In this regard, consider the theoretical bases for Nazi propaganda. What was Hitler's view of the masses? According to Hitler, why would the masses submit to terror? Recall the account of the brawl in the Pharus Hall in Source 7. What effect might this event have had on Hitler's opponents? Reexamine the graph of violence in Northeim. Why did Nazi violence break out when it did? How did it affect the party's image?

Examine the party's use of media technology for propaganda. What was the response of the Italian journalist to Nazi propaganda, according to Goebbels (Source 16)? What new electronic media did the Nazis employ? What do you think the Nazis'

level of success would have been without such modern technology as the microphone? What features of Nazi campaign technology have become part of modern campaigning?

As you consider these questions, you should have a better understanding of the Nazi seizure of power in Germany. The Nazis used technology and methods of political manipulation that were new to the modern world. To understand fully the magnitude of their political revolution in winning the German masses, conclude your examination by referring to Chapter 1 of this volume. Which social groups was Louis XIV of France trying to influence? What was his message? How have Western political strategies changed in the almost three centuries separating Louis XIV and Hitler?

EPILOGUE

Nazi media mastery and propaganda worked well enough by January 1933 for the party to secure the chancellorship for Hitler. In free elections, however, the Nazis never secured more than 44 percent of the vote.[15] Once Hitler became chancellor, the task for the party and Goebbels was to use modern media and propaganda either to win the support of

the majority of Germans or at least to convince them that opposition to the new political order was futile. As had been the case with the Nazi drive for power, implicit in this effort was the threat that force would be used against the recalcitrant. But Hitler did seem to keep his promises. The communist party was outlawed in 1933; building projects and eventually rearmament stimulated the economy and created jobs; and Germany restored its military power and defied the Treaty of Versailles. Ominously, Hitler's promises also pointed to the terrible tragedy of the Holocaust for European Jews, and to World War Two. But Goebbels's propaganda machine never let Germans forget the regime's successes.

---

15. In the last free Reichstag elections held in March 1933, the Nazis won only 43.9 percent of the vote, despite S.A. intimidation of voters and the great political advantage accruing to the party from Hitler's position as Chancellor. The Nazis finally secured a Reichstag majority only when Hitler expelled the communist members from the Chamber.

The Hitler government centralized control of all information and media in a new Ministry of Public Enlightenment and Propaganda, headed by Goebbels, which closely regulated Germany's press, film, and radio after 1933. Especially significant was Goebbels's understanding of the role of radio as a propaganda device and his use of it once in power. He said, "With the radio we have destroyed the spirit of rebellion,"[16] because the radio could burn the Nazi message into every German home. The regime saw to it that cheap radios were made available to Germans, and the number of receivers increased from 5 million in 1932 to 9.5 million in 1938. A system of government wardens notified citizens to tune in important programs and the Propaganda Ministry increased their impact still further by setting up loudspeakers in the streets and squares of Germany during key broadcasts.

Goebbels's ministry also sought to sway opinion via the medium of film. After some early crude and unpopular efforts, Goebbels's understanding of film as a propaganda device grew greatly. He wrote in 1942 of the subtle possibilities inherent in the medium:

> Even entertainment can be politically of special value, because the moment a person becomes conscious of propaganda, propaganda becomes ineffective. However, as soon as propaganda as a tendency, as a characteristic, as an attitude remains in the background and becomes apparent through human beings, then propaganda becomes effective in every respect.[17]

Armed with such methods, the Nazi regime was able to retain power, mobilize its citizens for war, and sustain their morale throughout much of World War Two. There was opposition to the dictatorship and a number of plots against Hitler himself, but the regime managed to contain such active resistance within a minority of the population. Modern media and propaganda techniques and a message that attracted many, combined with the omnipresent threat of state police power, proved to be effective devices that aided the regime in maintaining its ascendancy.

17. Joseph Goebbels, *Tagebuch*, unpublished sections, in Institut für Zeitgeschichte, Munich, entry for March 1, 1942. Quoted in David Welch, *Propaganda and the German Cinema, 1933–1945* (Oxford: Clarendon Press, 1983), p. 45.

16. Quoted in Roger Manvell and Heinrich Fraenkel, *Doctor Goebbels: His Life and Death* (London: Heinemann, 1960), pp. 127–128.

CHAPTER THIRTEEN

THE IDEOLOGIES OF COLD WAR:

THE BERLIN BLOCKADE

(1948–1949)

On April 1, 1948, Russian troops stopped a trainload of American soldiers leaving West Germany for Berlin, approximately 110 miles inside the Soviet zone of Germany (see map on page 339). Gradually the Russians tightened their stranglehold on the city; by June 23 no rail or highway traffic was permitted between West Germany and the vulnerable city of Berlin. Berliners in the American, British, and French sectors of the city had been cut off from food, fuel, and medical supplies from the West. The Berlin Blockade had begun.

The Berlin Blockade of 1948–1949 dramatized the fact that the world had entered the era of the Cold War. The two superpowers, the United States and the Soviet Union, were no longer allies as they had been in World War Two; instead, they were grappling with each other for control of wartorn Europe and Asia. In that contest, Germany in general and Berlin in particular became key factors.

Precisely when the Cold War started and which nation or nations should bear the principal responsibility for starting it remains the subject of considerable debate even today. Though they had been allies in the war against Germany, each side had regarded the other with considerable suspicion and distrust. To Soviet Premier Josef Stalin, whose nation had twice been invaded by Germany in the twentieth century, the West posed a constant threat. In Stalin's eyes, the Soviet Union had carried the burden of the fight against Germany since 1941, a situation that was altered only with the Allied invasion of Normandy in mid-1944. During that struggle the death toll inflicted on Russians truly had been staggering and whole areas of the Soviet Union had been utterly devastated.[1] To guard against future

1. Russian military deaths are estimated to have exceeded 7 million. In contrast, Germany suffered approximately 3.5 million military deaths, China 2.2 million, Japan 1.3 million, Great Britain and the Commonwealth 500,000, and the United States 350,000. Indeed, when civilian deaths are added to military deaths,

invasions from the west, Stalin believed the Soviet Union must dominate the nations of eastern Europe and not allow a strong Germany to emerge from World War Two. Increasingly suspicious of the intentions of Great Britain and the United States toward the Soviet Union, Stalin felt that he needed to keep those nations as unaware as possible of his country's economic and military vulnerability. Stalin's fears resulted in a policy of secrecy toward these Western powers.

For their part, many policymakers in the United States and Great Britain were as suspicious of the Soviet Union as Stalin was of them. Prime Minister Winston Churchill had distrusted the Russians since the Bolshevik Revolution of 1917, believing that Russian communists had a policy for European expansion and eventual world domination. During World War Two, Churchill advocated a joint British-American invasion of the Balkans (Europe's "soft underbelly") instead of Normandy, reasoning that Allied advances from the Balkans by the end of the war would leave Great Britain and the United States in control of eastern Europe to block Soviet expansion.[2] But U.S. President Franklin Roosevelt, while harboring few illusions about the Soviet Union, hoped to lessen Stalin's

fears and gain the Soviet premier's cooperation in forming the United Nations by making some concessions. At the Yalta Conference, Roosevelt, Churchill, and Stalin agreed that the postwar governments of eastern Europe would be freely elected but pro-Russian. The three powers also agreed on the temporary partition of Germany into three zones of occupation to be governed cooperatively by the three victorious powers, who eventually would merge these zones into one reconstructed and reformed German state. The city of Berlin, well within the projected Soviet zone, likewise would be divided into three administrative sectors.[3] In addition, the Soviet Union was given the right to exact heavy reparations from a defeated Germany, which ultimately amounted to the dismantling of German industry within the Russian zone for shipment to the Soviet Union. Even so, amid joint declarations of unity at Yalta, considerable distrust remained on both sides.

The death of President Roosevelt on April 12, 1945 (less than a month before the end of the war in Europe) brought a change in relations between the Western allies and the Soviet Union. The new president, Harry Truman, held views of the Soviets considerably closer to those of Churchill. Although he honored agreements made by his predecessor

the Soviet Union lost a total of 40 percent of all people killed in World War Two, or approximately 20 of 50 million.

2. Because of the mountainous terrain in the Balkans, American military experts believed that such an invasion was unfeasible and the plan was scrapped. The "second front" was opened in Normandy, France in June 1944.

3. At the insistence of the United States and Great Britain, France was given a small zone in Germany and a sector in Berlin. These areas, however, had to be carved out of the U.S. and British zones and sectors because the Soviet Union refused to relinquish any of its territory of occupation.

Chapter 13
The Ideologies
of Cold War:
The Berlin
Blockade
(1948–1949)

(on reparations, the partition of Germany and Berlin, the return of Russian "traitors" to the Soviet government) and ordered the U.S. Army (which had advanced beyond the line separating the Soviet zone from those of the United States and Great Britain) to withdraw back to the line agreed on, in other ways Truman made it clear that he intended to follow a different policy from that of his predecessor. In May 1945, even before the Potsdam Conference, the new president cut off aid to the Soviet Union, using the justification that because the war against Germany had been won further assistance was unnecessary. At Potsdam, Truman demanded that free elections be held immediately in eastern Europe, a demand Stalin unhesitatingly rejected. After the United States had dropped two atomic bombs on Japan (thus bringing the war in the Pacific to a rapid conclusion), the president announced that the United States would not share the secret of the atomic bomb, a move that undoubtedly raised Russian apprehensions.

In 1946 Truman unofficially approved an anti-Soviet speech delivered in Fulton, Missouri by former British prime minister Winston Churchill (Source 1). The next year he issued his important Truman Doctrine (originally intended to apply only to Greece and Turkey but later extended worldwide), in which the president pledged U.S. military aid to any nation attempting to resist communism from within or without. Also in 1947, U.S. Secretary of State George Marshall offered the countries of Europe economic assistance to help them rebuild, soon known as the "Marshall Plan." Marshall Plan aid had strings attached, however. Nations receiving economic assistance had to agree to purge communists from positions of power and open their economic ledgers to the United States. Speaking for the Soviet Union and eastern Europe, Stalin brusquely rejected Marshall Plan aid and countered with the similar but not so effective Molotov Plan. Clearly the Cold War had begun.

One can see that fear and suspicion on both sides were a critical factor in bringing on the Cold War. Stalin's policy of secrecy toward the West, his refusal to honor the spirit of the Yalta agreement on eastern Europe, his encouragement of espionage activities to gain atomic bomb secrets, and his establishment in 1947 of the Communist Information Agency (Cominform) to coordinate worldwide communist party activities—including sabotage—caused the Western allies to view the Soviet Union as a dangerous threat to peace and stability. Believing that their appeasement of Hitler had helped to bring on World War Two, the Western allies proposed to take a harder line toward Stalin. At the same time, the actions of the Western leaders, and especially those of President Truman, doubtless added to Stalin's fears that Hitler had been replaced by another foe, more powerful and hostile than the Nazi dictator. Thus, in many ways all the nations involved must bear some responsibility for the Cold War.

Largely because of its location, Germany became a focal point for competing nations and ideologies in the Cold War. By March 1948, when

Europe After World War Two

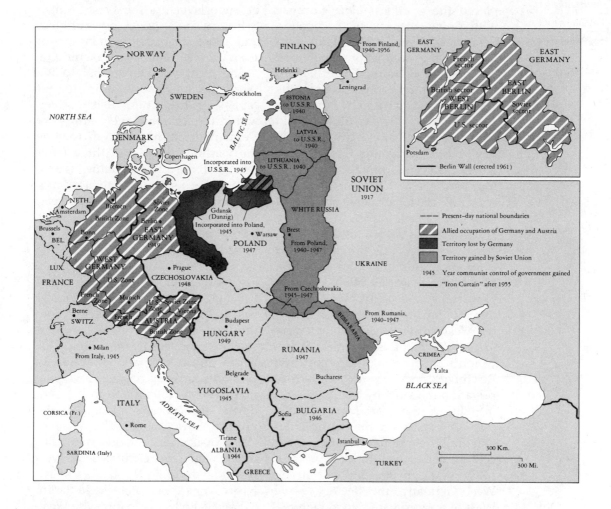

the Soviet Union withdrew from the Allied Control Council,[4] it appeared that an eventual reunification of Germany would be nearly impossible. Convinced of this, the Western allies

4. Established at Yalta, the Allied Control Council was composed of the military commanders of the three (later four) German zones and was intended to coordinate zonal administration.

planned to merge the American, British, and French zones into the Federal Republic of Germany (known informally as "West Germany"), which would receive massive amounts of Marshall Plan aid.

Furthermore, to restore West Germany's war-ravaged economy, the Western allies announced a thoroughgoing currency reform. At the

Chapter 13

The Ideologies
of Cold War:

The Berlin

Blockade

(1948–1949)

war's end the United States, Great Britain, and the Soviet Union had replaced the worthless Nazi currency with a new currency, the occupation Reichmark. Some of the plates used to print the occupation Reichmark had been given to the Soviet Union, which in turn printed enormous amounts of the new money, partly to pay their troops. The result was rapid and severe inflation. Unwilling to accept the occupation Reichmarks, whose value was rapidly deteriorating, farmers and retailers hoarded goods. Prices for available goods shot upward, leading in turn to bartering and a rampant black market in which cigarettes cost between $1.50 and $2.00 *each*.[5] Although introducing a new currency was clearly in violation of wartime agreements about the administration of postwar Germany, the Western allies believed they were forced to do this by the Soviet Union's inflation of the occupation Reichmark and by real conditions of privation in Germany.[6]

Stalin was now faced with the disastrous results of the 1946 Berlin mayoralty elections (in which the communists polled under 20 percent of the vote), the creation of a strong West Germany, the fleeing to the West of approximately 10 million refugees from the Soviet zone and Czechoslovakia,[7] and his failure to topple the independent Marshall Tito of Yugoslavia. As the West seemed to be growing stronger, more unified, and more aggressive, Stalin's own position seemed to be weakening.

The most vulnerable spot to the West, of course, was Berlin, former capital of the Third Reich. Deep within the Russian zone, Berlin, like Germany itself, had been divided by the wartime Allies into three (later four, with the addition of the French) sectors. Each sector was to be administered by one of the great powers, with the Kommandatura (Berlin's counterpart to Germany's Allied Control Council) coordinating the city's overall administration. In 1948, just as they had created the Federal Republic of Germany, the Western allies merged their three sectors into the single sector of West Berlin. Marshall Plan aid was transforming West Berlin into a dramatic showcase of Western Europe's postwar rejuvenation, a prosperous island in the middle of the more economically depressed Soviet zone. The Western allies' insistence that their new currency would be circulated in West Berlin made Stalin feel he had to act. His response was to blockade Berlin.

Was Stalin trying to force the Western allies out of Berlin? To what lengths would he be willing to go? As a drastic means of putting pressure on the West, would he allow West Berliners and the occupation troops of the Western allies in the city to starve to death? Under the most meager of rations, West Berlin

5. A pack of cigarettes, worth roughly $30 to $40 in Germany, could be purchased for under 25¢ in the United States. Many U.S. servicemen made a great deal of money by sending for cigarettes, Mickey Mouse watches, candy, and other items from home and then selling them on the black market. The U.S. Army and the Treasury Department were obliged to convert servicemen's Reichmarks into dollars.

6. The new currency the Western allies issued was the Deutschmark, pegged at a ratio of 10 occupation Reichmarks to 1 Deutschmark.

7. In February 1948, a communist coup in Czechoslovakia had brought that nation under the control of the Soviet Union.

needed 3,000 tons of coal and 2,500 tons of food *daily*. Would President Truman send troops through the Soviet zone to relieve West Berlin? If so, would that move precipitate World War Three? At the time many feared this would be the case.

Your task in this chapter is to use the evidence to analyze the positions of the West and the Soviet Union at roughly the time of the Berlin Blockade, with a view to understanding the ideological origins of the Cold War. How did each side portray itself? How did each side portray the other? What justifications did each side give for its actions in Berlin in 1948?

SOURCES AND METHOD

In this chapter, the evidence can be broken down into two categories, Western and Soviet. In the first category, Source 1 is taken from a speech titled "Alliance of English-Speaking People," delivered by former British Prime Minister Winston Churchill at Westminster College in Fulton, Missouri on March 5, 1946. Churchill (1874–1965), was first elected to the House of Commons in 1900. In 1940 he became prime minister and is credited with organizing Great Britain's war effort, inspiring the British people, and cultivating strong ties with the United States. Defeated by the Labor Party in 1945, Churchill was known as a strong opponent of the Soviet Union.

Selection 2 consists of excerpts from an anonymous article, "The Sources of Soviet Conduct," which appeared in the July 1947 number of *Foreign Affairs* and was actually written by George Kennan. Kennan (born 1904) joined the U.S. Foreign Service in 1926 and is credited as the architect of Truman's policy toward the Soviet Union, known as "containment." He was U.S. ambassador to the Soviet Union from 1952 to 1953.

Selections 3 through 6 are taken from the transcripts of telephone conferences and cables made by U.S. General Lucius Clay, commander-in-chief of the U.S. forces in Europe and military governor of the U.S. zone of Germany. Director of Materiel of Army Service Forces under General Dwight Eisenhower during World War Two, Clay (1897–1978) retired in 1949, after the lifting of the Berlin Blockade.

In the Soviet evidence, Source 7 presents selections from a 1947 speech delivered by Andrei Zhdanov (1896–1948). Made leader of the Cominform in 1947, he attacked the Truman Doctrine and the Marshall Plan as the "twin forks" of U.S. imperialism. At one time, it appears that Zhdanov might have been designated as Stalin's successor. Source 8 consists of portions of an October 4, 1948 speech by Soviet ambassador to the United Nations Andrei Y. Vyshinsky (1883–1954). A lawyer, Vyshinsky was active as a jurist in Stalin's purges of the 1930s. The Soviet Union's policy of de-Stalinization damaged Vyshinky's posthumous reputation. Source 9 is taken from an anonymous article published in the

[341]

Chapter 13

The Ideologies

of Cold War:

The Berlin

Blockade

(1948–1949)

February 11, 1949 issue of the *USSR Information Bulletin*, an English-language periodical issued by the Soviet government. As such, it can be seen as an organ expressing official Soviet government policy.

As you read the evidence, you will see very quickly that each side has its own opinion about the origins of the Cold War, and you will rarely have to read between the lines to find it. According to Western government spokesmen, what brought about the Cold War? According to the Soviets? How does each side perceive the other? In what ways are those perceptions similar? In what ways are they different?

How governments perceive each other becomes part of each side's *ideology*, a body of ideas that reflects a person's or group's aspirations and justifies actions. Why was each side's perceptions of the other in the Cold War an important part of its ideology? What role did those perceptions play in determining policy?

Because almost all the evidence is accusatory in nature (that is, it spends more time attacking its opponent than characterizing its own position), identifying each side's self-perception is a difficult task that will take some inference on your part. Yet self-perception is a crucial part of a person's or group's ideology. Can you infer how one side perceives itself by how it characterizes the other side? If so, what was the West's perceptions of itself? The Soviet Union's? In what ways were those self-perceptions similar? In what ways did they differ?

As noted, ideology often is used to justify action. How did the West justify its actions at the time of the Berlin Blockade? How did the Soviet Union? In what ways were these justifications alike? In what ways were they different?

Having examined and analyzed the evidence from both sides, can you now describe the ideological origins of the Cold War?

THE EVIDENCE

THE WESTERN PERSPECTIVE

Source 1 from Vital Speeches of the Day, *vol. 12 (March 15, 1946), pp. 329–332.*

1. From Winston Churchill, "Alliance of English-Speaking People," March 5, 1946

The United States stands at this time at the pinnacle of world power. It is a solemn moment for the American democracy. With primacy in power is also joined an awe-inspiring accountability to the future. As you look around you, you must feel not only the sense of duty done but also feel anxiety lest you fall below the level of achievement. Opportunity is here now, clear and shining, for both our countries. To reject it or ignore it or fritter it away will bring upon us all the long reproaches of the aftertime. It is necessary that constancy of mind, persistency of purpose and the grand simplicity of decision shall guide and rule the conduct of the English-speaking peoples in peace as they did in war. We must and I believe we shall prove ourselves equal to this severe requirement. . . .

[*Here Churchill called for a "special relationship between the British Commonwealth and Empire and the United States" to preserve peace and resist tyranny. He added that this alliance would not be in conflict with the United Nations but instead would help that body accomplish its work.*]

A shadow has fallen upon the scenes so lately lighted by the Allied victory. Nobody knows what Soviet Russia and its Communist international organization intends to do in the immediate future, or what are the limits, if any, to their expansive and proselytizing tendencies. I have a strong admiration and regard for the valiant Russian people and for my war-time comrade, Marshal Stalin. There is sympathy and good will in Britain—and I doubt not here also—toward the peoples of all the Russias and a resolve to persevere through many differences and rebuffs in establishing lasting friendships. We understand the Russians need to be secure on her western frontiers from all renewal of German aggression. We welcome her to her rightful place among the leading nations of the world. Above all we welcome constant, frequent and growing contacts between the Russian people and our own people on both sides of the Atlantic. It is my duty, however, to place before you certain facts about the present position in Europe—I am sure I do not wish to, but it is my duty, I feel, to present them to you.

From Stettin in the Baltic to Trieste in the Adriatic, an iron curtain has descended across the Continent. Behind that line lie all the capitals of the ancient states of central and eastern Europe. Warsaw, Berlin, Prague, Vienna, Budapest, Belgrade, Bucharest and Sofia, all these famous cities and the populations around them lie in the Soviet sphere and all are subject in one form or another, not only to Soviet influence but to a very high and increasing measure of control from Moscow. Athens alone, with its immortal glories, is free to decide its future at an election under British, American and French observation. The Russian-dominated Polish government has been encouraged to make enormous and wrongful inroads upon Germany, and mass expulsions of millions of Germans on a scale grievous and undreamed of are now taking place. The Communist parties, which were very small in all these eastern states of Europe, have been raised to pre-eminence and power far beyond their numbers and are seeking everywhere to obtain totalitarian control. Police governments are prevailing in nearly every case, and so far, except in Czechoslovakia, there is no true democracy. Turkey and Persia are

Chapter 13

The Ideologies

of Cold War:

The Berlin

Blockade

(1948–1949)

both profoundly alarmed and disturbed at the claims which are made upon them and at the pressure being exerted by the Moscow government. An attempt is being made by the Russians in Berlin to build up a quasi-Communist party in their zone of occupied Germany by showing special favors to groups of Left-Wing German leaders. At the end of the fighting last June, the American and British armies withdrew westward, in accordance with an earlier agreement, to a depth at some points 150 miles on a front of nearly 400 miles to allow the Russians to occupy this vast expanse of territory which the western democracies had conquered. If now the Soviet government tries, by separate action, to build up a pro-Communist Germany in their areas this will cause new serious difficulties in the British and American zones, and will give the defeated Germans the power of putting themselves up to auction between the Soviets and western democracies. Whatever conclusions may be drawn from these facts—and facts they are—this is certainly not the liberated Europe we fought to build up. Nor is it one which contains the essentials of permanent peace.

The safety of the world, ladies and gentlemen, requires a new unity in Europe from which no nation should be permanently outcast.

It is impossible not to comprehend—twice we have seen them drawn by irresistible forces in time to secure the victory but only after frightful slaughter and devastation have occurred. Twice the United States has had to send millions of its young men to fight a war, but now war can find any nation between dusk and dawn. Surely we should work within the structure of the United Nations and in accordance with our charter. That is an open course of policy. . . .

On the other hand I repulse the idea that a new war is inevitable; still more that it is imminent. It is because I am so sure that our fortunes are in our own hands and that we hold the power to save the future, that I feel the duty to speak out now that I have an occasion to do so. I do not believe that Soviet Russia desires war. What they desire is the fruits of war and the indefinite expansion of their power and doctrines. But what we have to consider here today while time remains, is the permanent prevention of war and the establishment of conditions of freedom and democracy as rapidly as possible in all countries. Our difficulties and dangers will not be removed by closing our eyes to them. They will not be removed by mere waiting to see what happens; nor will they be relieved by a policy of appeasement. What is needed is a settlement and the longer this is delayed the more difficult it will be and the greater our dangers will become. From what I have seen of our Russian friends and allies during the war, I am convinced that there is nothing they admire so much as strength, and there is nothing for which they have less respect than for military weakness. For that reason the old doctrine of a balance of power is unsound. We cannot afford, if we can help it, to work on narrow margins, offering temptations to a trial of strength. If the western democracies stand together in strict adherence to the principles of the United Nations Charter, their influence for furthering these principles will be immense and no one is likely to molest them. If, however, they become divided or falter in their duty, and if these all-important years are allowed to slip away, then indeed catastrophe may overwhelm us all.

Last time I saw it all coming, and cried aloud to my fellow countrymen and to the world, but no one paid any attention. Up till the year 1933 or even 1935, Germany might have been saved from the awful fate which has overtaken her and we might all have been spared the miseries Hitler let loose upon mankind. There never was a war in all history easier to prevent by timely action than the one which has just desolated such great areas of the globe. It could have been prevented without the firing of a single shot, and Germany might be powerful, prosperous and honored today, but no one would listen and one by one we were all sucked into the awful whirlpool. We surely must not let that happen again. This can only be achieved by reaching now, in 1946, a good understanding on all points with Russia under the general authority of the United Nations Organization and by the maintenance of that good understanding through many peaceful years, by the world instrument, supported by the whole strength of the English-speaking world and all its connections.

Let no man underrate the abiding power of the British Empire and Commonwealth. Because you see the forty-six millions in our island harassed about their food supply, of which they grew only one-half, even in war time, or because we have difficulty in restarting our industries and export trade after six years of passionate war effort, do not suppose that we shall not come through these dark years of privation as we have come through the glorious years of agony, or that half a century from now you will not see seventy or eighty millions of Britons spread about the world and united in defense of our traditions, our way of life and of the world causes we and you espouse. If the population of the English-speaking commonwealth be added to that of the United States, with all that such co-operation implies in the air, on the sea and in science and industry, there will be no quivering, precarious balance of power to offer its temptation to ambition or adventure. On the contrary, there will be an overwhelming assurance of security. If we adhere faithfully to the charter of the United Nations and walk forward in sedate and sober strength, seeking no one's land or treasure, or seeking to lay no arbitrary control on the thoughts of men, if all British moral and material forces and convictions are joined with your own in fraternal association, the highroads of the future will be clear, not only for us but for all, not only for our time but for a century to come.

Chapter 13
The Ideologies
of Cold War:
The Berlin
Blockade
(1948–1949)

Source 2 from Foreign Affairs, *vol. 25 (July 1947), pp. 566–582.*

2. From "X" (George Kennan), "The Sources of Soviet Conduct," July 1947

The political personality of Soviet power as we know it today is the product of ideology and circumstances; ideology inherited by the present Soviet leaders from the movement in which they had their political origin, and circumstances of the power which they now have exercised for nearly three decades in Russia. There can be few tasks of psychological analysis more difficult than to try to trace the interaction of these two forces and the relative rôle of each in the determination of official Soviet conduct. Yet the attempt must be made if that conduct is to be understood and effectively countered.

It is difficult to summarize the set of ideological concepts with which the Soviet leaders came into power. Marxian ideology, in its Russian-Communist projection, has always been in process of subtle evolution. The materials on which it bases itself are extensive and complex. But the outstanding features of Communist thought as it existed in 1916 may perhaps be summarized as follows: (a) that the central factor in the life of man, the factor which determines the character of public life and the "physiognomy of society," is the system by which material goods are produced and exchanged; (b) that the capitalist system of production is a nefarious one which inevitably leads to the exploitation of the working class by the capital-owning class and is incapable of developing adequately the economic resources of society or of distributing fairly the material goods produced by human labor; (c) that capitalism contains the seeds of its own destruction and must, in view of the inability of the capital-owning class to adjust itself to economic change, result eventually and inescapably in a revolutionary transfer of power to the working class; and (d) that imperialism, the final phase of capitalism, leads directly to war and revolution. . . .

Now it must be noted that through all the years of preparation for revolution, the attention of these men, as indeed of Marx himself, had been centered less on the future form which Socialism would take than on the necessary overthrow of rival power which, in their view, had to precede the introduction of Socialism. Their views, therefore, on the positive program to be put into effect, once power was attained, were for the most part nebulous, visionary and impractical. Beyond the nationalization of industry and the expropriation of large private capital holdings there was no agreed program. The treatment of the peasantry, which according to the Marxist formulation was not of the proletariat, had always been a vague spot in the pattern of Communist thought; and it remained an object of controversy and vacillation for the first ten years of Communist power.

The circumstances of the immediate post-revolution period—the existence in Russia of civil war and foreign intervention, together with the obvious fact that the Communists represented only a tiny minority of the Russian people—made the establishment of dictatorial power a necessity.

Now it lies in the nature of the mental world of the Soviet leaders, as well as in the character of their ideology, that no opposition to them can be officially recognized as having any merit or justification whatsoever. Such opposition can flow, in theory, only from the hostile and incorrigible forces of dying capitalism. As long as remnants of capitalism were officially recognized as existing in Russia, it was possible to place on them, as an internal element, part of the blame for the maintenance of a dictatorial form of society. But as these remnants were liquidated, little by little, this justification fell away; and when it was indicated officially that they had been finally destroyed, it disappeared altogether. And this fact created one of the most basic of the compulsions which came to act upon the Soviet régime: since capitalism no longer existed in Russia and since it could not be admitted that there could be serious or widespread opposition to the Kremlin springing spontaneously from the liberated masses under its authority, it became necessary to justify the retention of the dictatorship by stressing the menace of capitalism abroad.

This began at an early date. In 1924 Stalin specifically defended the retention of the "organs of suppression," meaning, among others, the army and the secret police, on the ground that "as long as there is a capitalist encirclement there will be danger of intervention with all the consequences that flow from that danger." In accordance with that theory, and from that time on, all internal opposition forces in Russia have consistently been portrayed as the agents of foreign forces of reaction antagonistic to Soviet power.

By the same token, tremendous emphasis has been placed on the original Communist thesis of a basic antagonism between the capitalist and Socialist worlds. It is clear, from many indications, that this emphasis is not founded in reality. The real facts concerning it have been confused by the existence abroad of genuine resentment provoked by Soviet philosophy and tactics and occasionally by the existence of great centers of military power, notably the Nazi régime in Germany and the Japanese Government of the late 1930's, which did indeed have aggressive designs against the Soviet Union. But there is ample evidence that the stress laid in Moscow on the menace confronting Soviet society from the world outside its borders is founded not in the realities of foreign antagonism but in the necessity of explaining away the maintenance of dictatorial authority at home.

Now the maintenance of this pattern of Soviet power, namely, the pursuit of unlimited authority domestically, accompanied by the cultivation of the semi-myth of implacable foreign hostility, has gone far to shape the actual machinery of Soviet power as we know it today. Internal organs of administration which did not serve this purpose withered on the vine. Organs which did serve this purpose became vastly swollen. The security of Soviet power came to rest on the iron discipline of the Party, on the severity and ubiquity of the secret police, and on the uncompromising economic monop-

Chapter 13

The Ideologies

of Cold War:

The Berlin

Blockade

(1948–1949)

olism of the state. The "organs of suppression," in which the Soviet leaders had sought security from rival forces, became in large measure the masters of those whom they were designed to serve. Today the major part of the structure of Soviet power is committed to the perfection of the dictatorship and to the maintenance of the concept of Russia as in a state of siege, with the enemy lowering beyond the walls. And the millions of human beings who form that part of the structure of power must defend at all costs this concept of Russia's position, for without it they are themselves superfluous.

As things stand today, the rulers can no longer dream of parting with these organs of suppression. The quest for absolute power, pursued now for nearly three decades with a ruthlessness unparalleled (in scope at least) in modern times, has again produced internally, as it did externally, its own reaction. The excesses of the police apparatus have fanned the potential opposition to the régime into something far greater and more dangerous than it could have been before those excesses began.

But least of all can the rulers dispense with the fiction by which the maintenance of dictatorial power has been defended. For this fiction has been canonized in Soviet philosophy by the excesses already committed in its name; and it is now anchored in the Soviet structure of thought by bonds far greater than those of mere ideology.

So much for the historical background. What does it spell in terms of the political personality of Soviet power as we know it today?

Of the original ideology, nothing has been officially junked. Belief is maintained in the basic badness of capitalism, in the inevitability of its destruction, in the obligation of the proletariat to assist in that destruction and to take power into its own hands. But stress has come to be laid primarily on those concepts which relate most specifically to the Soviet régime itself: to its position as the sole truly Socialist régime in a dark and misguided world, and to the relationships of power within it.

The first of these concepts is that of the innate antagonism between capitalism and Socialism. We have seen how deeply that concept has become imbedded in foundations of Soviet power. It has profound implications for Russia's conduct as a member of international society. It means that there can never be on Moscow's side any sincere assumption of a community of aims between the Soviet Union and powers which are regarded as capitalist. It must invariably be assumed in Moscow that the aims of the capitalist world are antagonistic to the Soviet régime, and therefore to the interests of the peoples it controls. If the Soviet Government occasionally sets its signature to documents which would indicate the contrary, this is to be regarded as a tactical manœuvre permissible in dealing with the enemy (who is without honor) and should be taken in the spirit of *caveat emptor*. Basically, the antagonism remains. It is postulated. And from it flow many of the phenomena which we find disturbing in the Kremlin's conduct of foreign policy: the secretiveness, the lack of frankness, the duplicity, the wary suspiciousness, and the basic unfriendliness of purpose. These phenomena are there to stay, for the foreseeable future. There can be variations of degree and of emphasis. When there is something the Russians want from us, one or the other of these features of their policy may be thrust temporarily into the background; and when that happens there will always be Americans who will leap forward with gleeful announcements that "the Russians have changed," and some who will even try to take credit for having brought about such "changes." But we should not be misled by tactical manœuvres. These characteristics of Soviet policy, like the postulate from which they flow, are basic to the internal nature of Soviet power, and will be with us, whether in the foreground or the background, until the internal nature of Soviet power is changed.

This means that we are going to continue for a long time to find the Russians difficult to deal with. It does not mean that they should be considered as embarked upon a do-or-die program to overthrow our society by a given date. The theory of the inevitability of the eventual fall of capitalism has the fortunate connotation that there is no hurry about it. The forces of progress can take their time in preparing the final *coup de grâce*. Meanwhile, what is vital is that the "Socialist fatherland"—that oasis of power which has been already won for Socialism in the person of the Soviet Union—should be cherished and defended by all good Communists at home and abroad, its fortunes promoted, its enemies badgered and confounded. The promotion of premature, "adventuristic" revolutionary projects abroad which might embarrass Soviet power in any way would be an inexcusable, even a counter-revolutionary act. The cause of Socialism is the support and promotion of Soviet power, as defined in Moscow. . . .

But we have seen that the Kremlin is under no ideological compulsion to accomplish its purposes in a hurry. Like the Church, it is dealing in ideological concepts which are of long-term validity, and it can afford to be patient. It has no right to risk the existing achievements of the revolution for the sake of vain baubles of the future. The very teachings of Lenin himself require great caution and flexibility in the pursuit of Communist purposes. Again, these precepts are fortified by the lessons of Russian history: of centuries of obscure battles between nomadic forces over the stretches of a vast unfortified plain. Here caution, circumspection, flexibility and deception are the valuable qualities; and their value finds natural appreciation in the Russian or the oriental mind. Thus the Kremlin has no compunction about retreating in the face of superior force. And being under the compulsion of no timetable, it does not get panicky under the necessity for such retreat. Its political action is a fluid stream which moves constantly, wherever it is permitted to move, toward a given goal. Its main concern is to make sure that it has filled every nook and cranny available to it in the basin of world power. But if it finds unassailable barriers in its path, it accepts these philosophically and accommodates itself to them. The main thing is that there should always be pres-

Chapter 13
The Ideologies
of Cold War:
The Berlin
Blockade
(1948–1949)

sure, unceasing constant pressure, toward the desired goal. There is no trace of any feeling in Soviet psychology that that goal must be reached at any given time. . . .

It is clear that the United States cannot expect in the foreseeable future to enjoy political intimacy with the Soviet régime. It must continue to regard the Soviet Union as a rival, not a partner, in the political arena. It must continue to expect that Soviet policies will reflect no abstract love of peace and stability, no real faith in the possibility of a permanent happy coexistence of the Socialist and capitalist worlds, but rather a cautious, persistent pressure toward the disruption and weakening of all rival influence and rival power.

Balanced against this are the facts that Russia, as opposed to the western world in general, is still by far the weaker party, that Soviet policy is highly flexible, and that Soviet society may well contain deficiencies which will eventually weaken its own total potential. This would of itself warrant the United States entering with reasonable confidence upon a policy of firm containment, designed to confront the Russians with unalterable counter-force at every point where they show signs of encroaching upon the interests of a peaceful and stable world.

Sources 3 through 6 from Jean Edward Smith, editor, The Papers of General Lucius D. Clay: Germany, 1945–1949, *vol. 2 (Bloomington: Indiana University Press, 1974), pp. 568, 580–581, 602–605, 622–623.*

3. Cable from Gen. Lucius Clay to Lt. Gen. Stephen Chamberlain,[8] March 5, 1948

TOP SECRET

For many months, based on logical analysis, I have felt and held that war was unlikely for at least ten years. Within the last few weeks, I have felt a subtle change in Soviet attitude which I cannot define but which now gives me a feeling that it may come with dramatic suddenness. I cannot support this change in my own thinking with any data or outward evidence in relationships other than to describe it as a feeling of a new tenseness in every Soviet individual with whom we have official relations. . . .

8. Director of Intelligence, U.S. Army General Staff.

4. Teleconference Between Clay and Gen. Lawton Collins,[9] March 17, 1948

CLAY: Received your subject notice, re: flow of dependents [to Europe]. From strictly military viewpoint, stoppage of flow and gradual reduction here is logical and cannot be argued against.

Nevertheless now that dependents are here believe stoppage and reduction would be politically disastrous and perhaps harmful to military situation by creating new problems.

For instance, withdrawal of dependents from Berlin would create hysteria accompanied by rush of Germans to communism for safety. Withdrawal from zone first would create panic in dependents in Berlin.

This condition would spread in Europe and would increase Communist political strength everywhere and particularly Italy unless as we withdrew dependents, we concurrently brought in new military strength. Bringing in more soldiers as dependents were withdrawn would indicate strength whereas removal of dependents without such action indicates weakness.

COLLINS: We note from a Berlin I[nternational] N[ews] S[ervice] report that Russians are to remove dependents from Berlin and Dresden in May and June. Have you confirmation of this report?

CLAY: Soviet papers have published statement that Soviet dependents are being evacuated from Berlin 1 June but this is not verified. It may be just a part of "war of nerves." . . .

CLAY: From military viewpoint, stoppage desirable but from political and psychological viewpoints bad. I doubt if temporary stoppage would deceive anyone. If it would, plan has merit. If not, and I think it would not, the following are my views:

Reaction of Soviets—they would use as propaganda that we plan war. Otherwise, it would have little effect.

Morale of our forces—if they knew why, it would not hurt our morale except it might panic dependents.

German people—would be frightened elsewhere but in Berlin might become hysterical and rush to communism for safety.

Neighboring countries—they would be alarmed and would lose some of present courage.

All of above would be offset if during period new troops arrived. Since this cannot be done, believe stoppage would do more harm now than good. Would be all in favor if it did mean additional strength.

---

9. Deputy Chief of Staff to the Secretary of the Army.

Chapter 13

The Ideologies

of Cold War:

The Berlin

Blockade

(1948–1949)

5. Teleconference Among Clay, Sec. Kenneth Royall,[10] and Gen. Omar Bradley,[11] March 31, 1948

ROYALL: Realizing that any incident involving shooting or other heavy violence might precipitate war, some consideration has been given here to the President sending an immediate note to Stalin informing him that requirements of [Soviet] Berlin commander is violation of existing agreements and stating that traffic will continue to move pending discussions as to any proper regulations. In that event traffic would start moving in the usual manner after 24 hours, even if no reply has been received from Stalin. What do you think of this procedure? Another suggestion is that traffic trains move but that in no event shall there be shooting. What do you think of this?

CLAY: Any weakness on our part will lose us prestige important now. If Soviets mean war, we will only defer the next provocation for a few days. For that reason, I do not think either [suggestion] realistic. I do not believe this means war but any failure to meet this squarely will cause great trouble. I realize our train resistance would be token. I am convinced it is only possible course of action. . . .

I would prefer to evacuate Berlin and I had rather go to Siberia than to do that. However, [the proposed letter to Stalin] would be better of two but I think it should await our own test. If Soviets do open fire, perhaps U.S. and U.K. Governments could close certain world trade routes under our control until normal condition restored here. . . .

Legalistic argument no longer has meaning. We are now faced with a realistic and not a legalistic problem. Our reply will not be misunderstood by 42 million Germans and perhaps 200 million Western Europeans. We must say, we think, as our letter does, "this far you may go and no further." There is no middle ground which is not appeasement.

BRADLEY: The letter to [Maj. Gen. George] Hays [Deputy Military Governor] has been carefully studied by the Secretary of Defense [Forrestal], Secretary of the Army and Under Secretary of State [Lovett]. It was considered important that no action be taken different from what has been in practice recently. If our action now should provoke war we must be sure that the fault is not ours.

CLAY: I do understand. Please understand we are not carrying a chip on our shoulder and will shoot only for self-protection. We do not believe we will have to do so. We feel the integrity of our trains as a part of our sovereignty is a symbol of our position in Germany and Europe.

10. U.S. Secretary of the Army.

11. U.S. Army Chief of Staff. During World War Two, Bradley was an effective aide to Eisenhower and extremely popular with the troops.

6. Teleconference Between Clay and Bradley, April 10, 1948

BRADLEY: At present with our passenger trains completely stopped, Russians in effect have won the first round unless some way to get this changed. Do you see any such likelihood? If not, will not Russian restrictions be added one by one which eventually would make our position untenable unless we ourselves were prepared to threaten or actually start a war to remove these restrictions? Here we doubt whether our people are prepared to start a war in order to maintain our position in Berlin and Vienna.

What are your comments and if you agree should we now be planning how to avoid this development and under what conditions say for example setting up trizonia[12] with capital at Frankfurt we might ourselves announce withdrawal and minimize loss of prestige rather than being forced out by threat.

CLAY: Relative to your first question, I do not believe anything will come from protest to Moscow except rejection accompanied by legal argumentation. Nevertheless, I believe that for the record a protest at Moscow is desirable, particularly if it can be given concurrently with similar protests from British and French Governments. Both of latter are weakening and apt to give in to Soviet position. This is particularly true in case of French who really lack means to support their Berlin contingent by air. An approach to British and French Governments by our Government relative to protest might at least serve to hold their positions for time being.

Reference to your second question. I do not believe that we should plan on leaving Berlin short of a Soviet ultimatum to drive us out by force if we do not leave. At that time we must resolve the question as to our reply to such an ultimatum. The exception which could force us out would be the Soviet stoppage of all food supplies to German population in western sectors. I doubt that Soviets will make such a move because it would alienate the Germans almost completely, unless they were prepared to supply food for two million more people. I do not believe they can do this now, although they may be able to do so by harvest time in late summer. Nevertheless, I am slowly reducing the number of dependents in Berlin and also the number of civilian employees. This comes in substantial part from the transfer of certain functions to Frankfurt as a result of Bizonal fusion.[13] This transfer will be completed in May. There are certain other functions now being performed in Berlin which can better be performed in the zone and these transfers will be made after May. Also, I am giving serious consideration to replacing married officers and commissioned officers, as their tours of duty expire, with unmarried officers and non-commissioned officers, thus further

12. **trizonia:** unification of the American, British, and French zones.

13. **Bizonal fusion:** the West was planning to merge its zones into the Federal Republic of Germany, resulting in only two zones ("bizonia"), the Western and the Soviet.

Chapter 13

The Ideologies

of Cold War:

The Berlin

Blockade

(1948–1949)

reducing the number of dependents. These steps are logical and can be done, I am sure, without creating any impression that we are abandoning Berlin. Further, we are allowing the return of any dependents who desire to go, and this will result in a small decrease. I think any decision beyond this should not be planned, although events may necessitate otherwise. We will, of course, get in touch with you before making any such decision and, in fact, it will really have to be tough going here before it would be made. Again my apprehension is a detection of weakening in the intent to remain on the part of both British and French. There can be no question but that our departure would represent a tremendous loss of prestige and I would greatly deplore incurring such a loss of prestige unless it were forced by military action. Of course, I realize that this final decision is a matter of high Government policy. Nevertheless, I cannot believe that Soviets will apply force in Berlin unless they have determined war to be inevitable within a comparatively short period of time.

You will understand, of course, that our separate currency reform in near future followed by partial German government in Frankfurt will develop the real crisis. Present show probably designed by Soviets to scare us away from these moves.

Why are we in Europe? We have lost Czechoslovakia. We have lost Finland. Norway is threatened. We retreat from Berlin. We can take it by reducing our personnel with only airlift until we are moved out by force. There is no saving of prestige by setting up at Frankfurt that is not already discounted. After Berlin, will come western Germany and our strength there relatively is no greater and our position no more tenable than Berlin.

If we mean that we are to hold Europe against communism, we must not budge. We can take humiliation and pressure short of war in Berlin without losing face. If we move, our position in Europe is threatened. If America does not know this, does not believe the issue is cast now, then it never will and communism will run rampant. I believe the future of democracy requires us to stay here until forced out. God knows this is not heroic pose because there will be nothing heroic in having to take humiliation without retaliation.

THE SOVIET PERSPECTIVE

Source 7 from The Strategy and Tactics of World Communism *(Washington, D.C.: U.S. Government Printing Office, 1948), pp. 212–230.*

7. From Andrei Zhdanov, "The International Situation," September 1947

The war[14]—itself a product of the unevenness of capitalist development in the different countries—still further intensified this unevenness. Of all the

14. World War Two.

capitalist powers, only one—the United States—emerged from the war not only unweakened, but even considerably stronger economically and militarily. The war greatly enriched the American capitalists. The American people, on the other hand, did not experience the privations that accompany war, the hardship of occupation, or aerial bombardment; and since America entered the war practically in its concluding stage, when the issue was already decided, her human casualties were relatively small. For the U.S.A., the war was primarily and chiefly a spur to extensive industrial development and to a substantial increase of exports (principally to Europe).

But the end of the war confronted the United States with a number of new problems. The capitalist monopolies were anxious to maintain their profits at the former high level, and accordingly pressed hard to prevent a reduction of the wartime volume of deliveries. But this meant that the United States must retain the foreign markets which had absorbed American products during the war, and moreover, acquire new markets, inasmuch as the war had substantially lowered the purchasing power of most of the countries. The financial and economic dependence of these countries on the U.S.A. had likewise increased. The United States extended credits abroad to a sum of 19,000 million dollars, not counting investments in the International Bank and the International Currency Fund. America's principal competitors, Germany and Japan, have disappeared from the world market, and this has opened up new and very considerable opportunities for the United States. Whereas before World War II the more influential reactionary circles of American imperialism had adhered to an isolationist policy and had refrained from active interference in the affairs of Europe and Asia, in the new, postwar conditions the Wall Street bosses adopted a new policy. They advanced a program of utilizing America's military and economic might, not only to retain and consolidate the positions won abroad during the war, but to expand them to the maximum and to replace Germany, Japan and Italy in the world market. The sharp decline of the economic power of the other capitalist states makes it possible to speculate on their postwar economic difficulties, and, in particular, on the postwar economic difficulties of Great Britain, which makes it easier to bring these countries under American control. The United States proclaimed a new frankly predatory and expansionist course. . . .

Although the U.S.A. suffered comparatively little from the war, the vast majority of the Americans do not want another war, with its accompanying sacrifices and limitations. This has induced monopoly capital and its servitors among the ruling circles in the United States to resort to extraordinary means in order to crush the opposition at home to the aggressive expansionist course and to secure a free hand for the further prosecution of this dangerous policy.

But the crusade against Communism proclaimed by America's ruling circles with the backing of the capitalist monopolies, leads as a logical consequence to attacks on the fundamental rights and interests of the American working people, to the fascization of America's political life, and to the dissemination

Chapter 13

The Ideologies

of Cold War:

The Berlin

Blockade

(1948–1949)

of the most savage and misanthropic "theories" and views. Dreaming about preparing for a new, a third world war, American expansionist circles are vitally interested in stifling all possible resistance within the country to adventures abroad, in poisoning the minds of the politically backward and unenlightened American masses with the virus of chauvinism and militarism, and in stultifying the average American with the help of all the diverse means of anti-Soviet and anti-Communist propaganda—the cinema, the radio, the church, and the press. The expansionist foreign policy inspired and conducted by the American reactionaries envisages simultaneous action along all lines: 1. strategical military measures, 2. economic expansion, and 3. ideological struggle.

Realization of the strategical plans for future aggression is connected with the desire to utilize to the utmost the war production facilities of the United States, which had grown to enormous proportions by the end of World War II. American imperialism is persistently pursuing a policy of militarizing the country. Expenditure on the U.S. army and navy exceeds 11,000 million dollars per annum. In 1947–1948, 35 per cent of America's budget was appropriated for the armed forces, or eleven times more than in 1937–1938.

On the outbreak of World War II the American army was the seventeenth largest in the capitalist world; today it is the largest one. The United States is not only accumulating stocks of atomic bombs; American strategists say quite openly that it is preparing bacteriological weapons.

The strategical plans of the United States envisage the creation in peacetime of numerous bases and vantage grounds situated at great distances from the American continent and designed to be used for aggressive purposes against the USSR and the countries of the new democracy. America has built, or is building, air and naval bases in Alaska, Japan, Italy, South Korea, China, Egypt, Iran, Turkey, Greece, Austria, and Western Germany. There are American military missions in Afghanistan and even in Nepal. Feverish preparations are being made to use the Arctic for purposes of military aggression.

Although the war has long since ended, the military alliance between Britain and the United States and even a combined Anglo-American military staff continue to exist. Under the guise of agreement for the standardization of weapons the United States has established its control over the armed forces and military plans of other countries, notably of Great Britain and Canada. Under the guise of joint defense of the Western Hemisphere, the countries of Latin America are being brought into the orbit of America's plans of military expansion. The United States government has officially declared that it has committed itself to assist in the modernization of the Turkish army. The army of the reactionary Kuomintang is being trained by American instructors and armed with American material. The military circles are becoming an active political force in the United States, supplying large numbers of government officials and diplomats who are directing the whole policy of the country into an aggressive military course.

Economic expansion is an important supplement to the realization of America's strategical plan. American imperialism is endeavoring like a usurer, to take advantage of the postwar difficulties of the European countries, in particular of the shortage of raw materials, fuel and food in the Allied countries that suffered most from the war, to dictate to them extortionate terms for any assistance rendered. With an eye to the impending economic crisis, the United States is in a hurry to find new monopoly spheres of capital investment and markets for its goods. American economic "assistance" pursues the broad aim of bringing Europe into bondage to American capital. The more drastic the economic situation of a country is, the harsher are the terms which the American monopolies endeavor to dictate to it.

But economic control logically leads to political subjugation to American imperialism. Thus the United States combines the extension of monopoly markets for its goods with the acquisition of new bridgeheads for its fight against the new democratic forces of Europe. In "saving" a country from starvation and collapse, the American monopolies at the same time seek to rob it of all vestige of independence. American "assistance" automatically involves a change in the policy of the country to which it is rendered: parties and individuals come to power that are prepared, on directions from Washington, to carry out a program of home and foreign policy suitable to the United States (France, Italy, and so on).

Lastly, the aspiration to world supremacy and the anti-democratic policy of the United States involve an ideological struggle. The principal purpose of the ideological part of the American strategical plan is to deceive public opinion by slanderously accusing the Soviet Union and the new democracies of aggressive intentions, and thus representing the Anglo-Saxon bloc in a defensive role and absolving it of responsibility for preparing a new war. During the Second World War the popularity of the Soviet Union in foreign countries was enormously enhanced. Its devoted and heroic struggle against imperialism earned it the affection and respect of working people in all countries. The military and economic might of the Socialist state, the invincible strength of the moral and political unity of Soviet society were graphically demonstrated to the whole world. The reactionary circles in the United States and Great Britain are anxious to erase the deep impression made by the Socialist system on the working people of the world. The war-mongers fully realize that long ideological preparation is necessary before they can get their soldiers to fight the Soviet Union.

In their ideological struggle against the USSR, the American imperialists, who have no great insight into political questions, demonstrate their ignorance by laying primary stress on the allegation that the Soviet Union is undemocratic and totalitarian, while the United States and Great Britain and the whole capitalist world are democratic. On this platform of ideological struggle—on this defense of bourgeois pseudo-democracy and condemnation of Communism as totalitarian—are united all the enemies of the working

[357]

Chapter 13

The Ideologies
of Cold War:

The Berlin

Blockade

(1948–1949)

class without exception, from the capitalist magnates to the Right Socialist leaders, who seize with the greatest eagerness on any slanderous imputations against the USSR suggested to them by their imperialist masters. The pith and substance of this fraudulent propaganda is the claim that the earmark of true democracy is the existence of a plurality of parties and of an organized opposition minority. On these grounds the British Laborites, who spare no effort in their fight against Communism, would like to discover antagonistic classes and a corresponding struggle of parties in the USSR. Political igno-ramuses that they are, they cannot understand that capitalists and landlords, antagonistic classes, and hence a plurality of parties, have long ceased to exist in the USSR. They would like to have in the USSR the bourgeois parties which are so dear to their hearts, including pseudo-socialistic parties, as an agency of imperialism. But to their bitter regret these parties of the exploiting bourgeoisie have been doomed by history to disappear from the scene. . . .

Source 8 from Jessica Smith, editor, The USSR and World Peace: Andrei Y. Vyshinsky *(New York: International Publishers, 1949), pp. 41–46.*

8. Speech of Andrei Y. Vyshinsky Before the U.N. Security Council, October 4, 1948

The Soviet government deems it necessary to declare that the proposal of the three governments—the United States, Great Britain, and France—to put the question of the situation in Berlin on the agenda of the Security Council is devoid of any ground, since this question does not come within the competence of the Security Council and, therefore, cannot be discussed by the Security Council. The actions of the Soviet authorities against which the governments of the United States, Great Britain, and France are complaining were taken only in reply to the latter's actions. The Soviet authorities were compelled to take these actions as a result of the fact that the above three governments carried out in the western zone of Germany a separate currency reform which placed Berlin and simultaneously the entire Soviet occupation zone in a position in which the mass of money notes cancelled in the western zone threatened to pour into Berlin and the Soviet occupation zone of Germany.

Under these circumstances absolutely essential steps were taken in order to protect the economy of the Soviet occupation zone of Germany from disorganization with which it was threatened by the governments of the United States, Great Britain, and France, which refused to consider the interests of the national economy of this zone and its population. The steps taken in this connection by the Soviet military authorities are of a defensive nature against the offensive actions of the three governments which should bear the responsibility for the situation that has arisen in Berlin. Were it not for these offensive actions of the governments of the United States, Great Britain, and France, the Berlin question itself would not have existed, for there would have been no need for the above-mentioned defensive measures.

Beyond any dispute, the question of the Berlin situation is closely connected with the question of Germany as a whole, and the separation of the Berlin problem from the German problem as a whole would be utterly artificial and could result only in wrong decisions not in conformity with the real state of affairs. The placing of the Berlin problem before the Security Council would constitute a direct violation of Article 107 of the U.N.O. Charter which says that "Nothing in the present charter shall invalidate or preclude action in relation to any state which during the second World War has been an enemy of any signatory to the present charter, taken or authorized as a result of that war by the governments having responsibility for such action."

Thus the Berlin question which forms part of the German problem as a whole, in accordance with Article 107 of the U.N.O. Charter, is to be settled by the governments which bear the responsibility for the occupation of Germany and hence is not to be placed before the Security Council.

Indeed we have a whole series of very important international treaties and agreements with regard to Germany and in particular with regard to Berlin concluded among the four powers—the Soviet Union, the United States, Great Britain, and France. The most important of these international treaties are the agreements among the Great Powers concluded at the Yalta and Potsdam conferences and formulating the political and economic principles to be adhered to in the treatment of Germany. Among these documents we have such important ones as the declaration on Germany's defeat and the agreement on the quadripartite control machinery for Germany. These documents, which represent international treaties and agreements, were signed by the great powers that assumed supreme authority in Germany for the period during which Germany was to carry out the principal provisions of unconditional surrender. . . .

In their note addressed to the Secretary-General of the U.N.O. the governments of the United States, Great Britain, and France assert that the situation in Berlin endangers international peace and security. The note says that the above governments decided to place the Berlin problem before the Security Council so as to eliminate the threat to peace and international security, thus alleging that at present peace and international security are endangered in connection with the Berlin situation. Such statements are, however, unfounded and absurd. As stated in the Soviet government's note of October 3, the assertion of the United States government to the effect that the situation in Berlin endangers international peace and security does not correspond to the real state of affairs and is nothing but a means of pressure and an attempt to utilize the U.N.O. for achieving its own aggressive aims. . . .

[359]

Chapter 13

The Ideologies

of Cold War:

The Berlin

Blockade

(1948–1949)

Allegations concerning the threat of famine are similarly utterly untenable and constitute merely a method of hostile propaganda. At the request of the Soviet military administration in Germany, as far back as the beginning of July, the Soviet government decided fully to ensure the supply of all the Berlin population.

Marshal Sokolovsky in a published statement to several correspondents of Berlin newspapers, says that hundreds of thousands of tons of grain and more than ten thousand tons of fats were brought to the western sectors of Berlin from the Soviet Union. According to rather incomplete data, up to nine hundred tons of food products, not including coal, textiles, etc., are delivered daily from the Soviet zone into the western sector of Berlin by various means. Nothing endangers the supply of the occupation forces either.[15]

Thus all the above accusations against the U.S.S.R. have no basis, and all rumors of this kind are circulated for the sole purpose of fanning uneasiness, alarm, and war hysteria and by no means for settling the Berlin situation.

The note of the three governments also contains the groundless allegation that the Soviet authorities in Berlin permitted a minority of the Berlin population to try forcibly to overthrow the Berlin municipality. The Soviet government has officially refuted these unfounded accusations. The Soviet authorities in Berlin received from the Soviet government firm instructions, despite the discontent of the Berlin population at the situation that has arisen, to ensure peaceful conditions for the work of the local Berlin bodies, which was confirmed by V. M. Molotov, Foreign Minister of the Soviet Union, on August 30, during the interviews with the representatives of the United States, Great Britain, and France. The absurd nature of the above allegations with regard to the Soviet authorities is also evident from the fact that the disturbances mentioned in the note of the three governments occurred in those parts of Berlin which are not within the jurisdiction of the Soviet command and the responsibility for which is consequently not borne by the Soviet command but by the military authorities of the other three sectors of Berlin. Thus the assertion of the three governments similarly does not correspond to reality. Consequently the argument that the situation in Berlin endangers peace and security should also be regarded as utterly untenable. It should also be rejected as one which does not correspond to fact. On the basis of the motives I have expounded, we object to the proposal on the inclusion of the Berlin problem into the agenda of the Security Council.

15. About one month after the blockade started, the Soviets offered to supply West Berliners with food and fuel. To receive goods, however, citizens would have to go into the Soviet sector to secure new ration cards. The West claimed that few Berliners did so and that Vyshinsky's figures were exaggerated.

Source 9 from USSR Information Bulletin, *February 11, 1949.*

9. Reaction to Formation of
NATO, February 11, 1949[16]

Carried away by their aggressive plans for world domination, the ruling circles of the United States and Great Britain failed to understand that the so-called "new departure" of their policy, running counter to their recent obligations towards the USSR and other members of the United Nations, far from being able to increase the consolidation of their political and economic positions, will be condemned by all peace-loving nations, will be condemned by all the champions of the consolidation of universal peace, who constitute the overwhelming majority in all countries.

Main conclusions. First conclusion. The Soviet Union is compelled to reckon with the fact that the ruling circles of the United States and Great Britain have adopted an openly aggressive political course, the final aim of which is to establish by force Anglo-American domination over the world, a course which is fully in accord with the policy of aggression, the policy of unleashing a new war pursued by them.

In view of this situation the Soviet Union has to wage an even more vigorous and more consistent struggle against each and every warmonger, against the policy of aggression and unleashing of a new war, for a worldwide, lasting, democratic peace.

In this struggle for the consolidation of universal peace and international security the Soviet Union regards as its allies all other peace-loving states and all those numberless supporters of universal democratic peace who voice the genuine sentiments and aspirations of the peoples who bore on their shoulders the unbelievable burden of the last World War and who with every justification reject each and every aggressor and instigator of a new war.

Second conclusion. Everyone sees that the United Nations organization is now being undermined, since this organization, at least to a certain extent, hampers and curbs the aggressive circles in their policy of aggression and unleashing of a new war.

In view of this situation the Soviet Union has to struggle, with even more firmness and persistence, against the undermining and destruction of the United Nations organization by aggressive elements and their accomplices, and must see to it that the United Nations organization does not connive with such elements as is often the case now, that it values its authority more highly when the matter consists in giving a rebuff to those pursuing a policy of aggression and unleashing a new war.

---

16. **NATO:** the North Atlantic Treaty Organization (NATO), an anti-Soviet military alliance of the West formed in 1949.

Chapter 13

The Ideologies

of Cold War:

The Berlin

Blockade

(1948–1949)

QUESTIONS TO CONSIDER

Begin by analyzing the origins of the Cold War from the Western perspective. The 1946 speech by Winston Churchill has been nicknamed the "Iron Curtain Speech" because in it he coined that now-famous phrase. In Churchill's view, who started the Cold War? Why? What does he believe are the goals of the Soviet Union? In what ways does he see the Soviets attempting to accomplish these goals? What does Churchill believe the U.S. response should be? Why does he not think this will lead to World War Three? Churchill also compares the rise of Hitler in the 1930s to the situation in 1946. What lessons does he think should be drawn?

U.S. State Department official George Kennan's perspective differs somewhat from Churchill's. How does Kennan see the history of the Bolshevik Revolution as leading to a Cold War with the West? What, in his view, motivated the Soviet Union to choose this course in its foreign policy? More fundamentally, why did the Soviet Union evolve into a dictatorship, according to Kennan? Is this situation likely to change? And how vulnerable is that dictatorship? In response, what does Kennan appear to suggest the West should do? Why? Finally, what does Kennan believe were the ideological origins of the Cold War?

Kennan advocated an American foreign policy of containment, in which the United States would not seek to destroy the Soviet Union but would not allow its power and influence to expand beyond the limits already reached in 1947 (in other words, to "contain" the Soviets). Would Winston Churchill have agreed or disagreed with such a policy?

General Lucius Clay was the commander of U.S. military forces in Germany at the time of the Berlin Blockade. Why, in his view, did the Russians blockade Berlin? What does he believe was the role of currency reform in this crisis? Of the merging of the three Western zones? What does he suggest the West's response should be? Why does he see this response as important (see his ideas on the evacuation of American dependents)? What do you think Clay would have done, had he had his way? Finally, what can you infer from Clay's statements about his own view of the origins of the Cold War?

The Soviet perspective, predictably, is somewhat different. Or is it? What are the similarities between Zhdanov's ideas and Kennan's? Kennan saw why the Soviets clung to a dictatorship. How is Zhdanov's view of the West, especially of the United States, similar to Kennan's view of the Soviets, in terms of motivation and strategy? How does Zhdanov view the origins of the Cold War? How does his view differ from (or resemble) that of Kennan?

Andrei Vyshinsky gave the official Soviet interpretation of the Berlin situation. In his view, what started the crisis? What role did the West's currency reform play? In his eyes, how did the West behave?

The governments of the United States, Great Britain, and France attempted to bring the situation in Berlin before the United Nations Security Council, and, in essence, the speech excerpted as Source 8 is Vyshinsky's veto message. How does he deal with Western allegations against the Soviet Union? In other words, how does he wish the Soviet Union to be perceived?

The Berlin Blockade was still in progress when the article you read originally appeared in the *USSR Information Bulletin*. In the opinion of the article's author, what were the origins of the Cold War? Who started it, and why? Compare this article to Churchill's speech. In what ways are the two similar?

Once you have analyzed the Cold War from the U.S. and Soviet points of view, you should be able to draw some interesting conclusions. How did each side portray itself? How did each side portray the other? Are there similarities between those views? Differences?

Now, having analyzed the evidence from both sides, what do you think were the ideological origins of the Cold War?

EPILOGUE

President Truman chose to respond to the Berlin Blockade with an airlift. Cargo planes would leave West Germany to relieve the desperate population of Berlin. Truman saw the airlift, which was actually the idea of Britain's Air Commander Reginald White, as a way to put the Soviet Union on the defensive: if the Soviets did not interrupt air traffic, then Berlin would stand, a model of the West's postwar rebuilding efforts in the midst of communism. If, however, the Soviets chose to shoot down a U.S. military transport plane, then World War Three might begin right there. By adopting the Berlin airlift, Truman had moved his piece on the world's chessboard. The next move was up to Stalin.

At the time of the plan's inception, it was by no means clear that an airlift to supply a city of 2 million people would work. Yet fliers, principally from the United States and Great Britain, accomplished the near impossible. From June 1948 to September 1948,[17] U.S. and British pilots flew a total of 277,000 flights into Berlin, carrying flour, coal and other needed provisions. In all, 689 cargo planes flew roughly 124 million miles and airlifted 2.3 million tons of provisions to the city. On the average, these planes landed in Berlin every 8 minutes; a C-54 transport was unloaded every 45 seconds.

At Christmastime 1948, U.S. fliers wrote home for toys for the children of Berlin. Over 53,000 baskets of toys were distributed. One flier who regularly dropped chocolates and candy to Berlin children became an international hero.

This is not to say that Berliners grew fat on the airlift. Most of the

---

17. The Soviets, admitting defeat, lifted the blockade in May 1949, but the West continued to supply the city by air, stockpiling for another anticipated blockade, until September 1949.

Chapter 13
The Ideologies
of Cold War:
The Berlin
Blockade
(1948–1949)

coal brought in was for use in industries, power plants, and bakeries; the average Berliner received only about one teaspoonful of coal per day. Electricity usage was cut to three hours per day. The winter months of 1948–1949 saw considerable privation and, according to U.S. personnel, even some cases of starvation. Yet overall the Berlin Airlift was a success. The West did not withdraw from the city and world opinion shifted sharply against the Russians. Finally, on May 12, 1949, the Soviets lifted the blockade. The U.S. policy of containment seemed to have worked.

The Cold War, however, continued. Europe was divided into two hostile camps and mutual distrust did not abate, even after the death of Stalin in 1953. Indeed, even when Soviet Premier Nikita Khrushchev attacked Stalin's brutal excesses and announced that "peaceful coexistence" with the capitalist West was possible, the ideologies of the Cold War remained not far from the surface. When reformers in Hungary attempted to chart a more independent course for their nation in 1956, Russian troops invaded the country and crushed the reforms as brutally as Stalin would have done. Five years later, Khrushchev ordered a wall built between East and West Berlin, a physical structure symbolic of the Cold War itself.

As the situation in Europe stabilized, the Cold War spread to other parts of the world, notably Asia and Latin America. In 1949 a successful communist revolution took place in China, an event that ultimately spurred communists in North Korea and Vietnam to similar efforts. Although worldwide communism was by no means a monolithic movement directed from Moscow (at some periods, communists in various nations have been more suspicious of each other than of the West), during the 1950s the West experienced a renewed wave of fear, leading in the United States to the outrages of McCarthyism. In areas such as Korea and Vietnam, the Cold War became very hot indeed.

It would take a new generation of world leaders, leaders not so deeply influenced by the ideology of the Cold War, before anything close to a warming of East-West relations could begin. Even into the 1980s, a good deal of distrust remained. Given the strength and durability of the ideologies that had brought on the Cold War in the first place, it would have been naive to expect more from the leaders of the East and the West.

CHAPTER FOURTEEN

POWER, POLITICS,

AND RESOURCES:

OIL AND

THE WORLD ECONOMY

THE PROBLEM

From October 3–5, 1979, over one hundred participants gathered in Vienna, Austria to attend a seminar on future energy markets sponsored by the Organization of Petroleum Exporting Countries (OPEC). Nearly every Western nation was represented, as were most of the world's major oil companies and all of the principal oil-producing nations.[1]

Highlighted by frank and open discussions of problems facing the oil-producing and oil-consuming nations, the three-day seminar was marked by considerable tension under the surface amenities. The oil-importing countries of Western Europe and the United States[2] had seen the

price of oil jump from $1.80 per barrel in 1970 to almost $18 per barrel in 1979, a factor that threatened the economies of these industrialized nations. On the other hand, many OPEC members felt that oil prices should rise even higher to compensate for world inflation and for their rapidly dwindling reserves. Both sides, therefore, were experiencing a good deal of frustration, anxiety, and anger.

The 1979 Vienna seminar clearly represented a shift in world power and politics. In the late nineteenth century, the West had moved to undertake imperialistic ventures, acquire colonies, and dominate the world's resources and markets (see Chapter 8). Those impulses had obliged the countries of the world to draw closer together, to the benefit of the industrialized West. After World War Two, however, anti-imperialist impulses weakened the West's hold on these valuable resources and demonstrated how dependent the Western economies

1. The Soviet Union, the world's second largest producer of oil in 1970, was not invited. The United States was officially represented by Dwight R. Ambach from the U.S. embassy in Vienna.

2. By 1979 oil imports to the United States exceeded 8 million barrels per day, roughly 40 percent of its total oil consumption.

were on resources that few of them could produce themselves. Thus, a state of interdependence emerged wherein the West relied on the imports of natural resources and the non-West on Western manufactures. Yet unlike the "new imperialism" of the late nineteenth century, the West and the non-West now came to meet each other as equal powers in a shrinking and interdependent world—a new relationship that many in the industrialized West clearly did not relish.

By the outbreak of World War One in 1914, much of Western Europe and the United States had become industrialized. Increasingly, the economic health and standards of living in those nations depended on the manufacture and distribution of goods as well as on the extraction of raw materials to process and power the burgeoning factories. As we have seen in earlier chapters, the Industrial Revolution had altered Western demographic, social, and political trends; accelerated urbanization; changed relations between and composition of socioeconomic classes; and played a major role in the imperialist surge of the late nineteenth and twentieth centuries. Along with a general rise in the standard of living, industrialization also helped to bring on wars (the Spanish-American War of 1898 between the United States and Spain, for example), revolutions, and diplomatic crises. Industrialization contributed as well to new ways in which some Westerners thought about history, economics, and politics (Marxism is an excellent example). Finally, in the scramble for

world resources and markets, by the mid-twentieth century industrialization had helped to produce a world order in which nations and their national economies were more interdependent than ever before, locked together to help Western industries and nations prosper and grow.

Nowhere is this phenomenon better demonstrated than in the evolution of oil as the West's principal source of industrial energy. The early stages of the Industrial Revolution were powered by water, wood, and coal. Indeed, by 1925 coal still represented 81 percent of the world's primary energy consumption. This was a circumstance that greatly benefited Western Europe and the United States, where coal reserves seemed almost inexhaustible.

By the outbreak of World War One, however, it had become clear that oil would soon replace coal as the primary industrial power source. Further, it was recognized that oil, processed into gasoline, would be needed for the West's rapidly growing automobile industry, to say nothing of its military vehicles. This prospect presented a major problem for all the Western nations except the United States, where oil reserves were plentiful. Other industrialized countries would have to find their oil elsewhere.

Exploration for oil had been carried out in the United States, Russia, Indonesia, Latin America, and the Middle East since the late nineteenth century. In the Middle East, where it was thought—correctly, as it turned out—that large oil reserves existed, the British took an early lead. In 1901 a

British syndicate (which in 1909 became the Anglo-Persian Oil Company) was granted concessions by the Shah of Persia to search for and extract oil from much of present-day Iran. This action touched off fierce competition among European companies for rights to drill for oil elsewhere in the Middle East, and dealings with the ruler of that part of the Ottoman Empire, the Grand Vizier of Mesopotamia, were haphazard and unpredictable. To form a united front and to lessen competition, early in 1914 the three government-controlled oil companies—Anglo-Persian (British), Royal Dutch–Shell (Netherlands), and Deutsche Bank (German)—signed an agreement that they would unite in obtaining oil exploration and drilling concessions from the Vizier (in return for modest royalties) and would apportion the oil production among them. After World War One, the French replaced the defeated Germans in the triumvirate, and in 1928 (at the insistence of the U.S. government, which sought entry for American oil companies into the Middle East), the United States was admitted to this favored group.

Although the agreement of 1914 applied only to the oil reserves in what was to become Iraq, the pattern of relations between the industrialized nations and the oil-producing nations had been set, thus ushering in a new kind of Western imperialism in which the extraction of natural resources was more important than outright political control or national status. Government-controlled or government-aided oil companies in Western Europe and the United States collectively signed the same sorts of leases and royalty agreements with the new nations that emerged from the destroyed Ottoman Empire. The amount of oil extracted, the percentage of each company's share of that oil, and the market price essentially were determined by the companies themselves. In addition, the system of mandates set up by the treaties ending World War One tended to reinforce the power of the Western nations, especially Britain, in the Middle East.

As new oil reserves were discovered and exploited in Iraq (1928), Saudi Arabia (1938), and Kuwait (1946), this general method of operations continued to be followed. In the interval, as a result of World War Two, U.S. interest and influence in Middle East oil increased, owing largely to the fact that U.S. oil companies realized that their nation would emerge from the war for the first time as a leading importer of oil. By 1946 Middle East oil was controlled by seven Western companies (Exxon, Mobil, Texaco, Socal, Gulf, British Petroleum, and Shell), known collectively as the "Seven Sisters." By 1949 the Seven Sisters controlled 92 percent of the known oil reserves outside the United States, the Soviet Union, and Mexico; by 1960 they had revenues exceeding those of the governments of Great Britain, France, West Germany, and Italy combined. The oil tankers of the Seven Sisters accounted for 37 percent of the world's total shipping. These *multinational companies* (public and private corporations with headquarters in many nations) had grown as powerful as governments themselves. In truth, their power was immense, aided in part by Western governments committed to a steady flow of oil to the factories and automobiles of the West. By 1950 oil represented 27.4 percent of all world energy consumed and coal had slipped to 61.6 percent. Concessions, royalties, and oil prices were extremely low, further accelerating the switch from coal to oil.[3]

Clearly, the West was becoming dependent on imported oil. That dependence marked an important watershed in the relations between the industrialized West and the oil-producing areas of the non-West. In many ways, World War Two was that watershed. With the exception of the United States, all the Western nations were considerably weakened by the war. With the economies of these countries virtually in shambles, their overseas empires were extremely vulnerable to nationalistic movements that sought to throw off the reins of their former colonial masters. This nationalistic and anti-Western movement was especially strong in the Middle East.

At the same time that former colonies or protectorates were throwing off their imperialistic yokes, the West was becoming more dependent on imported oil from the Middle East. In 1948 Venezuela—at the time the world's third largest oil producer—demanded and received a new agreement with the oil companies whereby it would receive half of all oil profits from Venezuelan oil. This move caused the oil companies to rely even more on the cheaper oil of the Middle East, even as Western demand for oil was rapidly increasing. Indeed, between 1948 and 1972, noncommunist nations doubled their oil consumption every 6.5 years, rising elevenfold during that period.[4] Thus, in many ways the Middle East held the key to Western industrial growth and postwar prosperity.

Finally, the rise of the Cold War between the West and the Soviet Union caused the West to fear that Soviet intrusion into the Middle East would cut off the flow of oil to the West. However much the Western nations disagreed over the apportioning of Middle East oil among themselves, they were united in their desire to keep the Soviet Union out of the region's rich oil fields. To do that, the West believed, "friendly" governments (that is, noncommunist governments willing to deal favorably with Western oil companies) had to be propped up and uncooperative governments overthrown.

Meanwhile an increased sense of nationalism had led the Middle Eastern nations to the conviction that Western oil companies had taken advantage of them and that one style of Western imperialism had merely been replaced by another. In Iran, Prime Minister Dr. Muhammad Mossadegh (Mōs a DĒK) attempted to renegotiate concessions paid by the British-controlled Anglo-Iranian Oil

3. On November 1, 1950, Saudi Arabian light crude oil was selling for $1.75 per barrel and Texas crude oil for $2.51 per barrel, thus encouraging some U.S. companies to import oil rather than produce it domestically.

4. The statistics exclude the United States and Canada, where oil consumption tripled between 1948 and 1972.

Company (British Petroleum) and, failing that, in 1951 nationalized all the property of that company in Iran and expelled British diplomats from the country.[5] Fearful that this new spirit would spread throughout the Middle East, Western oil companies boycotted Iranian oil and in 1953, aided by British Intelligence and the CIA, overthrew Mossadegh and replaced him with the more amenable and pro-Western Reza Shah Pahlavi (the Shah of Iran, who ruled that nation until his own overthrow in 1979 by the Ayatollah Khomeini). The Shah signed a new agreement and oil exports flowed again from Iran.

Far from suffocating Middle East nationalism, however, the overthrow of Mossadegh very probably increased it, as it did anti-Western opinion and the growing determination of these nations to control their own oil reserves. In 1959, faced with unexpectedly large surpluses, the oil companies cut the price they were willing to pay for Middle East oil. The next year, five nations—Iran, Iraq, Kuwait, Saudi Arabia, and Venezuela—joined together to form OPEC in an effort to raise oil prices.[6] Actually the brainchild of Perez Alfonzo, Venezuelan Minister of Mines and Hydrocarbons, OPEC was an at-

tempt by these oil-producing nations to stand united against the cartel of oil companies that had been able to play the oil-producing nations off against each other. As Alfonzo stated, the 1959 price cuts constituted a "tactic of taking unfair advantage of the underdeveloped countries." Clearly a new spirit had emerged that combined nationalism with a realization of the underdeveloped nations' common interests.

To Alfonzo and other early OPEC leaders, raising oil prices was linked to control over the amount of oil extracted. The key, however, was the ability of the OPEC nations to act in concert, something they had not previously been able to do. In OPEC's first ten years, therefore, the rising tide of nationalism tended to work against a unified front and made the organization less than effective.[7] Even so, OPEC nations controlled over two-thirds of the world's known oil reserves; it was only a matter of time, if they could learn to work together, before OPEC's influence would be felt.

Several factors added to the increase of OPEC's prestige and power in the late 1960s and 1970s. In 1966, the U.S. Congress enacted the Environmental Protection Act, which restricted the burning of high sulfur coal and oil. Nations in Western Europe were also moving to meet the problems of sulfur-produced air pollution. These acts caused the West to become even more eager to purchase the high-quality oil of the Middle

---

5. In 1938, the Mexican government expropriated all foreign oil properties in that nation and created Petroleos Mexicanos (PEMEX), a government agency that took charge of oil production and marketing. In the 1940s, 'EMEX settled claims against it from the oil companies. By 1951, however, it was not clear that Mexican nationalization had been a success.

6. The original five OPEC nations subsequently were joined by Qatar (1961), Libya (1962), Indonesia (1962), United Arab Emirates (1967), Algeria (1969), Nigeria (1971), Ecuador (1973), and Gabon (1975).

7. Although OPEC could set production quotas (and therefore oil prices), it was the prerogative of each nation to agree to abide by those suggested quotas and prices.

East. Then, in 1969, the Libyan government of King Idris was overthrown by Colonel Muammar al-Qadhafi (Ka DA fē), who raised prices on Libyan oil without consulting OPEC and used the threat of boycott for his own political purposes. Some OPEC nations followed suit.

As the oil-producing nations began to sense their power and common interests, the Western oil companies did not stand united against them. In the urge to extract as much oil as they could, Western oil companies had abandoned their united front to make private deals with Middle East nations on pricing, the amount of oil to be extracted, and the number of non-Westerners who would be employed by the oil companies. Thus, as the nations of the Middle East were beginning to recognize their common advantages, the Western oil companies showed little inclination to unite against them.

In October 1973, Syria and Egypt invaded Israel, thus setting off the "Yom Kippur War." This Arab-Israeli war gave the Middle East nations the chance to test their newly found power. As a blow against Israel's allies (especially the United States), the Arab members of OPEC imposed an oil embargo on all nations, using concessions won in 1973 from the oil companies that host nations could determine the amount of oil extracted. Immediately oil prices shot up, from $3.63 per barrel in 1973 to $11.45 per barrel in 1974. Although the oil embargo formally ended in mid-March 1974, the OPEC nations, now fully aware of their own advantageous position, were able to hold

prices roughly at 1974 levels until the 1979 coup in Iran forced prices up again.

This was the situation the participants in the OPEC seminar faced when they gathered in Vienna in the month of October, 1979. Oil prices were already over $20 per barrel and rising.[8] It was too soon to tell whether the energy conservation measures of U.S. President Jimmy Carter would have much effect, and the wholesale shift to alternative energy sources seemed years away. In addition, the rapid industrialization of Japan meant that competition for oil would remain high (by 1970 Japan consumed 10 percent of the noncommunist world's total oil production). Finally, the U.S.-initiated treaty between Israel and Egypt of March 1979 had angered many in the Arab world and had increased anti-American sentiment in portions of the Middle East. In Vienna, therefore, great courtesy and deference mingled with an air of fear, anxiety, and distrust.

Your task in this chapter is to analyze the evidence in order to answer the following questions: How would you characterize the changing relationship between the industrialized West and the Middle East in the twentieth century? What were the problems faced by the West *and* the Middle East at the time of the Vienna meeting (1979)? What alternatives were open to the nations of the industrialized West and the Middle

8. The price of Saudi Arabian light crude continued to rise: $26 (January 1980), $32 (November 1980), finally to $34 (October 1981). Libyan oil, of a better quality and geographically closer to Western Europe, was even higher, peaking at $40 per barrel in January 1981.

East in 1979? Using your understanding of the history and the relationships between both regions, what do you think were the best alternatives for the West? For the Middle East? For both regions collectively?

SOURCES AND METHOD

The evidence in this chapter is extremely diverse, thus giving you the opportunity to use many of the techniques you have learned in analyzing the sources in earlier chapters.

Source 1 consists of excerpts from some of the formal addresses given at the 1979 Vienna seminar, with some biographical information on each speaker. Note that although almost all concerned parties (industrialized Western nations, major oil companies, and others) attended the seminar, no representative from either a Western government or one of the Seven Sisters was invited to speak; they were there principally as observers. As you examine each excerpt, ask yourself the following questions: Who is the speaker? What perspective does he represent (OPEC, oil companies)? How does he perceive the changing relationships among the Western governments, the oil companies, and the Middle East in the twentieth century? (You may have to infer this information from the speakers' remarks because few of them dealt with that question directly.) What principal problem does each speaker address? Does he offer a solution?

In completing your task, it would be helpful for you to divide the speakers at the Vienna conference into two groups: spokesmen for the oil-producing nations (Ortiz, Otaiba, Abdul-Karim) and those for the oil-consuming nations (Mabro, Montaigu, Akins). First, read carefully the remarks from the oil producers, making a list of major problems each speaker identifies. Note also if the speaker offers a solution to each problem. For example, Rene G. Ortiz identifies four major problems faced by oil-producing nations and offers what to him is an acceptable solution for each problem. What are the problems and their solutions?

As you read the speeches of other representatives of the oil producers, do they agree with Ortiz on the major problems? How many, for example, mention rapid depletion of reserves? Which speakers identify problems not mentioned by Ortiz? Are their proposed solutions the same as his?

As you examine each excerpt, keep in mind the ways in which each side perceives the other. What adjectives would you use to characterize those perceptions?

Source 2 offers nine sets of statistics. These figures are important for two reasons. For one thing, they can be used either to corroborate or refute the speakers' assertions. For example, one of the major points made by some of the speakers is that the industrialized West had grown dependent on OPEC oil. Do the statistics support this conclusion? Specifically, how do they do so (or not do so)? Another point made repeatedly was that oil was not a limitless natural resource but was being depleted at an alarming rate. Do the statistics bear out this warning?

Statistics can also be used to detect historical trends. For example, Table 2 surveys the oil production from 1860 to 1980 of the United States, the Soviet Union, and the OPEC nations. What historical trends appear? Has the balance of world oil production shifted? If so, when did that shift take place? According to the speakers, what might be some of the major results of that shift?

The last pieces of evidence, gathered as Source 3, represent Western perceptions of the oil situation and of the Middle East, drawn from selected U.S. news stories and editorial comments, an advertisement of a major multinational oil company (Mobil, one of the Seven Sisters), and British cartoons. Because all the concerned parties were not invited to speak at the OPEC-sponsored Vienna seminar, these sources are in-tended to give some Western views of the problem. How do these perceptions differ from those presented at the 1979 seminar? How is the industrialized West depicted? The oil companies? The Middle East?

As you examine and analyze the evidence, keep in mind the central questions you must answer. In what ways has the relationship between the industrialized West and the Middle East changed in the twentieth century? In turn, what problems has that changed relationship presented to the West? To the nations of the Middle East? As you identify these problems, it would be helpful if you divided them into two categories: the problems faced by the West and those faced by the Middle East. What problems confront the non-Western oil-producing nations? How does each side perceive the other's problems? How does each side react to these problems? You will find that the real issues often are expressed subtly or indirectly, so be prepared to infer answers.

THE EVIDENCE

Source 1 from OPEC and Future Energy Markets: The Proceedings of the OPEC Seminar Held in Vienna, Austria, in October 1979 *(New York: St. Martin's Press, 1981), pp. ix–x; 3–4; 9–12; 104–105; 134–138; 216–234.*

1. From the OPEC Seminar, Vienna, Austria, October 3–5, 1979

RENE G. ORTIZ[9]

Secretary General
OPEC

It is not for me . . . to comment on the issues raised in the course of the Seminar: the views of the distinguished speakers, as well as my own, are recorded in the following pages. I would like, however, to make the following observations. It must be clearly understood that OPEC Member Countries are not prepared to discuss the price of oil outside the OPEC forum, since this would mean surrendering their hard-won right to price an indigenous resource which belongs to them and to no one else: no industrialized country would even contemplate such an act of misguided altruism. In the case of OPEC Member Countries, especially, it would be suicidal, since the oil represents, for the overwhelming majority of them, the main marketable commodity they possess, the revenues from which are essential to the developement [sic] of their economies, which development, in turn, is vital if the producers are to emerge from their state of industrial backwardness *before* the oil runs out.

OPEC Member Countries are engaged in a race against time, and as things stand at present, we do not appear to be winning that battle. The rate of increase of real income from a barrel of oil export of the Middle East producers is already "below zero," due to inflation and dollar weakness, despite high production levels that are generating unneeded revenues. Obviously, unless producers can be assured of a reasonable rate of return on their foreign investments *above* the inflation rate the incentive to continue such high rates of production will simply disappear: the producers will conclude (indeed, some already have concluded) that oil left in the ground is the best investment for the future.

This attitude on the part of OPEC Countries is likely increasingly to harden in the face of rapid depletion of existing reserves, on the one hand, and the

9. **Rene G. Ortiz:** a chemical and industrial engineer from Ecuador who had held several posts in the Ecuadorian State Petroleum Corporation before representing his nation in OPEC, Ortiz was appointed Secretary General of OPEC in 1977. This selection is taken from his foreword to the seminar's published proceedings.

apparent unwillingness of the industrialized countries to exploit the potential for further exploration, on the other. Indeed, some of our Member Countries have already made it plain that further concessions will be tied to an undertaking on the part of the operators to invest more in exploration and secondary recovery techniques. But this is not all. The time is fast approaching when monetary remuneration alone will no longer be acceptable as payment for OPEC oil: technology transfer will become a mandatory part of the price. OPEC Countries will be compelled to take this step because all pleas to the industrialized nations to meet this vital need on our part have fallen on deaf ears.

MANA SAEED OTAIBA[10]

Minister of Petroleum
United Arab Emirates

I would like to touch on the pricing issue. We hear a lot about the prices of oil and how high OPEC Member Countries raise these prices. At our last Meeting in Geneva, in June, we increased the prices of oil to a level which brought the real purchasing power of the price of the barrel of oil to that of 1973/74. However, the reduction in the value of the dollar, the inflation which has eroded the purchasing power of our oil revenues, continues; since June Meeting the purchasing power of our oil revenues has dropped by more than 5 percent. Until our next Meeting in December, in Caracas, I am sure it will go down further. I cannot see an end to this trend in the foreseeable future, but there is a certain fact—that we are the losers in the end. Therefore, the price of oil should be linked to the cost of alternative sources of energy. The purchasing power of our oil revenues must be protected one way or another. This is our humble demand. We do not want more than that. I hope that the industrialized countries will understand our position and cooperate with us. OPEC is ready to enter into a constructive dialogue with the consuming countries in order to find a new order for the world economy.[11]

Before 1973 the industrialized countries used to price raw materials, including oil—and decided the volume of production from each commodity. The world economy was based on that fact which I regard as not justifiable. If I am the owner of a wealth, how can I accept that someone else, who is thousands of miles away from me decides the price of my national wealth and the quantities I should produce? It was an odd situation.

Since 1973, however, a group of developing countries have moved forward, put their hand on their national wealth and started pricing their oil, deciding its value and the production levels. Since we are looking for a new interna-

10. **Mana Saeed Otaiba:** from Abu Dhabi, United Arab Emirates, Otaiba held an M.Sc. and Ph.D. in Petroleum Economics from Cairo University and was the UAE's first Minister of Petroleum and Mineral Resources. He was appointed President of OPEC in 1978.

11. **new order:** i.e., a more equitable relationship between the industrialized West and the oil-producing countries.

tional economic order we have to allow the owners of the wealth to say their word. We, in OPEC, are doing our utmost in this connection—producing more than we need for our own development and financial requirements. This is purely in order to meet the world demand, to prove that we are indeed playing a constructive role in the world economy.

The United Arab Emirates, for example, produce 1.85 million barrels per day. We do not need this amount of oil, if we have to consider only our own requirements; we should produce something in the order of 500,000 barrels a day. But by producing at a level of 1.8 million we are exhausting our reserves, producing the wealth which should be kept for coming generations. Future generations will blame us for this and even the consumers' future generations will blame us as well, because we will not have enough to produce. I hope this constructive role which we are playing is appreciated by the consumers, and by the industrialized countries in particular. . . .

Dialogue is always the best way. If we do not have a dialogue then we shall be left with confrontation. Since the problem of supply and demand is becoming greater—we had it last winter and we shall have it again this winter—unless we sit around the table and try to understand the problems of one another, help one another, we might have to face a situation where we shall be confronting one another. I have to say, in an open manner, that if there is going to be another World War it will be an oil war. We have the Great Powers talking to each other and making SALTS[12], SALTS I and II—and maybe a SALT III. If *we* do not have oil SALTS here we might be faced with another World War on oil.

TAYEH ABDUL-KARIM[13]

Minister of Oil
Iraq

The sacrifices of OPEC assume a special importance because the members of the Organization are developing countries which find no economic and moral considerations to justify their making sacrifices in order to support the prosperity of more developed economies. Yet OPEC, by virtue of its sense of responsibility and belief in the importance of continued growth of the world economy, preferred to continue making these sacrifices in order to give the industrial countries time to rationalize[14] their consumption of oil, develop alternative sources of energy and review their whole attitude towards the Third World. It was hoped that the sacrifices of OPEC would be met by minimum concessions from the major industrial countries to establish a new,

12. **SALTS:** Strategic Arms Limitation Treaties.

13. **Tayeh Abdul-Karim:** a native of Iraq and a former teacher and attorney, Abdul-Karim was a Socialist and a member of Iraq's Revolutionary Command Council as well as Iraq's Minister of Oil and President of the Iraq National Oil Company, which took over oil production when Iraq nationalized its oil industry.

14. **rationalize:** probably "to ration."

just international economic order and by true efforts to limit wasteful consumption of oil, especially in the United States, which alone consumes more than 29% of world oil production.[15] But unfortunately, nothing of this was achieved. The major industrial countries met the sacrifices of OPEC with the escalation of their information campaigns, threats of military occupation of oil fields and continuous attempts to cause dissension among the developing countries. . . .

The industrial countries consume around 85% of world oil production and get a similar percentage from the exports of OPEC. The continuous supply of oil by OPEC to meet the fundamental needs of industrial countries must be met by many guarantees, foremost of which are the taking of serious measures by the industrial countries to limit their oil consumption and eliminate the character of waste in this consumption, developing alternative sources of energy in order to extend the life of world oil reserves as long as possible, and directing increasing proportions of oil production to noble uses as a raw material in industry. This will also make it possible to provide a fair percentage of production to meet the needs of developing countries. In spite of the fact that the major industrial countries recently announced programmes to curtail their consumption, the targets of these programmes are still below the level of our ambitions as oil exporters and are still characterized by political propaganda.

The second guarantee is to maintain the purchasing power of the revenue of the exported barrel at a fair level which takes into consideration, year after year, the need to raise the levels of income in the Member Countries at rates which provide the possibility of narrowing the wide gap between them and the levels of income in the industrial countries. The statistics of the World Bank show that the average per capita income in the Member Countries of OPEC was $956 in 1976 compared with $6,310 in the industrial countries (as defined by the said Bank), i.e., approximately seven times OPEC's average. . . .

The third guarantee which must be provided by the industrial countries is the support of endeavours to establish a new, just international economic order. As a first step towards achieving this target, we insist that the major industrial countries should immediately abandon their negative attitudes towards this matter and take the necessary measures to achieve the following aims within the framework of international economic cooperation:

1. Abolish the discriminatory and restrictive commercial policies.[16]

2. Guarantee the stabilization of prices of raw material exported by developing countries at just levels.

15. For the singling out of the United States, see Table 6 in Source 2.

16. This probably refers to trade policies that forced Middle East nations to trade great amounts of oil for Western manufactured goods, which remained at high prices.

3. Support the process of economic development in developing countries and facilitate the process of transferring modern technology to these countries at a fair price.

4. Reconsider the structure of the debts owed to them by the developing countries and reduce the burdens of servicing and repayment of these debts.

5. Facilitate the flow of capital to developing countries under conditions which are far from being exploitative.

6. Curb the practices of multinational [oil] companies in the Third World.

Finally, the major industrial countries must abandon the method of confrontation and provocation which they pursue towards OPEC, whether through the International Energy Agency or through the misleading information campaigns which have recently assumed serious dimensions, and the methods of political and military pressure and threats which reflect the remnants of the jaded colonialist mentality.

ROBERT MABRO[17]

Director, Middle East Centre
St. Antony's College
Oxford, England

But if you went through the speeches of politicians since 1973, the leading articles of the major newspapers, and the pronouncements of commentators, you would be led to believe that if OPEC pegged the price of oil, inflation, balance of payments deficits, unemployment, political instability, communist subversion, debasement of currencies and malfunctioning of the monetary system would all be cured. This cannot be so. All these ills require other remedies. The sooner governments of consuming countries, backed by a better-informed public opinion, decide to face these problems on their own merit, the sooner they forget the easy alibi of the price of oil, the sooner they devise specific policy packages which are relevant to the solution of these problems, the better off the world will be. Before engaging in a dialogue, for which I am sorry and saddened to report that officialdom in consuming countries is not ready, we might as well agree implicitly on a division of labour, leaving the administration of the price of oil to OPEC and leaving it to them to administer it, without political hindrance.

Governments of industrial consuming countries in this division of labour would have to take care of the other problems: inflation, the international monetary system, and all that. They are equipped for this task. Let us hope they will get on with it and spare us all the unconvincing excuses.

17. **Robert Mabro:** an economist who wrote extensively on the Egyptian economy and on oil production, Mabro was a pioneer in trying to bring the two sides together to talk about energy problems. His Middle East Centre was sponsored in part by OPEC.

ROLAND DE MONTAIGU[18]

President, Total American, Inc.

It is also an honour for me to be the only oil company representative asked to say a few words, although I belong to what used to be called the "Eighth Sister." We have yesterday and this morning heard all sorts of things about multinational corporations—that they are evil animals, greedy for profit. It is true that multinationals do not have a soul; it would be innocent indeed to imagine that one can get soul music out of them. Nevertheless, I must say a word in defence of the major companies, not only because they have fed me all these years, but because, when a job needs to be done, the companies—and probably only the companies—can do it. Everything that exists on earth has been done by companies or groups of individuals, and as jobs get bigger and bigger, companies, too, have to get bigger and bigger in order to do these jobs. They may be a necessary evil, but they are certainly not "unnecessary" as was pointed out yesterday. . . .[19]

Seen from the consumer point of view, during the many years in which I have been involved with Middle East oil, the . . . market value of oil has risen from a low of $1.30 per barrel in 1969 to the present figures, which range from $18 for the market crude to $40/b on some spot sales. When Mr. Ait-Laoussine talks of the great downward leap-frogging, I think it is worthwhile to observe that the rebates offered by certain producers in periods of glut never exceeded 25 cents, while the producing countries' income on the sale of an additional barrel was in the region of $12. This provided a considerable temptation for some countries to sell extra barrels. This has been the prevailing attitude among producers, with the exception of Saudi Arabia and Kuwait over the years, certainly from the end of the 1973 war until recently. There is now, however, among producing countries, a new, sober outlook with regard to the rate at which reserves should be exploited: production rates depleting reserves in one hundred years have been mentioned. I am totally incapable of addressing my mind so far ahead. If production rates were adjusted to that low level, chaos would follow. On the other hand, it is quite understandable that the real value of a barrel of oil should increase in a period when energy shortages are the topic of the day. . . .

With regard to alternative energies, industrialized countries have not done what they should have during the last five years. For fear of displeasing some voters, Governments do not provide the strong leadership required

18. **Roland de Montaigu:** a French geologist who had held several offices in Compagnie Francaise des Petroles (CFP) in Paris, Algeria and Canada. Although he was an officer at CFP when Algeria nationalized its oil industry in 1967, it appears that Montaigu was both liked and respected by the Algerians. **Total American, Inc.:** a French oil company located in Alberta, Canada.

19. Montaigu is probably referring to the remarks of Saudi Arabian Abdulhady Hassan Taher, who urged cooperation between OPEC's national oil companies and Western oil companies.

and projects seem to get bogged down in red tape and ill-guided ecology. Massive investment in alternative forms of energy requires high technology and some element of risk; every consuming country is a special case. In fact, only one country, the United States, has a variety of choices—and possibly because of that, no decision is reached. The investment required to create one million barrels a day of nonconventional oil is not yet known: it may be in the range of $20–$30 possibly $40 billion. The present high prices of crude oil, and the possibility of reduced supplies, will eventually motivate the American economy, and action will be taken to develop coal, synfuel, solar, etc.

Nuclear is a different kettle of fish: fears and mismanagement have rendered this form of energy unpalatable to—surprisingly enough—a large segment of the younger generation. In a sense, this is strange, as they are the ones who would suffer most if insufficient energy is available. Producing countries complain that inflation imported from consuming countries erodes their oil income. Everyone wants to reduce inflation, but this will be difficult to achieve at a time when consuming countries are having to pay more for imported energy while spending considerable sums to develop alternative sources of energy. So we shall have to live with a high rate of inflation and a very low rate of growth. Growth can only exist when there are increases in productivity. Unfortunately, the whole economic world is a little out of breath and seems to be incapable of knowing which way it wants to grow— or indeed, whether it wants to grow at all.

JAMES E. AKINS[20]

Former U.S. Ambassador to Saudi Arabia
Private Consultant

It is perhaps inevitable that we should talk about an "oil era" or an "oil age"—we are in the middle of it. But by any historical criteria this brief period cannot be considered an "age" or "era." Oil was discovered somewhat over a hundred years ago and the period of great use started during the First World War. The growth in consumption was rapid in the inter-war period, throughout and after the Second World War, reaching its apogee in 1973 when a leveling began. Current world oil consumption is around 65 million barrels/day and the production of conventional oil may not ever rise much above that level. It *could* do so if a handful of the oil producing countries in the Middle East decided to raise production to physical capacity quickly but this would advance the onset of the ultimate decline. In any case, the decline in production of conventional oil will almost certainly start before the end of

---

20. **James E. Akins:** entering the U.S. Foreign Service in 1954, Akins held senior posts in Rome, Paris, Damascus, Kuwait, and Baghdad. From 1973 to 1975, he was U.S. ambassador to Saudi Arabia. He retired from the Foreign Service to become a private consultant on international trade and oil, often working for OPEC nations.

this century and by 2025 will be of relatively little importance in the world total energy scene. . . .

This period we call "the oil age" will last, at the outside, only three or four human generations. The heart of the period, its golden years, is a scant thirty years from 1970–2000—only a bright flash on the chart of history. It may not even be as important a flash as we now think. It will be viewed by historians as a time when a handful of countries located in the Gulf basin were given immense wealth and potential for immense power. How these countries will ultimately be judged will depend on whether they use this opportunity to restore their proud and ancient civilizations or whether they waste their treasures and heritage through fear, greed and ignorance. One-third of this period of high potential has passed and the signs are not encouraging. No one could maintain that the decade has been well used. . . .

OPEC was formed in 1960 to prevent the oil cartel (that is, the major oil companies) from again unilaterally reducing oil prices. It was able to do this but did not succeed until 1972 in its other goal of restoring oil prices, in real terms, to the 1960 levels. OPEC was not taken seriously for a decade after its founding. The oil companies thought it was a joke. Most consuming countries thought it would soon collapse and disappear. The American State Department ordered its diplomats to ignore it; no official American had contact with OPEC as it was an "unauthorized organization," whatever that might mean. . . .

I have until now avoided mention of the ultimate consumer reaction: Invasion. It would be good if we could dismiss this concept as an aberration of an obsessively anti-Arab former Secretary of State, but it keeps coming back with distressing regularity. The idea was first launched by Henry Kissinger in early 1975; it was nurtured by him in background press interviews during the course of that year. It has reappeared this year repeatedly. The basic formulation is this: OPEC and the Arabs are our enemy; they have something we need, therefore we take it. It all sounds so simple.

A bumper sticker in California reads "We need oil, not scapegoats. Let's go for it." It shows an American eagle taking over an Arabian oil rig. A Columbia Broadcasting System television poll in late June asked a sample of Americans "Would you favor the use of force to take oil if our heating oil supplies are inadequate next winter?" Sixty-two percent responded, "Yes." I was on a CBS news program in June devoted to the same subject. I said I thought invasion would be catastrophic; that we would have to consider genocide, the expulsion of the native populations in the areas we took over, the drafting of American workers to man the entire oilfields, and even so we would have to count on the loss of oil from the Gulf for a period of two years. Only the Soviet Union would benefit. Unfortunately, the editors did not give the reasons for my view but switched immediately back to the announcer who said, "Other experts disagree," and then turned to Admiral Elmo Zumwalt, former American Chief of Naval Operations, who said that invasion would be simple. With modern technology, he said, we could get the oilfields restored within three months. An NBC program on September 4th examined at length the same subject, and although my views were given rather considerably greater play, the idea of invasion is far from being dismissed. . . .

The proponents of invasion do not bother with the moral aspects. Moral considerations never affected the considerations of Henry Kissinger. It is strange that they are still ignored in a country which has prided itself on the morality of its foreign policy, particularly under this President. We must admit frankly that few American politicians would allow moral consideration alone to block invasion, provided the answers to the other two questions were positive. . . . Admiral Zumwalt is probably right; we *could* take over the oilfields, we *could* occupy the Arabian Peninsula by ourselves or with Israel. But Zumwalt is dead wrong when he maintains that the fields could be occupied intact or that they could be put back into operation within three months. Kuwait, Saudi Arabia and others have spoken of the smoldering ruins that would greet any invader. As long as such warnings are taken seriously in the United States, there can be no question of invasion. The question here is: *Are* they taken seriously?

The Arab technicians of Aramco[21] have told me, and the Americans in the company have confirmed, that Saudi Arabian production could be utterly destroyed by Arabs currently employed by the company; the gathering stations, the pipeline nexuses, the refineries, the piers could be restored only after two years and then *only* with the cooperation of the local population. With the opposition of the local population, which certainly must be expected under such circumstances, the shut-off of oil would be indefinite. We must assume that the same is true of the Emirates, of Kuwait, of Iraq and of Iran. Furthermore, we must assume that *in extremis* the oilfields in the Gulf itself would be sabotaged, that the resulting flow of oil into the Gulf could cut off exports from the Gulf for an indefinite period. Mexico lost one well in the Gulf of Mexico and it has been burning for 3 months. How would the world handle the flow of 300 wells, most of which would catch fire? What then would the world do without this oil?

21. **ARAMCO:** Arabian American Oil Company. In 1933 Standard Oil of California (Socal) signed an agreement with Saudi Arabia, giving that company exclusive rights to extract oil from that region. In 1933 almost no one else suspected that Saudi Arabia had any oil, so the agreement went almost unnoticed. In 1936 Socal joined with Texaco in this venture, and in 1948 Exxon and Mobil, under pressure from the State Department, became part owners of what in 1944 had been renamed ARAMCO. ARAMCO worked closely with the U.S. State Department.

2. Statistics and Statistical Projections

TABLE 1   SELECTED INFORMATION ON OPEC NATIONS

OPEC Nations	Year Joined OPEC	Year Oil First Produced in Commercial Quantities	Known Oil Reserves 1980 (billions of barrels)	Annual Oil Production 1980 (millions of barrels)	Estimated Year of Oil Exhaustion[b]	Per Capita Gross National Product 1979	1980 Population (millions)
Saudi Arabia	1960	1938	165.0	3,613.50	2026	$9,500	8.1
Iran	1960	1913	67.5	606.63	2091	2,170	36.9
Kuwait	1960	1946	64.9	604.44	2087	18,390	3.0
Iraq	1960	1928	30.0	917.61	2013	2,730	12.8
Venezuela	1960	1917	17.8	790.96	2003	3,370	12.7
Qatar	1961	1949	3.6	172.28	2001	29,900	0.2
Libya	1962	1961	23.0	652.26	2015	6,960	2.6
Indonesia	1962	1893	9.5	575.61	1997	350	142.0
United Arab Emirates[a]	1967	1962	30.4	623.79	2029	24,360	0.8
Algeria	1969	1958	8.2	372.30	2002	1,720	18.0
Nigeria	1971	1958	16.7	748.25	2002	620	84.5
Ecuador	1973	1918	1.1	74.46	1995	1,100	7.3
Gabon	1975	1957	0.5	63.88	1988	5,250	0.6

[a]Includes Abu Dhabi, Dubai, Sharjah, Ras Al-Khaimah, and Umm Al Qaymayn.
[b]Based on known reserves in 1980 and constant production at 1980 levels. By 1987 additional reserves had been discovered in Saudi Arabia, Kuwait, and Iraq and the years of oil exhaustion had been recalculated in other nations as well.
Source: Compiled from statistics in Albert Danielsen, *Evolution of OPEC* (San Diego: Harcourt Brace Jovanovich, 1982).

TABLE 2   AVERAGE DAILY OIL PRODUCTION, UNITED STATES, U.S.S.R.,
OPEC, AND TOTAL WORLD, 1860–1980
(MILLION BARRELS PER DAY)

Year	United States	U.S.S.R.	OPEC	Total World
1860	0.000	0.000	0.000	0.001
1870	0.014	0.001	0.000	0.016
1880	0.072	0.008	0.000	0.082
1890	0.126	0.079	0.000	0.210
1900	0.174	0.208	0.006	0.409
1910	0.574	0.193	0.030	0.898
1920	1.214	0.070	0.084	1.887
1930	2.460	0.349	0.659	3.868
1940	3.707	0.610	1.004	5.890
1950	5.407	0.748	3.432	10.419
1960[a]	7.055	2.943	8.800	21.026
1970	9.648	6.976	23.408	43.210
1980[b]	8.597	11.720	26.890	59.455

Sources:
1860–1950, American Petroleum Institute, *Petroleum Facts and Figures, 1971 ed.*, pp. 548–557.
[a]1960–1970, Central Intelligence Agency, *Handbook of Economic Statistics*, Washington, D.C.: 1979, p. 135.
[b]1980 (1979), U.S. Department of Energy, *Monthly Energy Review*, August 1981, pp. 88–89.

TABLE 3   AVERAGE POSTED PRICE AND PERCENTAGE CHANGE IN
PRICE OF SAUDI LIGHT CRUDE OIL, 1970–1980

Date	Average Posted Price *(dollars per barrel)*	Year-to-Date Percentage Change
1970	1.80	0.0
1971	2.23	24.0
1972	2.48	11.1
1973	3.63	46.3
1974	11.45	215.7
1975	12.18	6.4
1976	12.13	−0.5
1977	12.40	1.0
1978	12.70	2.4
1979	17.26	35.6
1980	28.67	66.1

Source: Exxon, *Middle East Oil*, 2nd ed., New York: 1980, p. 25.

TABLE 4 RELIANCE OF INDUSTRIALIZED NONCOMMUNIST NATIONS ON IMPORTED OIL, 1980

Nation	Crude Oil as Percentage of Total Energy Consumption[a]	Percentage of Total Energy Consumption that Is Imported Crude Oil	Imported Crude Oil as Percentage of Total Crude Oil Consumption
United States	43	17	40
Western European	53	44	82.5
Japan	68	68	100

[a] Total energy consumption also includes coal, natural gas, hydropower, nuclear power, and synthetics.
Source: *British Petroleum Statistical Review of the World Oil Industry, 1980.*

TABLE 5 SOURCES OF IMPORTED CRUDE OIL FOR INDUSTRIALIZED NONCOMMUNIST NATIONS, 1979
(percent)

Nation	Persian Gulf	Africa	Latin America	Indonesia	OPEC Nations
United States	28.4	31.1	11.8	5.0	76.3
Western European	48.0	14.9	4.2	0.1	67.1
Japan	69.4	0.3	0.1	13.6	83.4

Source: Central Intelligence Agency, *International Energy Statistical Review,* August 20, 1980, p. 4.

TABLE 6 TEN LEADING PETROLEUM CORPORATIONS IN NONCOMMUNIST NATIONS, 1980

Corporation	Nation	Net Sales *(billions of U.S. dollars)*
Exxon[a]	United States	103.1
Royal Dutch–Shell[a]	Netherlands-Britain	79.4
Mobil[a]	United States	59.5
Texaco[a]	United States	51.2
British Petroleum[a]	Britain	49.5
Standard Oil of California (Socal)[a]	United States	40.5
Standard Oil of Indiana	United States	26.1
Ente Nazionale Idrocarburi	Italy	25.0
Gulf Oil[a]	United States	22.3
Cie. Francaise des Petroles	France	22.3

[a] Member of the Seven Sisters.
Sources: "It's OPEC's Turn to Worry Now," *Fortune,* vol. 103, May 4, 1981, p. 47; "The Year the Red Ink Flowed Deeply," *Business Week,* July 20, 1981, p. 86.

TABLE 7   UNITED STATES ENERGY DEMAND AND SOURCES OF SUPPLY, 1965–2000

	1965	1979	1990	2000
ENERGY SOURCE	*(percentage distribution)*			
Nuclear	—	3	8	11
Hydropower and other	4	4	6	6
Coal	22	19	24	31
Gas, domestic production	30	25	18	15
Oil, domestic production	35	27	18	17
Synthetics	—	—	2	9
Oil and gas imports	9	22	24	11
Total	100	100	100	100
TOTAL OIL EQUIVALENT DEMAND				
Million barrels per day	26	39	41	46
Billion barrels per year	9.5	14.2	15.0	16.8

Source: Figures for Tables 7 through 9 have been adapted from Exxon, *World Energy Outlook*, December 1980, pp. 31, 33, and 35.

TABLE 8   EUROPEAN ENERGY DEMAND AND SOURCES OF SUPPLY, 1965–2000

	1965	1979	1990	2000
ENERGY SOURCE	*(percentage distribution)*			
Nuclear	1	3	11	16
Hydropower and other	9	8	8	8
Coal, domestic production	39	16	16	15
Gas, domestic production	2	12	10	8
Oil, domestic production	2	9	12	10
Oil imports	44	46	28	24
Gas and coal imports	3	6	15	19
Total	100	100	100	100
TOTAL OIL EQUIVALENT DEMAND				
Million barrels per day	18	27	32	37
Billion barrels per year	6.6	9.9	11.7	13.5

TABLE 9   JAPANESE ENERGY DEMAND AND SOURCES OF SUPPLY, 1965–2000

	1965	1979	1990	2000
ENERGY SOURCE	*(percentage distribution)*			
Nuclear	—	4	10	18
Hydropower and domestic fossil fuels production	34	8	8	8
Oil Imports	60	73	54	43
Gas and coal imports	6	15	28	31
Total	100	100	100	100
TOTAL OIL EQUIVALENT DEMAND				
Million barrels per day	38	7.5	9.5	11.5
Billion barrels per year	1.1	2.7	3.5	4.2

Source 3 from the New York Times, *October 17, 1979; October 26, 1979;* Time, *October 29, 1979;* Newsweek, *February 4, 1980;* Punch, *October 24, 1979; November 14, 1979.*

3. Western Media Accounts

Editorial, "A Gas Tax or Deeper Trouble Still," *New York Times*, October 17, 1979

Already worried by the cost of oil, Americans had better worry some more. Libya and Iran have raised their prices 7 cents a gallon and other exporters will probably follow. What's more, supplies are so tight and the major producers are so reluctant to accommodate importers that even a recession is unlikely to relieve the pressure. Only a crash conservation effort—the kind Congress has bitterly resisted—can save the country from runaway energy inflation.

The pretext for the latest increase in price is the high cost of oil on the "spot" market. Once the world markets settled down after the Iranian crisis, the spot price fetched for individual tanker loads was widely expected to fall to the $23-a-barrel average charged by OPEC. But spot prices have remained well above $35, probably because refiners are stockpiling supplies against the *next* crisis. Given such demand, the exporting nations are understandably looking to capture some of the windfall.

If the spot price alone were the problem, the process would be self-limiting: stockpilers would eventually meet their goals and the spot prices would fall. But a more ominous force is at work. Saudi Arabia, Kuwait and Venezuela have all announced plans to cut production in the near future. They may or may not mean what they say. But with Iran unable to keep exports flowing smoothly, the threat of cutbacks by other major producers must be taken seriously. At best, the Libyan-Iranian price rise will be the last shock until spring. But it may also trigger another chain reaction of price increases and supply cutbacks, limited only by the fears of the more conservative Arab exporters about political and economic instability in the West.

The United States would have some room to maneuver if in 1973–74 it had adopted strong incentives for American conservation and production. Now there is almost no room. President Carter's proposed synfuels program couldn't produce a drop until 1985. Decontrol of domestic oil will slow the decline of production at home, but it can hardly reduce dependence on foreign supplies. The rightly popular kinds of oil conservation—incentives to insulate buildings, to produce more efficient automobiles, to generate power and heat together and to harness solar energy—*can*, cumulatively, make a big difference over the years. But such progress will be measured in inches. Another Great Depression would certainly help. Needless to say, a victory over OPEC achieved by the collapse of Western living standards would be no victory at all.

The only practical way that the United States can gain a restraining influence on the oil prices charged abroad is through large and rapid changes in the way Americans consume fuel. Some immediate gain can be achieved by accelerating the conversion of oil-fired power plants to coal. A similar benefit (without similar consequences for air quality) could be achieved by reforming utility rates to reflect the high cost to the nation of producing electricity from oil. But the most promising and least explored route to reducing oil imports now is a tax on gasoline.

Gasoline represents about 40 percent of all oil consumed in the United States. A gasoline tax that discouraged demand by 10 percent would reduce oil imports by three-quarters of a million barrels a day. It would take a $1-a-gallon tax to induce that much conservation. But larger taxes than that have still left life tolerable for Europeans. And, what is most promising, the burden of such a gas tax on the cost of living could be nullified by reducing other taxes dollar for dollar. State sales taxes and Federal withholding taxes are prime candidates for reduction. Those who absolutely need to drive would save enough on other taxes to afford it. Those able to save gasoline would have extra money to spend on other goods.

Congress brushed aside President Carter's 1977 proposal for a gas tax. The American people, most politicians reckon, are less willing to accept a tax on auto power than a tax on mothers' milk. Perhaps they are right; perhaps Americans are too benighted to pay themselves instead of paying Colonel Qaddafi and the Ayatollah. But it would be salutary to take a vote and find out for sure.

Leonard Silk, "How to Curb OPEC's Power," *New York Times,* October 26, 1979

The problem of restraining the power of the Organization of Petroleum Exporting Countries urgently demands a solution. Instead of growing feeble with time and breaking down, as some free-market economists had predicted, the oil cartel appears to have learned how to exploit its monopoly-exporting position for all it is worth. Instead of waiting for "accidents," such as the Arab-Israeli war or the Iranian Revolution, to disrupt supply and put intense pressure on the price of oil, nation after nation in OPEC has learned to be careful to restrain supply to keep prices and earnings rising.

Thus, with better communication among its members and better understanding of how to manipulate price by controlling supply, OPEC looks stronger than ever—and the West weaker.

Formerly, Saudi Arabia, as the largest producer, with the greatest reserves and the least need for extra income in the short-run, was the cartel master. But now that other countries have learned to increase their take by controlling supply, the Saudis have less power to run the cartel. Other nations are forcing the pace of price increases by putting more oil into the spot market, where the scramble for short supplies drives prices up even faster.

Because the power of OPEC is the power of each member to control production, within its borders, there is no way that the United States or other oil-importing countries—without resorting to war or clandestine subversion and violence—can make OPEC members produce more oil than they believe is in their self-interest.

The simplifying axiom of economics that a monopolist will seek to maximize profits over time by restricting supply appears to fit OPEC to a T. All the pleading in the world will not avail, but will only convince the monopolist of the strength of his position.

The United States has tried that approach where it thought it would work. President Carter has had heavy correspondence with Saudi leaders going back to late 1976, before he was sworn in as President, and the contents have been kept confidential. The President sent James Akins, a former American Ambassador to Saudi Arabia who has been highly sympathetic to the Saudis, to Riyadh to talk oil prices with them. The United States has exported vast quantities of military goods and expertise to the Saudis.

In return, the Saudis have portrayed themselves, and been portrayed by the United States Government, as "price moderates," who have tried to hold OPEC oil prices down—while restricting their own output and deciding not to expand their oil capacity, which was the only way they could have held prices down.

Similarly, the United States sought to win moderation from Shah Mohammed Riza [sic] Pahlevi of Iran, before he was deposed, by sending him sympathetic ambassadors and even greater quantities of arms, without noticeable restraining effect on the oil price. The Ayatollah Ruhollah Khomeini appears to be beyond the reach of such friendly persuasion.

Short of war, is there any way for the United States to shield itself from excessive dependence on OPEC and to curb that cartel's monopoly power? Threatening to impound the bank accounts or other assets of Arabs in the United States would do no good because, as Prof. Maurice A. Adelman of the Massachusetts Institute of Technology observes, the impounding of huge sums would have serious, possibly disastrous, repercussions as other foreign-exchange holders feared for the safety of their deposits.

The tax on so-called "windfall" oil profits, which is a misnomer for an excise tax on domestic oil production, will have no effect on OPEC, whatever it may do to redistribute income from American oil producers to some American consumers. Indeed, the net effect of the tax may be to reduce American oil investment and development, thereby increasing United States dependence on OPEC and other foreign production.

A more effective approach would be to impose an ad valorem tariff on oil imports, levying a tax on oil from abroad proportional to the price charged for that oil. Since a higher price would result in a higher tax, this would shift the incentive for American companies from producing abroad to producing at home. It would also start to capture the monopoly profits of OPEC for the United States Treasury, to be distributed to Americans.

When the United States oil price reaches the world market level, as it will under Mr. Carter's decontrol plan, further efforts by the OPEC monopoly to increase prices would increase taxes and reduce their sales below the profit-maximizing point. They would finally have an incentive to reduce prices to hold onto the huge American market, especially if, in the longer run, greater price incentives for energy conservation and production changed the oil supply and demand situation adversely for OPEC.

From *Time*, October 29, 1979

In Concord, N.H., it took the form of an automobile "honk-in" outside Jimmy Carter's re-election campaign office. In Nashville, a 500-lb. pig with BIG OIL painted on its side was led to city hall to munch slops from a dish labeled AMERICAN WEALTH. In Washington, D.C., elderly citizens bused in to join a picket line outside the American Petroleum Institute.

In more than 100 cities and towns in 35 states last week, hundreds, and in some cases thousands, of demonstrators joined in the biggest protest ever against what the country is targeting as "Big Oil." They voiced fears of a winter of low temperatures and high fuel costs, passed out "Big Oil Discredit Cards" and waved banners declaring, "I don't want to freeze in the dark." For most, the principal peeve was not gasoline prices or petroleum industry profits but the 60% rise in the cost of heating oil in the past 2½ years.

Whether justified or not, the Big Oil protest, which was sponsored by a number of diverse labor and political groups, came at an odd time. As it happened, the most visible oil price gougers last week were not the oil companies but some of the more militant price hawks in the Organization of Petroleum Exporting Countries. Iraq, Libya and Iran all announced boosts of 10% or more in the overall cost of their crude, and other producers seem likely to follow suit. What really alarmed oil consumers was that the Libyan and Iranian rise, like that announced by Mexico a week before but unlike those announced by Iraq or earlier by Kuwait, broke through the $23.50 per bbl. price the cartel set in June as a "ceiling" for at least six months. . . .

The dismal outlook was spelled out in blunt terms last Thursday by Jimmy Carter. Addressing delegates to a national energy conference, the President warned that "in the future, supplies are going to be shorter and prices are going to be higher." He added: "My own judgment is that OPEC is probably producing at a maximum level, and the tendencies are toward reduced production."

This tight balance means that the consuming countries can do little but swallow further price increases and almost nothing at all to ward off the possibility of future shortages. Last week the Senate approved and passed to the House Carter's stand-by gasoline rationing plan, which now seems certain to become law; even so, it can only be used in times of severe shortages. The President also agreed to support congressional moves to grant funds to help middle- and lower-income people pay their higher energy bills. A plan approved by the Senate Finance Committee last week would extend tax credits for high home heating costs to 9 million families with incomes of $22,000 a year or less; they would get an average credit of $62 a year, though it would be available only to homeowners using high-cost heating oil or natural gas from Canada or Mexico.

The main concern in Washington now centers on just what will happen at the oil cartel's next price meeting, to be held in Venezuela in December. Last week the current president of OPEC, the Oil Minister for the United Arab Emirates, said that he personally would prefer that there be no formal increase, but it seems much more likely that the militant producers will push through some rise, perhaps to the $25 or $26 level.

As worrisome as the price situation is the fact that the OPEC countries are once again speaking openly of wielding the "oil weapon" for geopolitical purposes. In his Thursday address, Carter buttressed a call for greater emphasis on conservation with a warning that the U.S. must be able to protect itself from nations "like Libya, who in time of crisis cut back on production for political punishment, or harassment, or perhaps even blackmail."

In fact, the cutback weapon was being waved last week by other, more influential, OPEC governments. Iraq's President Saddam Hussein said in a Baghdad speech that the Arab world is "threatened by fragmentation more than ever before," and declared that the threat of a new oil embargo would remain the Arabs' chief weapon against their enemies. Yamani himself did not hesitate to drop some hints of a direct link with U.S. Middle East policy. Said he: "If we have peace in the area, you will be amazed at how many beautiful and healthy results you can get from that, including in the field of oil." Translation: the cost of crude oil will increasingly be reckoned in terms of diplomatic cooperation as well as dollars.

Advertisement from *Newsweek*, February 4, 1980. Reprinted with permission of Mobil Corporation.

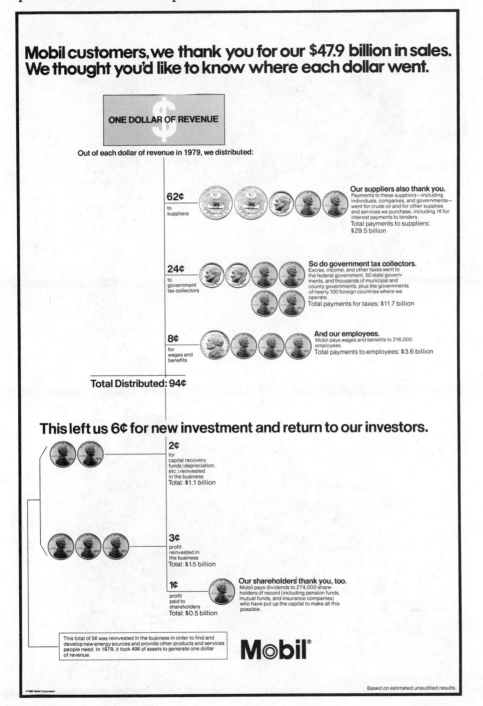

Mobil customers, we thank you for our $47.9 billion in sales. We thought you'd like to know where each dollar went.

ONE DOLLAR OF REVENUE

Out of each dollar of revenue in 1979, we distributed:

62¢ to suppliers

Our suppliers also thank you.
Payments to these suppliers—including individuals, companies, and governments—went for crude oil and for other supplies and services we purchase, including 1¢ for interest payments to lenders.
Total payments to suppliers: $29.5 billion

24¢ to government tax collectors

So do government tax collectors.
Excise, income, and other taxes went to the federal government, 50 state governments, and thousands of municipal and county governments, plus the governments of nearly 100 foreign countries where we operate.
Total payments for taxes: $11.7 billion

8¢ for wages and benefits

And our employees.
Mobil pays wages and benefits to 216,000 employees.
Total payments to employees: $3.6 billion

Total Distributed: 94¢

This left us 6¢ for new investment and return to our investors.

2¢ for capital recovery funds (depreciation, etc.) reinvested in the business
Total: $1.1 billion

3¢ profit reinvested in the business
Total: $1.5 billion

1¢ profit paid to shareholders
Total: $0.5 billion

Our shareholders thank you, too.
Mobil pays dividends to 274,000 shareholders of record (including pension funds, mutual funds, and insurance companies) who have put up the capital to make all this possible.

This total of 5¢ was reinvested in the business in order to find and develop new energy sources and provide other products and services people need. In 1979, it took 49¢ of assets to generate one dollar of revenue.

Mobil®

© 1980 Mobil Corporation

Based on estimated unaudited results.

Cartoons from *Punch*, October 24, 1979; November 14, 1979. Reproduced by permission.

"Those in favour of the new Islamic constitution raise their hands—those against, wave what's left."

"It's fool-proof. We use the money from the price increase to buy up all the BP shares."

QUESTIONS TO CONSIDER

Remember that your central task is to analyze the evidence in order to answer the following four questions: How would you characterize the changing relationship between the industrialized West and the Middle East in the twentieth century? What were the problems faced by the West and by the Middle East at the time of the Vienna seminar (1979)? What alternatives were open to both sides in 1979? What were the best alternatives for the West? For the Middle East? For both regions collectively?

Question 1 is intended to provide you with sufficient historical background to answer the subsequent questions. Yet almost immediately you will recognize a major problem: only one speaker, James Akins, dealt directly with the historical background of the situation. Therefore, you will have to *infer* how both OPEC speakers and speakers from the industrialized West perceived the changing relationship between the two groups in the twentieth century. For example, Otaiba twice referred to what he called a "new international economic order." By inference, what did he see as the "old order"? What was his opinion of it? Review the statistics and chapter introduction. To what, precisely, was Otaiba referring? Using all the material at your disposal, you should be able to explain how the relationship between the industrialized West and the Middle East changed in the twentieth century, and why. What were the roles of the Western governments? The Western oil companies? When

did the relationship change? What factors were responsible?

Questions 2 and 3 can best be answered by listing the problems and alternatives mentioned by the Vienna speakers and by checking these statements against the statistics. What do the OPEC speakers see as the principal problems (that is, what problems are mentioned by all or most of the speakers)? For example, many of the speakers refer to "inflation" as a major problem confronting both the West and the OPEC nations. According to the OPEC speakers, what were the causes of this inflation? Who was most hurt by it?

As you identify each problem mentioned by OPEC speakers, consult the statistics. How do (or do not) the statistics reflect that problem? For example, several speakers claimed that the industrialized noncommunist nations were insatiable in their appetite for more and more oil. Do statistics bear this out? On another note, do statistics support the contention that OPEC oil is being rapidly depleted? Once you have identified problems noted by OPEC speakers and then checked the statistics to corroborate those claims, list the solutions suggested by OPEC speakers. Are the speakers in agreement on pricing, exploration, and similar issues?

Having identified and analyzed the problems and suggested solutions from OPEC's point of view, now do the same for the speakers from the oil-consuming nations (here you should include the Western newspaper accounts and cartoons to get a fuller picture). How different is this group's perceptions from those of the OPEC speakers?

The newspaper accounts can be seen as reflecting the opinions of intelligent Americans. How do they portray OPEC? The oil companies? The United States government? What do they see as the problems? The solutions? The advertisement by Mobil was designed to appeal to an American audience. Why did Mobil choose the type of advertisement it did? What was its main theme? The *Punch* cartoons are intended to show Western perceptions of the Middle East. How do they portray people of the Middle East? How might this portrayal have affected Westerners' view of the problems? The solutions?

Now you are ready to deal with the fourth question, which asks you to project the paths the industrialized West and the OPEC nations should follow from now on. Up to this point in your study of history, you have not been asked to use your understanding of the past to devise strategies to deal with specific contemporary problems. Indeed, many historians believe that this should not be their task at all, but that they should be concerned only with an-

alyzing and understanding those trends and events that have already happened. Yet several governments and private corporations (the multinational oil company ARAMCO, for example) actually employ historians to help policymakers reach decisions. Based on their understandings of the past as well as of other cultures and key individuals, these historians create what are known as *scenarios*, projections of what may happen if certain policies are pursued.

In this chapter you are not asked to produce scenarios. Your task instead is to use your understanding of history and the skills you have acquired to draw up a set of alternatives that the oil-producing and oil-consuming nations might realistically pursue. What are these alternatives? What might be the results if each is adopted? To be sure, history is not an exact science and should not be thought of as a certain predictor of the future. Nevertheless, an understanding of the past can help us better to understand the present as well as to perceive the range of possibilities open in the near future.

EPILOGUE

The period following the 1979 Vienna OPEC conference was one of considerable tension and instability in the Middle East, a situation that was to have serious ramifications in the West. Barely one month after the Vienna meeting, approximately 500 Iranian youths, angered by the sanctuary given to the deposed Shah by the United States and excited by the anti-

American diatribes of the Ayatollah Khomeini, occupied the U.S. embassy in Teheran and held more than fifty American diplomats and embassy personnel for over a year. An ill-fated attempt by the Carter administration to rescue the hostages only deepened the chasm between the U.S. and Iran.

Because the uninterrupted flow of oil to the West depended on political stability in the Middle East, Western nations watched in shock and horror as the political situation in the Middle

East deteriorated. In 1980 war broke out between Iran and Iraq, with each nation trying to hurt the other by destroying oil-drilling equipment, refineries, and tankers in the Persian Gulf. Efforts by the United States and its Western allies to keep the sea lanes open resulted in incidents that only heightened tensions, the most unfortunate being the mistaken shooting down of an Iranian passenger jet on July 3, 1988, with a loss of nearly 300 civilian lives.

Indeed, the West increasingly was drawn into the unstable situation in the Middle East. In 1983 over 200 U.S. Marines were killed in a terrorist attack on their headquarters in Lebanon. In 1986 relations between Libya and the United States collapsed completely and, in a response to the bombing of a West Berlin nightclub, President Ronald Reagan sent U.S. bombers into Libya to retaliate against what the U.S. regarded as Libyan-inspired terrorist activity. Yet, dependent as it was on Middle East oil, the West found withdrawal from the region unthinkable.

As the Middle East remained unstable during the 1980s, oil prices began to decline from their 1981 high points. Alternative sources of energy in the West were beginning to have some effect on oil imports. By 1984, for example, Western Europe was producing more than 8 percent of its power by nuclear energy, the equivalent of over 104 million tons of oil. Oil fields in Alaska, Mexico, and the North Sea also began producing at full capacity, thereby lessening the West's reliance on OPEC. Lack of unity among the OPEC nations themselves created an oil "glut," causing many people, especially in the United States, to forget that oil was a finite energy source. Some oil-producing nations allowed prices to fall, reasoning that they could grab a larger share of the oil market; others continued to produce in large quantities simply to maintain their revenues. Finally, OPEC nations themselves came to appreciate the fact that the inflation rate in the West caused by high oil prices was hurting them, too, especially when they sought to buy goods and services from the West at inflated prices. In short, even as the Middle East situation remained terribly unpredictable, oil continued its flow to the West.

Today the citizens of the West live in an increasingly shrinking world, one far different from the world of their grandparents. Frustration and anger with the Middle East continues. Yet the two regions are almost permanently interlocked, with the oil-producing nations of the Middle East investing profits in Western banks, stock exchanges, corporations, and real estate and importing over $63 billion annually from the industrial West and Japan. Similarly, Middle East anger at Western "imperialists" remains in every nation of the region. Yet the economies—and governments—of these very nations are shored up by Western oil customers. Indeed, as the world continues to shrink, it is the responsibility of all its citizens to recognize the interdependence of nations, regions and peoples, and to live both sanely and responsibly on the ever-smaller planet.

Text acknowledgments continued from page ii.

Page 68: Table reprinted from John D. Post, "Climatic Variability and the European Mortality Wave of the Early 1740s," *The Journal of Interdisciplinary History*, XV (1984), 10, with the permission of *The Journal of Interdisciplinary History* and the MIT Press, Cambridge, Massachusetts. © 1984 by The Massachusetts Institute of Technology and the editors of *The Journal of Interdisciplinary History*. Page 69: Tables reprinted from John D. Post: *Food Shortage, Climatic Variability and Epidemic Disease in Preindustrial Europe: The Mortality Peak in the Early 1740s*. Copyright © 1985 by Cornell University. Used by permission of the publisher, Cornell University Press. Page 71: Figures from Pierre Goubert, "Legitimate Fecundity and Infant Mortality in France During the Eighteenth Century: A Comparison." Reprinted by permission of *Daedalus*, Journal of the American Academy of Arts and Sciences, Historical Population Studies, vol. 97, no. 2, Spring 1968, Boston, MA. Page 71: Table from E. A. Wrigley, "Mortality in Pre-Industrial England: The Example of Colyton, Devon, Over Three Centuries." Reprinted by permission of *Daedalus*, Journal of the American Academy of Arts and Sciences, Historical Population Studies, vol. 97, no. 2, Spring 1968, Boston, MA. Page 73: Tables from Pierre Guillaume and Jean-Pierre Poussou, *Demographie historique*. Used by permission of Armand Colin Éditeur, Paris. Page 90: Figures from George Rudé, "Prices, Wages and Popular Movements in Paris During the French Revolution," *Economic History Review*, 2 ser., vol. 6 (1953). Used by permission of Basil Blackwell Ltd. Page 92: Tables from George Rudé, *The Crowd in the French Revolution*. Copyright © 1959. Used by permission of Oxford University Press (Oxford). Pages 93–94: Extract from Darline Gay Levy, Harriet Branson Applewhite, and Mary Durham Johnson, eds. and trans., *Women in Revolutionary Paris, 1789–1795*. Copyright © 1979 by University of Illinois Press. Pages 110–111: Dates from Alain Lottin, *Chavatte, ouvrier Lillois, un contemporain de Louis XIV*. Used by permission of Flammarion (Paris). Pages 111–113: Extracts from Sidney Pollard and Colin Holmes, eds., *Documents in European History*, vol. 1, *The Process of Industrialization, 1750–1870*. Copyright © 1968 by St. Martin's Press. Used by permission of Sidney Pollard. Pages 121–123: Extract from E. O. Hellerstein, L. P. Hume, and K. M. Offen, eds., *Victorian Women: A Documentary Account of Women's Lives in Nineteenth-Century England, France, and the United States*. Used by permission of Stanford University Press. Pages 130–131: Extract from Sidney Pollard and Colin Holmes, eds., *Documents in European History*, vol. 2, *Industrial Power and National Rivalry*. Copyright © 1968 by St. Martin's Press. Used by permission of Sidney Pollard. Pages 143–150: Extracts from pp. 3–5, 231–233, 610–611, 613, 618, 665, 667–669, 674–675 from DEMOCRACY IN AMERICA by Alexis de Tocqueville. English translation copyright © 1965 by Harper & Row, Publishers, Inc. Reprinted by permission of the publisher. Pages 151–152: Extract from J. P. Mayer, ed., Alexander Teixeira De Mattos, trans., *The Recollections of Alexis de Tocqueville*. Copyright © 1966 Columbia University Press. Used by permission. Pages 152–153: Extract from Roger Boesche, ed., James Toupin and Roger Boesche, trans., *Alexis de Tocqueville: Selected Letters on Politics and Society* (Berkeley: University of California Press, 1985). © 1985 The Regents of the University of California. Pages 160–164: Extract from Karl Marx, *The Class Struggles in France (1848–1850)*, edited by C. P. Dutt. Used by permission of International Publishers. Page 170: Figures from B. R. Mitchell, *European Historical Statistics, 1750–1970*, abr. ed. Copyright © 1978 Columbia University Press. Used by permission. Pages 200–203: Extract from Joseph Chamberlain, M.P., *Foreign & Colonial Speeches*. Used by permission of Associated Book Publishers (UK) Ltd. Pages 212–214: Extract from Henri Brunschwig, FRENCH COLONIALISM, 1871–1914: *Myths and Realities* (Praeger Publishers, New York, 1966), pp. 35–36. Copyright © 1966 by Frederick A. Praeger. Reprinted with permission. Pages 251–252: Poem from BASIC VERITIES, by Charles Péguy, translated by Ann and Julian Green. Copyright 1943 by Pantheon Books, a Division of Random House, Inc. Reprinted by permission of the publisher. Published in the United Kingdom by Routledge & Kegan Paul. Used by permission of Associated Book Publishers (UK) Ltd. Pages 252–253: Poem from *The New York Times*, Oct. 15, 1914, trans. by Barbara Henderson. Copyright © 1914 by The New York Times Company. Reprinted by permission. Pages 253–259: Extract from Henri Barbusse, *Under Fire: The Story of a Squad*, trans. by Fitzwater Wray. Used by permission of J. M. Dent & Sons/Weidenfeld & Nicolson Ltd. Pages 259–263: Excerpt from ALL QUIET ON THE WESTERN FRONT by Erich Maria Remarque. "Im Westen Nichts Neues" copyright 1928 by Ullstein A. G.; Copyright renewed 1956 by Erich Maria Remarque. "All Quiet On The Western Front" copyright 1929, 1930 by Little, Brown and Company; Copyright renewed 1957, 1958 by Erich Maria Remarque. All Rights Reserved. Pages 263–264: Poem from Wilfred Owen, *Collected Poems*.

To the Student

Now that you have worked with this book, we would like to give you a chance to do some grading. The comments you make will be instrumental to the next edition of DISCOVERING THE WESTERN PAST: A LOOK AT THE EVIDENCE. Please answer the following questions and mail this sheet to:

History Editor
College Division
Houghton Mifflin Company
One Beacon Street
Boston, Massachusetts 02108

1. In general, how would you rate DISCOVERING THE WESTERN PAST: A LOOK AT THE EVIDENCE?

   Excellent ☐   Average ☐   Poor ☐

   Above Average ☐   Below Average ☐

   Please comment on your decision. _____
   _____
   _____

2. Did you like the organization of the text? Please explain. _____
   _____
   _____

3. Which chapters did you find the most helpful? _____
   Why? _____
   _____

4. Which chapters did you find the least helpful? _____
   Why? _____
   _____

5. Are there any topics or types of evidence you feel should be added or deleted? _____
   _____

6. Is the material presented clearly? _____
   _____

Are any topics or types of evidence particularly easy to understand?

_____

_____

Are any topics or types of evidence difficult to understand? _____

_____

_____

7. Are the "Sources and Method" and "Questions to Consider" sections helpful? Why or why not? _____

_____

Are "The Problem" and "Epilogue" sections helpful? Why or why not?

_____

_____

8. Do you think the physical format of the book is effective? Why or why not? _____

_____

9. Name of course for which you read DISCOVERING THE WESTERN PAST: _____

_____

What year did you take this course?

Freshman ☐   Sophomore ☐   Junior ☐   Senior ☐

Name of your college or university: _____

Why did you decide to take this course? _____

_____

Name of main textbook assigned for course: _____

10. Please describe your teacher's approach to this book. For example, were chapters used for individual assignments, class discussions, exams, or papers? Were all chapters assigned? _____

_____

_____